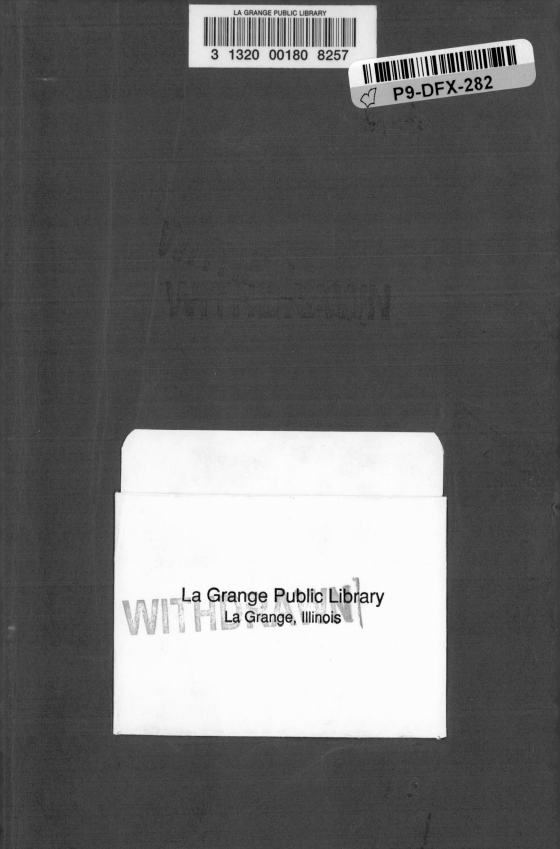

SHAKESPEARE
His Life, Work, and Era

DENNIS KAY

WILLIAM MORROW AND COMPANY, INC.
New York

First published in Great Britain in 1992 by Sidgwick & Jackson Limited

It is the policy of William Morrow and Company, Inc., and its imprints and affiliates, recognizing the importance of preserving what has been written, to print the books we publish on acid-free paper, and we exert our best efforts to that end.

Library of Congress Cataloging-in-Publication Data

Kay, Dennis.
    Shakespeare : his life, work, and era / Dennis Kay.
      p.   cm.
    Includes bibliographical references and index.   DEC   1992
    ISBN 0-688-12024-5
      1. Shakespeare, William, 1564–1616—Biography.   2. Dramatists,
English—Early modern, 1500–1700—Biography.   I. Title.
PR2894.K34   1992
822.3'3—dc20
    [B]   92-21603
                                                            CIP

Printed in the United States of America

First U.S. Edition

1   2   3   4   5   6   7   8   9   10

BOOK DESIGN BY PAUL CHEVANNES

Contents

Preface

Every age creates the Shakespeare, or Shakespeares, it needs. He remains, for good or ill, a powerful cultural icon, as his appearance on one British bank's "cheque-guarantee" cards testifies most eloquently. But in this book I am not concerned with what later ages and other cultures have made of him, fascinating though the subject is. In the following pages I have attempted to tell the story of Shakespeare's life within the context of his age, and to weave into that narrative a chronological study of his writings.

This is not a biography in the conventional sense, primarily because the evidence that usually underpins biography—diaries, journals, letters—simply does not exist in Shakespeare's case. Most of what is directly known about him concerns his business and family affairs. We know almost nothing about his physical appearance, and about his personality we are left with little more (though it is better than nothing) than the image of an amiable, sweet, and gentle disposition. We know that he was not writing for the approval of later generations; often he was not writing for a reading public. He seems to have been much more concerned to consolidate his business interests and preserve his estates in Stratford than to prepare his works for publication that would enable him to speak to posterity. And it is unfortunate but true that we know least about him when his writing career is at its peak. We know plenty about his last years in retirement in Stratford, but next to nothing about the circumstances of his life when he was writing *King Lear* or *The Tempest*. This book tries to fill in some of the gaps.

Perhaps because the hard evidence seems so patchy, some of the most rewarding evocations of Shakespeare as man and writer have come from poets, novelists, and dramatists rather than academic writers: I am thinking of Jorge Luis Borges, Anthony Burgess, John Mortimer, and A. L. Rowse. As Peter Ackroyd has shown in his recent study of Dickens, a novelist brings special gifts to the task of literary biography.

But my ambitions are somewhat more modest. I am writing for anyone who is curious to know a little more about Shakespeare, his life and times, or who might want to investigate how different plays and different parts of Shakespeare's writing career relate to each other. As I guide such a reader through Shakespeare's life and works, I would hope to make available some of the fruits of generations of scholars and critics in the academic Shakespeare "industry." But I have tried to avoid the specialized jargon that makes even some of the best academic writing incomprehensible to those not initiated in its private language. In this enterprise, I have been guided by the example of my Oxford colleagues John Carey and the late Richard Ellmann.

I have tried to hold back from pushing the reader toward my own understanding, such as it is, of Shakespeare and his works. This book is not written to persuade or convince its readers of the justice of a particular point of view: Rather, it is designed to make available in a single volume both a biographical narrative and a chronological introduction to Shakespeare's works in the context of their age. I am certainly not trying to provide a key that will unlock the mystery of Shakespeare's art, an explanation that will unravel the secrets of his genius. As Harry Levin once wrote in a similar context: "We are less acquainted with what went into his work than with what came out of it." And so, as with any work of genius, it must be.

Indeed, there would be no reason for a book such as this if Shakespeare had become irrelevant to us, if his works had lost the capacity to speak to us across the centuries. Yet, as recent scholarship has shown, Shakespeare's achievement is not diminished—how could it be?—by the recognition that it is inescapably part of the culture from which it sprang. Quite the reverse. If he is universal, his universality is a function of his particularity. To adapt Ben Jonson's phrase, he would not be a writer for all time if he were not so emphatically the writer of his own age. That is why, in the pages that follow, I have tried to recover the vital, animated connections between the man, his age, and his art.

In writing this book I have perched unsteadily on the shoulders of several giants of Shakespeare scholarship and criticism. Above all, for the details of the life, I have returned repeatedly to E. K. Chambers, to Samuel Schoenbaum, and to Mark Eccles. My debts to the editors of the major editions are very considerable, and those to generations of Shakespeare critics are too numerous to rehearse here; I apologize to them for relegating them to endnotes. My aim has been to produce a readable text, as uncluttered as possible with the scholarly paraphernalia of notes and references. At the end of the book I provide what I hope will be sufficient information to enable those who wish to check sources or pursue arguments to do so. I have also included a chronological table of the main events in Shakespeare's life, and a family tree.

If this book takes its readers back to Shakespeare, it will have done its job. When Shakespeare's friends and colleagues John Heninge and Henry Condell gathered his works together after his death to make the handsome volume known to history as the First Folio, they expressed a similar hope. They wrote:

> . . . it is not our province, who only gather his works, and give them to you, to praise him. It is yours that read him. And there we hope, to your divers capacities, you will find enough, both to draw, and hold you: for his wit can no more lie hid, than it could be lost. Read him, therefore; and again, and again.

SHAKESPEARE

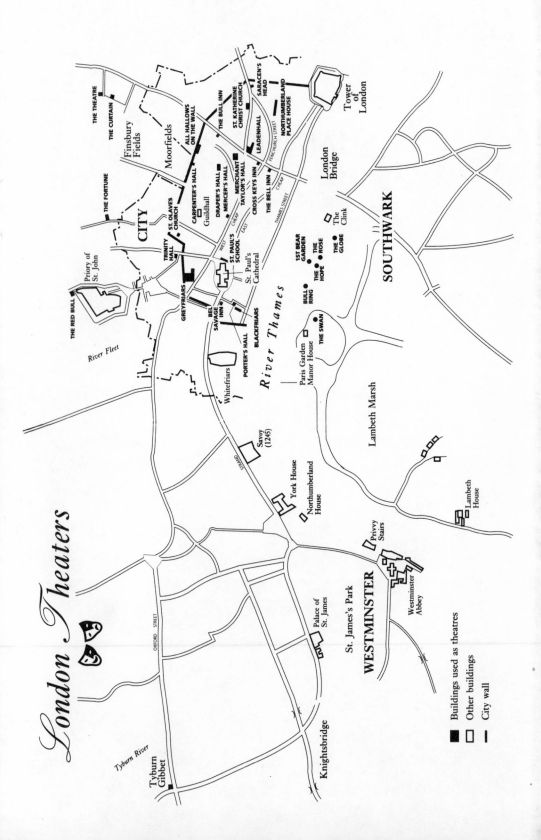

London Theaters

Principal Dates

November 24, 1556	Will of Robert Arden
November 17, 1558	Accession of Queen Elizabeth
February 10, 1561	Administration of Richard Shakespeare
April 26, 1564	Christening of Shakespeare
September 4, 1568	Election of John Shakespeare as bailiff
November 27, 1582	License for marriage of Shakespeare
May 26, 1583	Christening of Susanna Shakespeare
February 2, 1585	Christening of Hamnet and Judith Shakespeare
March 3, 1592	Production of *Part 1 Henry VI*
September 3, 1592	Death of Robert Greene
April 18, 1593	Registration of *Venus and Adonis*
May 30, 1593	Death of Christopher Marlowe
September 25, 1593	Succession of Ferdinando Lord Strange as earl of Derby
April 16, 1594	Death of earl of Derby
May 9, 1594	Registration of *Lucrece*
July 22, 1596	Death of Henry Lord Hunsdon
August 11, 1596	Burial of Hamnet Shakespeare
October 20, 1596	Grant of arms to John Shakespeare
November 9, 1596	Burial of George Peele
March 17, 1597	Appointment of George Lord Hunsdon as lord chamberlain
May 4, 1597	Fine on purchase of New Place
September 7, 1598	Registration of *Palladis Tamia*

May 1599	Opening of Globe Theatre
February 8, 1601	Revolt of Robert, earl of Essex
September 8, 1601	Burial of John Shakespeare
May 1, 1602	Conveyance of land in Old Stratford
September 28, 1602	Copy for cottage in Chapel Lane
March 24, 1603	Death of Queen Elizabeth
May 19, 1603	Patent for King's Men
July 24, 1605	Conveyance of tithes in Stratford
June 5, 1607	Marriage of Susanna Shakespeare to John Hall
February 21, 1608	Christening of Elizabeth Hall
September 9, 1608	Burial of Mary Shakespeare
1608–9	Acquisition of Blackfriars Theatre by King's Men
May 20, 1609	Registration of *Sonnets*
1610	Probable migration of Shakespeare to Stratford
February 14, 1613	Marriage of Princess Elizabeth to Frederick, elector palatine
March 10, 1613	Conveyance of Blackfriars Gate-House
June 29, 1613	Fire at Globe Theatre
February 10, 1616	Marriage of Judith Shakespeare to Thomas Quiney
March 6, 1616	Death of Francis Beaumont
March 25, 1616	Will of Shakespeare
April 23, 1616	Death of Shakespeare
1619	Printing of Jaggard's Quartos
August 6, 1623	Death of Anne Shakespeare
November 8, 1623	Registration of First Folio
April 22, 1626	Marriage of Elizabeth Hall to Thomas Nash
November 25, 1635	Death of John Hall
April 4, 1647	Death of Thomas Nash
June 5, 1649	Marriage of Elizabeth Nash to John Bernard
July 11, 1649	Death of Susanna Hall
February 9, 1662	Burial of Judith Quiney
February 17, 1670	Burial of Elizabeth Bernard

Family Tree

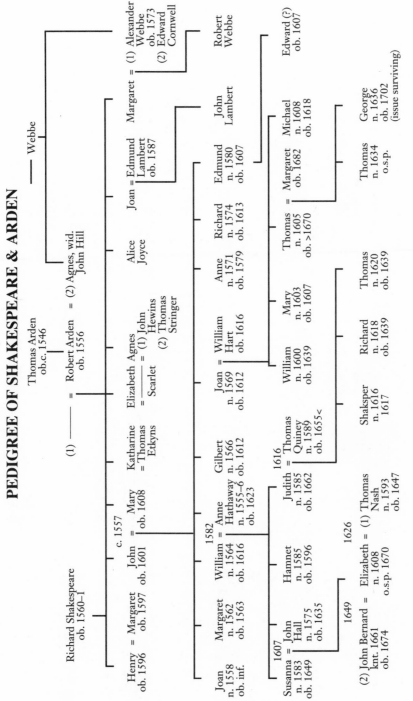

PEDIGREE OF SHAKESPEARE & ARDEN

SHAKESPEARE

CHAPTER ONE

Stratford and the Shakespeares

William Shakespeare's grandfather had been a tenant farmer; his daughter's husband was offered a knighthood; and his granddaughter died as Lady Bernard. His father rose to be one of the chief men—with a coat of arms to confirm the fact—of a prosperous town, and he himself was a man of considerable means, as we will see. The Shakespeare family history is a textbook case of that upward social mobility that was so common in Renaissance England. Contrary to the myth that all we know about Shakespeare could be written on a postcard, there is plenty of evidence to help us reconstruct the story in some detail. So it is with the written evidence, the documents that survive, that I begin.

"I shall keepe the register booke according to the Queenes Majesties injunction": This was the oath to which Elizabeth I required every parish priest in England to subscribe. Although Thomas Cromwell in 1538 and Edward VI in 1547 had instituted similar measures, examples of the Tudor relish for centralized bureaucratic reform, the records kept at Holy Trinity church in Stratford-upon-Avon run only from the beginning of Elizabeth's reign in March 1558. Baptisms, marriages, and burials are recorded in a great leather-bound volume decorated with the Tudor rose.

The handsome book is perhaps a little neater than one might expect; it also bears the date 1600 on the cover of the first volume. There is no great mystery about this; it does not represent some dark plot to doctor the records, to create an elaborate cover-up. What happened was that right at the end of the sixteenth century the Archbishop of Canterbury issued an instruction obliging parish priests to make their records more durable by transferring all those compiled since 1558 from paper to parchment. The task of laboriously transcribing all the information would have fallen on Richard Byfield, who became vicar of Stratford-upon-Avon in 1597, and so the records of the major events in the lives of the Shakespeare family and their neighbors during Elizabeth's reign are almost certainly in his hand. As a check on their accuracy, the vicar and churchwardens had to examine and certify each page that was copied into the new book.

But back to the bare records, and what they do—and do not— reveal. One of the few "facts" that every child at school used to know was that Shakespeare was born and died on the same date, April 23, St. George's Day. There is a very obvious and special fitness in the symmetry whereby the national poet was born and died on the feast day of the nation's patron saint. He certainly died on that date, but his date of birth is not so easily established. The inscription on his monument might imply that he was born on the twenty-third, but we cannot be sure what was in the mind of the author of those much-scrutinized words. And there is a tradition, dating from the eighteenth century, that points in the same direction. But what do the records say?

Byfield's transcript records the baptism, on Wednesday, April 26, 1564, of William, the son of John Shakespeare, *"Gulielmus filius Johannes Shakspere."* The records are, as usual, silent about the actual date of the birth, but we know what normal practice was at the time. According to the Book of Common Prayer, parents were required to arrange for the baptism of their child on the nearest Holy Day or Sunday following the birth, unless they could satisfy the curate of a "great and reasonable cause" to justify a delay. If Shakespeare was indeed born on Sunday, April 23, the next feast day would have been St. Mark's Day on Tuesday the twenty-fifth. There might well have been some cause, both reasonable and great, for a delay—or perhaps, as has been suggested, St. Mark's

Day was still held to be unlucky, as it had been before the Reformation, when altars and crucifixes used to be draped in black
cloth, and when some claimed to see in the churchyard the spirits
of those doomed to die in that year—the tradition was still available
to Keats in his poem "The Eve of St. Mark." We cannot hope to
know, though we might observe how strange it is that such a remarkable coincidence—that the leading poet of the monarch's own
troupe, the King's Men, had died on his birthday and on the feast
of the nation's patron—was not mentioned in any surviving contemporary account. In the nineteenth century Thomas De Quincey
noted that Shakespeare's granddaughter was married on April 22,
1626, and speculated that she was perhaps honoring her famous
relation. But that does not help to explain the christening on the
twenty-sixth. We are left, then, with the negative conclusion that
the researches of scholars over the centuries have yielded nothing
in the way of hard evidence to confirm or contradict the traditional,
unashamedly Bardolatrous dating. It is perhaps inevitable, given
the enduring power of myths that have grown up around him, and
have sustained one another over the centuries, that the question of
Shakespeare's date of birth has been elevated into a topic of grave
importance. Neither he nor his contemporaries nor his family left
any record of the matter. But born he was, in that spring of 1564,
into a harsh world in which he was lucky to survive his first months
of life.

Just how harsh a world it was we can judge from the register of
burials in Stratford-upon-Avon for 1564. On July 11 there is a
chilling note next to the entry which records the burial of Oliver
Gunne, an apprentice. The note reads, *"hic incepit pestis"*—on this
day the plague began. Stratford was ravaged by the pestilence for
the rest of the year, and only the onset of winter in December
brought an end to its destruction. From the evidence that survives
it looks as though some two hundred people—out of a population
only six or seven times that number—perished as a result of the plague
during the second half of 1564. Like the elderly and the infirm,
newborn babies and infants were most at risk. In Henley Street,
a couple of doors from John Shakespeare's house, four of the children of the miller Roger Green died, as did two sons and a daughter
of the town clerk, Richard Symons. When that August the council
(including John Shakespeare, who was at that time a burgess) met

in emergency session—in the open air to reduce the chances of infection—the most they could do was to make rudimentary provisions to relieve the hardship of the sick and dying. The plague was a cruel fact of life in sixteenth-century England, and there was little that could effectively be done when faced with its horror, other than to wait for the healthier, cooler air of winter. John and Mary Shakespeare had already lost two children: Joan, who was born in 1558 and died in infancy; and Margaret, who was born in 1562 and died a year later. It requires no great leap of imagination to conjure up an image of their anxiety for the safety of their new son as the children of friends and neighbors died all around them.

The Shakespeares' fourth child, their second son, was christened Gilbert on October 13, 1566, at Holy Trinity. He was probably named for Gilbert Bradley, who was, like John Shakespeare, a glover, a neighbor in Henley Street, and—as of 1565—a burgess of Stratford. Like his older brother, Gilbert was to divide his time in adult life between London and Stratford. The solidity of his infant credentials as a bourgeois, with a father and godfather prominent in local government and trade, gives a good indication of the course his life would take: His career was to be that of a respected and responsible tradesman. He was to die unmarried in February 1612.

As was quite common practice in those times of high infant mortality, the Shakespeares named their third daughter as they had named their first. Joan Shakespeare was baptized on April 15, 1569. As with the previous Joan, she was probably named for her aunt, Joan Lambert. She was to be the longest-lived of the eight Shakespeare children, dying in 1646, and the only one—apart from William—to marry and produce children. Of the next two Shakespeare offspring little is known. There was a final daughter, Anne, who was baptized on September 28, 1571, and was buried at the age of seven on April 4, 1579. A boy, Richard, was baptized on March 11, 1574, and buried on February 4, 1613—a year and a day after the burial of his brother Gilbert.

The last of the children was Edmund (presumably named for his uncle Edmund Lambert, Joan's husband), whose life shadowed that of his oldest brother. The boy was christened on May 3, 1580, and in due course followed William to London and embarked on a career as an actor. His illegitimate child, probably called Edward, was buried at the church of St. Giles without Cripplegate on August 12, 1607. Edmund himself was buried on the last day of the same year in the great church of St. Mary Overy in Southwark, just a few yards from the Globe Theatre. He was not yet thirty, and had made no great reputation for himself on the stage. But he had a great and expensive funeral, with the bells tolling out over crowds thronging on the Thames, which had been frozen solid by the severe early frost of that terrifying winter. Whoever paid for the funeral specified the "forenoon knell of the great bell" (funerals were more normally held in the afternoon); presumably the chief mourner was the young man's oldest brother, and the morning funeral was arranged so that the actors could attend the interment of their fellow.

Edmund was the only one of the eight children of John and Mary Shakespeare to be buried away from Stratford-upon-Avon. The four sons and four daughters were statistically quite normal—their ages at death ranged from one to seventy-seven and their average lifespan was just over thirty, broadly in line with the national average life expectancy of the period. We know nothing about Mary Shakespeare's inner life; as far as we can tell she was illiterate. The unvarnished records of her married life tell a story typical of her age, sex, and class: She bore eight children whose births were spread over twenty-two years, and only three years separated the birth of her youngest child from that of her first grandchild.

However grand the circles in which he moved, and however strong his ties with London and the court, William Shakespeare would never lose contact with Stratford. At a very simple practical level, of course, he had a growing family there, and expanding property and business interests that required his presence from time to time. Many of the most reliable pieces of evidence relating to his life derive from this side of it, from the man of business, as will become apparent in later chapters. Less tangibly, but hardly less important for that, the sights, sounds, and places of his boyhood remained vividly in his mind throughout his writing career, and the experiences of his early life—and those we can reconstruct most readily are his schooling and his religious education in the Church— can be seen surfacing time and again in his plays and poems.

To try to understand what the place of his birth and upbringing might have meant to him, it is necessary to show the depth of his roots—on both sides of his family—in the communities of modestly well-off tenant farmers in the Warwickshire countryside. His name is an obvious starting point. Shakespeare was a relatively common name—spelled in a variety of ways—in Warwickshire and Gloucestershire in the later Middle Ages. In 1248, for example, a William Sakspere of Clopton in Gloucestershire was hanged for theft; in 1385 a William Shakespeare served on a coroner's jury at Balsall. Almost all the early occurrences of the name seem to derive either from the great city of Coventry or from a cluster of four villages—Balsall, Baddesley Clinton, Wroxhall, and Rowington—inside what was then the Forest of Arden, a few miles northwest of the town of Warwick, rather fewer to the west of Kenilworth, and about a dozen or so miles north of Stratford-upon-Avon. There is more than just a hint that in more sophisticated circles the name (whose bawdy, phallic connotations link it with names like Shakestaff and Wagstaff) was regarded as something of an embarrassment—it may have seemed excessively provincial, or too lower-class, or unseemly for a celibate don, for example, when one Hugh Shakespeare became a fellow of Merton College, Oxford. In 1487, the College Register records that he had changed his name to Hugh Sawnders: It reads, *"Hugo Sawnder alia dictus Shakspere, sed mutatum est istud nomen eius, quia vile reputatum est"* (Hugh Sawnders, elsewhere called Shakespere, but this name of his has been changed, because it has such a base repute).

From the early part of the sixteenth century onward the name is found more extensively in Warwickshire, but despite the most laborious scrutiny of the records, the furthest back that William Shakespeare's line can be traced with confidence is to his grandfather. Richard Shakespeare lived and worked on the land in a couple of manors around the village of Snitterfield as a husbandman—essentially a tenant farmer—from 1529 to his death in 1560 or 1561. Snitterfield, on a low hill not far from the main road to Warwick, is about four miles from the center of Stratford. Some of his land he held as a tenant of the collegiate church of St. Mary in Warwick; as a college tenant, he was required to attend the manor court at Warwick, held annually at Hocktide after Easter and at Michaelmas. The penalty for unexplained nonattendance was a fine of two pence; and Richard Shakespeare, like many other tenants from the district, regularly opted for the fine rather than waste a day tramping six miles to Warwick, though his excuses were accepted and no fine was imposed in 1532, 1538, and 1550. From the records of this manor—in which he is variously named Shakspere, Shakespere, Shakkespere, Shaxpere, and Shakstaff—we also learn that in 1538 he was ordered to mend the hedges between his land and that farmed by one Thomas Palmer, and we can probably assume, since no more is heard about it, that he duly did so.

Richard Shakespeare also farmed the land belonging to the chief manor in the Snitterfield district, the "Warwikeslands and Spencerslands" estate, which had at one time been in the possession of the earls of Warwick. In its surviving records, now kept at the Birthplace in Stratford-upon-Avon, there are further traces of his farming enterprises. In 1535, for example, Shakespeare was in trouble for overburdening the common pastureland with his beasts. Twenty-five years later—in the last months of his life, as it turned out—he was fined for not yoking or ringing his pigs and for keeping his animals on the "leez," the meadows. On the same day, October 3, 1560, all the tenants of the estate were given until the eighteenth day of the month to make a hedge and ditch *"inter finem venelle Ricardi Shakespere"* (between the end of Richard Shakespeare's lane) *"et sepem vocatam Dawkyns hedge"* (and the hedge called Dawkins hedge). In the nineteenth century a "Dawkins Close" was identified on a farm called the Wold, on the north of a lane leading from Snitterfield to Warwick, and that may be the place where the old man's neighbors rallied round to help him keep his beasts under control, and to stop his land from flooding in the winter rains. Richard Shakespeare was an important figure in his village: On several occasions he was called upon to value the estates of neighbors who had died. He was also known in the world outside. In 1543 Thomas Atwood (alias Taylor), a prosperous alderman of the Stratford guild, bequeathed him a team of four oxen which were then in his possession, and when in January 1560 Thomas Lucy held an inquisition at Warwick into the estates of Sir Robert Throckmorton, "Richard Shakyspere" served on the jury. His house, on the High Street of Snitterfield, had land which ran down to the stream that flows through the village. When he died his estate was valued at £38 17s.—a long way from poverty in those times; the estate of the vicar, Sir Thomas Hargrave, had been valued at £34 in 1557. His landlord was Robert Arden of Wilmcote, whose daughter Mary was to marry Richard's son John.

Apart from John, the child of Richard Shakespeare who has left the most traces in local records is Henry, William's scapegrace uncle. Like his father he was a tenant farmer, and held land at Ingon, near Stratford; he was similarly lax in his later years about keeping his fences and ditches in good repair, and was rebuked for not participating in communal road maintenance. He spent various periods in prison for trespass and for debt, and was for a time excommunicated for refusing to pay his tithes. In 1574 he fell into a brawl with Edward Cornwell (later to be the second husband of Margaret Arden, Mary Arden's sister), and was fined *in absentia*. More puzzling, he was fined with two other men in 1583 for deliberately flouting the Statute of Caps (introduced to protect the declining cap-making industry) by provocatively wearing a hat—rather than a cap—to attend church on Sundays and holidays. While it may be tempting to see the episode as a gesture of sympathy with the widespread, and essentially puritan, opposition to the statute, it is just as likely to have been an act of bloody-mindedness from a man who seems to have found authority an irritant throughout his life. He had two children baptized at Hampton Lucy (Lettice on March 10, 1581 and James on October 16, 1585—the little boy was buried at the same church on September 25, 1589) and was himself buried in Snitterfield on December 29, 1596. He died with debts unpaid, and it took some time to set his affairs in order; but at his death he had his own house, a full barn, and some livestock. His wife Margaret survived him by less than two months.

John Shakespeare, William's father, was a man of very different stamp from his prickly and wayward brother. But he makes an incongruous and ignominious first appearance in the records of Stratford-upon-Avon, the town in whose affairs he was to play such a prominent role. On April 29, 1552, at the court leet of the king's manor of Stratford, he was fined, along with a group of his fellow townsmen, for making an unauthorized dunghill in Henley Street. After that, as the records show, relations between the elders of the town and the young newcomer from Snitterfield improved markedly.

Where his brother Harry had evidently been content to remain in the same way of farming as their father, John found himself drawn to the nearest large town, and to a trade. He was to be a glover and "whittawer"—one who dresses white leather. He would have prepared the hides of sheep and goats, deer and horses, and then imbued them in a solution of alum and salt. His business would have involved making and selling a wide range of leather goods—gloves, bags, belts, and so forth. In Stratford-upon-Avon, the glovers had the best "pitch" in the market square, under the clock at the Market Cross. Glovers were also shielded from foreign competition by a protectionist Act of Parliament, so the young man's choice of career was a sound one. What else moved him can only be guessed at, but the chances are that some personal connection facilitated his apprenticeship. Richard Shakespeare had business dealings with a prominent figure in the town, Thomas Atwood, and he may have helped. Another Stratford alderman, Thomas Dickson alias Waterman, was married to Joan, a daughter of John Townsend, a neighbor of the Shakespeares in Snitterfield. Certainly this Dickson was a glover, and he was probably John Shakespeare's master in his new craft.

On this journey from the old world of agriculture to the new age of industry, from feudal courts and tithes to capitalist enterprise, from tilling others' land and tending others' beasts to owning property, workshops, and a coat of arms, the forward-looking John Shakespeare picked up little education—he was to all intents and purposes illiterate—but he obviously understood and desired social status, as would become evident during his time as a prominent man in the public life of his new hometown. We can also probably see in his choice of a wife an attempt to graft the Shakespeares on to a family tree that had pretensions to gentility and antiquity.

Mary Arden, who was to be William Shakespeare's mother, was one of the daughters of the farmer Robert Arden of Wilmcote. Robert Arden's great-grandfather was probably Robert Ardene, bailiff of Snitterfield in 1438. More significantly for genealogists—and Elizabethans relished such matters—there is a possibility that these Ardens were related to the ancient Arden family of Park Hall in Castle Bromwich, now a suburb of Birmingham; these Ardens claimed to be able to trace their descent beyond the Norman Conquest into Saxon times, to the family of the sheriff of Warwick in the days of Edward the Confessor. In the Domesday Book the properties of "Turchillus de Eardene" (elsewhere "Turchill of Warwick") are matched by few other Englishmen in extent or value. There can be little doubt that, even if the connection was not strong enough for them to claim to be gentry in their own right, the farming Ardens of Wilmcote derived prestige from association with such a wealthy and long-established family.

Robert Arden was a farmer on quite a large scale; by the time he married Agnes Hill, the widow of another comfortably-off husbandman, he had accumulated a sizeable holding. He had also managed to father no fewer than eight daughters (for six of whom he would be able to provide husbands), and his new wife brought with her two sons and two daughters. The old man and his numerous dependents certainly lived in Wilmcote, but regrettably not in the solid two-story farmhouse in Featherbed Lane near the village green which tourists visit as "Mary Arden's House." The tradition associating the house with the Ardens can be traced precisely to the fanciful assertions of the mythologizer John Jordan, writing in 1794. The property, together with the manor of Great Wilmcote, was sold in 1561 by Thomas Finderne of Nuneaton to Adam Palmer and George Gibbs. Not an Arden in sight. Nevertheless, the house cannot be very different in scale from the one in which the Arden tribe lived, and it preserves many characteristic features of a farmhouse of that time; the Birthplace trustees have also assembled a fine collection of farming and domestic artefacts of the sixteenth century, so that visitors can gain a fair impression of the physical circumstances of a Warwickshire farming family from Shakespeare's lifetime.

Robert Arden made his will on November 24, 1556. His daughter Mary, though little older than sixteen, was named one of his executors: In that capacity she supervised the inventory made on the old man's death the following month. Robert left Mary ten marks and some valuable property—"all my land in Willmecote cawlide Asbyes and the crop apone the grounde, sowne and tyllide as hitt is." His goods were valued at £77 11s. 10d. and the inventory shows a well-stocked and prosperous farming operation, from the "bacon in the roof" down to the bees in the hive, from the bullocks, oxen, weaning calves, swine, and colts in the field to the implements and woodpile in the yard. Not everything was simply utilitarian: We learn that the house boasted no fewer than eleven wall hangings of painted cloth. These were canvas strips on which were depicted scenes from legend or from the Bible, usually with an appropriate caption or motto underneath to interpret the image. In *Lucrece*

William Shakespeare would refer to the way simple people could be "kept in awe" by such hangings. And in *As You Like It*, when Orlando and Jaques bandy clichés with each other, Jaques scornfully asks if Orlando has been learning his wisdom from sentimental mottoes inscribed on the inside of rings. Orlando replies in the same vein: "Not so, but I answer you right painted cloth, from whence you have studied your questions." These mottoes seem to have been all the book learning that Shakespeare's mother and her family had, and whether Shakespeare saw the painted cloths at home in Stratford or in his grandmother Arden's house in Wilmcote, he would have seen their naïve and crude simplicity as tokens of the gulf that was separating him from his parents' mental world as a result of the education he was rapidly acquiring at the grammar school.

Mary Arden married John Shakespeare at some point between her father's death in late 1556 and the birth of her first child in September 1558. Robert Arden was buried in the churchyard at Aston Cantlow, and it is probable that his daughter's wedding took place in the same parish of St. John the Baptist (the records are lost). She then moved to Stratford, where she would spend the rest of her days.

Stratford-upon-Avon as it is today preserves the general shape, and many of the buildings, of the small market town it was at the beginning of Elizabeth's reign. But a striking difference, and one which relates directly to the way the Shakespeare leather business operated, is the disappearance of the wooden Market House with its elaborate cupola and clock, consisting of a large room held up in the air by four supporting pillars, beneath which tradesmen— including John Shakespeare—sold their goods at the weekly market on Thursdays. All that remains now is a patch of grass on a traffic island at the junction of Bridge Street, High Street, and Henley Street. But the town's chief functions derive, like its name, from its location, as a place where a highway (Anglo-Saxon *stræt*) can be provided with a crossing or *ford* over a river (originally Welsh *afon*, retained by succeeding generations). And that has not changed.

In Tudor times, it was believed that the church of the Holy Trinity stood on the site of an ancient monastery established during the ascendancy of the kingdom of Mercia. In the pre-Reformation of Worcester, who secured for the townsfolk the right to hold fairs, the longest of which lasted for sixteen days. There was also, from the time of Richard I, a weekly market held on Thursdays. In fact there were three markets: cattle were sold at the Rothermarket; the chief market was the Market Cross; and dairy produce was to be sold outside the Gild Chapel. As time went by, the occupations of the townspeople became more specialized, and commerce became increasingly important as ever greater numbers came to the markets or passed through Stratford on their way north to Birmingham or Coventry or south to Bristol or London. With the Reformation, responsibility for the town's affairs was thrown on to the population; the local people were compelled to come up with a system of self-government. And the evidence suggests that the task took some time. But from the seventh year of Edward VI's reign, 1553, the town became independent and acquired a seal and a charter. Its corporation consisted of a bailiff together with fourteen aldermen who had the right to choose fourteen burgesses to serve with them.

There are some illuminating accounts of Stratford in the six-teenth century. In about 1540, shortly after the trauma of the Dissolution of the Monasteries, the antiquarian John Leland, keeper of Henry VIII's libraries, perambulated around England recording what he found. He noted that Stratford was a town of some fine broad streets and solid timber houses "reasonably well builded." He also gives a glimpse of what the Warwickshire countryside was like in those harrowing times. He traveled up into the county from Banbury—along what is now the A41—and set out for Warwick, "twelve miles by champaign [i.e., *campagne*, countryside] ground, fruitful of corn and grass, barren of wood, and two miles by some enclosed and woody ground." He marveled, as generations of visitors have, at the Beauchamp tomb in Warwick chapel, and he saw the ruined monastic buildings that were to be restored by the earl of Leicester during Elizabeth's reign. His relish for ancient stories caused him to wax rhapsodic in recording a visit to Guy's Cliff, where the Avon passes through a gorge associated with the legendary Guy of Warwick ("a place of pleasure, a house meet for the Muses"). When he left Stratford he left behind the Arden woods and rode across the open grassy plain.

William Camden, Ben Jonson's schoolmaster and one of the

great scholars of the age, visited Stratford during the years of Shakespeare's early childhood. He came from the north, from Warwick, following the course of the Avon, as he toured the country in his quest for hard fact, nuggets of information (in contrast with Leland's delight in legends and folklore) on which to build his majestic *Brittania*. To him also, the contrast between woods and plain—between the Forest of Arden and the fertile plain of Feldon—was marked, and he found the best vantage point from which to observe it. As he remarked, "The Feldon lieth on this side Avon southward, a plain champaign country, and being rich in corn and green grass yieldeth a right goodly and pleasant prospect to them that look down upon it from an hill which they call Edghill." Camden found Stratford "a fine small market town, which is indebted to two of its sons for all its glory"; those sons being Archbishop John de Stratford and Sir Hugh Clopton the builder of Clopton Bridge.

Clopton, in one of those Dick Whittington-style stories with which the fifteenth century abounds, had been a younger son who left Stratford to ply his trade as a mercer in London, where he was in succession alderman, sheriff, and (in 1491) lord mayor. He was a great benefactor of Stratford, and his mark is still on the town in the shape of the great bridge over which all who make the journey between London and Stratford must pass. He also lavishly decorated the great Gild Chapel to the glory of his Maker, attracting the admiration of Leland for its splendor, and built for himself a fine house opposite. This house would in due course come to be occupied by another Stratford man who made his fortune in London: By William Shakespeare's time the house had come to be known as New Place.

John de Stratford, appointed chancellor of England in 1330 and on two subsequent occasions, provided for the expansion and augmentation of Holy Trinity Church, essentially to the plan as we see it today—although the present site is an eighteenth-century replacement of the smaller, wooden one which Shakespeare would have known. He widened the aisles, built chapels (including the one now filled with Clopton monuments and known as the Clopton Chapel) and a chantry, as well as providing an endowment for five priests to sing masses forever for him, his family, the monarch, and the bishop of Worcester.

William Shakespeare was to travel south over Clopton Bridge many times, was to take possession of Clopton's great house, and would be laid to rest in John de Stratford's beautiful church.

What of Shakespeare's father? It is possible to draw up a full schedule of his activities covering much of his career. But there are gaps in the record, and there is much that can never be recovered. As far as the factual record is concerned, we have seen already that by the spring of 1552—some half-dozen years before his marriage— John Shakespeare was living in Henley Street (whether as tenant or not is not certain), in the western part of the large double-fronted house now known reverently as the Birthplace. In 1556 he acquired the other half of the house (the part known as the Woolshop) and over the years arranged for the two parts to be joined together to give the appearance of a single structure. He subsequently had a rear wing built out into the garden, and further property was acquired. In 1556 John Shakespeare bought a house with garden and croft (enclosed patch of ground) in Greenhill Street (nowadays called More Towns End) from a man named George Turner. We know that Shakespeare's father was living in Henley Street at least until 1597, when he sold off some land at the edge of his property, including a patch of ground on which the Bell Inn was to be built; and that his wife shared the house with him from about 1558.

As mentioned earlier, in 1553—within a year or so of John Shakespeare's arrival in town—the borough of Stratford-upon-Avon received from the Crown its Charter of Incorporation. And for almost a quarter of a century the rising fortunes of the increasingly prosperous town were mirrored by those of the young man from Snitterfield.

On Richard Shakespeare's death, his eldest son might have been expected to take over his farming enterprise—and the records refer to the young man as a farmer (*agricola*) at the time the will was proved. A few months later, in October 1561, John Shakespeare was fined for failing to keep his hedges in good condition, and the inference that his heart was not in farming is supported by his disappearance from the records. It looks as though he made over the land, and sold the copyhold, well before 1574, probably to his brother-in-law Alexander Webbe, who was married to Margaret Arden, Mary Shakespeare's sister. He had plenty to keep him occupied in Stratford.

In the town records he is referred to on several occasions as a glover (as when he was unsuccessfully sued for eight pounds in 1556, or when he stood bail for a local itinerant tradesman in 1586) and on others (as in 1573 and 1578) as "whyttawer." But tradition has always maintained that Shakespeare's father was a wool trader—and the designation of his property as the "Woolshop" has strengthened this belief. The Woolshop later became an inn, and in the early years of the nineteenth century its landlord told a visitor that "when he re-laid the floors of the parlour, the remnants of wool, and the refuse of wool-combing, were found under the earth of the foundations"; Shakespeare's earliest biographers lined up behind the local tradition that the elder Shakespeare had been "a considerable dealer in Wool." In this century, bits and pieces of documentary evidence have been turned up to support this tradition. We know that in 1599 John Shakespeare sued John Walford, a clothier from Marlborough, in the Court of Common Pleas for failing to pay £21 for 21 tods of wool (a tod was 28 pounds). More recent research in the public records has unearthed some further evidence that shows that John Shakespeare was a businessman on a substantial scale, and that, as well as trading in large quantities of wool, he was also involved in lending money.

The evidence consists of "informations"—claims made by informers that individuals were committing offenses—and there is little doubt that such a system encourages frivolous or malicious accusations. Indeed, one of John Shakespeare's accusers, a man named John Langrake, was at different times fined and imprisoned for striking a deal with people he had accused before the case came to court; being an informant could be a lucrative business at the margins of legality. On the other hand, the very sums involved in the Shakespeare accusations are indicative of the scale of John Shakespeare's enterprises. What is also evident is that the law had failed to keep up with developments in the sphere of commerce. Sixteenth-century businesses were increasingly reliant upon credit, but they operated after 1552 in the context of an archaic piece of biblical literalism, a fundamentalist law against usury, and always ran the risk that a zealot with an eye for the main chance would bring information before the court, in the hope that the accused would be willing to buy him off in an out-of-court settlement. Those convicted of usury forfeited both loan and interest and ran the risk of further fines or imprisonment. Before 1552, interest had been permissible up to a level of 10 percent, but after that date businessmen were faced with what has been called "a random tax on trade," where they were at the mercy of some distinctly shady individuals.

In 1569, for example, one John Harrison of Evesham claimed that John Shakespeare had lent a business partner, John Mussom, the sum of one hundred pounds to be repaid a year later with twenty pounds interest. Such a loan would have been regarded as usury, and would have been in breach of a statute of 1552. Likewise with a similar accusation—this time from the notorious Langrake—of the same year, to the effect that Shakespeare had lent eighty pounds and had charged twenty pounds interest. In each of these accusations Shakespeare is referred to as a glover of Stratford.

Langrake pointed the accusing finger at John Shakespeare on at least two other occasions. The context of the accusations was a statute of 1552 which restricted the buying of wool to authorized dealers, to manufacturers and merchants of the "staple." The purpose of this legislation was twofold. First, the major dealers, known as staplers, faced difficulties in the export market because of the high price of English wool, and it was hoped to bring prices down by reducing competition. Second, by restricting the operations of middlemen the spread of industrialization might be contained, since manufacturers would have fewer sources of supply for their raw material. As with the usury legislation, this statute was enforced partly by the activities of informers, as Langrake's accustions exemplify.

In 1571, John Shakespeare was accused of engaging in two illegal transactions. In the first, he was said to have bought 200 tods (that is, 5,600 pounds) of wool for 14 shillings per tod. In the second, he was accused of buying 100 tods at the same price. Since the records say no more, it looks as though Langrake and Shakespeare came to some sort of understanding and the matter was dropped.

What is interesting is less the detail of these transactions than what they tell us about the scale and range of John Shakespeare's business activities. He ran a cottage industry, manufacturing leather goods, then selling them in the Stratford market. He owned property in the town, which he rented out (indeed, at one time he let a house to a William Burbage—we can only speculate as to their connection with the theatrical Burbages with whom William was to work). He was in a position to advance considerable sums to business partners, and he traded in wool, a valuable local commodity. We know from other records that Shakespeare also dealt in timber—he sold some to the town corporation for three shillings; and in barley—the raw material for the local ale- and beer-brewing industry. He probably used the "Woolshop" as a store for these goods. The overall picture is of a busy and enterprising man, seizing the trading opportunities presented to him and apparently embodying in his own career his movement from tenant farming to capitalism, the energy of that diverse and broad swathe of society which the Elizabethans thought of as the "middling sort of people." He also, as we have seen, ran many risks, and it may well be that his overextension was a cause of the downfall he was to suffer in 1576. But for the quarter-century before that the value the corporation placed on his enterprise was signaled by the succession of offices he held.

In the years after 1553, the borough was organizing itself to exercise the new powers it had acquired; people were needed to perform a range of duties. John Shakespeare's first appointment— which came in September 1556, when he had been living in Stratford for four or five years—was as one of the two ale tasters, as a guardian of basic trading standards. His chief function was to check that brewers sold beer of the proper quality at the approved price and in the prescribed manner, and that bakers made loaves of the standard weight. Twice a year the leet, or manor court, would try offenders. As with most such offices, the duties were enforced by fines; and we know that John Shakespeare was fined in June 1557 for having missed, in his official capacity as taster, three sittings of the Court of Record. His absence might indicate that he did not take the job particularly seriously; it might also suggest that his last months of bachelorhood held other attractions for him.

In the autumn of 1558, round about the time of the birth of his first child, Joan, John Shakespeare became one of the four constables of the borough, charged with keeping the peace, confiscating weapons, stamping out street brawls, enforcing local by-laws, making sure the townsfolk behaved themselves during divine service, and performing the very necessary task of supervising fire-fighting precautions. In 1559 he became an affeeror, that is to say the official whose job it was at the leet to assess fines that were not laid down by statute. He was evidently taking on a range of increasingly significant responsibilities, and his standing in the community was reflected in two notable ways. First came his election as one of the fourteen principal burgesses in about 1561, and then his appointment, with John Taylor, as one of the two chamberlains who had official charge of borough finances and property.

The accounts clearly indicate that John Shakespeare had the trust of his colleagues. While the actual documents were drawn up by an official, the deputy steward, Richard Symons, they were endorsed by Shakespeare and Taylor, and supervised by them. And even after his stint as chamberlain was over, John Shakespeare—first with Taylor (1564–5) and later (1565–6) alone—marked the accounts to show his approval. His deep involvement in local government—and in particular his responsibility for the accurate maintenance of the town's financial records—cannot be matched among his contemporaries. As well as being a far-sighted and enterprising entrepreneur, he seems to have had an enthusiastic commitment to the orderly running of his adopted home and to have inspired the confidence of his fellows. And it was in this time that William was born, that the plague struck, and that the council met in the open air to plan its response to the disaster.

In May 1565 the prickly and widely disliked William Bott, one of the aldermen and the owner of William Shakespeare's eventual house, New Place, was summoned to appear to answer the charge that he had allowed it to be understood that "ther was never a honest man of the Councell or the body of the corporacyon of Stratford." Bott, according to his own son-in-law a false harlot and a false villain, and who may well have been a murderer, did not attend and was duly expelled. In his place the popular and efficient newcomer, John Shakespeare, was elected on July 4 and took office on September 12. From that day on Master Shakespeare, as he would have been addressed, was entitled to wear in public the aldermanic thumb ring and black gown trimmed in fur. So the earliest years of his son's life coincided with the completion of John Shakespeare's transformation from migrant worker to respected local grandee.

And still his rise continued. On the first Wednesday of September 1567 he was one of three nominees for the post of bailiff—the chief elected official of the borough. In the following year he was elected to the post, which he took up on October 1, 1568. During his year in office he presided at council meetings and at sessions of the court of record as a justice of the peace. Every week, on Thursday night, he fixed the weekly price of corn—to which the prices of bread, ale, and so on were necessarily linked. The town granted many dignities to its bailiffs. On his journey from his house to the Gild Hall, sergeants bearing maces would go before him; the same officers would escort the bailiff as he took his walk of inspection through the market on Thursdays, and processed with his wife to church on Sundays. In church the bailiff and his wife had a prominent pew, as likewise in the Gild Hall when sermons were given or plays performed. We know that troupes of players acted in Stratford-upon-Avon—it seems for the first time—toward the end of John Shakespeare's year of office, probably in August 1569. The Queen's Men, who received nine shillings for their work, and the Earl of Worcester's Men, who received just a shilling, gave shows in the Gild Hall, where John and Mary Shakespeare would have been sitting in all their finery in the front row of the audience. They had touched the highest point of their greatness.

It was possible to hold the office of bailiff on more than one occasion; indeed, a brewer called Robert Salisbury held the post for three terms. But John Shakespeare, for whatever reason, was not elected again. Nevertheless, he still played a major role in the borough's affairs. In 1571, for example, he was chosen to act as chief alderman, to serve as justice of the peace alongside the new bailiff, Adrian Quiney (his neighbor from Henley Street), and to deputize for him when necessary. In January 1572 the two men, granted plenipotentiary powers by the corporation to proceed "according to their discretions," set off on horseback to London to try to push forward borough business in the courts and elsewhere. Again the impression is of a man trusted by his colleagues and regarded as capable of securing deals in the best interests of his fellow merchants. Meanwhile, he was continuing to build up his collection of properties in Stratford—two more houses were purchased in October 1575, and in the same year he took on another fourteen acres of land at Ingon. We also know that at about this time John Shakespeare thought about applying to the College of Heralds for a coat of arms, as his tenure of the office of bailiff entitled him to do.

So in the space of two decades John Shakespeare had established himself in the close-knit business community of his adopted home, a thriving market town. He had made himself central to the commercial life of the town, not just in his own manufacturing and trading operations (which were quite extensive), but also by offering storage space and rudimentary banking facilities, by representing a locally based alternative for the wool traders, and so on. In addition, he owned a good deal of land and a number of properties within Stratford itself. He was evidently, in the terms of the late sixteenth century, a modern, entrepreneurial spirit. He was also trusted by his fellow townsmen, not just with ceremonial offices but with the conduct of town business and the oversight of its finances. All of William Shakespeare's early life was set in the context of growing wealth, promise for the future and, perhaps most influential, unchallenged social respectability.

But then the picture changes suddenly, and nobody has ever been able to say exactly why. The facts are pretty striking. After 1575, for example, John Shakespeare bought no more property or land in Stratford or anywhere else. If we look at the records of the corporation, we find that whereas he had been present at every single council meeting for which attendance is recorded from his election as bailiff until 1576, he only attended one more meeting, on September 5, 1582.

Despite these absences, John Shakespeare's name remained on the aldermanic register for ten more years—nobody else was so favored for such a long time. So the desire for his return was evidently genuine. And consideration was regularly shown to him. When other absentees were fined, he was let off; and when men were taxed, he was taxed at the level set for burgesses, not at the double rate the aldermen had to pay. When they collected for poor relief, everyone had to contribute four pence, except John Shakespeare and Robert Bratt, "who shall not be taxed to paye any thinge." Then, at last, on September 6, 1586, two new aldermen were elected: John Wheeler was to be replaced because he wished "to be put out of the Companye," and Master Shakespeare because he "dothe not Come to the halles when they be warned nor hathe not done of Longe tyme."

The most likely explanation of John Shakespeare's decline is economic. A whole series of transactions from the late 1570s and early 1580s indicate that he was selling off land and property to raise hard cash. Compared to what we have already seen of the scale of his business operations, the sums of money realized by these transactions were frequently pitifully small, and the sentimental associations of some of the property—especially for Mary Shakespeare—must have made their loss especially painful. And other adversities—fines, law suits, arguments with neighbors— came in the wake of the financial problems. Throughout the West Midlands, it is now thought, the latter part of the sixteenth century was a period of sharp economic recession, and just because we know a lot about John Shakespeare we should not think that his plight was unique. Far from it. The Stratford records tell a tale of increased disorder, drunkenness, illegitimacy, begging, and destitution. The most extraordinary statistic is that in 1601 the poor of the borough (i.e., those without work or means of support in the terms of the so-called Poor Laws) numbered some seven hundred souls—a figure close to half the entire population.

John Shakespeare's decline, though abrupt, did not plunge him, as far as we can tell, into the most abject poverty. But he was one of a group of nine men who in the early 1590s kept away from church for fear of being sued for debt (the officers of the sheriff could make arrests on Sundays, and tended to combine attendance at divine service with pursuit—and public embarrassment—of their quarry), so even his reduced circumstances must have seemed somewhat precarious. On the basis of nonattendance at church he has been seen as some sort of religious nonconformist, either Puritan or (more usually) Catholic. The evidence is not strong enough to support either conclusion. We should remember that Stratford seems to have been a tolerant enough place, with recognized Puritans and Catholics involved in town affairs and in local business.

John Shakespeare continued after his fall to play some part in the life of the town, and managed to hold on to his large house in Henley Street and pass it on to his son. It does not look as though he was ostracized or persecuted for religious or political views.

Indeed, in 1601 Richard Quiney wrote a note naming seven men who could testify to the rights of the borough, which were being challenged by Sir Edward Greville, the lord of the manor. Among the small group of town officials and old men appeared John Shakespeare's name, although he died before he had a chance to give his evidence. He was buried at Stratford on September 8, 1601, in the churchyard of Holy Trinity, having achieved the great age for those times of seventy years, and having lived long enough to dandle his grandchildren and to see his eldest son establish himself as a fashionable and successful playwright. All we know of his personality derives from an anecdote of dubious authenticity. Thomas Plume, the archdeacon of Rochester, recorded this observation about William Shakespeare in his notebook sometime in the late 1650s: "He was a glovers son—Sir John Mennis once saw his old Father in his shop—a merry Cheekd old man—that said—Will was a good Honest Fellow, but he durst have crackt a jeast with him at any time." It is with the image of this "merry Cheekd old man" in mind that I will turn to the early years of his son.

CHAPTER TWO

Upbringing in Stratford

Nobody has seriously questioned the assumption that the young Shakespeare was a pupil at the King's New School in Stratford. It remains an assumption nevertheless, since no registers survive; nor, for that matter, do we know exactly what the curriculum in Stratford was. But we can reconstruct a good deal from what is known about comparable schools of the period, and from official prescriptions of standard textbooks and editions. We can also begin the process of sketching in the mental world that became available to him as he grew up—in school, in church, at home, within Stratford and in contacts with the wider world.

The burgesses of Stratford were serious about education. They were not alone. All over the country, small businessmen were putting money into new schools and were enthusiastically promoting godly learning, creating what we would call an educated work force, a population geared to deal with rapid social, economic, and technological change. In the 1553 charter it was decreed that the schoolmaster of Stratford would be housed rent-free and receive a stipend of twenty pounds per annum, of which four pounds were to be set aside to pay for the usher to look after the junior classes and to cover repairs and maintenance. This was a handsome arrangement

(Eton, as champions of the grammar school have often pointed out, paid less), and Stratford was able to attract highly qualified teachers. We know who they were, and can identify six men who were teaching at the school during Shakespeare's boyhood.

From 1565 to 1567 the master was John Brownsword, a native of Cheshire. Brownsword was a friend, and probably a former pupil, of the vicar, John Bretchgirdle; when he left Stratford he moved back north, to Macclesfield. His Latin verses were to be published in 1590 by his own pupil, Thomas Newton, translator of Seneca; and John Brinsley, in *Ludus Literarius: or, The Grammar Schoole* (1612), would praise him as "that ancient schoolemaster . . . so much commended for his order and Schollers."

Brownsword was succeeded for a short time by John Acton, a scholar of Brasenose College, Oxford, before the post went to a more eminent man, Walter Roche, a fellow of another Oxford College, Corpus Christi. Roche too was a northerner, a Lancastrian. He took on the duties of rector of Droitwich at about the same time as he started work in Stratford, in 1569, and schoolmastering was only a brief interlude in his career. He held on to the Droitwich position after giving up teaching in 1571, and moved into law. He acted for Robert Webbe of Snitterfield, Shakespeare's cousin, and lived until at least 1582 in Chapel Street near New Place; he witnessed deeds with John Shakespeare in 1573, and evidently had some contact, even if only on a professional level, with his neighbors. It is unlikely, however, that he had much to do with the instruction of the youngest pupils—however promising—during his time.

If Shakespeare did indeed attend the school, the chances are that he was taught for a while by the next master, Simon Hunt, who worked at the grammar school from 1571 to 1575. He received his license from the bishop of Worcester on October 28, 1571, paid toward the repair of windows in 1573, and paid rent for a room for twelve months from Michaelmas 1574. So far, so good. Insuperable complications arise, however, when one tries to find out more about the man charged with "disciplinating the juvental fry" (Philip Sidney's phrase) during Shakespeare's first years in school. There were two Simon Hunts, and one of them provides ammunition for the pro-Catholic interpretation of these years. He matriculated in 1575 from the University at Douai, intellectual center of émigré English Catholic life, became a Jesuit in 1578 and held the post of English penitentiary at St. Peter's in Rome (in succession to the celebrated Jesuit Robert Parsons), where he died in 1585. The second Simon Hunt lived a less public life, at least as far as surviving records indicate. All we know is that he lived in Stratford and died there in about 1598 leaving an estate valued at a hundred pounds; we do not know why, if he continued to live in Stratford for more than twenty years, he gave up teaching when he did.

We are on surer ground with the next master, Thomas Jenkins, who held the post from 1575 to 1579. Jenkins was not, as used to be supposed, a Welshman; he was born to a poor family in London, the son of an old servant of Sir Thomas White, founder of St. John's College, Oxford. Jenkins was evidently a bright young man. He acquired a B.A. in 1566 then an M.A. in 1570 at St. John's, and held a fellowship there from 1566 to 1572, when the college allowed him to lease "Chaucer's House" in the village of Woodstock, ten miles north of Oxford. It seems that Jenkins had an abiding interest in teaching—Sir Thomas White asked the college to grant him leave in 1566 so that he could learn the craft—and some time later he took up a teaching post at Warwick. In 1575 his expenses were paid to travel from Warwick to Stratford, and he seems to have married at about this time. His daughter Joan was buried in 1576 and his son Thomas was christened in 1578.

In the following year Jenkins amicably parted company with Stratford, having lined up a successor in the shape of John Cottom, an Oxford graduate from Brasenose. Cottom's younger brother Thomas was a Jesuit who was sent on a mission to England, bearing a letter addressed to John Debdale of the village of Shottery near Stratford. He was arrested in June 1580, arraigned (along with Edmund Campion) on November 14, 1581, and on May 13, 1582, was subjected to the hideous death by hanging, drawing, and quartering prescribed for traitors. John Cottom resigned from his teaching position—we do not know if he did so voluntarily—some time after Michaelmas 1581, presumably at about the time of his brother's trial. He retired in 1582 to Tarnacre in Lancashire where his family had some land which he eventually inherited and administered, living openly as a Catholic and paying his recusant fines (fines imposed for nonattendance at church) until his death in 1616.

The next master, Alexander Aspinall, who lasted from 1582 to

1624 in the job, can hardly have had much to do with Shakespeare's education, but he became a prominent figure in the life of the small town. He is chiefly remembered because of his connection with an occasional verse atrributed to Shakespeare. In 1594 Aspinall, long a widower, married the widow Anne Shaw (one of whose sons would eventually witness William Shakespeare's will). In the following century Sir Francis Fane of Bulbeck (1611–80) recorded in his commonplace book a "posy" said to have been given by Aspinall to Mrs. Shaw to accompany a present of a pair of gloves, and attributed the lines to "Shaxpaire":

> The gift is small:
> The will is all:
> Asheyander Asbenall.

We are on more stable ground in trying to establish what the young bard might have learned at school. The curriculum would have been the authorized, standard fare of the time, and would have taken the boy far away from his parents in intellectual attainment and training. The process started very young.

We know, for example, that it was normal for education to begin in the so-called petty school at the age of four or five, where the pupils (all males—such a system was closed for girls) would work under the supervision of the school usher or *abecedarius* (so called because of the emphasis placed on learning the alphabet). The boys brought with them to school a hornbook, a sheet of paper or parchment with a protective cover of transparent horn; the paper would show the alphabet, the Lord's Prayer, and some simple guides to spelling. Once the hornbook had been worked through, they went on to *The ABC with the Catechism*, in which the hornbook page was included, as well as the Catechism from the Book of Common Prayer and a set of graces to be said before and after meals.

The school day was long, and it was framed by morning and afternoon prayers. The children were at work early, at six or seven in the morning, and their first session—uninterrupted except for a short pause for breakfast—lasted until eleven. They would come back from dinner at one, and work through, with a fifteen-minute break, to five. The staple activity of this eight-hour school day was

Latin grammar, and a great deal of effort went into rote-learning of conjugations, declensions, and the rest, as set out in the officially authorized textbook, William Lily's *Short Introduction of Grammar*. The experience was one which Shakespeare would dramatize in many of his plays; most directly in *The Merry Wives of Windsor*, where Lily's *Grammatica Latina* forms the basis of a comic interrogation of a schoolboy called William by the Welsh schoolmaster-parson Sir Hugh Evans.

A major objective of the educational system was to encourage fluency and eloquence in Latin composition. The theory was that, having been thoroughly schooled in the principles and structures of Latin grammar through study of Lily, students would then be introduced to storehouses of Latin eloquence and wisdom. These might be in the form of proverbs, *sententiae*, aphorisms from individual authors (such as Cato in the edition by Erasmus, or the stories of Aesop), collection of memorable phrases, words, constructions, or observations. The boys would eventually, it was hoped, be equipped to imitate, improvise, and invent spoken and written Latin of a high order. For scholars up to Newton's time, for men like Bacon and Milton, Latin was the language of learned discourse, a language that offered some fleeting hope of survival in a world of flux and instability. The most famous and influential of these collections was Erasmus's great anthology called *De Copia*.

So the first couple of years were devoted to Latin grammar and to simple collections of commonplaces and proverbs; the German Protestant reformer Martin Luther commended this material as second only to holy scripture. Into this program other kinds of writing were gradually introduced, notably (and of greatest relevance to Shakespeare's upbringing) dramatists like Plautus and Terence, and Erasmus gave careful instruction to the teacher to ensure that the correct pedagogical message was conveyed by such light-hearted texts. In some schools there was even a tradition of performing scenes from these plays, and for composing English versions of classical plays for performance by the boys. When Shakespeare, in *The Comedy of Errors*, one of his earliest plays, went out of his way to double the complexities of his already complicated source in Plautus *Menaechmi*, his audience would have recognized straightaway the familiar schoolroom material of wit, trickery, and deception; they would also have recognized the ambition, virtuosity, and difficulty of the task this latter-day Plautus had set himself.

At the age of nine or ten, in the third form (so in 1573–4 in Shakespeare's case), pupils would be introduced to some more modern authors—among them Palingenius and Mantuan, both quoted in the plays. They would also be put to work to enrich their vocabulary by learning lists of words and definitions, and would be set English passages from the Geneva Bible to translate into Latin. For practice in conversational Latin they would use the colloquies of various humanist educators, of whom the most important in England were Juan Luis Vives and Erasmus; these works contained dialogues, brief dramas exploring an idea or situation, or illustrating contrasting attitudes. Only recently have we come to recognize how the sensibilities of writers, readers, and patrons were shaped by their shared early experience of such works.

To modern eyes this is already a challenging curriculum, even if—apart from the plays—generally void of imaginative stimulation for the pupils. In the following year, though, they moved from the care of the usher into the hands of the master. In the Upper School training in rhetoric and composition continued, and students were introduced to some elementary logic. As well as Erasmus, the chief writers set before them were Cicero and Quintilian. On the basis of these models, the boys were set increasingly complicated compositions to perform, and in their final year at school might be told to invent speeches on particular occasions, to imagine what some famous person might or should have said at some crucial moment in history. As with so much of this Elizabethan system, we can see connections between a golden age of drama and an educational program constructed on the basis of dialogue, colloquy, and imagined speeches, and which so prized eloquence and verbal inventiveness. These older boys received a certain amount of imaginative nourishment as well. Virgil and Horace, and sometimes the satires of Juvenal and Persius, were studied. But the most important and vital text for many of the boys, to judge from its ubiquitous influence on their creative writings, and unquestionably the classical text nearest to Shakespeare's heart, was the *Metamorphoses* of Ovid. Alongside this the boys studied Caesar and Sallust as historians, and began some work on moral philosophy based on the *De Officiis* of Cicero. Those who made a start on Greek would have done so by study of the Greek text of the New Testament.

That, alongside the instruction from the pulpit and the tales and fables that would have been exchanged in bakehouses, alehouses, and other places where people met, was the extent of the education available to Shakespeare. To argue, as some do, that a man of Shakespeare's background could not have been sufficiently learned to write the works attributed to him, is to fly in the face of the evidence. And if we look at other writers of the time, many of them had the same grammar school training and came from the same or similar social class. What is more, there was nothing about the prescribed courses, whether at the universities or at the Inns of Court, that would have been especially beneficial to a fledgeling writer. These institutes were concerned to prepare men for the professions—the Church, the law, medicine—or to train them up to administer estates or hold office in government. Literature, as we would call it, was an extracurricular diversion, an entertainment extraneous to the serious business of life. And Shakespeare's approach to writing, to acquiring the secrets of a writer's craft, was as professional as that of any young lawyer or doctor.

Shakespeare's experience of drama might in any case have been more direct, more mind-forming, more central than the fragmentary surviving evidence can demonstrate. Let me suggest why. Of the Stratford schoolmasters listed earlier, Richard Jenkins (1575–9) and John Cottom (1579–82) were those most likely to have taught Shakespeare. Cottom was recommended to the town by Jenkins, so we may assume that they saw eye to eye on matters of educational practice; and one aspect of that practice involved drama.

Jenkins, born in London, was assisted at every stage of his career by Sir Thomas White, the founder of St. John's College, Oxford, and a substantial benefactor of the Merchant Taylors' School, which Jenkins presumably attended. The school was under the guidance of one of the great Elizabethan pedagogues, Richard Mulcaster, whose enthusiasm for the English language is well documented. He wrote: "I love Rome, but London better. I favour Italy, but England more. I honour the Latin, but I worship the English." To cultivate eloquence in English composition, and to inculcate what he called "audacity" as well as "good pronunciation" among his charges, he advocated teaching through drama, more specifically,

through acting. The Merchant Taylors' Boys regularly put on plays
at court before Queen Elizabeth; another of their plays, put on
before Sir Thomas White, consisted of an appeal for him to provide
more scholarships for them at St. John's. We know that many
writers came from this tradition, the greatest being Edmund Spenser; Mulcaster's system produced scholars and teachers also, of
whom it seems likely that Jenkins was one and Cottom another. In
other words, during the time Shakespeare was a schoolboy, education at Stratford was probably based on the principles set down
by Mulcaster and implemented by his followers, and consequently,
it laid stress on eloquence, performance, and "audacity."

There was undoubtedly some acting in the town in that time.
At Whitsun in 1583 the corporation paid 13s. 4d. "to Davi Jones
and his company for his pastime." Davy Jones, on the death of his
first wife Elizabeth Quiney (daughter of Adrian Quiney), had married Frances Hathaway (perhaps a cousin of Anne's) in 1579, and
William Shakespeare married Anne Hathaway in November 1582.
It seems likely that Shakespeare was glancing back at this Pentecost
play or one of its unrecorded predecessors when, in *The Two Gentlemen of Verona*, he has the disguised Julia reminisce about the time

When all our pageants of delight were play'd,
Our youth got me to play the woman's part,
And I was trimm'd in Madam Julia's gown;
Which serv's me fit, by all men's judgments . . .

There is also a fair chance that, as well as being exposed to a
small amount of drama during his schooldays, the young Shakespeare saw some plays performed during his formative years. I have
already mentioned that troupes of actors performed in Stratford in
the Gild Hall during John Shakespeare's year of office as bailiff
(1569, when William was just five years old), and from then onward
the town frequently staged performances by touring companies,
especially in the 1580s, as we shall see in the next chapter. Other
sorts of theatrical representation might have been available to the
boy during his second decade. In 1575, for example, the earl of
Leicester entertained Queen Elizabeth at his castle at Kenilworth,
just a dozen miles northeast of Stratford. The shows were of extraordinary magnificence and length—they lasted nearly three

weeks—and the local population thronged into the castle precincts
to see the great pageants and water shows, marvels and firecrackers
whose lights were reflected in the waters of the great lake that lapped
against the castle walls. There are undoubtedly moments in the
plays that can be plausibly connected with the astonishing spectacles with which the "great lord" pursued his political, religious,
and erotic courtship of the queen. Leicester was the lord of the manor
of Stratford, and it is perfectly conceivable that Alderman Shakespeare would have attended, and that he would have brought his
eleven-year-old son. In particular, some scholars have found traces
of the pageants of July 18, 1575. It has, for example, been suggested
that Shakespeare is recalling a childhood experience when the captain in *Twelfth Night* describes how Sebastian was delivered from
shipwreck by riding "like Arion on the dolphin's back"; or when,
in *A Midsummer Night's Dream*, Oberon reminds Puck how he once

> . . . sat upon a promontory,
> And heard a mermaid on a dolphin's back
> Uttering such dulcet and harmonious breath
> That the rude sea grew civil at her song.

For evidence, we need to turn to Robert Laneham, whose eyewit-
ness account of the "princely pleasures," tells of a water pageant:

> *Arion* that excellent and famous musician, in tyre and appointment
> strange well seeming too his person, riding aloft on his old friend
> the Dolphin (that from head to tail was a four and twenty foot long)
> and swimmed hard by these islands: herewith Arion . . . after a few
> well couched words unto her Majesty . . . bean a delactable ditty
> of a song well apted to a melodious noise, compounded of six several
> instruments all covert, casting sound from the Dolphin's belly
> within, *Arion* the seventh sitting thus singing (as I say) without.

One might go further and find in Oberon's reference to stars which

> . . . shot madly from their spheres,
> To hear the sea-maid's music.

—an allusion to the fireworks with which Leicester astonished the
beholders, and which were all the more extraordinary for being
aquatic.

Another large-scale dramatic performance that Shakespeare could have seen was the revival of the Coventry mystery cycle in 1579. The Coventry cycle had been the most famous of the great biblical dramas of the Middle Ages in England. Of the ten plays that made up the sequence only two survive: the Shearmen and Taylors' play of *The Annunciation, Nativity and Massacre of the Innocents*, and the Weavers' play of *The Purification and the Doctors*. Four other titles and subjects are recorded: The Smiths put on *The Trials of Jesus and the Crucifixion;* the Cappers staged *The Harrowing of Hell and the Appearances to the Disciples;* the Mercers, *The Death and Assumption of Mary and Mary's Appearance to Thomas;* and the Drapers were responsible for a play of *Doomsday.* There were four further plays of which nothing is known, though presumably at least two will have treated Old Testament subjects. The scale and scope of each guild's production is striking; indeed each seems to be a mini-sequence in itself. The fame enjoyed by the Coventry cycles was considerable.

In a collection of anecdotes, *A Hundred Merry Tales* (1526), there is an account of an unlearned priest in Warwickshire who, though "no great clerk nor graduate of the University," preached the Twelve Articles to his congregation, and ended by advising his illiterate flock: "If you believe not me, then for a more . . . sufficient authority, go your ways to Coventry, and there ye shall see them all played in Corpus Christi play." No cycle was as popular with royalty. Kings and queens were regular visitors to these great pageants that combined doctrine and spectacle. The antiquary William Dugdale, who was born in 1605, wrote that Coventry

was very famous for the *Pageants* that were play's therein, upon *Corpus-Christi*-day; which occasioning very great confluence of people thither from far and near, was of no small benefit thereto: which *Pageants* being acted with mighty state and reverence . . . had Theaters for the severall Scenes, very large and high, placed upon wheels, and drawn to all the eminent parts of the City, for the better advantage of Spectators: And contained the story of the New-Testament, composed into old English Rithme . . . I have been told by some old people, who in their younger years were eye-witnesses . . . that the yearly confluence of people to see that shew was extraordinary great, and yielded no small advantage to the city.

These plays were very lavish and heterogeneous, and they utilized a variety of dramatic modes and playing-spaces, ranging from elaborate wheeled scaffolds and *tableaux vivants* to having King Herod run up and down in the street among the audience. The cycles survived the Reformation in some form, and it is known that they were performed as late as 1579; clearly the city valued the events as tourist attractions and as expressions of civic and guild pride quite independently of their doctrinal functions. A few years later, in 1584, a new play called *The Destruction of Jerusalem* (by the Oxford scholar John Smythe of St. John's, a former colleague of Shakespeare's teacher Jenkins) was installed and scheduled for performance on Midsummer's Day and St. Peter's Day—dates which made it effectively a replacement for the Corpus Christi celebrations. Also to be performed was *The Conquest of the Danes*, a Hock-Tuesday pageant staged before the queen as part of the 1575 Kenilworth entertainment. Other plays were to be suppressed, and maypoles to be taken down. The council's decision smacks of compromise, of a way of maintaining the lucrative midsummer pageant without running the risk of being condemned as idolatrous and papist. At about the same time as *The Destruction of Jerusalem* was established as a regular feature at Coventry, Shakespeare was constructing his own secular equivalent, a cycle of plays setting out a historical narrative displaying a similar interplay of human detail and massive historical sweep. But did he see them? There is no way of being certain, though a single phrase in *Richard II* provides a tantalizing clue. When the king, in the process of being deposed, is called to appear before the assembled peers, he notes the silence of his sometime followers, and asks:

> Did they not sometime cry "All hail!" to me?
> So Judas did to Christ.

In no Gospel text available to Shakespeare does Judas say "All hail," but he does in the York play of *The Agony in Gethsemane*, and perhaps he used the same words in the (now lost) Coventry play on the same subject. As with the Cain story, whose details Shakespeare never shook out of his mind, the Judas episode, with its drama of recognition and betrayal, may have fixed itself in his memory through the resounding hypocrisy of this formal greeting.

Of course nothing that Shakespeare or his English contemporaries saw, read, discussed, experienced, wondered at, or understood existed outside a Christian context. More specifically, that context was Anglicanism. From his earliest days Shakespeare was brought up in a community that organized its religious life in accordance with the prescriptions of the state. Thus he would have been expected to receive instruction in his catechism from the parish priest before Evensong on Sundays and Holy Days as a child; to have attended Matins and Evensong; and to have received Communion on three occasions in the course of the year. He would have heard the Homilies set out in the Book of Common Prayer; and after 1570, when Queen Elizabeth was excommunicated by Pope Pius V and when there was a rebellion in the north of England, those prescribed sermons included the three-part *Exhortation to Obedience* and the six-part *Against Disobedience and Wilful Rebellion.*

From regular attendance at these services, with their systematic progression through the Bible, as well as from study of the Bible at home and at school, Shakespeare derived a good general knowledge of scripture. To judge from references within the plays, the first three chapters of Genesis were known almost by heart. Allusions to or quotations from more than forty books of the Bible, as well as the Apocrypha have been identified. Some parts of scripture were apparently particularly important to Shakespeare, notably Ecclesiasticus and the Book of Job, while the story of Cain surfaces in his writings on more than twenty-five occasions. The Prayer Book, and its texts of the Psalms, as well as the Catechism (in its English version) can be discerned frequently in the plays and poems. Much of Shakespeare's biblical knowledge indicates that the text of the Bible he used most was the so-called Geneva Bible, an enduringly popular translation, which carried convenient interpretative glosses next to the verses. But he knew other texts as well, and was aware of problems of translation and interpretation.

Shakespeare read widely, remembered acutely, and was especially apt to be struck by a memorable phrase. That, given what he went on to do, is hardly surprising. Some kinds of phrase or story—including those of betrayal and dissimulation, and those that reveal the shaping hand of providence behind the apparently random tragedies of human life—were particularly prominent in his consciousness. At another level, we might note that it is the early Books of the Bible, and the early books of Ovid's *Metamorphoses*, upon which Shakespeare draws most frequently; evidence here of the limitations of his education, perhaps, or a sign of his reading habits. But we should beware of such a conclusion, based as it is on a romantic view of the Bard leafing through classics or scripture and being struck by the beauty of their choicest phrases. He knew the whole stories of these texts, he understood and recognized literary structures, and imitated patterns and orders and kinds of composition just as much as the local felicities of eloquent clusters of words.

We have now seen something of the mental world in which Shakespeare grew up, though so far I have dwelt chiefly on its official and formal components. In later chapters I will attempt to show how men and women of Shakespeare's day tried to make sense of the world and the universe and their place in the system of things. But for the moment we can leave him, having taken note of the resources available to him through his church, his school, and the life of the town.

Only one of the twenty-six males christened in Stratford in 1564 carried on with full-time education. He was William Smith (born on November 22, 1564—six months later than Shakespeare), who spent some time at Winchester College before attending Exeter College, Oxford, from 1583. In later years he became a schoolmaster in Essex, and we can imagine that in his later career he put into practice the precepts and advice of the Mulcaster/Jenkins tradition.

As for Shakespeare, he would have left school with a good knowledge of scripture and would have had a thorough indoctrination in the Catechism and orthodox Anglicanism from church, whatever other influences might have been met at school or at home; he also had a solid grounding in Latin, and already knew some of the authors who would nourish his imagination throughout his life. From school, and perhaps from the town, he would have experienced the special quality of drama—he would have witnessed the transformation that overtakes words when they are performed, the control of an audience's imagination through staging, in other words, the miracle of performance. As his father's fortunes declined, Shakespeare's horizons widened. In a culture in which there was no adolescence for the middle classes, Shakespeare was pre-

paring to enter the world of adulthood armed with the best education that Stratford could provide, with a set of family
circumstances which, though now financially rocky, were better
than those of most of his fellows, and with a combination of the
roving spirit and entrepreneurial drive of his father and his mother's
sentimental attachment to homely proverbs on painted cloth. The
synthesis of sentiment and upward mobility was soon to bear fruit.

CHAPTER THREE

The "Lost Years"

This chapter deals with the years of Shakespeare's life in which one or more of the following—singly or in combination—might have happened. He may have traveled, worked as a schoolmaster, a soldier, or a lawyer, trained as an actor, embraced (or left) the Roman Church, poached deer, or indulged in bouts of heavy drinking. Whatever he did, he found some way of passing the time between leaving school in the late 1570s and springing into action—and celebrity—on the professional stage in London at some time in the late 1580s.

The most certain and best-documented (which is not saying very much) events in his life took place in and around Stratford: his marriage to Anne Hathaway and the subsequent birth of their children Susanna, Judith, and Hamnet.

Shakespeare was a minor when he married—he was eighteen, and would have needed the approval of his father. Anne, twenty-six and pregnant at the time of the marriage in November 1582, was to give birth the following spring to Susanna, who would be christened on Trinity Sunday, May 26, 1583, in Stratford. In those days the main legal requirement was that banns be published on three successive Sundays or Holy Days, in order to make it possible for any objections to the proposed match to be heard. After that it was customary for the wedding to be held in the bride's parish church before assembled families and neighbors, and obligatory for the details of the event to be recorded in the parish register. This standard procedure was not followed in Shakespeare's case.

The reason is fairly straightforward. Anne was pregnant, so the marriage needed to be arranged in a hurry. Banns could not be published during Advent or the twelve days of Christmas, or indeed for a week after that (in other words, between December 2 and January 13 in 1582–3). If the plan had been to have the banns read in the normal way before this off-season, the last dates available would have been the last two Sundays in November and St. Andrew's Day (November 18, 25, and 30). For some reason the parties involved did not meet this deadline. So on November 27 two friends of the Hathaway family traveled the twenty miles to Worcester to attend the consistory court, a body empowered to grant a marriage license even if, as in this case, the normal regulations could not be observed.

Consistory courts had a good deal of discretion in such matters, and could stipulate special conditions to meet the circumstances of particular cases. Sometimes, for instance, they could dispense with the banns altogether. But the bishop's officials would require more than mere attendance. They needed to be supplied with a statement on oath of the names, addresses, and occupations of the couple and their parents, a bond, a certificate testifying to the consent of the parents or guardians on both sides when this was necessary, and, of course, a fee. And Shakespeare, of course, also required the consent of his father.

All was presumably in order, since the bishop of Worcester's register for November 27, 1582 records the grant of a license for a marriage *"inter Willelmum Shaxpere et Annam whately de Temple grafton."* The mistake over the woman's name is one of a series of errors made by the scribe of the register. Elsewhere he wrote "Darby" where he should have written "Bradley," for example; it is not repeated in the text of the bond, dated the next day. There we read that "William Shagspere" and "Anne hathwey of Stratford in the Dioces of Worcester maiden" have been given license to marry after just one reading of the banns. The terms of the bond specified that the two sureties, Fulke Sandells and John Rychardson (each identified as *"agricola"*—that is, husbandman—of Stratford), would be obliged to pay forty pounds if the requirements laid down for the marriage were not satisfied. These requirements were that there should be no impediment (precontract, consanguinity, affinity), and no pending lawsuit relating to such matters; that if any legal action were brought against the bishop or his officials for providing the license, the costs of the action would be borne by William Shakespeare; that the marriage should not be solemnized without securing the consent of Anne's "friends." Sandells and Rychardson were friends of the bride's father: In 1581 Sandells was appointed an overseer of Richard Hathaway's will, and Rychardson witnessed the document. It seems to have been normal practice in Worcester, when the bridegroom was a minor, for friends or kinsmen of the bride to stand as surety, and generally to make sure her interests were safeguarded. The Shakespeares, and in particular their eldest son, would be held to their agreement.

What sort of family did Anne come from? Like Sandells and Rychardson, Richard Hathaway was a husbandman. He lived and worked at Shottery, in Hewland's Farm (known more picturesquely since 1795 as Anne Hathaway's Cottage), about a mile across the fields to the west of Stratford parish church. In his will in 1581, Richard left to his daughter Agnes (Agnes and Anne were more or less interchangeable names at the time) the sum of ten marks, which was to be paid to her on the day of her marriage. The will is dated September 1, 1581, not much more than a year before Anne's marriage to Shakespeare. There is no record of Anne's birth, since baptismal records did not begin until the new reign in 1558; she was probably born a couple of years before that, as the inscription on her grave brass suggests (she died on August 6, 1623, "of the Age of .67. yeares").

The Hathaway family house in Shottery was right at the boundary of the parish of Stratford, at the point where the farmland gave way to the Forest of Arden. Hathaways had lived in Shottery for some time. Anne's grandfather, John, had been a prominent Stratford figure in the early part of the sixteenth century. Muster-rolls of 1536 list him as an archer, and he went on to serve as constable in 1548 and to hold a variety of other posts of responsibility—beadle, affeeror, and so on. In the means test for the subsidy (tax) of 1549–50 he was assessed on an income of ten pounds—a considerable sum in the context of Stratford.

John was succeeded by his son Richard, who continued farming and seems to have operated on holdings in the Shottery area that amounted to between 50 and 90 acres, an acreage comparable to the Shakespeare holdings of about 107 acres in Stratford itself. The best evidence for his prosperity, and for his circumstances generally, is provided by the will. In that document he refers to seven children (three daughters and four sons) who were living in 1581, and made arrangements for them to be well provided for. His wife Joan was to act as executrix and residuary legatee, and was clearly expected to play an active role in the day-to-day running of the farm. Meanwhile, his oldest son, Bartholomew, was left to carry on the farming business. Provision was made for a financial settlement in the event of a dispute with his mother—Joan would be obliged to pay him £40 in compensation for the loss of his interest in the farm—and the will expresses the hope that the young man "shallbe a guyde unto my saide wife in her husbandrie. And also a Comforte unto his Bretherne and Sisters to his power." Of the other children, the youngest son, William, was to receive £10, and the remaining five were to be given ten marks (£6 13s. 4d.); the boys Thomas and John immediately; Margaret when she was seventeen; Agnes (Anne) and Catherine on the day of their marriages. As far as can be told, it looks from the phrasing of the will as though Anne was the oldest of Richard Hathaway's children. And she was, of course, a good deal older than her husband.

"O spite," as Hermia says in *A Midsummer Night's Dream*, "too old to be engaged to young!" Shakespeare's play contains several passages that speak regretfully of lovers "misgraffed in respect of years." In particular, we find older women twinned sadly with younger men. Whether this meant that Shakespeare was generalizing on the basis of his own experience, or whether his deep understanding of his wife, and of what commonplace wisdom would have made of her marriage, led him to write with sensitivity and sympathy of such unions, we can only guess. But there is enough material to feed the suspicion that Shakespeare felt trapped, that his youthful folly with a woman already moving rapidly out of the marriageable range was something for which he was conscious of having to pay, and pay dearly. And if he thought of trying to wriggle out of his responsibilities, Sandells and Rychardson, and no doubt others of their friends associated with recreational archery and part-time policing, would have kept him to his promise.

On the other hand, there may be a less confrontational, though admittedly less dramatic, way of reading these events. To take a particular instance, we might well be justified in interpreting the way Anne was left to look after the Stratford end of Shakespeare's business as a powerful indication that she was not some kind of predatory virago, out to snare anyone foolish enough to wander into her influence. Rather she may have been a competent manager, as her mother was, and someone who could be relied on to act as steward during the husband's absence. Neither John nor William Shakespeare was committed to husbandry, though each owned land. The two men found careers and fulfillment outside the family home, engaged in pursuits of which their ancestors could have had no conception. Each married into a degree of social pretension (the father more than the son), but it may have been equally important that they married into farming, that they took wives who had been brought up to manage the land. If we try to imagine what the big house in Henley Street was like, we need to conceive not just of noise and bustle and the external signs of small-scale manufacturing industry. The house was also the center of a small farming business, as well as being crammed with people—dependents, children, workers, servants, and others. The community, the extended family, was governed not by the preoccupied, upwardly mobile Shakespeare men but rather by Mary and Anne, whose upbringing fitted them well for such responsibilities.

Of course we can still speculate: We can imagine, for instance, that the relationship outgrew its passion (as the lack of further children after the birth of the twins Hamnet and Judith in January 1585 could show) and turned instead into that Protestant ideal of a union that provided its participants with companionship, with "mutual society." As his daughters moved into their teens (the boy Hamnet by then being dead), and his wife into her forties, Shakespeare's texts show traces of a concern that others should not fall into the snares of an unequal match—especially that they should avoid a union where the wife was much older than her husband. In *Twelfth Night*, for example, the Duke Orsino, sick of love-melancholy, offers advice to what he thinks is a young man (actually

the cross-dressed Viola). He gives general guidance on the choice
of partner:

> . . . Let still the woman take
> An elder than herself; so wears she to him;
> So sways she level in her husband's heart:
> For, boy, however we do praise ourselves,
> Our fancies are more giddy and unfirm,
> More longing, wavering, sooner lost and won,
> Than women's are . . .
> . . . let thy love be younger than thyself;
> Or thy affection cannot hold the bent:
> For women are as roses, whose fair flow'r
> Being once display'd, doth fall the very hour.

Much of what he says is engagingly commonplace: the duke,
however much he may appear to the infatuated Viola an oracle, a
fount of profound wisdom, is presented to the audience as one of
several examples in the play of narcissistic excess in love. On the
other hand, it is difficult to resist the sensation—so rare in Shakespeare's works—that behind this comic creation of a pitiable jumble
of amatory clichés and stereotypes there lies something a good deal
sharper, more intimate, more painful. We should note, though,
that the blame is placed on the male. It is man's inconstancy that
is at fault. Men's nature renders absurd all the conventional protestations of love, of faithfulness, and devotion. And these demons
are unleashed from the bottle most readily when the man is much
younger than his wife.

Let us now turn from marriage to the rest of the "lost years."
After all, the missing years would be a crucial period in the life of
any individual. In the case of Shakespeare they represent the transition from an evidently unremarkable student at a provincial gram-
mer school first into an actor, and then into a dramatist who was
instantly recognized as distinctive, extraordinary, a phenomenon.
The context for the period seems to me to have been set by Shakespeare's father, a man who, like so many other fathers, was concerned to give his son the advantages in life he felt he had missed.
Where he had forged a career for himself in a growing community,
had carved out a place in the commercial and industrial life of
Stratford, his son would start out as the eldest child of a prominent

man, as the heir to a substantial estate. And, unlike his brother Gilbert, for example, William was driven onward and outward, to emulate the mobile vigor and energy that had made (and perhaps broken) old John Shakespeare. On the surface, at least, it does not look as though the young man married as well—from a social point of view—as his father. Anne Hathaway was an heiress right enough, and the Shakespeare family was not as well placed in the early 1580s as it had been eight or nine years previously. But John Shakespeare can hardly have regarded it as a glittering match— and he would have had plenty of time to regard it, since he ended up sharing a house with Anne Hathaway for many more years than his son ever did. If William fell short of his father's expectations in that central aspect of his life, how else did the eldest son shape up in his attempts to make his way in the world?

The short answer is that we have no idea; or that we have plenty of ideas but precious little evidence. Scholars have taken positions on these "lost years" (and the implicit parallel with the period in the life of Christ between his discussions with the elders in the temple and the beginning of his public ministry hardly needs to be dwelt on too closely) that depend on certain beliefs based more on faith than on evidence. To some, an early start on the stage, probably in a touring company, is congenial. To others, the (sometimes associated) notion of employment in a Catholic household in the north of England fills the bill. Others imagine he was kept busy around Stratford with his growing family, a father who was a shadow of the man he had been, and a group of brothers and sisters who needed a firm, older presence to keep them in order. There are attractions in all of these views.

We need to remember that the "lost years" is a term that covers a longer period than is sometimes conceded. Until the printed attacks on Shakespeare by fellow dramatist Robert Greene in 1592, all we know for certain is that William Shakespeare was christened, took out a marriage license, and fathered three children. So we could take the lost period to be everything before 1592. More sensibly, I think we can assume that a writer of Shakespeare's accomplishment was educated, and that a boy of his social background would have attended the grammar school in Stratford up to the age of fifteen or sixteen. Thus, the missing period stretches, with the exception of the wedding and christening of his children, from about

1579 to 1592. Some of the stories that have grown up around the Shakespeare legend over the centuries have found this blank in the narrative a hospitable resting place.

The legends tell us precious little about William, John Shakespeare's son, Anne Hathaway's husband. But they tell us a good deal about the developing Shakespeare myth. The two most celebrated legends concern the story of Shakespeare's poaching deer belonging to Sir Thomas Lucy, and his boisterous drinking bouts. Three things should be said at the outset. First, they do not in any way retrieve the "lost years," since they deal with supposed events that must, even if we believe them to have been based on truth, have been marginal, recreational episodes. They do not explain how Shakespeare spent his time, fed his family, or acquired the skills he was to deploy in his writing career. Second, these stories conform to an oddly anachronistic—and certainly un-Jacobean—image of Shakespeare as a quintessentially English, robust, nononsense, virile fellow, a cross between his own Prince Hal and Robin Hood. They participate in that extraordinary late seventeenth- and early eighteenth-century shaping of Shakespeare's legend and status as the national poet. Indeed, they seem calculated to foster the notion of his rustic, unlearned, native wit, his spontaneous, artless brilliance that would have been held to contrast so markedly with the decayed, neoclassical, and formulaic achievements of clever (but suspect) foreigners like Molière and Racine. Third, the stories gave focal points for tourism. They furnished the world with a reason to visit such shrines as the Shakespeare Crab Tree and the Lucy estates at Charlecote and, later, at Fulbrooke.

The poaching stories begin to appear more than seventy years after Shakespeare's death. Richard Davies, a clergyman, perhaps at that time the chaplain of Corpus Christi College in Oxford, and certainly later the Archdeacon of Coventry, jotted down some observations about Shakespeare:

> William Shakespeare was born at Stratford upon Avon in Warwickshire in about 1563–4. Much given to all unluckiness in stealing venison & rabbits particularly from Sr———Lucy who had him oft whipt & sometimes Imprisoned & at last made Him fly his Native Country to his great Advancement. But his reveng was so great that

he is his Justice Clodpate and calls him a great man & yt, in allusion
to his name bore three lowses [luces; fish] rampant for his Arms.
From an Actor of Playes, he became a Composer. He dyed Apr.
23. 1616, probably at Stratford, for there he is buryed, and hath a
Monument on wch He lays a Heavy curse upon any one who shal
remoove his bones. He dyed a papist.

Davies lived all his life in Shakespeare territory—in Sandford,
four miles down river from Oxford; in Sapperton in Gloucestershire; and in Coventry. The credence given to his memorandum
about Shakespeare is not traditionally great. To the relief of those
who find the final unequivocal statement about the national poet's
religion unacceptable, Davies's reliability as a witness is damaged
by his faulty memory (he forgets Lucy's first name, Thomas) and
by his inaccurate recollection of literary texts. Clodpate is a character in Thomas Shadwell's play *Epsom Wells* (1672), and has been
confused in Davies's mind with Justice Shallow in *The Merry Wives
of Windsor*. Professor Schoenbaum, Shakespeare's most fastidiously
dispassionate biographer, goes a stage further in casting doubt on
Davies's standing. As a character witness he summoned Anthony
Wood, that sharp-tongued recorder of the Oxford of his day: Wood
depicted Davies as "red and jolly, as if he had been at a fish dinner
at C.C.C. [Corpus Christi College], and afterwards drinking—as
he had been": Schoenbaum implicitly attributes the mistakes in
Davies's mote to overindulgence of some kind. And of course the
effect is to render the final assertion as doubtful, as lacking in
authority, as is the rest of the material.

But before dismissing it, it might be an idea to look more closely.
What do we know of Sir Thomas Lucy, for example? Lucy (1532–
1600) had been a pupil of the martyrologist John Foxe, from whom
he derived a resolutely anti-Catholic set of views. At the age of
fourteen he married the twelve-year-old heiress Joyce Acton, who
brought with her extensive lands in Worcestershire. With this prosperity he built at Charlecote the first and one of the finest of the
great Elizabethan houses in the county. He was host to the earl of
Leicester, who knighted him (doubtless with the queen's approval)
at Charlecote in 1565, and to Queen Elizabeth in 1572. Records
associate him with drama twice. In 1555, "Master Luce" saw a play
at Banbury and then in 1584 a troupe called "Sir Thomas Lucies

players" were paid ten shillings at Coventry. The rest of his public
life conforms more closely to the expectations of someone schooled
by Foxe. As a Member of Parliament, in 1571 he presented a
petition on behalf of Puritan ministers, and was involved in drawing
up penalties for saying and attending Mass. In 1583, on the in-
structions of the Privy Council, he arrested Edward Arden at Park
Hall and conducted a search of the property of Edward Grant at
Northbrooke. He was a zealous seeker-out and hunter-down of
recusants, and was rewarded in the usual way when, in 1584,
Parliament granted him lands that had been confiscated from Catholics. On a more incidental level, he drew up a bill (which never
surfaced after its committee stage) to make poaching a felony. What
is clear from these facts is that, if Shakespeare was indeed a papist
(and, since Lucy died in 1600, that would mean that Shakespeare
was a Catholic early in his life), he would have had every reason
to fear Lucy, and every temptation to make him look a fool. The
occurrence of Davies's unambiguous assertion at the conclusion of
a story that involves a vigorously Protestant justice of the peace is,
to say the least, intriguing; it may well contain some elements of
truth—it may take us back to some disagreement between Shakespeare and Lucy that was transformed and mangled into the jumbled Davies records.

Shortly after Davies wrote, Nicholas Rowe published in 1709
both his great edition of Shakespeare and his two-volume edition
of Spenser. Each of these monuments of the scholarly standards of
their age represents an attempt to canonize, to invest with authority,
the writers so edited. We see the elaborate apparatus of the edition
of a classical text—biography, glossary, notes, textual commentary,
and so forth. The two editions show how the England of Queen
Anne, of the post-1688 settlement looked back at the England—I
am tempted to write "Merrie England"—of the last great queen.
Rowe had not read Davies, but his informant, the celebrated actor
Betterton, had a good deal of credibility, since an apparently unbroken line of theatrical succession could be traced back to men
who knew and worked with Shakespeare. Concerning the poaching
episode, introduced into the narrative as an "Extravagance" which
resulted in Shakespeare's being "forc'd out of his Country and that
way of Living which he had taken up," Rowe wrote that the young
Shakespeare:

. . . had, by a Misfortune common enough to young Fellows, fallen into ill Company, and amongst them, some that made a frequent practice of Deer-stalking, engag'd him with them more than once in robbing a Park that belong'd to Sir *Thomas Lucy* of *Cherlecot*, near *Stratford*. For this he was prosecuted by that Gentleman, as he thought, somewhat too severely; and in order to revenge that ill Usage, he made a Ballad upon him. And tho' this, probably the first Essay of his Poetry, be lost, yet it is said to have been so very bitter, that it redoubled the Prosecution against him to that degree, that he was oblig'd to leave his Business and Family in *Warwickshire*, for some time, and shelter himself in *London*.

Later in the edition, in the notes on the character of Falstaff in *The Merry Wives of Windsor*, Rowe seems to be closer to the mark than Davies had been in relating the youthful escapade to Shakespeare's text. He is unhesitating in his identification of the historical "source" of the celebrated comic episode in the play, when Falstaff is accused by Justice Shallow from Gloucestershire of having insulted him, "beaten my men, kill'd my deer, and broke open my lodge." Shallow comes to the court at Windsor to take the case before the Star Chamber. We have already learned that Shallow is a man to be reckoned with. He is praised by his cousin Slender because he can sign himself "Armigero" in legal documents; more significantly, the coat of arms he is entitled to wear displays a dozen white luces— a species of freshwater fish in the pike family. This fact inevitably gives rise to puns on "luces" and "louces." For Rowe, the connection is quite clear. He writes of Falstaff: ". . . in *The Mery Wives of Windsor* he has made him a Dear-stealer, that he might at the same time remember his *Warwickshire* Prosecutor, under the Name of Justice *Shallow:* he has given him very near the same Coat of Arms which *Dugdale*, in his Antiquities of that County, describes for a Family there . . ."

In fact, several families in the Stratford area had pike or similar fish on their coats of arms. More substantially, the events that lurk behind the evident allusiveness of the passage in Shakespeare's play are probably much closer in time to the text's composition, and closer in place to the London stage. This is hardly surprising, since it would have been an extremely private allusion, the most obscure of in-jokes, if Shakespeare had chosen to allude so obliquely to events that had occurred over a decade before, in the distant Warwickshire countryside. The barb, the poet's revenge nursed for so many long years, would have been wholly inaccessible to the metropolitan theater audience. Nevertheless, the fact that two independent witnesses made the identification indicates that it was current by the end of the seventeenth century—which shows, if nothing else, that there had arisen an interest in decoding Shakespeare's fictions, in uncovering the "reality" behind his allusions, of piercing his disconcerting veil of anonymity. By that time a great hunger to know more about "Shakespeare the man" was developing, and great feasts were made of the slenderest biographical scraps.

Rowe's account of the poaching, though composed without reference to Davies's anecdote, paints a similar picture. For him the youthful Shakespeare is to be conceived of as a young man of high spirits, with an interest in manly sport. His repudiation of authority is far from total: He objects primarily to Lucy's excessive severity, not to his defense of his property. And we should note that his reaction is a literary, rather than a social, rebellion: According to Rowe, he retaliates by composing a satirical ballad to shame his persecutor, and lampooned Lucy on the stage later in his career. Rowe was evidently reading Shakespeare in the light of his own day, placing him in a literary London much closer to Grub Street than to the circumstances of the 1590s.

Of course, we cannot establish conclusively that as a young man Shakespeare did not engage in some poaching—it would have been a common enough thing to have happened. What is more, Rowe claimed to have had sources for his biographical information that took him back almost to those who had known and worked with him. So there may be some basis to the story. On the other hand, memories might have been defective. We now know, for example, that in 1610 another Sir Thomas Lucy brought a Star Chamber suit against men who poached in his park and damaged his property; this obscure incident could well have been recalled when biographical interest in Shakespeare's life began to dig into memories of old Warwickshire folk.

The poaching story evidently struck a chord. It stimulated further research into Shakespeare's life in Stratford—rustic nonogenarians were quizzed assiduously by eminent literary pundits from London, and some duly obliged with vivid recollections that found their way into editions and celebrations of the national poet's life and work. Narratives of Shakespeare's youth were constructed on the basis of a feud between the young poet and the crusty squire; the location of the episode was fixed at Charlecote and then moved to Fulbrooke, a few miles away. Sites, such as a barn (formerly Lucy's Keeper's Lodge) where Shakespeare was supposed to have been imprisoned, were identified for the benefit of visitors to the district, and these places would have added credibility and given physical corroboration to the stories. Those who published such material often did so with every appearance of tentativeness, but argued that even the possibility of a connection with Shakespeare was sufficient reason to suspend scepticism. Samuel Ireland, describing a view of the Keeper's Lodge, remarked, "This supposition, how slight soever the foundation of it may be, I yet thought sufficient to give an interest to the spot in which it is presumed to have passed." And these stories satisfy a natural desire on the part of those exposed to the Shakespeare myth—whether at school or at home or even on a check-guarantee card—by effecting a link between the immortal, mythologized Bard and the Warwickshire countryside in which he lived. Undoubtedly, the commercial opportunities for the townspeople of Stratford that have sprung from Shakespeare's renown were in the minds of some who helped to fashion it, just as at the time of the Reformation the citizens of Coventry defended their mystery plays not only as spiritual festivities but also as tourist attractions.

There are not, alas, many local references in Shakespeare's plays. Even the Forest of Arden in *As You Like It* is in Belgium. A notable— and often noted—exception is that peculiar episode where Christopher Sly is tricked at the opening of *The Taming of the Shrew*. Sly is identified as "old Sly's son of Burton Heath," and he refers to "Marian Hacket, the fat ale-wife of Wincot." Wincot, half a dozen miles southwest of Stratford, was home to several Hackets in Shakespeare's day, while Barton-on-the-Heath, farther south still, was where Shakespeare's aunt Joan and her husband Edmund Lambert lived. From this slender information legends grew.

In 1762 the *British Magazine* featured an article on Stratford; the anonymous author described the various sights to attract the sophisticated literary tourist. As so often in that period, the good

people of Stratford were immensely accommodating to their learned
and gullible visitors, furnishing them with local legends in abundance. In this case, the landlord took his guest to a tree where
Shakespeare had sheltered for the night in the course of an expedition to test the drinking prowess of the inhabitants of the nearby
village of Bidford. The Londoner was solemnly assured that Shakespeare, "like Ben Johnson, loved a glass for the pleasure of society,"
and that the tree had ever since been known as "Shakespeare's
canopy." The fate of the unfortunate tree was thereby sealed. In
just a few years "the depredations of pious votaries" (as one contemporary put it) had reduced it to a lifeless stump, after pieces
had been broken off and carried away as souvenirs. In addition,
the image of a Bibulous Bard, a Shakespeare who drank with the
best and could find a bed under the stars, was consistent with the
other strands in the legend. The tree, like so much else that was
celebrated in those days, was a way of bringing Shakespeare down
to earth, of making him less miraculous and other-worldly and more
reassuringly normal, human, and English. And, whatever one may
think of the deer-hunting stories, the attraction of visiting Charlecote, like that of going to see "Mary Arden's House" or the Hathaways' cottage in Shottery, remains. These are places that the real,
historical Shakespeare—whatever he was like, whatever his feelings
for his wife, whether he started his plays early or late, whatever
his relationship with the young man of the Sonnets or the identity
of the Dark Lady—knew and saw and visited. They can stand for
a kind of certainty, for a certain point of reference, no matter how
much they have been "constructed" by later generations of wor-
shippers.

The big questions about the "lost years" remain unanswered—
we are no nearer knowing how and when Shakespeare began writing
plays, nor do we know how he acquired the skills and experience
to fit him for his profession. I have already suggested that his
schooling was a more important factor than is sometimes conceded,
and that the role played by drama in that process, and more generally in the dramatic events in Kenilworth, Coventry, and Stratford to which Shakespeare could have been exposed, needs to be
borne in mind. Perhaps we are today content to envisage the plays
as springing from imagination, from reading, from conversation,

and not necessarily from direct experience. We are less inclined to assume that because Shakespeare wrote of Italy he had been there, that because he wrote of war he had been a soldier, that because he wrote of politics he must have been a politician, and because he wrote of courts he must have been the earl of Oxford. There is still, however, a temptation to try to "explain" his eloquence as the consequence of pursuing some career that prizes it, such as the law or teaching—or even, of course, acting. In this, as in so many other matters, much depends on the preferences and predispositions of the biographer.

I have already tried to suggest that the use of drama in education played an important role in the formation of Shakespeare's literary experience. And as a consequence of such a connection we can conceive of the young Stratford man teaching and acting at the same time. In the last few years there has been an attempt to revive and circumstantiate one of the oldest anecdotes about Shakespeare's early years, and it merits very serious consideration. It goes back to John Aubrey, who claimed to have had his information from the actor William Beeston (died 1682). Beeston was the son of Christopher Beeston, who acted with Shakespeare in Ben Jonson's *Every Man in his Humour* in 1598—they were all members of the leading theatrical company of the time, The Lord Chamberlain's Company. Like Shakespeare's, Beeston's interests extended to the management and administrative side of the theater, and he became a prominent figure in the London theatrical world of the 1630s. So Beeston's son seems to represent a contact of sorts with the historical Shakespeare, and his report stated that "though as Benjamin Johnson says of him, that he had but little Latin and less Greek, he understood Latin pretty well: for he had been in his younger years a schoolmaster in the country." If the report is true, it probably means that Shakespeare was an assistant of some kind—we have already seen that the Stratford masters, for instance, were all graduates; and it would have been unusual—though not unprecedented—for a person of Shakespeare's more modest paper qualifications to set up independently as a schoolmaster. But a boy who had been brought up to act (and presumably showed some promise), and who could help out in the classroom, might well have attracted the attention of potential employers.

In 1581 the master of Lea Hall near Preston in Lancashire, a man called Alexander Houghton, made a will. In the document he made provision for a large number of retainers, including one William Shakeshafte, and he enjoined his heir, his half brother Thomas Houghton, to "be friendly unto" Shakeshafte, and either to find work for him or to help him to obtain another position. The household included players and musicians, and Thomas seems to have kept them on. Was Shakeshafte William Shakespeare? The name is hardly a problem, as there are plenty of references to the Stratford Shakespeares as Shakestaffe, Shakeshaft, and so on, and even at the height of his fame William appears in records as "Shaxberd." Nor is the age a drawback: There are numerous recorded instances of schoolmasters starting work in their teens (including Queen Elizabeth's doctor, Simon Forman), and seventeen was a normal age to act as an assistant. But is there any positive evidence to connect William with this actor in Lancashire?

One of the Stratford schoolmasters during Shakespeare's early years may represent a link. When Thomas Jenkins gave up the post in 1579 he recommended to the town a scholar from Brasenose, John Cottom. Cottom, as we saw, resigned in 1581, round about the time his younger brother, a Jesuit missionary priest, was arrested with Edmund Campion. John Cottom retreated to his native Lancashire, where he lived openly as a Catholic, paying the stipulated fines, in that northern stronghold of the old religion. The Cottom family were neighbors of the Houghtons—indeed, Cottom's father was their tenant. So, for this connection to work, some time between 1579 and 1581 the young Shakespeare has to be translated from Protestant Stratford to Catholic Lancashire, and achieve a position of some prominence in a large household—judging from the handsome financial provision made for Shakeshafte in the will. The suggestion of Professor Honigmann is that Cottom, shortly after arriving in Stratford, heard that his father's neighbor and landlord was looking for someone to teach the numerous children in his large household. Cottom's brightest pupil, whose father's financial fortunes have suffered a major reverse (thus ruling out university and setting back the project to make a gentleman of him), but who has no inclination to give up his books and involve himself in the family farming or commercial enterprises, is offered the chance of a post in the substantial household of a provincial grandee.

Once arrived in the north, the boy teaches his Terence and Plautus but also gets to know the group of players in the household, and begins to work with them too.

The major problem with this story is that the Lancashire connection implies a closer conjunction between Shakespeare and Catholicism than would be consistent either with the unimpeachably patriotic figure propagated by the Shakespeare myth or with the strong anti-Catholic sentiments articulated from time to time in the plays. On the other hand, as some have argued, the anti-Catholicism might equally mark the enthusiasm of a convert to repudiate and dismiss his former allegiances. A material objection is that the mere citing of names proves little—there were other Shakeshaftes in Lancashire, for example—though the career of John Cottom unquestionably connects Stratford Grammar School with both Catholicism and Lancashire. Whatever the facts may have been, Shakespeare was back in Stratford no later than August 1582 (when Anne Hathaway became pregnant), not long after Cottom returned to his native Lancashire. But Stratford and his young family need not have occupied his time entirely. If we subscribe to the Lancashire story, the likelihood is that it explains Shakespeare's route to the London stage. That is because Houghton's players probably went into the service of the Hesketh family, and thence into the service of Lord Ferdinando Strange, the earl of Derby. When Lord Strange died, his players were assimilated into the Lord Chamberlain's Men, and it is as a member of that company that William Shakespeare is first recognizable as a figure in the documentary history of the London theater companies. It is entirely consistent with what we know to suppose that Shakespeare worked in the theater—perhaps still doing some teaching—from about 1585 to 1595, though such a reading of his life has prompted some to reach striking conclusons about his religious beliefs and about the chronology of his plays.

The frustration of knowing so little about Shakespeare's formative years can hardly be wished or argued away. And the Shakespeare myth has its own vitality, its own self-sustaining energy. All we do know is that during the "lost years" Shakespeare married a woman much older than himself, that she bore him three children, and that she settled down to live out her life in the teeming Shakespeare household. Meanwhile, the "merry-cheek'd old man" had

his former glories to think on, and his ambitions for his family—
focused on his eldest son—to keep him warm. And as for Shakespeare himself, the period saw the schoolboy turn into a professional
actor, the student of Plautus and Terence turn into the author of
The Comedy of Errors, and the reader of Seneca and Ovid into the
poet of *Titus Andronicus*. No stuffed archives of biographical data
could chart or explain such a metamorphosis.

CHAPTER FOUR

From the Country to the City

Early modern England provides us with plenty of rags-to-riches stories, as young men, following Dick Whittington, sought their fortune in London. So whatever image we may wish to entertain of Shakespeare's momentous departure from his native heath— whether we wish to suppose that he set off on his own, on foot, after a tearful farewell to his wife, aging parents, and three young children, or alternatively that he was carried away in the midst of a bustling throng of actors hurrying to their next venue—the scene would have been a version of similar scenes being played out all over the country. Like his father before him, Shakespeare was moving onward and, he hoped, upward. Stratford can have held little for him now that his father's enterprises had faded, and it must have seemed better to seek a means of using his talents, of stretching his abilities, than to submit himself to the seasonal disciplines of a life his father had spurned many years before.

There was a choice of two routes to London, and from scattered local allusions in the plays it seems clear that over the years Shakespeare knew both of them. Whichever he chose, the trip would have taken at least four days on foot, assuming both a daily average trek of about twenty-five miles and good conditions underfoot. Doubtless he would have hired a horse if the means had been available to him, as they certainly were within just a few years of his arrival in London. But let us suppose that his first journey was undertaken on foot, carrying what he could—did he bring a few books (a New Testament, Ovid's *Metamorphoses*, perhaps?) maybe stored away, with clothes, provisions, and letters of introduction, in one of his father's fine leather satchels? The two routes diverged then, as they diverge today, on the far side of Clopton Bridge, the road to the right leading to Oxford, that to the left to Banbury; the modern roads follow those that Shakespeare knew fairly closely.

The Banbury route (today the A422) would have started with a fairly straight six miles down to the junction with the ancient Roman road, the Fosse Way, at Ettington. It continued through the wooded countryside toward the forbidding slope of Edge Hill, close to what was to be the site of the opening battle of the Civil War more than half a century later. Then it wended its way along the ridge through Wroxton and down into the prosperous (and Puritan) market town of Banbury. Carrying on to the east, the road passed through Brackley and then followed the valley of the Great Ouse for seven or eight miles to Buckingham before turning south, through Winslow and on to Aylesbury (close to today's A413). From Aylesbury the sixteenth-century traveler had to make the steep ascent of the Chilterns, probably above Wendover, and then pass down through Great Missenden, Amersham, Chalfont St. Giles, and Chalfont St. Peter to Uxbridge and so into London.

The Oxford route was, and is, shorter. In winter and spring it would have been wetter, colder, and vulnerable to falls of snow. It took the traveler directly south along the banks of the Stour through Atherstone and Newbold (the modern A34), across the Fosse Way, to Shipston-on-Stour. The road then moved up into the Cotswolds, along the bleak ridge that runs from the ancient and mysterious Rollright Stones through the market town of Chipping Norton and on through Enstone to the royal park of Woodstock, before dropping down into the Cherwell valley on the approach to the city of Oxford. Out of Oxford (on something like the modern A40), the road passed over Headington Hill and on through Wheatley, Tetsworth, and Stokenchurch, over the Chilterns and down into High Wycombe. From there the trail led through Beaconsfield and Gerrards Cross to Uxbridge.

The approach to London from Uxbridge, shared by both routes, was a weary trudge of a dozen miles or so, enlivened perhaps by an occasional glimpse of St. Paul's. Even at this period, the pall of smoke that was to hang over the city until the late 1950s would have been noticeable, and a thing of wonder to a traveler from a small provincial town. The road (close to the modern A4020) led through Shepherd's Bush and on past the gallows at Tyburn (modern Marble Arch), through pleasant fields and clusters of houses along the Oxford road, ignoring the Tottenham Court Road to the left and the lane down through St. Martin's Fields to the right. The road changed its name to St. Giles High Street as it passed through the village of St. Giles in the Fields (bounded on the south by the Reading road—now Shaftsbury Avenue), and then, passing a walled track to the right (modern Drury Lane), it led south into Holborn, a broad street with substantial and imposing buildings (including Gray's Inn, where *The Comedy of Errors* would be performed at Christmas 1594, across Ely place, over the Fleet River by means of Holborn bridge, and then via Snow Hill to Newgate.

We know from contemporary accounts that the scale, bustle, and prosperity of the city astonished even well-traveled foreign visitors. But a young man from a town whose population was not much more than a thousand souls, from a place where he and his family had been prominent and influential, where close ties of kinship, business, and friendship bound neighbors to each other, must have experienced this extraordinary phenomenon of the great metropolis as a profound jolt to his understanding of the world. Maybe his traveling companions strove to puncture his awe by pointing out the recently established suburban brothels in St. Giles (relocated from the city in response to the syphilis "epidemic") or by showing the filth and squalor of the Fleet River, where periodic efforts to restore the channel to the navigability of previous generations represented feeble shots in a losing battle against the city's ability to generate refuse on an unprecedented scale.

So we can assume that Shakespeare made his way into the city by way of Newgate, with any reverie at the majesty of the capital disrupted by the bustle of the crowds and by the limbs of executed criminals displayed on poles above his head. Elizabethan London was a walled city, whose inhabitants (in theory at least) were still regularly drilled in the use of weapons well into the 1590s. Although the most recent siege had been during Wyatt's rebellion in

1554, the extensive preparations for defense against the Armada in 1588 gave concrete expression to the city's pride in its inviolability. The city walls, like those of the Tower, so it was said, were bound together with a mortar that included human blood, and their strength derived from this grisly paste. Tudor Londoners were nourished on the legend that the city had been founded by Brutus (hence "British") and other survivors of the destruction of Troy. And when the Romans named the inhabitants of this region the Trinovantes, they were garbling the "real" name of the city—Troy Novant, or New Troy. The walls contained several substantial forts, numerous turrets and bastions, and stretched all around the city on the northern side, running for more than two miles.

Though the walls are gone, their route can still be traced—most easily by following the sites of the former city gates. Even in Shakespeare's time the southern stretch of the wall, along the shore of the Thames, had fallen into disuse and crumbled into the water, though Baynard's Castle, next to Puddle Wharf, still stood to dominate the waterfront. The castle, rebuilt in 1428 by Henry V's brother Humfrey, duke of Gloucester, was where Richard III had been offered the crown, and in Elizabeth's time was the London residence of the earls of Pembroke. Newgate, as its name implied, was one of the more recent gates to be constructed. The original ones had been Aldgate in the east, Aldersgate in the north, Ludgate in the west, and the Bridgegate over the Thames to the south. By the reign of Henry II three further gates had been permitted: Newgate, the Postern (immediately to the north of the Tower on Tower Hill), and Bishopsgate to the north. Other, less substantial, breeches in the wall in the form of posterns had been created, such as those at Moorgate, at Christ's Hospital (near Smithfield), and at Cripplegate.

This was still essentially the city that Chaucer would have known two hundred years before. Indeed, it was the city in which so many of the events that Shakespeare would dramatize in his English history plays had taken place. The monastic houses were gone, of course, and great nobles and merchants now created their mansions and apartments in them. A typical example is the complex of buildings in the Blackfriars area where, at the height of his fame and prosperity, Shakespeare would acquire a fashionable residence (as the artist Van Dyck would in the next generation) in the gatehouse of the old priory (whose hall housed the exclusive, expensive, modern theater for which he wrote his last plays). The number of major new constructions was small; as the population grew ever greater, gardens became houses and alleys, while spaces were filled with improvised structures. There were some open spaces, and some notable gardens, but much of the city was a rabbit warren of narrow, twisting lanes, thronged with people and animals, with carts and carriages, street vendors and the like. The city was bursting at the seams.

One of the few large-scale Renaissance buildings in the city was Sir Thomas Gresham's Royal Exchange, built at Cornhill in 1566–7 on the model of the Burse at Antwerp. It had a spacious courtyard and a distinctly cosmopolitan ambience. In the dramatist Thomas Dekker's words, "at every turn, a man is put in mind of Babel, there is such a confusion of languages." Within the city, the Guildhall stood as the focus of the local civil administration, while the growing power of trade and commerce was embodied in the numerous halls of the various livery companies, successors of the medieval guilds; there may have been up to fifty of them, many purpose-built. From maps that have survived we can see the handsome turreted hall of the Drapers, which stood in Throgmorton Street, and the halls of the Mercers in Cheapside and of the Fishmongers near London Bridge. Down by the river, as the maps show, docks and warehouses, quays and cranes gave concrete expression to the commercial foundation of the city—and their names (Hay Wharf, Timberhithe, Fish Wharf, Salt Wharf, Vintry Wharf) record the trades that took place there.

The West Midlands, Shakespeare's country, had already seen the beginnings of an industrial revolution. Travelers in Birmingham in the sixteenth century commented on the noise that the foundries made; perhaps Shakespeare had come across some industrial processes on a grander scale than that of the local brewers in Stratford, or of his father's leather works. But he had now come to an altogether more awe-inspiring place, with industrial operations on a massive scale. The maps depict few of the numerous factories that we know existed at the time, but they do show gun foundries. One was at the corner of Thames Street and Water Lane, and there was another, larger, factory north of Aldgate on the other side of Houndsditch. Stow reports that the noise generated by a group of

iron foundries at Lothbury was "loathsome . . . to the by-passers."
It is also possible to make out brick kilns—and these must have
declared their presence by the smoke that poured out of their lofty
chimneys. One was in the fields near Islington, while another is in
Scotland Yard and would have belched out smoke—depending on
the prevailing wind—over the adjacent palaces and mansions in
Westminster and along the Strand.

Londoners saw the "silver streaming Themmes" as their metaphorical lifeblood, their commercial link with the ever-expanding
world of Europe, the Indies, Africa, and America. It was a highway, connecting the city with Westminster by means of barges and
other small vessels. Unfortunately, they also depended on the
Thames in a more literal sense: Though the great river was a sewer,
people ate the fish that swarmed in it and relied on it for drinking
water. Professional water bearers took their pack-ponies down to
the Thames and loaded them with great wooden "cans" full of water
for delivery to individual houses. Water was additionally piped in
from wells and springs in the suburbs, and the carriers also supplied
their customers from the many conduits and pumps in the city.

The huge population was provided with food at the numerous
markets. Some were specialized: meat at Smithfield, fish and meat
at the Stocks Market (on the site of the present Mansion House),
poultry at Leadenhall. But others, like Newgate market or that at
Cheapside, sold a wide range of goods. For any wide-eyed migrant
from the country in those days there would have been two marketplaces above all to visit. Each was a building designed for other
purposes; each was a massive structure that dominated the skyline;
each was a center of exchange and commerce. One was London
Bridge, the other St. Paul's Cathedral.

London Bridge was one of the wonders of the kingdom, and a
sight that all tourists came to see. It was the only bridge across the
Thames, and the only direct access to the city from the south. Its
southern gate was decorated with the heads of criminals, whose
limbs were displayed on the city's other gates. It was broad and
majestic, built on twenty arches, and carried a road that had once
been wide enough to permit wagons to pass freely in both directions. But that had all changed by Shakespeare's day, and it was
permanently clogged with traffic and people—primarily because
the length of the bridge had by that time come to be occupied by

substantial houses built by "merchants of consequence," who would use the ground floor for their showrooms and have their apartments on the upper stories. Right in the center was a huge Tudor building known as Nonsuch because of its resemblance to the great royal palace of that name, but contemporaneous pictures show that there was a great deal of improvised, parasitical construction here as in the city, with structures sprouting from the solid houses and filling in the spaces. They made it almost impossible for the traveler to see the river beneath, with boats negotiating the narrow channels between the pillars. Along with the Tower, the bridge was a potent symbol of the city's uniqueness and endurance.

As a spectacle, St. Paul's was equally extraordinary. It was a place where God and Mammon met on more or less equal terms, with the balance tilted somewhat toward the latter. The cathedral church was still from a distance the most massive and splendid of all English cathedrals—even if by Shakespeare's day the 447-foot wooden steeple had been burned down in 1561 after being struck by lightning. Travelers on the road in from the west could have seen its huge bulk from many miles away, as some drawings show. It was at St. Paul's that great national occasions were staged in the heart of the capital. Here, for example, Sir Philip Sidney was laid to rest in February 1587; and here on November 24, 1588, was held the service of thanksgiving for the victory—the miraculous, God-given victory, as the English were encouraged to see it—over the Spanish Armada.

But a closer view, perhaps gained as the crowds gathered for a sermon at Paul's Cross, yielded a much less imposing image. To start with, the cathedral was falling apart. King James would eventually establish a Royal Commission (whose members included Francis Bacon, the duke of Buckingham, and Inigo Jones) to draw up a plan to remedy the structural damage and modernize the Gothic structure on neoclassical principles. But when Shakespeare arrived in London he would have seen the great edifice as a faded, crumbling ruin outside, and a scene of unique oddity inside. Parts of the building still performed the normal functions of a cathedral; services were held in the usual way, lavish tombs were constructed for the nobility, and the choir sang as it always had. But the nave (variously known as Paul's Walk or Duke Humfrey's Walk) was a riot of commercial life. If this temple was not full of moneylenders, it was because the moneylenders had lost the fight for breathing space with merchants, factors, tailors, lawyers, pickpockets, whores, and other dealers busily engaged in meeting clients, swapping information, selling services of all kinds, and hiring workers who advertised their availability. The rood loft, tombs, and even the baptismal font were used as counters for paying out money; and beer, bread, fish, and fruit could be bought there. In a limited attempt at reform, in 1554 the mayor and council had prohibited a few of the more egregious sacrileges, most notably the use of the church as a short-cut by deliverymen, and the practice of leading horses and pack-mules through the building. But the cathedral was, and remained, a magnet for all sorts and conditions of Londoners. Gallants, wits, and other hustlers loitered there to try to sponge a meal or some other invitation; in Gabriel Harvey's phrase, a penniless gallant would be compelled to "seeke his dinner in Poules with Duke Humphrey."

Outside, in the churchyard, was the hub of the publishing trade. Stationers lived in the streets around the cathedral close, and set up stalls and shops to sell their wares in the shadow of the church. If we look at the title pages of books from this period we can gain some idea of the number and variety of the booksellers, and of the colorful signs with which the stalls and shops were distinguished. To give just a few examples from Shakespeare's works, *Titus Andronicus* was printed for Edward White and Thomas Millington, and was "to be sold . . . at the little North doore of Paules, at the signe of the Gunne"; *Venus and Adonis* was to be sold "at the signe of the white Greyhound"; *Richard II* "at the signe of the Angel"; *Troilus and Cressida*" at the spred Eagle," and so forth. I will have more to say about the publishing business in later chapters, but we can be entirely confident that Shakespeare knew this area well; that, like most literate citizens, he browsed here for the books that would make up his small personal library; and of course, within a few years of his arrival in London, this was to be one of his marketplaces too, a place where his writings sought to effect a transition from the emphemerality of stage performance to the more abiding state of print.

The city, as befitted the fortress of the descendants of the ancient Trojans, had a fierce pride in its independence and traditions. But although it was preeminent in commerce and industry, its neighbor,

Westminster, was the seat of the crown, and of the government, as well as the main home of the court. Between the city walls and Westminster, between the Strand and the river, beyond the Temple Gardens, was a row of great mansions with gardens stretching to the water's edge. These were the city houses of various court grandees—York House, Bedford House, Arundel House, the Savoy, Durham House, Somerset House, Essex House (formerly Leicester House, and later to figure in Essex's abortive coup against Queen Elizabeth). The complex of palace buildings themselves stretched from Scotland Yard westward to Westminster Abbey, and they were linked by a walled street to St. James's Park to the north.

Opposite was Lambeth, a village surrounded by treacherous marshes, and then as now the London residence of the archbishop of Canterbury. Contemporaneous maps indicate several ferry crossing points at this relatively narrow part of the river, notably those on the sites of the modern Westminster Bridge and Lambeth Bridge. The other part of the south bank that sustained a population was the Southwark area around the southern end of London Bridge, and this was one of the suburban districts whose population grew most rapidly during Shakespeare's lifetime—indeed, he himself moved there round about the turn of the century, and it was there that the Globe Theatre would be built.

Let us imagine that the newly arrived Shakespeare has had his first sight of these great landmarks of the capital, that he has made his way from west to east, from north to south through the crowds, that he has crossed over the bridge to the south bank, and that he turns to look at the city. What he would have seen was a spectacular water frontage, from the huge bulk of the Tower in the east, past Baynard's Castle and St. Paul's to Blackfriars and the Temple, with the mansions of the Strand out of his line of sight. He would also have seen the spires and towers of a hundred churches within the city walls, the river teeming with small boats, the wharves alive with workers, the smoke belching from small factory chimneys and domestic hearths. To the north, he might not have been able to see the group of windmills built on top of rubbish dumps in Finsbury Fields, but he would have seen similar structures on the higher ground, like those at Highbury and Hampstead. Everywhere a combination of majesty and bustle, at every turn an illustration of how humans, whatever their power and pretension, are parts of a

much bigger, much older picture, and that they depend on forces—
the sea, the wind and, above all, the river—that are beyond their
control. And the city was many things: a collection of ancient
monuments, an encyclopaedia of the nation's history, an intensely
modern development, a social phenomenon that nobody at the time
was in a position to comprehend or manage. For if Shakespeare
crossed back over the bridge to the city, what did he find?

The simplest answer is that he found a very large number of
people, a population some hundred times greater than that of Stratford. In 1550, for example, when no other English city had more
than 5,000 inhabitants, London had something like 120,000. By
1600 that figure had grown to about 200,000, and by 1650 to
375,000. Shakespeare's time in London coincided with a period of
rapid growth and with the final bursting out of the city walls, when
the suburbs to the north and west and those on the south bank
expanded at an unprecedented rate.

Some of the physical and economic consequences of this increase
in population will be obvious. It posed a massive logistical problem
for the civil administration. These people had to be housed and fed
and employed; they and their horses needed to be watered in summer and kept warm in winter; they needed to be cared for when
they were ill, buried when they died, induced to obey the law, and
so on. For new immigrants, the city must have rocked the foundations of their understanding of themselves, of the world, and of
social relations. In the environment in which most of them had
been brought up, the countryside, Elizabethans lived with plenty
of room for each individual. In the great capital, on the other hand,
personal space was at a premium. Population density was so much
greater that it necessitated a redrawing of the boundaries of privacy
and identity. Tenements were constantly thrown up, houses,
rooms, and apartments squeezed into ever narrower spaces. Recent
studies have shown that London households did not just have less
living space; they were also considerably larger (on average by some
50 percent) than households in provincial towns or in more rural
areas. And this was not because there were different patterns of
family composition in the metropolis. If anything, as a result of
exceptionally high infant mortality in London, and because some
families sent their offspring into the countryside to be nursed, the
number of resident children was lower there than elsewhere. Lon-

don households were bigger because they contained more servants and lodgers. Given the importance attached to family and local ties, many immigrants found lodgings with members of their extended family, or with households connected in some way with the same provincial town or village—in just this way, a generation earlier, John Shakespeare had moved into Stratford from Snitterfield, and no doubt William Shakespeare had at least some names and addresses to look up when he arrived in London. In this way new citizens provided themselves with some kind of anchor, some familiar values, customs, and dialect in which to root their new urban identity.

But all around them the entire city was embarking on an involuntary and unprepared experiment in urban living, both as individuals and as a community. We do well to remember when noting "themes" in Shakespeare's writings—themes such as the nature of the individual, the relationship between the individual and society, the gulf between the public mask and the private self—that these matters were not just common Renaissance preoccupations. Rather they were among the most urgent concerns of the writer and of his London audience. Indeed, the very popularity and continued success of the public theater, which had no counterpart anywhere else in Europe, was a social phenomenon intimately bound up with the nature of the city in which he lived and worked.

Shakespeare's work was the city's play. The theater was one of the ways in which the population found recreation and amusement. But there were other diversions available to Londoners. To the north of the city, for example, in Finsbury Fields, there were stakes set up with colored targets. In what seems to have been a fairly hazardous cross between a modern golf driving range and a golf course, citizens would stroll, dressed in fetching short cassocks, and fire arrows at these targets. But maps indicate that these fields were also used for musket practice and for grazing and milking cattle. And while the musket range was behind a wall, accidents with arrows were common. The diary of the London undertaker Henry Machyn records the death of a woman who was "slain going in Finsbury Field with her husband with an arrow shot in the neck"; Dame Alice Owen founded her school in Islington to thank God for a narrow escape when a stray arrow passed through her hat. The danger became a joke, too: At the end of Francis Beaumont's comedy *The Knight of the Burning Pestle* (1609), the grocer's son Rafe comes onstage with an arrow through his head as a result of a walk in Moorfields. Rafe was a casual victim of that branch of archery known as Roving—shooting over open ground at unknown distances. The other archery practices of the time, namely "Prick" or "Clout" shooting (over measured distances of between 160 and 240 yards and designed to increase the length of shot), or "Butt" shooting (over distances between 110 and 140 yards and designed to foster accuracy) were more obviously military in their application. It is worth remembering that, although the musters gathered to defend London from the Armada were better armed with guns than their provincial counterparts, between 20 and 50 percent were armed with bows. So shooting in the fields, whether purely recreational or with a more sober purpose, was a common pastime. In other parts of the city, and especially on the south bank, quintains and other obstacles were set up to test equestrian skills—other facets of military training which had become exercises and pastimes for those who could afford the leisure and the equipment. There is a clear parallel with the revival of chivalry under Queen Elizabeth, and the consequent cultivation of martial arts that, in the real world of war, were being rendered obsolete by the gun and by the development of weapons of mass destruction such as the fireship.

Though literacy was on the increase, many of the systems of communication were preliterate—visual rather than verbal. Shops and inns were distinguished by signs, servants wore livery, and different social ranks and professions were marked by their dress. Public information was disseminated by proclamations. Changes in public policy were often conveyed by pageants, processions, and displays, and the surviving records show how crowds would assemble to watch such sumptuous displays as the queen's journey from palaces at Westminster or Greenwich to the city.

Of enduring popularity as a public diversion was the spectacle afforded by executions. Huge crowds gathered at Tower Hill for beheadings, at Smithfield for the burning of heretics, or at Tyburn for the hanging, drawing, and quartering of convicted traitors—which, by Shakespeare's day, usually meant Jesuits. Such events were inescapably theatrical: There was a stage, and an audience, and actors who could be judged on how well they played their parts. The officers were required to carry out their function with decency and solemnity, acting as the mere instruments of justice. The victim would be expected not to shake but to show steadfastness, to make a ritual gift of earthly possessions, to utter some resolute and/or penitent words expressing submission to the Almighty, and, perhaps, to make some final quip, some highly individual jest as the performance of his life was about to be brought to an end. The crowds became connoisseurs of these final scenes in the lives of famous men and women. As Montaigne said, "I have seen divers, by their death, give reputation to all their forepassed life." Where modern politicians are well advised to have their resignation letter always to hand, Tudor and Stuart statesmen rehearsed their gallows performance and their last words. Sir Walter Ralegh, who spent years under threat of execution, wrote a brief poem (later set to music by Orlando Gibbons) that sums up these matters:

> What is our life? A play of passion,
> Our mirth the music of division.
> Our mothers' wombs the tiring-houses be,
> Where we are dressed for this short comedy.
> Heav'n the judicious sharp spectator is,
> That sits and marks still who doth act amisse.
> Our graves, that hide us from the searching sun,
> Are like drawne curtains when the play is done.
> Thus march we, playing, to our latest rest—
> Only we die in earnest. That's no jest.

Ralegh's use of two ideas in particular—the world as a stage and life as a performance—may well strike modern eyes as somewhat commonplace. But on a very general level, his lines tell us a great deal about how people in the Renaissance saw themselves and their lives, and tried to make sense of their experiences. They also show how the theater had become, during the course of Ralegh's life, an accepted metaphor for human existence. That development coincided with—indeed was inseparable from—the extraordinary new phenomenon of the public stages in London, a phenomenon that grew to be one of the wonders of the age.

Apart from large-scale outdoor entertainment such as processions and executions, Elizabethan London provided numerous diversions for those with time on their hands, although the civic authorities were usually anxious to exercise a degree of control over the leisure pursuits of the population. Specifically, they ensured that certain kinds of merrymaking took place outside the city limits.

On the south bank of the Thames, for example, citizens could disport themselves in brothels or at the bear-baiting stadium. Bear-baiting by dogs was a pastime in which the English took some considerable pride, a sport in which they regarded themselves as superior to their effete continental cousins. In 1506, Erasmus commented on the great herds of bears maintained to supply the ring. From the reign of Henry VIII onward, the office of Master of the Royal Game was a significant court position. In 1526 a substantial amphitheater or circus (the classical precedent added to the dignity of these celebrations in New Troy) was constructed in the Paris Garden on the Bankside in Southwark. The building could hold about a thousand spectators, with admission later fixed at a penny for the cheap places and twice as much for the upper galleries. Both bulls and bears were baited by mastiffs in this building until in 1570 a second circus was constructed in an adjoining field and the bullfights were transferred there, leaving the bears in the older ring. And so they continued until they were suppressed by the Long Parliament in 1642, leaving behind a folk memory of the bulldog as the embodiment of indomitable patriotism.

There were also animal contests in great houses, royal parks, and in the court. Queen Elizabeth herself seems to have been an enthusiast. On April 25, 1559, for example, she entertained the French ambassador with bull- and bear-baiting by English dogs in Whitehall; and the ambassador followed this up with a trip to Paris Gardens for more of the same the next day. She put on a similar show for the Danish ambassador in Greenwich Park in 1586, and she herself visited Paris Garden as late as 1599. The earl of Leicester included such sports in his entertainment for the queen (which the young Shakespeare may have attended) at Kenilworth in 1575. King James expressed his imperial pretensions by organizing a match between some champion dogs from the south bank and one of the lions kept in the royal menagerie in the Tower. He wanted to see if the renowned English mastiffs deserved their reputation for bravery. The contest was somewhat unsatisfactory, ending in a draw with the advantage toward the lion. James pursued this enthusiasm for lion-baiting for a while, but then came up with the idea of a contest between a lion and a bear. A great assembly of notables was gathered at the Tower to witness this re-creation of an ancient Roman spectacle. In the event not very much happened. The animals refused to fight each other, and the bear was led away in disgrace to be baited upon a public stage some days later.

These royal combats were essentially private affairs, away from the public gaze. But they were similar to the shows that took place in the large stadia on the south bank. At its peak, Paris Garden had a complement of some seventy mastiffs, twenty bears, and (for variety) three bulls. The bear would be tied to a stake in the middle of the ring. A group of some half-dozen mastiffs would be loosed upon it. Dogs slain or mutilated would be replaced by fresh dogs until they brought the bear down (at which point a new bear would be produced) or until none could be found to challenge him. Usually the wounded bear would be tended back to health: It was rare for the dogs to kill their prey outright. Sometimes there would be a novel touch, such as a blinded bear, or perhaps the day's festivities would conclude with the dogs set upon a horse (running free) bearing an ape upon its back—a program might refer to "Pleasant sport with the horse and ape" as the comic conclusion of the day's entertainment.

The delights of the Bankside attracted large numbers—when full, each of these stadia would have held about 1 percent of the entire population of London—and the operation was clearly a major enterprise. It involved the construction of substantial buildings; creation of facilities for the animals and the garden staff; assembling, feeding, diverting, and dispersing considerable crowds; and so forth. The civic authorities were understandably anxious to exercise a measure of control over the businesses, but rarely managed to achieve very much. In a note from the lord mayor to Lord Burghley in January 1583, the harassed official reports to the Privy Council on a disastrous collapse of part of the stadium: "a great mishap at Paris Garden, where by ruin of all the scaffold at once yesterday a great number of people are some presently slain, and some maimed and greviously hurt." As far as the lord mayor was concerned, the explanation for the event was obvious. It had taken place on a Sunday, and therefore, he went on, "giveth occasion to acknowledge the hand of God for such abuse of the Sabbath day, and moveth me in conscience to beseech your Lordship to give order for redress of such contempt of God's service." Burghley replied smoothly that he would undertake to "treat with my Lords of the Council" and investigate the possibility of finding "some other day within the week meeter for bear-baitings and such like worldly pastimes." Behind this exchange lay a series of abiding hostilities between the city and the thriving Elizabethan "entertainment industry" as well as its sponsors and supporters in the court.

I have dwelt on the sport of bear-baiting partly because of its remoteness from modern culture. On the most basic level, it opens a window on to a world in which the English were not, as later generations have been, renowned as animal lovers, one in which a regular holiday pastime was to visit the Bedlam hospital for the insane and laugh at the merry antics of the wretched inmates. But these strange sports are more than a dash of local color, an exotic and eccentric oddity. Their story is wrapped up with Shakespeare's career, with the history of London theaters. For when theaters came to be built on the south bank of the Thames, their size, design, and organization were strikingly similar to those of the bear gardens, so similar that at least one contemporary illustration mistakenly labeled the Globe as "The Bear Garden." Such confusion of theatrical and animal-baiting enterprises is hardly surprising, given their many close connections. For example, the chief proprietors of the Rose, built about 1587, were Philip Henslowe and his son-in-law Edward Alleyn, the great actor. These men were major investors in the bear-baiting stadia from the 1590s onward, rising to official positions of control in the sport from 1603. Henslowe's last major business venture was the construction of the Hope Theatre in 1614, designed to double as a venue for both theatrical performances and animal shows.

This new theatrical business was the trade in which the young Shakespeare opted to make his way. As a career it had none of the security that apprenticeship promised to so many of his fellow immigrants to the city. Whereas his father seems to have had a sponsor or mentor to direct him and guide his first steps in the commercial life of Stratford, William Shakespeare can have had no such established assistance.

But two other reflections are worth making. The first is that John Shakespeare had been a man reluctant to confine himself to single or conventional enterprises: In particular, he evidently had a clear understanding of the financial realities of his time, an eye for emerging opportunities, and a willingness to range far beyond the borders both of Stratford and, at times, of strict notions of legality. Second, it was normal for immigrants to lodge with families with which they had some prior connection, whether by marriage or business or town of origin. So whatever model we entertain of Shakespeare's move to London—whether as a member of a troupe of actors (and thus enjoying both a degree of patronage and professional contact with established actors) or as an individual seeking to make his fortune, we can assume he had somewhere to stay when he arrived. If he was an actor, then in the actors' enclaves in the city; if not, then with some Stratford folk or perhaps business contacts of his father's. And even if he came south knowing of the theater only what he had encountered in Stratford, he was still his father's son. He would have seen ample evidence to suggest that the business of providing entertainment for the swelling population of the metropolis was moving from a random, *ad hoc*, disorganized phase into something altogether more substantial and commercially promising. He may have come to London with a dawning awareness of his acting and writing talent; or he may have come with some modest capital, salvaged from his father's decline, to invest in a developing new business. Whichever it was—and indeed it may have been a combination of these factors—we can readily imagine the kind of attraction that the new public stages would have held for him.

Purpose-built theaters were a striking novelty in Renaissance England, and they were recognized as such. The decision to build them grew out of a complex set of circumstances—it is not as if companies of players had suddenly appeared from nowhere. There had been a long tradition of staging plays and interludes in the halls of great houses, or of schools and colleges, and for many years troupes of players—often bearing the badge of some noble or gentleman—had performed in the yards of inns and other improvised, temporary settings. Such conditions were ideal for the strolling players of the period, small groups who took their talents from place to place, rarely performing in the same place on successive days; likewise for those entertainers attached to noble households, whose acting skills might be called on to mark the celebration of particular events, but whose duties were more various for most of the time. This state of affairs was changed at a stroke in 1572 by the promulgation of two Acts of Parliament.

The first, in January of that year, was prompted by what the queen deemed to be "the unlawful retaining of multitudes of unordinary servants by liveries, badges, and other signs and tokens (contrary to the good and ancient statutes and laws of this realm)." The consequence of the existence of such groups of retainers, the Act argued, was "stirring up and nourishing of factions, riots, and unlawful assemblies (the mothers of rebellion) besides such other great inconveniences that already are seen and more likely daily to follow if speedy remedy be not provided." Severe penalties were available to those charged with enforcing this law, a piece of legislation wholly consistent with a series of attempts by Tudor monarchs to curb the power of local grandees and bring the nation under more effective central control.

The second statute, of more immediate relevance to players, is clearly related to the first, and seeks to deal with some of the consequences of disbanding the provincial households. Its effect on subsequent theater history was profound. The "Acte for the punishment of Vacabondes" was a measure that set in train a sequence of developments that would quickly result in the disappearance of the strolling players and the eventual creation of large professional repertory companies based in purpose-built theaters, performing before audiences numbered in thousands, and ultimately enjoying the personal support of the king. The 1572 act specified that every company of players had either to be under the patronage of one noble of the rank of baron or above, or, alternatively authorized by two senior justices of the peace of the county in which they wished to perform:

> All and every person and persons being whole and mighty in body and able to labour, having not land or master, nor using any lawful merchandize [business], craft or mystery [trade or profession] whereby he or she might get his or her living; & all fencers, bear-wards, common players in interludes, & minstrels, not belonging to any Baron of the realm or towards any other personage of greater degree: all jugglers, peddlers, tinkers, and petty chapmen: which said fencers, bear-wards, common players in interludes, minstrels, jugglers, peddlers, tinkers, and petty chapmen, shall wander abroad

and not have licence of two Justices of the Peace . . . shall be taken, adjudged, and deemed rogues, vagabonds, and sturdy beggars.

The penalty for being so taken, adjudged, and deemed was severe. If nobody of good standing in the community came forward with an offer of a year's work for the vagabond, the wretched "sturdy beggar" would be "grievously whipped" and then "burned through the gristle of the right ear with a hot iron of the compass of an inch about." A second conviction would lead to two years of enforced work in the household of some respectable individual; a third conviction condemned the vagabond to death as a felon, with consequent confiscation of lands and goods.

So in 1572 an actor faced a future that was, to say the least, uncertain. If he joined the household of a noble, he might find himself penalized under the statute limiting numbers of retainers. If he tried to ply his trade as a freelance, outside the law, he would have to operate under constant threat of punishments that began with flogging and mutilation and could lead to death. And of course some of the great nobles faced a problem, too. They had to be able to demonstrate convincingly that their large households represented no threat to the central authority. Merely reclassifying their henchmen as servant-actors would fool nobody. If they claimed to be supporting a company of actors, it was now necessary to prove that they could act. If we look at the records of activity at court during the Christmas holiday season of 1572–3, we can see that there were three performances by a troupe calling itself the Earl of Leicester's Men. A group of the same name had previously performed at court during Christmas period in 1562–3, and they are recorded as playing in various provincial centers during the next decade. The idea that their sudden return to court was prompted by the new legislation is strengthened by the appearance of another company, the Earl of Sussex's Players, in a court performance on February 7, 1573. This group, like Leicester's, had been playing in the provinces since 1569, and their appearance at court, as well as showing one of the effects of the new laws, also probably owes something to the fact that the earl of Sussex had just taken on the post of lord chamberlain (he succeeded the elderly Lord Howard of Effingham, who had been in post since 1558) in late 1572. One of the functions of the lord chamberlain was to supervise the Revels Office, but

Sussex was the first personally to sponsor a theatrical company.

The records also suggest that Sussex's men may not have been quite up to the transition from rural inn-yards to the more demanding circumstances of court performance. Just before the Christmas season of 1574, for example, they were inspected ("perused") by officials of the Revels Office, with a view to being permitted to perform before the queen; but they did not perform. It was not until 1576 that they became a regular part of court entertainments.

So from 1572 onward the business of playing took place under the protective shield of noble patronage. But it would be wrong to suppose that all their efforts were directed toward performing before the queen, and putting on shows through which their sponsor could demonstrate his qualities and, at times, shape and influence policy. Their motives were more straightforwardly commercial. As the companies developed, they grew into quite substantial businesses. The usual organization involved a central group of shareholders (maybe a dozen, whereas traveling companies had had half that number) who determined policy; they were supported by a group of hired employees. More crucially, they tended to work with a proprietor or impresario, who could furnish them with cash up front in return for a share of the takings and who could provide a venue. Companies who could find work in London fought to remain in business there. That was where the largest audiences could be found, where it was not necessary to travel to a different venue every day, and where there were actors, technicians, and writers in abundance. The building of permanent theaters followed quite naturally from this.

To start with, the playing spaces in inn-yards were developed into more permanent structures. From the 1560s onward there are records of performances at such inns as the Bel Savage on Ludgate Hill, the Cross Keys and the Bell in Gracechurch Street, the Bull in Bishopsgate Street, and the Red Lion and Boar's Head in Whitechapel. But it was only a matter of time before someone came up with the idea of a purpose-built theater. That someone was James Burbage, and he brought with him a useful combination of talents and experience. A carpenter and joiner by trade, Burbage had become a player in the earl of Leicester's troupe and had also developed an eye for business opportunities.

As early as 1572 it was Burbage who wrote to Leicester to request patronage and (to use a term from analogous present-day practice) endorsement. In the letter he reminds Leicester of the statute limiting numbers of retainers. Then he proceeds:

> We therefore, your humble servants and daily orators your players, for avoiding all inconvenience that may grow by reason of the said statute, are bold to trouble your Lordship with this our suit, humbly desiring your honour that (as you have always been our good Lord and Master) you will now vouchsafe to retain us at this present as your household servants and daily waiters, not that we mean to crave any further stipend or benefit at your Lordship's hands but our liveries as we have had, and also your honour's licence to certify that we are your household servants when we shall have occasion to travel amongst our friends as we do usually once a year, and as other noblemen's players do . . . whereby we may enjoy our faculty in your Lordship's name as we have done heretofore.

The request is not for money or work, but rather for the protection of Leicester's name—embodied in the livery and the license—as the company goes about its business throughout the country. What is sought is a kind of sponsorship, through which Leicester's status as a great lord is enhanced by the magnificence and skill of these men who wear his livery, while they are licensed to ply their trade freely and lucratively. But the commercial value of Leicester's endorsement, however considerable, was put in the shade a couple of years later. In a patent of May 10, 1574, protection was granted from an even higher authority, the queen herself. She wrote:

> Know ye that we of our especial grace, certain knowledge, and mere motion have licensed and authorised, and by these presents do license and authorise, our loving subjects, James Burbage, John Perkyn, John Lanham, William Johnson, and Robert Wilson, servants to our trusty and well-beloved cousin and counsellor the Earl of Leicester, to use, exercise, and occupy the art and faculty of playing comedies, tragedies, interludes, stage plays, and such other like as they have already used and studied, or hereafter shall use and study, as well for the recreation of our loving subjects, as for our solace and pleasure when we shall think good to see them, as also to use and occupy all such instruments as they have already practiced, or hereafter shall

practice, for and during our pleasure. And the said comedies, tragedies, interludes, and stage plays, together with their music, to show, publish, exercise, and occupy to their best commodity during all the term aforesaid, as well within our City of London and liberties of the same, as also within the liberties and freedoms of any of our cities, towns, boroughs & whatsoever as without the same, throughout our Realm of England. Willing and commanding you and every of you, as ye tender our pleasure, to permit and suffer them herein without any your lets, hindrance, or molestation during the term aforesaid, any act, statute, proclamation, or commandment heretofore made, or hereafter to be made, to the contrary notwithstanding. Provided that the said comedies, tragedies, interludes, and stage plays be by the Master of our Revels for the time being before seen & allowed, and that the same be not published or shown in the time of common prayer, or in the time of great and common plague in our said city of London.

The possession of this warrant was a valuable and powerful defense against the hostility with which acting was viewed by the authorities in many cities, especially London. Its guarantees gave encouragement to seek a permanent home, and made the company appear attractive to potential investors. In Burbage's phrase, a permanent theater would give rise to "continual great profit"; his own modest fortune (though less than one hundred marks at his death, it was nevertheless more than he would have made had he remained an unenthusiastic carpenter) gave some evidence of that. But now, with the patronage of the greatest nobleman of the kingdom and the explicit protection of the monarch, the scale of the enterprise, and of the investment needed, were set to expand. Burbage borrowed from his brother-in-law John Brayne, and took out a lease on a site in the Liberty of Holywell, part of the parish of St. Leonard's, Shoreditch, in the fields just outside Bishopsgate. The land in this northern suburb—close to the modern Liverpool Street Station—had once formed part of a Benedictine priory; its southern boundary was marked by the lane known to this day as Holywell Street. The former monastic buildings were not in a good state of repair, and the eponymous Holy Well had come down in the world to feed a horse pond. The site that Burbage leased for this building was probably just to the east of present-day Curtain Street, which now runs along what was then a strip of vacant ground outside Burbage's property, in the angle that that street makes with New

Inn Yard. Construction began after the lease was granted on Lady Day 1576. The relationship between Burbage and his landlord was destined to be unhappy, as later chapters will show.

We can see that Burbage's choice of a site outside the city walls is important: It connects playing with bear-baiting as an activity that could be tolerated only on the margins of the city. The civic authorities could console themselves that this godless pursuit with its popular support and aristocratic patronage would be confined to a licensed space given over to recreation and sport. But as a man who had a good idea of the large potential audience in London for plays, Burbage could be confident that spectators would come, even if, because there was no right of way from Holywell Lane, they had to tramp across the open fields to get to the show. At least one contemporary referred to the "great press," a "concourse of unruly people," streaming out of the city to see the plays.

The building, to which Burbage, "the first builder of play-houses," gave the grand classical name of the Theatre, was probably an amphitheater, constructed largely of wood, though with some ironwork in places. There was a tiring-house for the players to dress in, and there were galleries, at least one of which offered the spectators the luxury of seats and privacy. Admission to the building cost a penny, with an extra penny or twopence payable for transfer to the galleries; these sums were collected and placed in locked boxes which would be opened and the cash shared out after the performance. The players would have shared the entrance pennies among themselves, while the proprietors, Burbage and Brayne, took the gallery money.

The success of the Theatre is attested by the prompt appearance of a second playhouse just two hundred yards closer to the city walls, on the other side of Holywell Lane. This building was called the Curtain, since it was in Curtain Close, and opened its doors to the paying public in the latter part of 1577. The Curtain was built by one Henry Lanman or Laneham, and as time passed he seems to have enjoyed a close business relationship with Burbage and his associates, with the Curtain serving as an "easer" for the Theatre, and with profits being pooled between the two sets of proprietors; Laneham's house also staged nondramatic shows such as fencing exhibitions. It was at the Curtain, as we will see, that Shakespeare's company, the Lord Chamberlain's Men, was performing in the late

1590s; this building may well be the "wooden O" where *Henry V* was performed. The presence of these two thriving theaters at the very gates of the city was predictably distressing to Puritan preachers. As early as November 1577 one of them urged his congregation: "behold the sumptuous theatre houses, a continual monument of London's prodigality and folly."

They were also a striking monument to the new age, a microcosm of the tensions and movements in Elizabethan society. These first theaters stand in the same relation to the itinerant drama as factories do to cottage industry. Or perhaps we might think of them as echoing the transition from a manuscript culture to one dominated by the mass productions of the printing press. Indeed, these playhouses can be seen almost as factories dedicated to the industrialization, even the mass production, of entertainment. Up until their construction, theatrical shows had been put on on a one-shot basis—made to order, to so speak—whether in court or in some country town where the actors were obliged to carve out a space for themselves to perform in, and pass around the hat for money. But now conditions were wholly transformed. These purpose-built theaters pumped out many performances of the same text, with large troupes of professional actors playing before spectators who had to pay for admission to the show. Every step in the process was suddenly better organized and coordinated; actors became more numerous, more competent, better dressed, and better rehearsed; the stages developed new resources, the potential for more elaborate effects; and the audience's taste was followed, but also modified as time passed. However, as in the early years of new modern media such as film and television, technological changes outstripped literary production. Companies had to expand their repertoires, and had to do so in difficult circumstance. Recent censorship legislation had removed a substantial portion of their stock, so they needed new material that could pass the censor's scrutiny and keep the crowds pouring in so that they could pay the rent. Writers were hired to scribble furiously—ancestors of the desperate hack radio dramatist in Mario Vargas Llosa's *Aunt Julia and the Scriptwriter*—to feed the medium's voracious appetite for new material. If the theater can be seen as a factory, the writer may be understood to be one of its suppliers, providing raw material for the industrial process; though, given the miserable financial rewards available to writers, they would have been justified in seeing these great wooden structures as monstrous machines geared up to devour the offspring of their brains.

This, very broadly, was the world into which Shakespeare came at some point in the late 1580s. In the next chapter we will try to reconstruct his early years in the theater. And we will see how he began to define his own identity as a writer in the context of the other writers whose work was being played on the public stages. But all the time we will need to remember that Shakespeare was committed to the theater in highly distinctive ways. He was an actor, a sharer, a member of a company. For him the contact with the stage was more than a simple financial transaction; for him the activity of writing plays was not a necessary piece of drudgery in the intervals between writing for some great patron or serving some elusive muse. At least to start with, his status, his security, derived more from his acting skill and his eye for business than from his pen.

CHAPTER FIVE

"The Only Shake-Scene in a Country"

The development of the public theaters in London was a piece with other social and cultural phenomena of the time. Things we now take for granted, including concepts like the state and the professions, for instance, were being forged, invented, improvised. The permanent professional theaters caused expectations and standards of performance and preparation to rise; the profession of player became, effectively for the first time, a career that a man might responsibly follow. The traveling, vagabond component of the job had been reduced by the construction of fixed stages, and the ties with great nobles were looser and less intimate. A player able to augment his natural acting talents with material ambition and some means might buy himself into a partnership and become a sharer in the company. This Shakespeare would eventually do, and the trajectory of his career, especially in the early years, was wrapped up in the organization and commercial success of his troupe. What I want to stress now is that his early plays need to be understood as the writings of an actor, of someone who had come to writing from the direction of practical theatrical experience. As the theaters digested all they were permitted to use from the previous repertoires, and as they hungrily devoured each new play that was staged to divert an audience that thirsted for novelty, Shakespeare emerged as a creature of this new environment. For him the business of the theater was neither a threat nor an unwelcome novelty. It was the medium in which he had elected to move, the sphere in which he was to excel. And it distorts the nature of his imagination and art, especially in his early works, to pretend that they are not saturated in the theatrical conditions, assumptions, and expectations of the day. His early works are pieces for the theater first and foremost, designed to keep the paying customers pouring through the doors and to keep them entertained as they crunched their hazelnuts in the afternoon sunshine.

But to "place" him as part of theatrical life is necessarily to place him in the wider context of what was happening in England at the time. What that time was like, and indeed when it was, are important questions that have divided scholars for many years. At times there is an almost Lilliputian flavor to their disputes. The traditional, so-called "late start" view was that the earliest plays date from about 1590. The "early start" party, on the other hand, held that Shakespeare began writing several years before that, possibly as early as 1586. All we can say for certain is that Shakespeare had become established as a popular writer by 1592, when Robert Greene poured scorn on him as a jack of all trades ("an absolute *Iohannes fac totum*") who was too big for his boots ("in his own conceit the only Shake-scene in a country"). How many plays did he need to have written to warrant this kind of attack? Estimates range from three to ten. Other sorts of evidence are even harder to assess: When Shakespeare's work is very similar to passages in Marlowe, for example, we have to make a leap of faith to decide who is borrowing from or being influenced by whom.

But we, like the Bard, have to make a start somewhere, and I will begin by looking at the sequence of plays printed in the First Folio as *Henry VI, Parts 1, 2,* and *3,* and *Richard III.* The form as they appear in the printed collection, and as they have been performed since then, is not the form they initially took, and it is worth pausing for a moment to reflect on this. Indeed, the history of the ordering of the sequence tells us a great deal about Shakespeare's developing conception of the project, and about his response to other writers and to the world outside the playhouse.

The first of the four plays to be written and performed was the

piece now called *Henry VI Part 2*. Clearly, it was not first presented
to the public under this name. In fact, its title was *The First Part
of the Contention of the two Famous Houses of York and Lancaster with
the Death of the Good Duke Humphrey*. Its sequel, the play now known
as *Henry VI Part 3*, had an even longer descriptive title: *The true
Tragedy of Richard Duke of York, and the death of good King Henry the
Sixth, with the whole Contention between the two houses Lancaster and
York*. Evidently these two plays were conceived as a pair, and set
a series of famous events against the backdrop of the conflict between Lancaster and York, the so-called Wars of the Roses. It was
only after this two-part work had appeared that Shakespeare's project developed into areas hitherto unexplored on the Elizabethan
stage. We know that two-part plays were reasonably common, and
continued to be popular throughout Shakespeare's career. But he,
in an unprecedented move, added two further plays, one at the
beginning and the other at the end. He wrote *Henry VI Part 1*,
then, as a kind of retrospective prologue to a sequence which
reached its culmination in the massive and artistically very ambitious *Tragedy of Richard III*. In the process he created a four-part
work whose scale was matched nowhere else in the drama of his
day, and which perhaps is more properly understood in relation to
contemporaneous epic, historical, and heroic works, such as Holinshed's *Chronicles* (1587), Spenser's *The Faerie Queene* (1590), Sidney's *Arcadia* (1590) and the translation by Sir John Harington of
Ariosto's epic romance *Orlando Furioso* (1591). As I have said, Shakespeare did not invent the two-part play, but he was very close to
inventing the genre of the English chronicle history. Records are
sparse, but apart from the anonymous *The Famous Victories of Henry
the Fifth* (which is earlier than 1588) and maybe Peele's *Edward I*,
Shakespeare's story of the English Civil Wars (and we should note
that his titles were more ample and less tied to a specific individual
than these other history plays) broke new ground. What is more,
his innovation was recognized at the time: from the surviving fragments of contemporary reactions to Shakespeare's arrival on the
scene, it seems that it was his innovation in the history play as a
new theatrical genre that most struck the theatergoers of the years
around the time of the defeat of the Spanish Armada. What was
so remarkable about this new form?

At the simplest level, Shakespeare responded to the theater's thirst for new material by creating dramas that tapped into current political questions, into more general anxieties aroused by the continuing threat of invasion by Spain, and, of course, into the current literary vogue for history and epic. But perhaps we need to go further back to find specifically dramatic models for the large-scale enterprise into which Shakespeare's plays rapidly developed; back to Warwickshire, to Coventry, and to William Shakespeare's teenage years, when the Coventry cycle of mystery plays was performed for the last time.

The great craft cycles involved processions of pageant wagons through the streets of the cathedral cities. Each wagon would carry a tableau depicting a biblical scene, and at set points the wagon would stop and the figures in the tableau would act out a play based on a Bible story: the Creation, Adam and Eve, Cain and Abel, Noah's Flood, Abraham and Isaac, Christ's Nativity, the Crucifixion, and so forth, up to the Last Judgment. At the end of the long summer day, all the wagons would be drawn up before the great west front of the cathedral and a final performance of the whole story of mankind, from the Creation to the Day of Judgment, would be played out in sequence. An observer from our century would be struck by the way the physical organization of the show was saturated with spiritual meaning. For instance, the backdrop to this narrative of human existence was the carved stone of a mighty building, generating a contrast between the ephemerality of the improvised wagons with their flimsy structures, on which tiny humans proclaimed words that were not their own, and the massive edifice bathed in the setting sun, on which perched Christ the King and his glittering court of angels and saints, innumerable statues painted in dazzling colors. In other words, human history was placed in the context of eternity: Time was played out before a screen of timelessness. It would be hard for a spectator to escape the message so powerfully articulated: that human history is providential, that the Bible tells the story of the working out of God's providential plan for humanity. But that was not all that the spectacle conveyed.

Some wagons had to double as locations for several plays. Partly this was a matter of space and logistics. But it also enabled another doctrinal point to be made nonverbally. For instance, if the same hill was employed for such events as, say, the expulsion from Paradise, Abraham's attempted sacrifice of Isaac, and the Crucifixion, the spectators stood to learn two lessons, one literal and one more poetic or indirect. The first was that it was believed in those days that (to quote John Donne): "Christ's cross and Adam's tree stood in one place"—literally, that Paradise and Calvary were the same location; and this would have had the status of a fact. And the meaning of this "fact," its more oblique sense, was that it established connections between the two events—between, so to speak, Paradise Lost and Paradise Regained. It showed that events such as the sacrifice of Isaac were designed to prefigure later episodes in the unfolding story. In biblical scholarship this kind of interpretation is known as "typology," where people and events are versions, shadows, or "types" of others. This understanding of history accounts for the way in which a number of episodes in Shakespeare's tetralogy are staged. But it also underpins the whole, albeit in a secular form, since the whole is presented as providential, as the enactment of God's will—instead of human history leading to the Last Judgment, it leads to the present, to the installation of the Tudors on the throne of England at the end of *Richard III*.

Now, while these large ideas were being expressed in this more or less architectural way, the details of the overarching narrative were filled in by flesh-and-blood citizens speaking English (rather than the clergy speaking Latin). So these great mysteries of faith, these epoch-making events in the human story, were brought to life by friends, neighbors, workmates. This dimension of vividness, of pathos, of humanity made a contrast with the stiff formality of the painted statues on the cathedral front. It accords with the theology and pragmatism behind these cycles. They were staged, after all, on the feast of the body of Christ, Corpus Christi, which celebrates both the way in which the son of God took on human flesh and blood and the capacity of Communion to reenact that direct physical intervention in mortal affairs.

The mystery cycles grew up as part of the celebration of the feast of Corpus Christi, which is movable, and occurs in the early summer between May 23 and June 24. The feast was instituted in the Middle Ages; planned by Pope Urban IV in 1264, it was promulgated by Pope Clement V in 1311 at the Council of Vienne. The ecclesiastical celebration played a major role in structuring the drama that was written to express it, and also, I would suggest, the drama of later generations—specifically Shakespeare's first history plays. The official explanation for introducing a new feast honoring the body of Christ—in other words, celebrating the sacrament of Communion—was that on the anniversary of the founding of the sacrament at the Last Supper, Maundy Thursday, the Church was too busy recalling the events leading up to the Crucifixion to pay adequate attention to the gift that Christ left behind for his disciples. The theological context for the new feast was the dogma of Transubstantiation—whereby the bread and wine are held actually to become the body and blood of Christ during the Mass—which was promulgated at the Lateran Council in 1215. This dogma generated stories and plays of its own. There are numerous accounts of miracles designed to show that the bread and wine were physically changed. Priests delivered sermons in which they described how a doubter or heathen was converted by seeing Christ in the bread, or by seeing blood run from the wafer. These little stories lent themselves to dramatic treatment all over Europe.

In England, there seems to have been a rather different understanding of the dramatic implications of the institution of the sacrament. Instead of anecdotal interludes showing single miracles, there were huge civic spectacles telling the narrative of humanity from the creation to the Last Judgment. These great cycle plays represented the whole of human history as saturated with the divine presence, transformed by the intervention of God in human shape in the person of Christ. The English understanding of the miracle of transubstantiation, then, seems to have involved a broader sense of its meaning, one which took the institution of the sacrament to be a moment that radically and permanently altered the shape of human history—changing it, so to speak, from a series of episodes to a coherent and structured symmetry. The dramatic implications are important. As events were played out on the wagons, they were inescapably part of larger narratives: No matter how local, topical, vernacular, or irreverent the material, no matter how fallibly human the speakers, they could not avoid implication in a massive celebration of the divine principle within human life and history. At the same time, part of the reason for the choice of early summer for the feast was the Church's recognition that that period is a pretty thin one for religious festivals. Here was a new and officially approved holiday, an excuse for merrymaking and recreation at a time of year when the weather and the agricultural cycle were propitious.

The parallel with the situation on the Elizabethan stage will be fairly obvious. That stage, like the cycle spaces, was a moralized arena. It represented, albeit crudely, the cosmos. The heavens were above the stage (often indicated by stars painted above the actors' heads), while hell and the devils were below (as both Hamlet's father and Malvolio were to testify), and humans were fated to play out their lives suspended between these two extremes. The theatrical conventions encouraged the dramatists to show huge events, mighty sweeps of history, great journeys, and discoveries, within the narrow compass of the stage. And alongside this capacity to deal with fundamental elements in the condition of humankind, the Elizabethan theater, like the cycles, was inescapably connected with ideas of play, of holiday, festival, and recreation. There were also parallels between medieval and Elizabethan modes of characterization, given the ways in which pathos and comedy were deployed in the cycles in order to demonstrate instances of the presence of the divine principle within human existence. That, as we shall see in a moment, is certainly what happens in the histories.

But it would be unwise to claim too many continuities. Even though there were some performances as late as the 1570s, the form belongs to the last days of Catholic England, to the period up to the Reformation. Yet there are connections, and they are significant. After the suppression of the cycles, the search was on for doctrinally respectable, morally improving, and spectacular substitutes; at Coventry, for example, this certainly meant historical dramas and pageants, battles between Danes and Saxons. In some cities, secular equivalents of the pageant-processions were readily found. The Lord Mayor's Show in London was, and still is, a splendid instance of this transfer of religious celebration into the secular sphere—a triumphal rehearsal of the excellence of the capital, crammed with allegorical and historical material presenting the modern city as the worthy descendant of mighty ancestors, as the culmination of an ordered, providential sequence of historical moments. Such translations of pre-Reformation forms, such secularizations of religious festivals, were common enough: In the most spectacular instance, of course, Queen Elizabeth and her advisers participated in the creation of a cult of the Virgin Queen that tapped into—at times in a very explicit fashion—the cult of the Virgin Mary.

A fifteenth-century writer who set out to script a play, or to organize the performance of a cycle, would have been able to rely on his audience's understanding of the broad principles on which his enterprise was based. There was no problem about asserting that history was providential, for instance, or that it constituted the working-out of a divine scheme. By Shakespeare's day, however, the situation had changed; and it would continue to change throughout his career. His own attitude to the subject underwent a series of transformations the longer he worked at it. But, to start with, he seems to have launched into the project without too much self-conscious reflection. He had hit on a repository of material from which to draw shows for his company, and enthusiastically set about converting this matter into dramatic units. It was only later, as the implications and possibilities of the genre he was inventing became apparent, that further complexities arose.

But even by the time he had rounded out his two-part play into a tetralogy, Shakespeare had begun to direct his mind to more general reflections. Every kind of historical narrative, whether a fragment of oral history or the catalog of the Public Record Office, constitutes an act of shaping, of interpretation. What we choose to remember about the past, and the way we choose to express and structure those memories, will express the way we understand the world and human nature. Though conveyed in different language, this was one of the more important intellectual discoveries of the Renaissance. As scholars were driven to discover more about the past—to excavate the origins of the Bible, for instance, or to recover hitherto forgotten classical authors—it dawned on some of them that the more they found out about the past, the greater the gulf that cut them off from it. And as his sequence took shape, Shakespeare seems to have moved from confident self-assurance to a more hesitant and cautious view. Nevertheless, it is fair to say that there were two main attitudes to history in the period. One was providential, the other antiquarian or evidence-based. Shakespeare's history plays show him moving from one to the other, just as his great contemporary Edmund Spenser did. In the first three books of Spenser's *The Faerie Queene*, published in 1590, history is presented in the approved Tudor providential mode, as a sequence leading to the fortunate accession of Queen Elizabeth. In the final three books, published in 1596, Spenser (probably influenced by the antiquarian writings of Ben Jonson's schoolmaster William Camden)

places much greater stress on evidence, and on the difficulties involved in adducing historical parallels and learning lessons from the
past. Even in the earliest plays, Shakespeare could not rely on a
shared view, even of the outlines of recent English history.

In this century we have created our own myths about Shakespeare's history plays. One is that they were written out of a terror
of civil war, that the memory of the Wars of the Roses was still so
strong as to make the audience long for order and stability. The
evidence is hard to find. There is no suggestion in the popular
literature of the time that there was an anxious folk memory of
distant battles. On the other hand, the Tudors were very enthusiastic propounders of a doctrine of centralized authority; from their
point of view—and it was an opinion they did their best to pop-
ularize—they themselves represented stability and national unity.
In the interests of their policy, the powers of local barons were
curbed. Shakespeare's histories show the negative consequences of
a weak center confronted by over-mighty subjects. But they do not
tap into a popular belief. They seem rather to be an attempt to
construct or convey such a belief, though how wholeheartedly is a
matter of critical debate.

Shakespeare's career as a dramatist began in the years immediately following the defeat of the Spanish Armada, but that was not
a period of unalloyed national triumph. Far from it. The Armada
had been providentially swept away by a great tempest, and there
was no guarantee that similar intervention would frustrate the inevitable second attempt to invade. Francis Walsingham, for example, remarked that "Our half-doings doth breed dishonour and
leaveth the disease uncured"; he was alluding to the halfhearted
way in which English troops were involved in the wars against the
Spanish on the Continent.

In such circumstances, the grim situation with which the first
part of *Henry VI* begins would have struck a chord with audiences
of 1591. It would have seemed intensely, almost subversively, topical. Shakespeare's play starts with the funeral of Henry V, an
exemplary interventionist, an active ruler waging war on foreign
soil to defend his title to his kingdom. His miraculous victory
against all rational odds at Agincourt was a parallel to the defeat
of the mighty Armada. And what happens as the play develops
becomes a pointed contribution to the political debate of the early

1590s. The world into which Shakespeare plunges the audience is not one of triumph but rather one of despair and death; after a victory which united the crowns of England and France came a rapid disintegration of the empire under a high-minded but fatally inactive and inadequate ruler.

Henry VI Part 1 is strikingly ambitious in its claim for artistic status—both for itself and for the sequence for which it has been constructed as a retrospective prologue (what we would call today a "prequel"). It is designed to ape the qualities of epic and history, to invoke for itself and for its sequence the grandeur of these elevated, inclusive forms, genres whose variety and comprehensiveness were revered in the Renaissance. If we look at the beginning and end of the play, for instance, we will see that it starts like the end of a tragedy and ends like the beginning of a comedy. The action onstage opens with the funeral processions of Henry V, as the great lords in whose charge the country has been placed during the minority of Henry VI accompany the coffin, and vie with each other to lament the king's death:

> Hung be the heavens with black, yield day to night!
> Comets, importing change of times and states,
> Brandish your crystal tresses in the sky,
> And with them scourge the bad revolting stars
> That have consented unto Henry's death.
> King Henry the Fifth, too famous to live long!
> England ne'er lost a king of so much worth.

These words sound like the conclusion of a lofty tragedy, but they immediately give way to squabbles among the nobles onstage, accusing one another of incompetence, of bad faith, of being henpecked. The silent corpse of the dead hero-king sits in its black-draped coffin as an eloquent reminder of the task these political pygmies are left to undertake, and the emptiness of their verbose rhetoric is soon revealed when a messenger brings from France news of the loss of numerous English possessions. The dramatic design is like that of the opening of *Titus Andronicus*, where the pageantry of the first scene creates a political map of the declining Roman Empire. Here the dissension among the English nobility lays bare tensions and rivalries that will soon flare up into civil war. So what looks like the end of something, like the stately conclusion of a tragedy, is rapidly dismantled and shown to be the starting point of new stories, new complicatons, and further tragedies.

Likewise with the end of the play. In Act V, the earl of Suffolk woos Margaret of Anjou on the king's behalf; as so often with such episodes in comic plays, the game turns serious as Suffolk determines to woo her for himself and to use his influence as a source of power over the cuckolded king. What is striking, at least initially, is the apparent lightness, almost frivolity, of their exchanges:

> **Suffolk:** I'll win this Lady Margaret. For whom?
> Why, for my king. Tush, that's a wooden thing!
> **Margaret:** He talks of wood: it is some carpenter.

But the implications of this banter are profound and open up further possibilities of death and rebellion. It is with these possibilities that the stage action concludes. The final words of the play are given to a triumphant Suffolk, alone on stage after the king has left with all his followers, having announced his determination to proceed to marry Margaret. Suffolk sums up the events gleefully:

> Thus Suffolk hath prevail'd; and thus he goes,
> As did the youthful Paris once to Greece,
> With hope to find the like event in love,
> But prosper better than the Troyan did.
> Margaret shall now be queen, and rule the king;
> But I will rule both her, the king, and realm.

So at the beginning and end of the play Shakespeare stages events—a funeral and a marriage—that conventionally signal that a story is over. But in each case he shows that these rituals set in train new waves of action, generating new complications. In Suffolk's words at the end, the allusion to the Trojan wars is partly an indication of the brash conceit and confidence of the speaker; but it also furthers Shakespeare's strategy of forging an epic story out of the unruly jumble of medieval dynastic squabbles. The audience is invited to see beyond the immediate event on the stage and to perceive larger narratives, a more inclusive and comprehensive kind of story that includes and embraces the individual incidents and voices.

So even from these two moments in the play we can see how

Henry VI Part 1 performs its role as a prologue to the tetralogy by signaling the epic dimensions of the story, and by showing how events possess significance outside the understanding of their participants. But as well as establishing this comprehensiveness as a principle, it also evokes two other key elements, each related to the model of the mystery cycles. These are continuity and pathos. Both can be seen in operation at a particularly remarkable moment in Act I, where action, spectacle, and heroic resolution were combined with touching humanity.

Scene IV of Act I calls for two opposed stations on the stage. One represents the besieged town of Orleans, the other a tower from which the English generals oversee the battle. The action begins with a conversation between the master-gunner of the town and his boy, in which the master explains that he has trained a gun on the English tower, with a view to shooting any of the English commanders foolish enough to present himself as a target. The care he has taken to line up his shot is contrasted with the boy's admission that he has "oft . . . shot at them. Howe'er unfortunate I miss'd my aim." This time there is to be no mistake. They both exit.

The chief English leaders, Salisbury and Talbot (newly ransomed from his French captors), attended by numerous others of their nobles, are then seen on top of the English tower on the other side of the stage. Talbot tells his fellows of his humiliating and degrading experience as a prisoner, and of his resistance to the French scorn:

> With scoffs, and scorns, and contumelious taunts,
> In open market-place produc'd they me,
> To be a public spectacle to all:
> Here, said they, is the terror of the French,
> The scarecrow that affrights our children so.
> Then broke I from the officers that led me,
> And with my nails digg'd stones out of the ground,
> To hurl at the beholders of my shame:
> My grisly countenance made others fly . . .

If we remember the physical space where these lines were spoken it is inevitable that the suggestion of a connection with bear-baiting would have been in the minds of some spectators; and the tone of mockery that is described recalls the mystery plays that dealt with the beating and degradation of Christ by the Roman soldiers who scourged, beat, and mocked him. Talbot remarks that his armed guard had been prepared to kill him: "Ready they were to shoot me to the heart." This line is instantly answered visually by what happens on the battlements of Orleans. As the stage direction puts it: *"Enter the Boy with a linstock."* While the boy prepares to fire his gun, Salisbury discusses with his fellow officers the likely weak points in the city's defenses.

The council of war is cut short by the sound of gunfire, and Salisbury and Sir Thomas Gargrave fall wounded. Talbot's reaction is to use the language of epic and tragedy—to interpret the blow as the operation of cruel fate:

> What chance is this that suddenly hath cross'd us?
> Speak, Salisbury: at least, if thou canst, speak.
> How far'st thou, mirror of all martial men?
> One of thy eyes and thy cheek's side struck off!
> Accursed tower! accursed fatal hand
> That hath contriv'd this woeful tragedy!

In terms of the medieval view of what tragedy is—in Chaucer's words, "a dite of prosperitee for a time that endith in wrecchednesse"—this little episode is indeed a "woeful tragedy". Indeed the physical movements of the scene—Salisbury climbs up the tower only to be shot down—encapsulates the suddenness of a tragic fall. But the moment is also emphatically of its age. The gun that struck down Salisbury was widely, and correctly, interpreted as a major threat to the idea of knightly chivalry. Since at least Roman times, the power and authority of the armed man on horseback had profoundly influenced the structure of society. Suddenly, with the advent of gunpowder, chivalry was under threat. Whereas the profession of knighthood required training for long years in the management of heavy weapons, riding the great horse, and so forth, it was a simpler and cheaper matter to learn how to fire a gun. Whereas it could be argued that the acquisition of knightly skills and disciplines was a morally beneficial thing for young men to do— indeed, if they believed their popular fictions, they might have supposed that only by being virtuous could a knight be certain of success in battle and with the ladies—expertise with the gun carried no such overtones. And this development was not merely a topic bewailed, as might be expected, in the pages of chivalric romances such as Ariosto's *Orlando Furioso*, which legitimately felt under threat from this new advance in military technology. As recently as 1586, the flower of English chivalry, Sir Philip Sidney, had been cut down by an anonymous sniper's bullet in the wars in the Netherlands. As the dying Sidney had passed on the torch of militant Protestantism to the earl of Essex, bequeathing to him both his wife and his sword, so a similar transition between generations is effected in the play. Talbot first describes the death agonies of his leader and then speaks words he supposes the great man to be intending by his gestures:

> Yet liv'st thou, Salisbury? Though thy speech doth fail,
> One eye thou hast to look to heaven for grace:
> The sun with one eye vieweth all the world. . . .
> He beckons with his hand and smiles on me,
> As who would say, "When I am dead and gone,
> Remember to avenge me on the French."
> Plantagenet, I will, and like thee, Nero,
> Play on the lute, beholding the towns burn:
> Wretched shall France be only in my name.

Dramatically, this is a fascinating moment, in which Shakespeare uses a device that was to become one of his trademarks. Before us on the stage are acted out different kinds of show, different ways of representation. Salisbury is a *tableau vivant*, Talbot a speaking character. The effect of the sight of Salisbury is to make Talbot eloquent, emotional, and active. It also turns him into a participant: His pity invests him with the skill of a chronicler or dramatist who imagines the words his historical figures might have said, or ought to have said, at crucial moments in history. The exchange between the two men derives from a particular view of how history works, of how continuities are created, as one hero passes on his glory and his purpose to the next generation. Shakespeare seems to be trying to demonstrate that such connection of the past to the present is achieved through the imaginative engagement, the emotional participation, of someone who might easily have been content to remain as a spectator. There may perhaps in any event have been an added sharpness to this scene when it was first staged, with its likely allusion to the recent death of George Talbot, sixth earl of Shrewsbury and descendant of the earlier Talbot, the terror of the French, in 1590.

So the play, which opens like the end of a tragedy and ends like the opening of a comedy, stages at its core a demonstration of the working of history. The piece is characterized by a remarkable variety of kinds of theatrical show. Since the eighteenth century this variety—together with the play's range of verbal styles—has been held to indicate multiple authorship. Some accounts of the play have found it to be largely the work of various university wits, with Shakespeare contributing only a scene or two. But other scholars hold, and I am inclined to agree with them, that the play shows the young Shakespeare operating in a range of styles, a range inevitably colored by the plays he had seen and acted in. A more positive argument is that it is inappropriate to nitpick the play on the grounds of inconsistencies. What Shakespeare was creating was something else, a different kind of drama altogether, based upon variety of forms and perspective. This procedure relates it to the educational practice of teaching students to examine problems from both sides of the question (*in utramque partem*). The application of such a technique to history is a major innovation on Shakespeare's part. What is more, it makes it much harder to interpret the first tetralogy as an unthinking, unreflective piece of propaganda for the "Tudor myth." The dramatic technique that Shakespeare deploys cannot help but show how difficult it is to discern large movements in history, to be certain of the operation of providence. His audience would have been conscious of the process of selection, editing, and distortion that lay behind the show; by his moments of artistic self-consciousness Shakespeare alerts them to the nature of his enterprise. He offers a reading of history rather than a chronicle, a work of art whose symmetries and orders (tragedy, comedy, and so on) are derived from art, from literature, rather than from the rough commerce of history.

Of course, whenever Renaissance writers claim that what they offer is art, and that their work cannot be applied to the world outside it, we know they are unlikely to be speaking frankly. The position I have just outlined would constitute an excellent defense against censorship. It is important to remember that Shakespeare's choice of subject was novel and potentially controversial. So there was a defense to be constructed, a justification of the whole enterprise; hence the stylized, high art flourishes, and the obvious invocation of the mystery cycles and their governing concept of providence.

But the more we look at the early plays, and especially at the development of the *Henry VI* sequence, the more troubled, problematic, and anxious becomes the England they depict. And the picture they paint of the human condition is no rosier, though the whole is shot through with moments of pathos—incidents that compel the audience to engage with the human predicaments played out before them.

A feature of late Elizabethan literature was an interest in the private lives of famous people of antiquity; to us such an interest—the staple of the romantic historical novel, the film biography, the television miniseries—is a commonplace of popular literary and dramatic culture. But then it was a novelty, affording a glimpse behind the public mask of the great. The most important and popular work that shaped and pandered to this taste was by Shakespeare's Warwickshire neighbor and exact contemporary, Michael Drayton. Called *England's Heroical Epistles*, it was first published in 1597 and many times reprinted. The book consisted of fictional verse letters exchanged between celebrated pairs of historic lovers—Henry II and fair Rosamund, Lady Jane Grey and Lord Gilford Dudley, and so on. They represent a very significant component in the literary culture in which Shakespeare was operating, and provided a vocabulary, and a method, with which to explore the intimate relations between celebrated historical figures. In *Henry VI, Part 1* the dealings between Margaret and the earl of Suffolk relate to this fashion. Other examples include the staging of the relationship between Duke Humfrey of Gloucester and his wife in *Henry VI Part 2*, between Edward IV and Jane Shore, and between Richard III and the Lady Anne. Where they differ from Drayton is in their integration within a larger design, whereby the plights of different pairs are shown in such a way as to epitomize the more general state of the nation at the time. In *Henry VI Part 2*, the action is organized around two contrasting movements: the fall of Duke Humphrey and the rise of the duke of York, and the set pieces—like the conjuring at St. Albans in Act I, Scene IV, and the execution of Suffolk in Act IV, Scene I—are cunningly woven into that larger shape. Yet Shakespeare still stresses the pathos in individual episodes. A good example is the presentation of the cynical plot designed to bring down Humphrey, duke of Gloucester. His duchess, Elinor Cobham, is sentenced to exile and disgrace for consorting with witches and encouraging seditious prophecies. Gloucester reacts by reaffirming his loyalty to the king and dismissing his wife:

> I banish her my bed and company.
> And give her as a prey to law and shame . . .

Shortly after this, Shakespeare stages a meeting between the couple. This time Humphrey appears less detached:

> But soft, I think she comes, and I'll prepare
> My tear-stain'd eyes to see her miseries.

And they address each other in familiar terms as "gentle Nell" and "Humphrey." Both figures stress, as so often, the theatricality of her disgrace:

> **Gloucester:** Sweet Nell, ill can thy noble mind abrook
> The abject people gazing on thy face,
> With envious looks laughing at thy shame,
> That erst did follow thy proud chariot-wheels
> When thou didst ride in triumph through the streets.
> **Duchess:** The ruthless flint doth cut my tender feet,
> And when I start, the envious people laugh. . . .
> Sometime I'll say, I am Duke Humphrey's wife,
> And he a prince, and ruler of this land;
> Yet so he rul'd, and such a prince he was,
> As he stood by, whilest I, his forlorn duchess,
> Was made a wonder and a pointing-stock
> To every idle rascal follower.

Her resentment at her husband's political innocence, at his reluctance to believe in the schemes set to entrap him, elicits no more than an exhortation to be patient, to endure what the law ordains. The exchange anticipates Drayton's poems. But Shakespeare never lets us lose sight of the developing political picture of which this moving spectacle is only a detail. When Gloucester willingly follows a royal summons to a parliament, apparently secure in the belief that he can be in no danger because he has done no wrong, it is the kind of assessment that the context makes ominous in the extreme. We can guess the fate that awaits him. As always in the play, the audience's sense of the vivid immediacy of a particular dramatic moment is suddenly and deftly augmented by an understanding of how it relates to wider circumstances.

At times the wider resonances are created in a more heavy-handed, more overtly allegorical way. An instance is Act IV, Scene X of *Henry VI Part 2*, when Alexander Iden, a gentleman of Kent, is interrupted in his garden by Jack Cade, leader of a savage rebellion. The clash between the men is clearly set up as a clash of value systems, a competition between order and anarchy, between discipline and riot. The garden's immediate status as a visual pun on Iden's name (Iden = Eden) reinforces its conventional role as a microcosm of the state, an image Shakespeare used constantly. Scenes set in gardens inevitably recall other garden episodes. So Iden's confrontation with the revolutionaries takes us back to the scene in the previous play where the great lords declared their enmity in the Temple Garden by plucking roses of red and white as their badges. On a formal level, the semi-pastoral scene exemplifies the mixture of different literary genres within the sequence. But the disruption of Iden's garden retreat, and his transformation from an unworldly scholar into a doughty fighter who challenges Cade and slays him, seems designed to stand for the malaise of the time. Like many such scenes it is essentially a brief sketch whose elements are—necessarily, perhaps—presented somewhat starkly.

But there are times when this rather static mode can be used elaborately. In *Henry VI Part 3*, Act II, Scene V, we see one of the most extraordinary pieces of invention of this phase of Shakespeare's career. It combines emblematic staging with pathos, and shows a magnificent conjunction between moments of dramatic intensity and a much larger overall design. The context of the scene is the savage battle of Towton, which flows back and forth across the stage in a series of short exchanges of violent combat and bombastic verbal challenge. Then suddenly the atmosphere changes. The simple-minded, possibly saintly king finds space for himself at the center of this vortex of destruction, and speaks in a markedly detached way about it:

This battle fares like to the morning's war,
When dying clouds contend with growing light,
What time the shepherd, blowing of his nails,
Can neither call it perfect day nor night.
Now sways it this way, like a mighty sea
Forc'd by the tide to combat with the wind;
Now sways it that way, like the self-same sea
Forc'd to retire by fury of the wind. . . .
So is the equal poise of this fell war.
Here on this molehill will I sit me down.
To whom God will, there be the victory!

This is a pastoral moment of rest and of recreation. But it also constitutes an abdication made all the more powerful by its situation within the clamorous savagery of a battlefield. And the point is then reinforced by moments of almost unendurable pathos. Each of the doors to the stage opens and spills out a tableau of the consequences of war, of the way that civil war has torn apart families as well as the kingdom. From each door comes a soldier carrying a corpse. The first, searching his victim for gold, removes the helmet and discovers he has killed his father. He laments what he has done and subsides into silent tears. The second, making a similar search, finds that he has killed his son, laments and weeps. The whole event is a remarkable combination of pathos and pageantlike formality. These soldiers, racked with sorrow, are also tokens of the wider conflict. And Henry's response is quite extraordinary: He, like the audience, can see both of the distraught soldiers, and he joins in their lamentation:

Son: Was ever son so ru'd a father's death?
Father: Was ever father so bemoan'd his son?
King Henry: Was ever King so griev'd for subjects' woe?
Much is your sorrow: mine ten times so much.

Henry sums up the spectacle by commenting, after the men have borne away their victims:

Sad-hearted men, much overgone with care.
Here sits a king more woeful than you are.

Then the action resumes and Henry is swept away by his supporters as the tide of conflict rises around him. The scene, which is dotted with scriptural echoes ("Pardon me, God, I knew not what I did"), recalls the strategies of the mystery cycles in relating these individual tragedies to broader circumstances—"O heavy times, begetting such events! . . . O pity, God, this miserable age!" Such cries are patterned, formulaic, static. But they also reach out to their audience and tell of how the family squabbles of the powerful are paid for in the blood of their subjects.

As Henry sits down on his molehill, his act visually recalls the earlier scene in which the duke of York had been humiliated on the molehill before being killed. In that scene Queen Margaret torments her captive, mocks him, and places on his head a paper crown. The episode echoes the torment of Christ, often staged in the mystery cycles. More immediately, it also prefigures the grisly episode just a few moments later when the fatally wounded Clifford is similarly tormented by the Yorkists.

In other words, the play's elements are connected by the reiteration of devices, by patterns and symmetries, by verbal, visual, and physical echoes. The implications are usually not available to the speakers onstage. It is for the audience to perceive the ironies, to comprehend that apparently diverse events are in some important ways related to each other. In *Richard III* this patterning is more obvious, more concentrated, and seems more unambiguously directed toward its conclusion. But the play also marks a change in direction and focus, as the audience's attention is guided instantly to a dominant central speaker, who both bestrides the stage action and serves as a bridge between that action and the spectators, functioning simultaneously as protagonist and impresario.

During the course of composition, Shakespeare's conception of the *Henry VI* plays grew from a two-part drama of rising and falling fortunes into a larger structure, something that aspired to the great sweep of the mystery cycles. *Richard III* can be seen as the climax of that sequence; many commentators have drawn attention to the parallel between the way the mystery cycles concluded by demonstrating the providential ordering of history, and the ending of Shakespeare's play, where the Tudor regime is installed to replace the twisted, satanic monster Richard. Such a reading also implies a parallel between Shakespeare's plays and the epic, because it was normal in epics to show how history led providentially to the present, usually to the author's patron. Virgil's *Aeneid* had told the story of Rome as a compliment to Augustus: Spenser's *The Faerie Queene* was an epic that praised Elizabeth. Just so, the argument runs, Shakespeare organized his history cycle as an account of the inexorable and praiseworthy historical process that produced Queen Elizabeth.

And there is no doubt that the formal and processional qualities of *Richard III* emphasize and reinforce such a view. The extraordinary nocturnal scene before the battle of Bosworth embodies this mode. There are two tents onstage, one each for Richard and Richmond. The ghosts of those whom Richard has slain come on in solemn procession and deliver hostile speeches to the sleeping king before lining up behind the man they wish to succeed him. Not long afterward, the two protagonists give parallel speeches to their forces. Each employs a rhetoric expressive of his historical reputation. It is as if, as the play draws to its close, the verdict of history is being delivered before our eyes.

But *Richard III* is also a tragedy, and within the stately patterns of its scenic structure roams the demonic force of the grotesque, hunchbacked king. He represents a model of power antithetical to the Elizabethan myth. Where she was praised as inviolable, inexpressible, ideal, Shakespeare's Richard is distorted, uncontrollable, almost inhuman. He collects within himself all of the anarchic powers that have been operating throughout the sequence—most of them up to now had been loaded on to females, who had been staged as the representatives of dark, unsayable things. Margaret of Anjou, Joan La Pucelle, and Elinor Cobham are just three instances of women who are associated with "otherness," with the supernatural, with prophecy. Richard likewise is represented as excluded from all conventional norms. But, like Marlowe's Tamburlaine, he nevertheless manages to fascinate, to seduce, to dominate, to rule.

One of the elements that have made the play so abidingly popular (there were six quartos between 1597 and the First Folio in 1623) is its competition between this dominant, scene-stealing individual and the shape of history which surrounds and eventually crushes him. The vitality of Richard's relentless verbal inventiveness is connected with the pressure under which it is forced to burgeon.

Richard, like Tamburlaine, tries to create an alternative reality, to construct a world out of his words, out of his profound theatricality.

The reason is declared at the outset. Richard announces that, given his deformity, there is no alternative:

> . . . I, in this weak piping time of peace
> Have no delight to pass away my time
> Unless to spy my shadow in the sun,
> And descant on mine own deformity.
> And therefore, since I cannot prove a lover
> To entertain these fair well-spoken days,
> I am determined to prove a villain,
> And hate the idle pleasures of these days.

The disarming frankness establishes a private contract between the demonic protagonist and the audience. As he lets us in on his schemes, we are ourselves in danger of being seduced by his persuasive arts (the parallel is probably with Chaucer's *Pardoner's Tale*). But we are not alone. We see his skills on a private stage first, with the seduction of Lady Anne in the presence of the corpse of Henry VI. Then we see them applied with equal zest in the political sphere. All the time, through a use of soliloquies matched elsewhere only in *Hamlet*, we are kept informed of the strategies we are about to see enacted.

As the play proceeds we perceive the gradual separation and isolation of Richard in a way that anticipates *Macbeth*'s final scenes. One consequence is to stress the almost ritual nature of the events, of the purgation after a national disease. But another is to generate a sense of admiration or pathos for the figure against whom all the odds stack with alarming power and inevitability as his life draws to its close. As his authority wanes, he expresses his weakness as an actor's forgetting his lines. And the political realities of Shakespeare's position were in fact conducive to this process of building up Richard into something more appealing than an amalgam of those ancient and modern theatrical stereotypes, the Antichrist, the Vice, and the Machiavel. The greater his stature as an opponent, then the greater and more providential would the ultimate victory of the Tudors appear.

In its final form, Shakespeare's sequence opens with the funeral of Henry V: "Hung be the heavens with black," and proceeds to show the passing of a generation of English commanders. It ends, four plays later, with an explicit staging of the triumph of the Tudor dynasty. Taken as a whole, it possesses an overall argument, a structural coherence unprecedented in English drama. But that is only part of the achievement of these plays. It is less for their scaffolding than for their range and variety, the fertility of their inventiveness, their combination of elevated rhetoric, spectacle, and deeply affecting pathos that these plays are remarkable. By the time the sequence ended, Shakespeare had shown himself the equal of Marlowe as a tragedian; a notable triumph in itself. But he was at the same time engaged in outstripping his contemporaries in a variety of other modes, too. And it is to them that we now turn.

Shakespeare's earliest plays are experimental, and would have seemed so to their first audience. One of the most striking features of Shakespeare's art is that he conducted his literary experiments in public, before the gaze of massed spectators, rather than in a safer, more private sphere. The status that drama went on to enjoy twenty years later—when nobles and kings professed a technical interest in theatrical composition and staging—was partly a response to the achievement of Shakespeare, Jonson, and their contemporaries. But when Shakespeare first began to write for the stage—whether in the late 1580s or early 1590s—he was directing his talent to a form that was a popular success, a social phenomenon, but not yet something that was taken very seriously as art. Most educated dramatists (and the majority were university men) seem to have written for the stage in the same spirit as European screenwriters approached prewar Hollywood. It was work, but it wasn't really art. Serious writing in late Tudor times was what you did for your patron. The whole point of literature was to get you noticed, to persuade a nobleman of your intelligence, eloquence, and mastery of the new print culture and to take you on to his staff. In due course you could then enact the humanist ideals of education applied to practical questions of government, judgment, and administration. The concept of making a career through writing did not yet exist—not surprisingly, since it was so poorly paid. And there certainly was not, until Shakespeare appeared, any precedent for basing and constructing a literary reputation on dramatic texts. During the early 1590s even Shakespeare was chiefly ad-mired—or at least chiefly praised in print—for his poems rather than his plays.

But his early plays are ambitious and experimental—some people at the time would probably have thought them pretentious and overblown, attempts to make "serious" what to them was inescap-ably a popular form of mass culture. Shakespeare did not have the financial pressures that broke Robert Greene, John Lyly, and oth-ers, nor the desperate need to secure patronage that dominated the minds and hands of so many of his contemporaries. He may not have been wealthy, but he had enough to live on. He also had a job as an actor—a career much better paid than writing—and a stake in the company he worked in. Of course, while these advan-tages sustained him they deprived him of one of the usual motives for writing that spurred on Nashe, Greene, and the rest to scribble desperately night and day to translate their words into harder cur-rency. Nor was he in a position in which elegies, epithalamia, panegyrics, dynastic histories, and antiquarian fantasies were re-quired of him to secure some scraps from the tables of potential patrons and sponsors.

So he was left with the public stage. And what he produced in those earlier years constitutes a remarkable portfolio, in which he tries his hand at most of the kinds of writing currently practiced on the professional stages and in each case attempts to push it to a new level of sophistication. His writings are saturated with the words, concepts, and methods of his contemporaries, but he re-peatedly charges his pieces with significances that enlarge their scope beyond the received conventions of the form. But these are large assertions. Let me try to illustrate what I mean by looking first at *The Comedy of Errors*.

Elizabethan schoolboys were taught rhetoric and literary analysis through the systematic and detailed study of a small number of canonical authors. And several of Shakespeare's earliest plays take school texts as their starting point. Every Elizabethan schoolboy knew, because any Elizabethan schoolmaster would have told him, that the master of comedy was Terence, who was, in Erasmus's words, "pure, concise, closest to everyday speech, and . . . congenial to the young." Erasmus cautiously went on to say that if some experts were to advocate that "a few, selected comedies of Plautus should be added to the above, I would personally not demur." It so happens that we can quite easily reconstruct how these works of Roman comedy were analyzed in the classroom, for Erasmus wrote a guide for schoolmasters called *De Ratione Studii* (On the Method of Study). After some general advice about making the lesson accessible and various, he becomes more specific:

> For example, take a comedy of Terence. Before translating this [the teacher] should first of all discuss briefly the author's circumstances, his talent, the elegance of his language. Then he should mention how much instruction and enjoyment may be had from reading comedy; next the significance of that form of literature, its origins, the number and types of comedy and its laws. Next he should explain as clearly and concisely as possible the gist of the plot. He should be careful to point out the types of metre. Then he should make a simple arrangement of these points and then explain each one in greater detail. In this respect he should carefully draw their attention to any purple passage, archaism, neologism, Graecism, any obscure or verbose expression, any abrupt or confused order, any etymology, derivation, or composition worth knowing, any point of orthography, figure of speech, or rhetorical passages, or embellishment or corruption. Next he should compare parallel passages in authors, bringing out differences and similarities—what has been imitated, what merely echoed, where the source is different, where common, inasmuch as the majority of Latin works have their origin in Greek. Finally he should turn to philosophy and skillfully bring out the moral application of the poets' stories.

The taste formed by such exercises was the taste for which the young dramatist wrote *The Comedy of Errors*. He constructed a show that would not have been out of place in a schoolroom, and his audience would have been struck instantly by its familiarity. But no sooner were they settled in, confident that they were seeing a restaging of their youthful study, than Shakespeare elaborated the material in various disconcerting ways, some hilarious, some confusing, some moving, some disturbing.

The fundamental structure of the plot derives from a school text, Plautus's *Menaechmi*, in whose Latin prologue lies a promise of a plot whose complexities can be "weighed not in pecks or bushels but by the barnful." But Shakespeare wove in a further full set of complications from another Plautus text, his most famous comedy, the *Amphitruo*. An Elizabethan would have been struck by the ingenuity with which this recognizable material was handled, by the virtuoso doubling of the story, and by the doubling of the challenge to the audience. We do not know what attracted Shakespeare to the *Menaechmi* story; he would almost certainly have read it in Latin—numerous texts were available—perhaps he saw the first English translation, by William Warner. Warner's version of this play of "much pleasant error" (which sounds like a source for Shakespeare's title) was not published until 1595, but was evidently circulating among his friends for their "use and delight" for a few years before that. Shakespeare presumably knew Warner, who in the late 1580s dedicated several works to Henry Carey, Lord Hunsdon, who was lord chamberlain from 1585 to 1596 and the patron of Shakespeare's troupe, the Lord Chamberlain's Men, from 1594. This seems to have been the company responsible for a performance of *The Comedy of Errors* at Gray's Inn in 1594, though the records are unhelpfully vague, as we shall see.

With all early Shakespeare it is advisable to try to create some kind of mental image of the stage for which he was writing. In this case there was a lengthy tradition of performing Roman comedy, whether in Latin or in modern vernacular languages. And there are plenty of descriptions and illustrations to show what their practice was. The evidence of the text suggests that the staging of *The Comedy of Errors* was typical of academic drama. That is to say, Shakespeare would have used an "arcade" stage which accommodated three "houses"; the Phoenix, the Porpentine, and the Priory. Each "house" was represented by a door with a sign on it, and the space in front would be designated the exchange, the forum, the "mart." Staging of this kind was available in the public theaters, and was normal in academic settings, such as at the Inns of Court or in the halls of Oxford and Cambridge colleges, whose architecture corresponded very closely to the arrangements of the neoclassical stage.

There is a mock-serious account of "a disordered Tumult and Crowd upon the Stage" at Gray's Inn on the night of Holy Innocents' Day (December 28) 1594, during the celebration of the Christmas revels—a time of the ritualized inversion of normal conventions

and behavior. The account tells—in a studiedly offhand way—of
the appearance of the professional players:

> . . . it was thought good not to offer any thing of Account, saving
> Dancing and Revelling with Gentlewomen; and after such Sports,
> a Comedy of Errors (like to *Plautus* his *Menaechmus*) was played by
> the Players. So that Night was begun, and continued to the end, in
> nothing but Confusion and Errors; whereupon, it was ever after-
> wards called, *The Night of Errors.*

The author goes on to tell of the "Sorceries and Inchant-
ments . . . a great Witchcraft used," to speak (tongue in cheek) of
complaints that there had been "great Disorders and Misdemean-
ours, by Hurly-burlies, Crowds, Errors, Confusions, vain Representations and Shews, to the utter Discredit of our State and
Policy." And he concludes: ". . . this was the end of our Law-
sports, concerning the Night of Errors." Our awareness of the
academic setting needs to include the sense of festival, of carnival
behavior, of the deliberate disruption of normality, where confusion
of identity merges with more ominous elements such as witchcraft
and sorcery. And however comic and high-spirited, the text goes
beyond confusion and farce to hint at altogether more serious concerns, as the Gray's Inn reporter, albeit jocularly, recognized.

Indeed, the play provides evidence that from the very outset of
his career Shakespeare had the remarkable gift of combining control
over the theatrical show—in this case staging a comedy to a time
of revelry, confusion, and hilarity—with a more serious, more
thought-provoking project. And in *The Comedy of Errors* he displayed
his art by other means than doubling the plots and providing a
comic complication of material remembered from school. Plautus
had set his play in Epidamnum: Shakespeare shifted the action to
Ephesus, a city familiar primarily for its role in the New Testament.
In that source it is presented as a kind of spiritual hothouse, dominated by the celebrated Temple of Diana (which Paul said should
be "nothing esteemed, and . . . shulde be destroyed" [text from the
Geneva Bible of 1560]) but also including a Christian community,
as well as Jews who had taken up practices of exorcism and magic.
So where Epidamnum was described in Warner's translation as "a
place of outrageous expences, exceeding in all ryot and lascivious-
nesse: and . . . as full of Ribaulds, Parasites, Drunkards, Catch-

poles, Cony-catchers, and Sycophants, as it can hold," Shakespeare's Antipholus of Syracuse describes Ephesus thus:

They say this town is full of cozenage,
As nimble jugglers that deceive the eye,
Dark-working sorcerers that change the mind,
Soul-killing witches that deform the body,
Disguised cheaters, prating mountebanks,
And many such-like liberties of sin.

So Plautus's evocation of a place of disorder and license is transformed and darkened. It becomes a grotesque, threatening, and morally dubious world, where corrupt and degenerate religious practices conflict with revealed truth. Dr. Pinch's exorcism in Act IV probably recalls the Christian triumph, described in Acts 19:19, at which the spread of the news about Christ caused magicians to burn their books ("many of them which used curious artes, broght their bookes, and burned them before all men"). Paul's Epistle to the Ephesians colors the text at some points, too. In particular, his recommendations about the marital relations ("Wives, submit your selves unto your husbands, as unto the Lord. For the houseband is the wives head, even as Christ is the head of the Church, and the same is the saviour of his bodie. Therefore as the church is in subjection to Christ, even so let the wives be to their housbands in everie thing") and between masters and servants ("Servants, be obedient unto them that are your masters. And ye masters, do the same things unto them, putting away threatening"). Diana's Temple is deftly transformed into the Abbey of Act V—Diana was one pagan deity who was rarely criticized in Elizabethan England at the height of the queen's cult as virgin-goddess.

Throughout the play Shakespeare places great stress on marriage and courtship. Hardly surprising, perhaps. But in order to achieve this focus—which we naturally assume to be the norm in a Shakespearean comedy—he had to replace the intrigues with a prostitute who had been central to the Plautine plot. Along with the scriptural allusions, this shift of emphasis Christianizes the story. Maybe the play represents an attempt to legitimize fiction, to invest it with a degree of respectability, by making it more sententious, more certain in its moral direction.

Nevertheless, the very obvious classical model gave the text its

chief characteristics. In *The Comedy of Errors* Shakespeare is closer
to adhering to the classical unities of time, place, and action than
in any other play he wrote, with the possible exception of *The
Tempest*. Indeed, Shakespeare makes powerful use of time as a force
within the action. The primary effect is to generate a sense of
urgency whose purpose seems to be (in line with the other Chris-
tianizing devices) to point to the need to gird loins, to repent. Again,
the echo is of Ephesians:

> Put on the whole armour of God that ye may be able to stand against
> the assaults of the devill. For we wrestle not against flesh and blood,
> but against principalities, against powers, and against the worldlie
> governours . . . against spiritual wickednesse, which are in the hie
> places . . . Stand therefore, and your loins girde about with verity.

Like many other Renaissance writers who reworked ancient comedy—notably Ariosto and Machiavelli—Shakespeare directed attention to the preoccupations of his day, to the relationships
between the sexes, between generations, between different social
groups. As I will try to explain when discussing *The Taming of the
Shrew*, Shakespeare tapped into a particular contemporary English
concern about marriage. But more generally he directed attention
to the human predicaments of the individuals enacting the absurdly
comic plot. In particular the framework story of Egeon, which
superficially seems little more than a plot device, becomes a means
of evoking pity and pathos in a way that would have been alien to
his source, and which must have brought the reveling lawyers up
with a jolt when the play was performed before them. The old
man, after all, is sentenced to death unless someone can be found
to redeem him; this provides an unequivocally serious and urgent
framework for the hilarious stage actions and mistakes. However
endless the complications and ramifications of confused identity
might be, there is always the grim finality of execution, the gloomy
specter of the scaffold, hovering behind the games. The Egeon
story comes not from Plautus but from the story of Apollonius of
Tyre told in John Gower's poem *Confessio Amantis*, from the turn
of the fifteenth century, and also draws on the world of Renaissance
fiction and romance, and on the all-too-real perils of sea travel of
the time. So Egeon is for Shakespeare's audience both a fictional

stereotype and a victim of recognizably "real" circumstances. And the extraordinary series of recognitions and coincidences which conclude the action, when the Abbess reveals that she is really Egeon's long-lost wife, combines literary convention with a scene of affecting pathos. Just before the Abbess declares her true identity, after all, Egeon had been heartbroken to discover that his son did not recognize him:

> Not know my voice? O time's extremity,
> Hast thou so crack'd and splitted my poor tongue
> In seven short years, that here my only son
> Knows not my feeble key of untun'd cares?

And the Ephesian Antipholus's words, "I never saw my father in my life," cut through the layers of fiction and confusion to bring the revels and tricks to a halt in the face of a moment of loss, of separation. It is an incident that anticipates the highly charged emotional exchange between parents and children in Shakespeare's last plays; as in those plays, the bleakest experiences are succeeded by the restoration prompted by the abbess. In the duke's words, "here begins our morning story right." The end of the play is a new beginning, an opening out of experience rather than a line drawn under it, less a revelation of something hidden than a new discovery altogether.

What I am stressing here is that *The Comedy of Errors* is, as well as being a very funny play, also extremely clever; and in its conclusion it aspires to touch and move its audience. A remarkable sureness of touch is displayed in managing the audience's response and in controlling the modulations of tone. Shakespeare used his understanding of the actor's craft to transform academic exercises into theatrical experiences, to translate from the page to the stage. This is a central quality of his approach to writing plays. To us there might seem nothing unusual about a playwright whose first concern was with what happened onstage; but to an Elizabethan writer the text was conceived outside the playhouse and he lost all control once it was taken on by the company. Further, he would have regarded such writing as hack work, doomed to ephemerality by the audience's ever-changing tastes. For Shakespeare circumstances were different. And we can see him taking on his major contemporaries throughout his early plays, rising to the challenge that their work posed. He created a very distinctive voice for himself, and developed a theatrical vocabulary that embraced wit, invention, cleverness, pathos, pity, and profound engagement of his audience's sympathies.

Some of Shakespeare's most daring experiments, his boldest innovations, are completely lost on us today. The dazzling novelty of his art—even at the very outset of his career, and it is possible that *The Two Gentlemen of Verona* is his first solo play—would have been instantly apparent to his contemporaries. Shakespeare's experiments were those of a practicing theatrical professional, someone who has found out firsthand what works onstage. So when he brought together disparate elements, whether court drama, low comedy, classical learning, folktale, or popular romantic novels, his ambition was to "please," to fill the theater. At this time in his writing life he did not write with half an eye on posterity, nor with an ambition to attract noble patronage. The patrons for whom he wrote paid their penny at the door.

Because it is rarely performed, and because the infrequent revivals have enjoyed relatively little theatrical success, *The Two Gentlemen of Verona* is perhaps inevitably treated as a written text, as something to be read and studied. It is above all, however, a script, and the script of a theatrical event that is both hilarious and at times arrestingly eloquent. It deals with a topic that Shakespeare worried away at all his life—the relationship between (male) friendship and heterosexual love. Proteus, true to his name, leaves his mistress Julia because he has fallen for Silvia, the mistress of his close friend Valentine. Valentine recovers Silvia, magnanimously forgives Proteus, and then gives up Silvia to him. At that moment the attendant page falls into a swoon and is revealed to be none other than Julia. Proteus is shamed into a recognition of his inconstancy and returns to Julia, and Valentine is united with the woman he had moments before been prepared to yield to his friend.

The mental world of the play is not our own. It is built—not uncritically, but certainly—on an idea of male friendship that many writers of the time articulated. In the words of John Lyly, from his hugely popular prose romance *Euphues, the Anatomy of Wit* (1578):

". . . well I believe it, that a friend is in prosperity a pleasure, a solace in adversity, in grief a comfort, in joy a merry companion, at all times an other I, in all places the express image of mine own person." Montaigne wrote of friends in similar terms: "All things being by effect common between them: wills, thoughts, judgements, goods, wives, children, honour, and life; and their mutual agreement being no other than one soul in two bodies, according to the fit definition of Aristotle, they can neither lend or give ought to each other."

In the context of such passages, the ending of the play is of a piece with Shakespeare's lifelong exploration of love, friendship, and selfhood. His constant return to it indicates that he was no nearer a solution in 1613 with his final play *The Two Noble Kinsmen* than in this very early play, or in the *Sonnets*. As so often, we should be alert to the way in which Shakespeare invariably uses exaggeratedly neat conclusions in plays that raise questions much wider than those within the narrow confines of the plot.

But it is not just that the central theme of the play is alien to us. We have also, unfortunately, lost touch with the traditions of theater and indeed of comedy in which Shakespeare operates this play. In particular, the writings of John Lyly (both in his prose fictions *Euphues, the Anatomy of Wit* and *Euphues and His England*, and in a remarkable sequence of short plays) are scarcely known today. His fiction was immensely popular, and his drama—performed both at court and by the boys' companies in "private" theaters—was extremely influential.

It is for his verbal artifice, his seemingly endless lists of parallels, antithetical constructions, puns, and quibbles that he is chiefly, if unfairly, known. And the verbal texture of Shakespeare's play owes a great deal to him, though Lyly's plays are all in prose. Also close to Lyly is the management of the relationship between the main plot and the subplot. In addition, the figure of Speed is unquestionably a version of one of Lyly's comic pages: His routines with Launce (and the dog Crab), for instance, recall the hilarious, quibbling exchanges between Licius and Putulus in Lyly's *Midas*.

The comic exchanges in *The Two Gentlemen* provide a critique of the behavior of the participants in the romantic main plot (which derives from fashionable continental romance, such as the Spanish Jorge de Montemayor's *Diana*, and perhaps in part from Sidney's

Arcadia). But they also, in the figure of Launce, give us a clown in
the unmistakably English tradition of Richard Tarleton. He has
some of the funniest moments in the whole canon—such as his first
appearance with his silent, still, scene-stealing dog Crab:

> I think Crab my dog to be the sourest-natured dog that lives: my
> mother weeping; my father wailing; my sister crying; our maid
> howling; our cat wringing her hands, and all our house in a great
> perplexity; yet did not this cruel-hearted cur shed one tear. He is a
> stone, a very pebble-stone, and has no more pity in him than a
> dog . . . my grandam, having no eyes, look you, wept herself blind
> at my parting. Nay, I'll show you the manner of it. This shoe is
> my father. No, this left shoe is my father; nay, that cannot be so
> neither. Yes, it is so, it is so: it hath the worser sole. This shoe with
> the hole in it is my mother; and this is my father. A vengeance on't,
> there 'tis. Now, sir, this staff is my sister; for, look you, she is as
> white as a lily, and as small as a wand. This hat is Nan our maid.
> I am the dog. No, the dog is himself, and I am the dog. O, the dog
> is me, and I am myself. Ay; so, so. Now come I to my father:
> "Father, your blessing." Now should not the shoe speak a word for
> weeping; now should I kiss my father; well, he weeps on; now come
> I to my mother. O, that she could speak now, like a wood woman!
> Well, I kiss her. Why, there 'tis: here's my mother's breath up and
> down. Now come I to my sister; mark the moan she makes. Now
> the dog all this while sheds not a tear, nor speaks a word; but see
> how I lay the dust with my tears.

Lyly wrote his plays for boys to perform. He could not display
on stage the interest in psychological introspection that underlies
the endless self-examination of his novels. Shakespeare wrote for
grown men, with greater professional expertise, wider vocal range,
and a developing penchant for creating characters who show more
than one face to the audience. In the soliloquies of Proteus, the
studiedly artificial, patterned verse is evidently an attempt to recreate Lyly's mode of interior debates. But unlike the extraordinary
energy of Richard III's asides to the audience, Proteus's speeches
have a metronomic regularity that keeps him frozen within the far-
off world of the play:

> To leave my Julia, shall I be forsworn;
> To love fair Silvia, shall I be forsworn;

To wrong my friend, I shall be much forsworn . . .
I cannot leave to love; and yet I do;
But there I leave to love, where I should love.
Julia I lose, and Valentine I lose;
If I keep them, I needs must lose myself;
If I lose them, thus find I by their loss;
For Valentine, myself; for Julia, Silvia.
I to myself am dearer than a friend,
For love is still most precious in itself . . .

In these speeches, especially as performed by a flesh-and-blood actor, the textbook dilemmas of the sort declaimed by prepubescent schoolboys in Lyly's theater inevitably acquire a much greater psychological weight. And we might feel, with some critics, that the style is not best fitted for such moments of inwardness. It might also be argued that the play's resolution similarly points up the difference between boys' theater and the adult companies. The illusion of actuality is that much more powerful, and makes it much harder to carry off the extraordinary transformation with which the play ends. But the disparity between the words and the characterization may have been part of Shakespeare's design, and if so, it was not the only time he took over the mode of the indoor theaters when creating scripts for his adult actors. Of the play's performance and reception we know nothing. There are no records of performance, though since it was not published before the Folio, and Francis Meres mentions it in his *Palladis Tamia* in 1598, we can assume it was staged probably in the early 1590s.

Critics have identified two central theatrical strategies in the drama before Shakespeare, and have shown how Shakespeare adopted and adapted them both. They can be summed up as "demonstrative" and "explorative." A demonstrative play is arranged to prove the truth of some proposition, usually a proverb, and moves toward a definite conclusion. An example is the morality drama *Everyman*, whose full title expresses its demonstrative character: "Here beginneth a treatise how the high father of heaven doth summon death to give account of every creature, and is in manner of a moral play." The explorative mode, in contrast, starts with a situation and then explores its various complexities and ramifications. The cast list of the morality *Play of Love* by John Heywood illustrates this form well. It reads: "A new and merry interlude concerning pleasure and pain in love. The actors' names: a man a lover not beloved; a woman loved not loving: a man a lover and beloved; the vice neither lover nor beloved." What ensues is a series of exchanges, usually dialogues, between these figures, which explore in an open-ended way the various facets of love as played out between these stereotypes. By the time Shakespeare began writing, the two modes could coexist within a single play, but they are helpful models of the kinds of interpretative systems and models his audience knew.

Simply from their titles, for instance, it would appear that *The Two Gentlemen of Verona* and *The Comedy of Errors* are explorative plays, developing the consequences of an initial situation, and carrying no expectation of a specific conclusion. The title of *The Taming of the Shrew*, on the other hand, appears to promise a demonstration, working out of an uncomplicated plot toward a specific objective. The title arouses no expectation of open-endedness. But as with the two earlier plays, it soon becomes clear that Shakespeare wants to make his audience work a bit harder.

The play's subject prepared audiences for that. The play was written at a time of renewed interest in marriage, in the way relations between the sexes were being redrawn by the consequences of the Reformation and by the socioeconomic conditions of contemporary England. The Anglican marriage service, with its claim that matrimony had been instituted for the usual procreative purposes but also for "mutual society," for companionship, had posed a new challenge for men and women. Alongside the Renaissance impulse to self-creation, to the development of the individual self as an autonomous being, came this new imperative: One's life partner was to be regarded not as a fellow combatant in an ancient and endless war between the sexes but as a friend and companion. The impact of this change can hardly be underestimated, even if in practice society remained emphatically patriarchal. At least as far as wooing and courtship were concerned, lovers, who had been trained to believe that they had interior personalities and identities quite separate from their external selves, now had to chart and explore similarly unknown territories within their prospective partners. These new challenges were staples of English culture after the Reformation; but for some reason the nature, purpose, and value of marriage were especially contentious subjects again in the late 1580s and early 1590s, and there was renewed discussion, argument, and speculation. Those who engaged in these arguments could lay their hands on reputable humanist guidebooks, of which three were of particular importance: Juan Vives's *The Office and Duty of a Husband* (1553); his *A Very Fruitfull & Pleasant Book Callyd the Instruction of a Christen Woman* (1523); and a colloquy by Erasmus called *Conjugium*, later translated into English anonymously as *A Mery Dialogue Declarynge the Property of Proud Shrews, and Honest Wyues* (1557). This last is especially relevant because it is a colloquy, an essentially dramatic form: It presents contrasting views of the subject through characters who embody those views and enact them in a series of exchanges.

The Taming of the Shrew stages various modes of love, wooing, and marriage. It also stages various kinds of education. Indeed, one of its themes is the connection between the two. Lucentio gains access to Bianca by securing employment as her tutor, and all of his "lessons" are transparent ruses, part of a strategy of seduction. The same is true of Hortensio, the teacher of music and mathematics. So these suitors use learning as a device, a means of securing a victory, of possessing Bianca. In other words, the humanist project, with all its lofty aspirations, is debased to an accomplishment, a stratagem. Which suggests that these lovers are unreconstructed "old" men, still to come to terms with the newly ordained relations between the sexes.

Indeed, Shakespeare seems to go out of his way to strip bare the pretenses of amorous rhetoric and role-playing, revealing the savagery of the struggle for power beneath. A good example of this process is Scene I, Act II, an extended scene of some 413 lines which encompasses four distinct movements, each consisting of a contest followed by a recovery. The four bouts are between Katharina and Bianca, followed by the reception of the suitors; between Baptista and Petruchio, followed by the reception of Hortensio; between Petruchio and Katharina, followed by Petruchio's announcement of his "victory" over Katharina; and then between Baptista and Gremio, the wealthy old man who is one of Bianca's suitors, followed by Tranio's delight at his victory over Gremio. At the core of the scene is Petruchio's soliloquy, an unrhymed sonnet of fourteen lines, in which he informs the audience

of his plan to tame Katharina by contradicting her. He ends, "But
here she comes, and now, Petruchio, speak." Where he speaks,
Katharina offers violence. She had opened the scene, we recall, by
striking her sister, and in this episode, at the center of the scene,
she hits Petruchio. His response is to tell her to stop; she does, and
resorts thereafter to verbal onslaughts. Throughout the scene the
events become increasingly fantastic, further and further removed
from an imitation of everyday existence. But at the same time we
see that, underneath the ever more elaborate rhetoric, women are
being sold, being fought over as if they were property. And though
violence is submerged, it does not go away.

Yet at the same time as revealing a "reality" behind words and
actions, he creates a profoundly and specifically theatrical experience. Despite her savagery in action and in words, for instance,
Katharina has two moments of powerfully silent eloquence, when
she is in sequence stunned into silent rage by her father and then
shocked into silence by the extraordinary behavior of Petruchio. A
consequence of these experiences is that everything is thrown open
to question, and that for the audience every category is infected
with uncertainty. So the contrast between brutal violence and romantic love is first made ambiguous in the contrasting final speeches
of Bianca and Kate, and then thrown open to the audience for
further thought. The play has a defining title, but it is open-ended.
Thus Shakespeare ends the play with the contrasting performances
of Bianca and Katharina. Their roles appear to have been reversed
as a result of their marriages. Where the play had opened with Kate
associated with action and Bianca with words, for instance, now it
is Bianca who acts and Katharina who speaks. The audience is
confronted with two very different models of wifely behavior, as
it had been faced with various courtship strategies throughout the
play. And Shakespeare leaves it at that. He offers no help, no guide
to the future lives of his creations. As I see it, he was providing a
topic for debate—something the Elizabethans prized highly, and
which they called, with some relish, "matter." He had set his play
in a folktale setting and had loaded it with the trappings of artifice—
disguise, trickery, farce, burlesque, the clash between head-in-the-
clouds, naïve romantic notions of love and hard-nosed commercial
transactions—but he brought it back resoundingly into contemporary England. The problems and questions that the drama leaves

behind are left for the audience to think about and to try to resolve, as the critical and theatrical responses to the play over the centuries demonstrate.

Renaissance writers, especially women, suggested that there were two ways of finding truth. One, the male way, was associated with traditional kinds of logic and rational argument, and ended with a definite single conclusion. The other, female, method was to encourage variety, to conceive of truth as a composite, diverse quality incapable of reduction to a simple formula. The title of Shakespeare's play arouses the expectation of the former, while the theatrical experience provides the audience with the latter.

That theatrical experience is set up by the extraordinary "Induction," in which an unnamed "lord" plays a trick on a drunken, sleeping beggar, Christopher Sly. The lord's attendants wait on Sly when he awakes, telling him he is their master, that he has slept for fifteen years, and revering one of their number (disguised as a woman) as Sly's "Lady." Sly is delighted at his good fortune, but also confused:

Am I a lord, and have I such a lady?
Or do I dream? Or have I dreamed till now?
I do not sleep: I see, I hear, I speak,
I smell sweet savours and I feel soft things.
Upon my life, I am a lord indeed.

His new "wife" asks him to postpone their physical reunion at least until it is dark. Meanwhile, the other servants appear and propose to while away the rest of the day with "a pleasant comedy. . . . For so your doctors hold it very meet"—the lord having hired players for that purpose, without telling them that their noble audience is his dupe. Sly, disappointed, asks if he is about to see "a Christmas-gambold or a tumbling-trick," but is told he will see more pleasing stuff, "a kind of history." He accepts this, and says to his wife, "Come madam, wife, sit by my side and let the world slip, we shall ne'er be younger." At that point *The Shrew* begins, and to that point Shakespeare does not permit his audience to return. He never shows Sly's discovery of the illusions staged for him. Instead, he plays endlessly with the idea of illusion and dissimulation, of confusions of categories. By leaving Sly suspended forever in a world of fiction, of fabrication, he leaves his play open-ended and then leaves his audience to experience contrast, variety, and multiplicity of possibilities rather than a conclusion. It is a characteristic Shakespearian paradox that so self-advertisingly artful a play should seem deliberately to shun a worked-out conclusion.

Sly is told that a comedy is "a kind of history"; history, as people of Shakespeare's generation had been taught to understand it, was a kind of comedy; that is, it was a story with a happy ending pointing to a moral. Tragedy, too, was a kind of history, as we saw in the previous chapter. The slipperiness of these generic labels is worth bearing in mind. Shakespeare and many other writers of his time had come to regard human experience as too various, too unruly, and too changeable to be conveniently pigeonholed into the categories prescribed by the ancients. And just as the comic plays contain tragic elements, so the tragedies shared some of the qualities of the comedies. One of Shakespeare's earliest commercial successes illustates this generic fluidity very well, and it is to that play that I turn now.

At the beginning of 1594 Philip Henslowe, the proprietor of the Rose Theatre, recorded the opening of a play new to his repertoire. The entry reads: "Rd [Received] at titus & ondronicus the 23 of jenewary iij *li* viij s." £3 8s. represented, by the standards of that season, a considerable commercial success. On February 6 the printer John Danter put down in the Stationers' Register, "a booke intituled a Noble Roman Historye of Tytus Andronicus," together with "the ballad thereof." Some months later the booksellers Edward White and Thomas Millington began to sell at their stall "at the little North doore of Paules at the signe of the Gunne" a volume entitled "The most lamentable Romaine Tragedie of Titus Andronicus," printed by Danter and claiming to be the text "As it was Plaide by the Right Honourable the Earle of *Darbie*, Earle of *Pembroke*, and the Earle of *Sussex* their servants." Scholars have inspected these fragments of evidence with diligence and imagination: They have speculated, for instance, as to the meaning of Henslowe's marginal note "ne" next to the record of the first performance. It can hardly mean "new," if the evidence of the subsequent title pages is to be believed, since they indicate a previous theatrical career in the hands of either several companies or of a group formed out of the plague-ravaged remnants of a number of companies.

It is clear that *Titus Andronicus* was immensely popular in its own day, and after several centuries of neglect has been rediscovered by the present generation as a theatrical experience of stunning force. While records of specific performances are sparse, the play held the stage for many years, so that by 1614 it had come to seem somewhat passé. Ben Jonson commented then that "he that will swear *Hieronimo* [Thomas Kyd's *Spanish Tragedy*] or *Andronicus* are the best plays yet, shall pass . . . as a man whose judgement shows it is constant, and hath stood still these five and twenty, or thirty years." Jonson's remark does not need to be taken literally (that would date *Titus* as early as 1584), and it tells us more about his snobbery than about changes in literary taste, but it does fix the play as one of the outstanding representatives of the vogue for spectacular historical tragedies that occurred around 1590.

The most important early evidence for performances is to be found in the library of the marquess of Bath at Longleat, in papers formerly belonging to Sir Michael Hicks, secretary to Lord Burghley in Elizabeth's time. Henry Peacham, an artist chiefly remembered for his books of emblems and for his conduct book *The Complete Gentleman* (1622), who was eighteen or nineteen years old in 1595, made a visual record of a performance of *Titus*. His pen drawing shows six figures: on the left Titus, flanked by two supporters (who may be sons or attendant lords); on the right Tamora and her sons Chiron and Demetrius kneeling, with Aaron the Moor behind, pointing at the sons. Beneath the picture are copied lines from the play, taken from the first and last acts. We cannot know if the picture corresponds to public or private staging practice, but evidently the visual aspect of the performance was sufficiently striking to warrant this most unusual pictorial record. We can also see that, whereas the soldiers or lords who attend Titus are dressed in Elizabethan fashion, some effort has been made to clothe the central actors in a version of classical dress. The illustration is not a "snapshot" of a moment in the play (for none corresponds to Peacham's picture), but rather a comprehensive illustration of aspects of that performance. A further indication of the importance of the visual quality of the play survives in a record of a private performance at Burley-on-the-Hill, in the household of Sir John Harington of

Exton, on New Year's Day 1596. Jacques Petit, who was employed
in the household as a French tutor, wrote: *"On a aussi joué la tragédie
de Titus Andronicus mais la monstre a plus valu que le sujet"*—the show,
the display (*la monstre*), is worth more than the idea or theme (*le
sujet*).

Nevertheless, the subject was hardly negligible. *Titus* was performed to public acclaim in the years after the Armada, and shares
many of the preoccupations of the *Henry VI* plays. As in those
plays, Shakespeare sets his treatment of political questions safely
in the past. Further, in *Titus* he chose a topic—and to some degree
its manner of treatment—that would have been familiar to the
audience from its schooldays. Partly that was derived from the
constant references to the *Metamorphoses* of Ovid, but alongside Ovid
Shakespeare drew upon other Roman writers, especially historians
such as Livy and Tacitus, as well as on Plutarch.

The raw material for the story probably came from a popular
(and now lost) prose history of Titus Andronicus—of which only
a chapbook printed in the 1730s survives to show what it consisted
of. Shakespeare seems to have augmented this simple source in
various major ways, most notably by restructuring the material
around the sort of antithetical conception he found so congenial.
The effect is to accentuate the contrast between the austere values
of Republican Rome, embodied in Titus himself, and the decadence
associated with the late Empire, and embodied in many figures in
the play.

The opposition between on the one hand decline, decadence,
and indecision at the seat of imperial government, and on the other
hand the personal and civic virtues associated with republican values, would have been impossible to treat in a contemporary English
context. These politically sensitive ideas could be argued about in
an educational setting, and they were. After all, schoolboys were
trained to compose speeches and arguments for and against propositions, imagining themselves in the shoes of famous historical
figures to invent speeches they should have made at some crisis in
history. These habits of mind meant that political thought was
often conducted in terms of dialogue, debate, and drama. In addition, as Queen Elizabeth grew older there was clearly an active
intellectual interest—in some cases going further than disinterested
investigation—in republicanism, not least for its association with

high personal standards of virtue. Republics in Venice and in the Netherlands provided attractive contemporary foreign models. But the only safe way to stage republican values was to restore them to their ancient context, to act out a clash of value systems in a suitably distanced, academically respectable context. Yet Shakespeare found the academic mode of competing arguments and set-pieces of only limited interest. Whenever he used it, he jumbled it up with a great variety of other elements and with other methods.

In *Titus*, for example, he wove in sensational blood-curdling material from Ovid and Seneca. From Ovid came the story of the rape of Philomel in which Philomel is raped by her brother-in-law Tereus in a cabin in the woods. He then cuts out her tongue to guarantee silence, and tells his wife Procne, his victim's sister, that Philomel is dead. Philomel weaves her tale into a cloth which she sends to her sister. The two women plan revenge. They take the son of Tereus and Procne, Itys, kill him, cook him, and serve him up for his father to eat. In the action that follows, Philomel is turned into a nightingale and Tereus and Procne also become birds.

A similar episode of cannibalism occurs in Seneca's play *Thyestes*, where Atreus tricks Thyestes into eating his own sons and tells him: "Thou has devour'd thy sons, and fill'd thyself with wicked meat." He goes further in exulting over his defeated enemy and boasting:

> Myself with swords the wounds them gave;
> I strake them down . . .
> . . . the carcase cutting then and lifeless limbs on ground
> I have in little parcels chopp'd, and some of them I drown'd
> In boiling cauldrons, some to fires that burn full slow I put . . .

Titus's torture of Tamora, presenting her sons to her "both baked in this pie," brings this Roman horror from the study to the stage. Likewise with Ovid. Indeed, there is a moment when a copy of Ovid's *Metamorphoses* is brought on to the stage. Lavinia, raped and mutilated, tells her story by opening the Ovidian text at the story of Philomel. Shakespeare makes vivid and theatrical that which his audience would have been more familiar with in the private world of the imagination or in the schoolroom. He forced them—as in all his earliest plays—to experience what they had merely studied before.

As well as drawing heavily on classical material, the play takes one of its plots from a thoroughly nasty story about a Moorish servant who seeks revenge on his master for a slight. When the master goes out hunting, the Moor rapes the master's wife and locks the doors of the house. When the husband returns he is confronted by the spectacle of the gloating Moor pointing to the wife and children. The Moor then proceeds to murder the children one by one before their parents' eyes, and drops the bodies into the moat. He offers to release the wife with no further injuries provided that the husband cuts his own nose off. When the distraught husband complies, the Moor responds by throwing the wife to her death. The husband dies of shock; the Moor laughs hysterically and jumps to his death in the moat to avoid capture. His delight in his wickedness survives in Shakespeare's Aaron: most notably in his unrepentant speech as he faces death in the last act:

> But I have done a thousand dreadful things
> As willingly as one would kill a fly.
> And nothing grieves me heartily indeed,
> But that I cannot do ten thousand more.

The tone of the play has posed problems for audiences. Shakespeare confronts us with a mixture of grand horror and low farce, juxtaposing poised, artful rhetoric and gross violence or slapstick, combining learning and crudity, barbarism and pathos. We do the play a disservice if we try to base interpretation or performance on one of these elements to the exclusion of others, or if we see it merely as a play of ideas, a competition between political ideologies safely displaced to an intellectual plane. Shakespeare was using the very fact of staging, working with the medium itself, to create experiences that were impossible to assimilate within simple categories or preconceptions. His view of existence resisted neat separation of tragedy from comedy, of great movements in history from personal experiences. Let me try to illustrate what I mean from the most theatrically risky and breathtaking moment in the play.

The qualities traditionally prized in the victims of a tragic story are endurance, stoicism, and patience. They pose problems for the dramatist, since they involve reaction rather than action. Revenge tragedies, like many of the historical tragedies of Shakespeare's day, offered an alternative path for tragic heroes, showing them abandoning patience in favor of a vendetta. *Titus* contains elements of each tradition, but at its core is a depiction of endurance that has lost none of its force over the centuries.

In the course of Scene I, Act III, there is an almost unimaginable heaping up of horrors, each jolting Titus further from his sanity. The scene is crafted with architectural skill, disposed into two equal sections of 150 lines each. Titus is onstage until the last dozen lines, when Lucius sums up the scene. Within those sections we should note the cumulative nature of the horror; and that material is organized to suggest that after each new event the list is complete. Thus the first movement, which begins with Titus flinging himself to the ground to plead for the lives of his sons, and then goes on to stage the pitiable reunion of Titus with his mutilated and abused daughter Lavinia, concludes with what seems a moment of some kind of stillness, a kind of family reunion, as father and daughter lament together convinced that no worse can happen to them. This saturation with grief is symbolized by the napkins, so wet with tears that they cannot be used to dry the tear-stained cheeks of Titus, Marcus, and Lavinia. But immediately new horrors come. Titus is told by a gloating Aaron that the emperor will save his sons if Titus or any of his group will chop off one of their hands. After the amputation, Aaron takes the hand away; but a messenger comes and brings onstage the heads of Titus's sons.

At this point the drama teeters on the edge of absurdity, partly because the events are so grotesque as to be beyond assimilation—audiences are often embarrassed, and think the only way to deal with the horror is to treat it as excessive, almost comic. But Shakespeare anticipates and exploits this reaction in order to generate an extraordinary sense of pathos. Even Titus acknowledges that the whole catalog of miseries is like a nightmare. He asks: "When will this fearful slumber have an end?" But Shakespeare effects a theatrical transformation, first by changing the role of Titus's companions. Whereas Marcus, for instance, had spent the first half of the scene urging Titus to display stoicism and fortitude—"let reason govern thy lament," now he encourages tears:

Ah, now no more will I control thy griefs;
Rend off thy silver hair, thy other hand
Gnawing with thy teeth, and be this dismal sight
The closing up of our wretched eyes.
Now is a time to storm . . .

But Titus does not cry. To the consternation of the others, he
laughs. And he explains: "I have not another tear to shed." His
laughter is, in context, a deeply shocking theatrical event, an incident which preempts and stifles any inclination that an audience
might have to relieve its discomfort by laughing. This brief moment
is the hinge upon which the play turns, the moment when Titus
is transformed from a stoic sufferer into an active avenger. From
being a victim, battered by successive waves of degradation and
sorrow, Titus finds the strength to construct meaning for himself
and his little group, staging an extraordinary ritual:

You heavy people, circle me about,
That I may turn me to each one of you,
And swear unto my soul to right your wrongs.
The vow is made. Come, brother, take a head,
And in this hand the other will I bear;
And, Lavinia, thou shalt be employed in this:
Bear thou my hand, sweet wench, between thy teeth.

Shakespeare challenges his audience to experience this spectacle
as a rebirth of dignity, of identity. But he also challenges himself
and his actors to bring off a very daring effect. At the most basic
and pragmatic level, the properties—the two heads and the hand—
need to be got off stage. But what he stages is a ritual, if not of
resurrection, then of reintegration—literally the pieces of Titus's
family are gathered together, formed into a circle, in some sense
reunited. And from that moment Titus is invested with the power
of the stage manager: He is given control over his destiny and over
the play in which he acts. If the episode is absurd, a delusion, a
self-deception, it is also a display of human resilience in spite of a
gale of misfortunes.

Titus typifies Shakespeare's art in his earliest plays. As in the
comedies, he takes material that his audience would have been
familiar with in other contexts—whether in books or in the school-

room—and he brings them to life in stage action. He adds a dimension of spectacle, of performance. Thus at the opening of *Titus*, to give a very simple example, the political situation in Rome—the kind of thing schoolboys might have written essays on, or been expected to compose partisan speeches for, is staged. So we have the first stage direction:

> *Flourish. Enter the Tribunes and Senators aloft: and then enter below Saturninus and his followers at one door, and Bassianus and his followers at the other, with drum and colours.*

This direction creates onstage the political topography of Rome—establishes a framework, so to speak, for the struggle for the imperial crown, and prepares the context for the appearance of the major players in the drama, which follows very shortly:

> *Sound drums and trumpets, and then enter two of Titus' sons, Martius and Mutius, and then two men bearing a coffin covered with black; then two other sons, Lucius and Quintus; Titus Andronicus in a chariot, and then Tamora, the Queen of Goths and her three sons, Alarbus, Chiron, and Demetrius, with Aaron the Moor, and others as many as can be. They set down the coffin, and Titus speaks.*

Throughout this play, as in the early comedies, the rhetoric of space, of action, is as important as the verbal rhetoric. Indeed, there are occasions when silence becomes the greatest eloquence. Thus Lavinia is most eloquent when silenced. She writes with her stumps, kisses her father, and bears his hand in her teeth. By their very presence onstage she and her suffering father unify the scenes in which they are tormented; and that unity stands for the personal integrity, that sense of self, with which they withstand their misfortunes. In these cases, meaning is invested in what is shown, in the display or spectacle, in the theatrical event.

And frequently the impact on the audience of such silent eloquence competes with other features of these plays, such as their highly artful verbal texture and their self-conscious theatricality. Shakespeare's plays seem designed to appeal on a visual, nonverbal level, alongside the speeches and arguments, and we flatten them out if we concentrate on one at the expense of the other. In the case of these very early plays, I would like to be a little more specific, and talk about one particular quality in them.

I have already tried to show how Shakespeare constructs and deploys a sense of the immediacy of what is being staged for the audience—how he shocks them into recognizing that situations they were familiar with from the printed page or from the schoolroom were happening here and now before their very eyes. A consequence is that he cultivates a connection between the audience and the actors.

To Sir Philip Sidney, eyesight was "the sense most subject to pity"—in the sixteenth century pity meant something more like "empathy" and it was usually depicted as the first step to love. In all the plays considered in this chapter, there are moments when our eyes are called upon—when our pity is evoked. The scene from *Titus*, or the occasion where Egeon goes unrecognized by his son in *The Comedy of Errors*, typify such incidents. What is especially striking is that such episodes commonly occur at points in the play where the artifice, the fictiveness, is stressed. It is as if the audience's awareness of the writer's skill—an aesthetic response—is meant to be inseparable from a shock of recognition, a jolt of fellow feeling at the predicament of his creations. And that is a much more visceral response, achieved in large measure through the spectacle and through Shakespeare's ability to make the audience encounter the events of stage before them as an experience.

Shakespeare did not invent this kind of device. Marlowe, for example, ended several of his tragedies very disconcertingly, by revealing to his audience that the monsters whose demise they have been encouraged to long for are in the end Everyman figures, versions of themselves. But Shakespeare's art, I think, is more specifically grounded in ideas of theatrical experience. On the one hand it represents a systematic, virtuoso restaging of nondramatic material within this novel and remarkable cultural phenomenon of the professional public stage. On the other, it constitutes an exploration of that experience itself and of the medium. Other dramatists probably saw writing for the stage as just one part of their labors, not to be confused with more prestigious projects. For Shakespeare the theater was not an option or a sideline. It was the medium in which he lived and moved and had his being, a medium whose resources he was uniquely placed to identify and exploit, and qualified to develop and extend. By the time he was thirty Shakespeare had shown himself the master of his art, and had opened up the possibilities of the forms in which he chose to operate. But he was about to be called upon to diversify, to display his gifts in other spheres, as a result of the vulnerability of the public theaters to the periodic visitations of that curse of London life in the Renaissance, the plague.

CHAPTER SIX

The Plague and the Poems

From 1594 the clouds lift and we can trace the outlines of Shakespeare's professional life with a degree of confidence. After that date his place in the theatrical world, for instance, is much less obscure and enigmatic. And yet by then he was thirty and had already written a substantial number of plays—perhaps as many as ten. So it makes sense to worry away at the evidence, such as it is, that can help us to construct some sort of narrative for his early years. I have already tried to trace the main strands of his artistic development, and have used the plays themselves as evidence; but, as I said earlier, that artistic development is inseparable from the theatrical circumstances, from the companies, the patrons, the regulations, the audiences, and so on. It is time to try to draw together some of these elements.

We do know that Shakespeare was connected in some ways with several of the numerous companies that flourished in the years up to 1593, though the details are elusive. Then, like everyone else in his profession, he found his business suppressed during a prolonged outbreak of the plague. During that time he wrote poems and sought the patronage of a prominent young nobleman. After that period of disruption, he rapidly established himself as a senior shareholding member of one of the only two dramatic troupes permitted in the changed artistic climate of the post-plague period. I will now try to add some light and shade to this stark, simple story of the years that marked Shakespeare's transition from one among many competing actors and writers to one of the leaders of his profession.

It will be clear, even from a casual perusal of the introductions to Shakespeare's early plays, or from some other biographical studies, that the questions of Shakespeare's first steps in the theater, and of his connections with the various dramatic troupes performing in London during the first years (whenever they were) of his professional career, are complex and knotty and give rise to savage scholarly disagreement. After 1594 we know pretty well where we are. Before that, all is conjecture, and it can be thoroughly confusing. So what I propose is to sketch what is known of each of the major companies, and suggest how Shakespeare's earliest years in the theater took shape in the context of that theatrical milieu.

The early 1580s had seen the proliferation of dramatic companies. Although Leicester's Men seems to have been the dominant group, and the one with a permanent home, settled membership, and apparently secure patronage from the powerful earl of Leicester, it had plenty of rivals. The records speak of numerous other companies—Essex's, Oxford's, Sussex's, Warwick's—whose normal pattern of operation was to tour in the summer and to play in the capital at other times if commissioned to do so. So the number and frequency of London performances increased, as did the vehemency of complaints from the city authorities. In time Sir Francis Walsingham intervened (there had been a delay—for some unknown reason—in appointing a new lord chamberlain to succeed the earl of Sussex, who died in April 1583). Walsingham got the Master of the Revels to cull out the best actors from the various troupes and form a company that would operate under the patronage of Queen Elizabeth herself. In the words of his orders, he was told to "choose out a companie of players for her majestie." Thus did the Queen's Men come into being.

Between 1583 and 1588 the Queen's Men were without dispute the leading company, and they dominated court performances at the holiday seasons until 1590–1. Their dominance was hardly surprising in view of their charter, and their annexation of the leading talents of the day, including at least three of the stars of

Leicester's Men: Wilson, Laneham, and Johnson. Unlike the great troupes that would dominate theatrical activity in the 1590, however, they were not a company of business partners, shareholders bound by a common material interest; nor did they have a permanent London base—they played at several different theaters.

What they did have was a very privileged position: Their names were lodged with the authorities, and they had undertaken not to perform except as members of the Queen's new troupe. They alone were authorized to play within the confines of the city, in private houses, or in other places where admission was not open to the public. They could put on public shows on any day except Sunday, and not before evening prayer on Holy Days (and their gates were to remain shut until evening prayer was ended). The times of performance (even on Holy Days) were to be arranged so that the entire audience could get home before nightfall. After an outbreak of plague they had to wait until the weekly death toll from the pestilence had been below fifty for three weeks. Apart from that, and apart from the threat that a single transgression was sufficient to annul the license, and apart from the threatening apparatus of state censorship, whose regulations could be enforced by suppression, imprisonment, and mutilations, they were free agents.

The repertoire of the company was markedly up-to-date, including the comedies of Greene and Peele, and a number of pieces treating the newly fashionable topic of English history. But their chief attraction was the archetypal Elizabethan clown, Richard Tarleton: He was the model for all other clowns, and probably the most famous theatrical performer of his day. His gifts included the ability to extemporize jokes and songs in response to promptings from the audience. One of his typical tricks was to deflate serious action onstage by poking his head out from behind a curtain or pillar. He had a comic fight-with-a-dog act (which apparently caused Queen Elizabeth to dissolve into helpless laughter), a drunk routine, and an unmatched ability to feed the seemingly insatiable appetite of Elizabethan audiences for jokes about (invariably phallic) animal horns or defecation. Or both. After his death in 1588 the fortunes of his company declined, but he was immortalized in a book, *Tarlton's Jests*, a compilation of anecdotes in which he is the leading actor. I invite you to guess the two most common subjects of the jokes.

Despite the preeminence of the Queen's Men, other companies continued to operate, though their membership seems to have been fluid and their practices variable. Touring was a major factor in encouraging movement between companies, and at times in precipitating the break-up of particular troupes. Whereas it was possible—indeed desirable, given the scale of the capital's theaters—to employ quite large numbers in London, touring bands were inevitably much smaller. They were also less well paid. In Henslowe's papers we can see that he paid hired men five shillings per week on tour as against ten shillings per week in London. So any hired man offered London work while his fellows went on tour was likely to stay where the money was, even if it meant changing companies.

The combined company created by the amalgamation of the Admiral's Men with Lord Strange's Men's lasted from about 1590 to 1594, when Lord Strange (Ferdinando Stanley, fifth earl of Derby) died; after that they were known as the Admiral's Men, under the patronage of the senior privy councillor, Lord Howard of Effingham, lord admiral from 1585. In the early 1590s they were built on the talents of a single dominating actor, Edward Alleyn. While the detailed contractual terms of the combination remain obscure, Alleyn retained his personal position as the servant of the lord admiral. Up to 1589 Alleyn had been one of Worcester's Men, at which point he went into the service of the lord admiral, whose players were suppressed in 1590 in the aftermath of the Marprelate controversy when the appearance of satirical, anti-Episcopal pamphlets from a secret press prompted even greater efforts to control all forms of publication and performance. It is conceivable that Lord Strange's Men—maybe just some of them—also suffered for allowing themselves to become involved in the same religiopolitical squabbles. At any event, the combined troupe began to perform at James Burbage's playhouse, the Theatre, in 1590–1.

From one of their earliest surviving "plots"—the single sheet listing exits, entrances, cues, properties, sound effects, and so forth—we know that one of the actors in the company was the young man who would challenge and eventually surpass Alleyn: Richard Burbage, son of James. And there were several others in the troupe whose paths were to cross Shakespeare's: actors such as John Holland and John Sincler, for example. Then, in May 1591, a quarrel broke out between the players and the elder Burbage. The proprietor was accused of withholding money taken at the gate of the playhouse, and had to stand by as Alleyn and his band left the Theatre. They soon found new venues, the Rose and the theater at Newington, under the aegis of the rival promoter Philip Henslowe—on the south bank of the Thames. In 1592 Alleyn married Henslowe's daughter and became increasingly involved in the business side of the operation as well as being the troupe's leading actor. Such a move was consistent both with Henslowe's habitual distancing of himself from the specialist aspects of the entertainments he presented, and with Alleyn's already well-developed business sense.

During the 1590s Alleyn created the parts of Orlando in Greene's *Orlando Furioso* (his personal copy of the script survives to this day among the Alleyn papers at Dulwich College, which he founded), and Marlowe's Doctor Faustus, Tamburlaine, and Barabas in *The Jew of Malta*, as well as other towering, heroic roles. The company also performed Kyd's *The Spanish Tragedy*, Greene's comedy *Friar Bacon and Friar Bungay*, and a host of other popular successes.

The short-lived company known as Pembroke's Men has attracted plenty of speculation from scholars over the years because of its teasingly shadowy connection with Shakespeare. The group probably came into being in 1591–2, at about the time the main body of the combined Admiral's/Strange's men decamped after the quarrel with the elder Burbage, though whether or not their formation resulted directly from the dispute we cannot know. Indeed, some recent evidence indicates a slightly later date for their formation, in the plague summer of 1592. The company performed. in Leicester in 1592 and made its only recorded court appearances during the holiday season of 1592–3, on St. Stephen's Day and at Epiphany. They toured the country during the plague months of the summer, performing at York, Rye, Ludlow, Shrewsbury, Coventry, Bath, and Ipswich. But by the end of September Henslowe wrote in a letter that the band had drifted back disconsolately to London some six weeks before; he reports that their gate receipts had been insufficient to cover their costs, and that they had been obliged to sell off their costumes to pay their bills. So their revels were ended. And other properties were put on the market, notably those most valuable assets, their scripts.

The company's name appears on the title pages of four very distinguished plays published immediately after its dissolution. They are Marlowe's *Edward II* (entered in the Stationers' Register as early as July 6, 1593); the so-called "Bad Quarto" *The Taming of the Shrew, Henry VI Part 3* (entitled *The True Tragedy of Richard Duke of York*), and *Titus Andronicus*. In addition, it is likely that the company had also performed *Henry VI Part 2*, published as *The First Part of the Contention* . . . in 1594. There has been constant scrutiny of these books over the centuries: They may, after all, contain clues that might help us to piece together the events of Shakespeare's early years in the theater, the chronology of his plays, their relation to the acting companies, and so forth. The qualities of the volumes are held by some scholars to indicate that Pembroke's Men had reconstructed the scripts, essentially from memory, in order to sell them off. Examination suggests that these texts could have been performed by a small group of eleven men and four boys—by a touring troupe, in other words—and that such slimming down for traveling performance may largely account for the numerous discrepancies between these scripts and those later published more officially. In other words, Pembroke's Men took on tour with them simplified and pared-down versions of plays that had been part of the repertoire of the larger London groups—groups with the human and material resources to stage them in their full splendor. A recently discovered will from an actor, Simon Jewell, of whom little had been known, suggests that Pembroke's Men may have been a company set up specifically to tour when the plague hit London in the summer of 1592.

So where do we suppose the young Shakespeare fitted into this shifting, chaotic world? We can conclude that Shakespeare, before becoming involved with the short-lived Pembroke's Men, was associated with the conglomerate of the Admiral's Company and Lord Strange's Men. This large group certainly would have had the human resources to stage plays like *Richard III* and *Titus Andronicus*. Samuel Schoenbaum, Shakespeare's most judicious and level-headed biographer, paints a picture of the young Bard of these years as a freelance. And indeed it may well be the most plausible explanation of Shakespeare's early years in the theater to suppose that he started off as a player in the company called the Queen's Men, and then moved on to be associated in various capacities with other groups, seeking to better himself, and to widen the range of opportunities open to him. As we have seen, the composition of the groups was fluid and uncertain in the extreme, and such movement would not have been without contemporary parallel. And while this account can never be more than conjecture in the present state of knowledge, it can hardly be an accident that three of Shakespeare's plays, written at different points in his career (*King John*, *Henry V*, and *King Lear*) are based on plays that had once been in the Queen's Men's repertoire.

In his pamphlet *The Wonderful Year* (1603), Thomas Dekker described the various remarkable events surrounding the death of Queen Elizabeth and the accession of King James. But then he turned to a matter more grievous and more urgent, namely the plague then raging in London:

> A stiff and freezing horror sucks up the rivers of my blood. My hair stands on end with the panting of my brains. Mine eye-balls are ready to start out, being beaten with the billows of my tears. Out of my weeping pen does the ink mournfully and more bitterly than gall drop on the pale-faced paper even when I do but think how the bowels of my sick country have been torn out.

Shakespeare's life had begun under the baleful shadow of the plague. In the summer of 1546 the borough authorities at Stratford-upon-Avon had done their best to alleviate suffering, to collect for the relief of the bereaved. They had taken rudimentary precautions such as holding council meetings out of doors in order to reduce the risk of infection. But still the plague had numbered its victims in the hundreds. In London, throughout Shakespeare's life, visitations of the plague were regular and on a scale that must have been almost beyond comprehension. The population of Stratford at this time was in the region of 1,200. There are numerous recorded instances of London plague deaths reaching this number in a single week during Shakespeare's day, though even this is put into the shade by the Great Plague of 1665, when in a single part of London (Stepney), on a single September day, no fewer than 11,154 plague victims had to be buried—by then London's population was close to a half million.

The plague was a fact of life, and of death, in Renaissance London, as it was indeed from the time of the Black Death in 1348 to that of the Great Plague in 1665–6. Thanks to the industry and assiduity of Tudor bureaucrats, sufficient evidence has survived, at least from the outbreak of 1563 onward, to chart its impact on the city and the suburbs. It looks as though, with the exception of only a couple of brief periods (perhaps in the 1550s, in 1616–24 or 1650–64), when there were hardly any deaths from the disease, its impact took one of two shapes: Either it struck in the form of a major epidemic (1563, 1593, 1603, 1625), followed by a year of relatively few deaths; or else the normal mortality rate was increased by up to 20 percent.

Gradually a series of public health measures was formulated by the authorities to try to contain the spread of the disease. They included isolation, quarantine, the establishment of plague hospitals ("pesthouses"), the creation of specialized medical teams (a plan realized only in the next century), and the formation of groups of officials to monitor observance of the regulations. These measures became more sophisticated as time passed, and as London's administrators introduced measures that had been successfully employed in cities such as Paris, Padua, and Venice. From Shakespeare's point of view, the most significant restriction was that on public assembly. It was recognized—even if not adequately understood—that bubonic plague was highly contagious, and that it spread when people were gathered together. Theaters were therefore suppressed, along with most forms of public entertainment. Other assemblies were harder to control: funeral processions, for example, or congregations praying beside plague pits. What is more, plague victims and those fatally trapped with them in quarantine did not always go quietly. Pepys would later record that some such unfortunates in Westminster would lean out their windows to "breathe in the faces of well people going by."

There were regulations limiting attendance at funerals to the immediate family, but some of the poor (especially mothers with babies in arms) would make a point of following the procession and standing by the open pit to show they did not fear the plague. And some preachers were determined to carry on with funerals despite official disapproval. We might feel they furnished a necessary and wholly understandable outlet for the city's grief, an opportunity for public mourning, for social and communal intercourse, while all around was suspicion, incarceration, silence, and death.

The plague that struck in 1592–3 was severe, though not quite on the catastrophic scale of 1563 or 1603. By the time it ran its course it had claimed almost 11,000 lives out of a total population of some 125,000. What is more, it was the first epidemic to establish the pattern for the next series by being most severe in the poorest and most crowded areas—notably in the northeastern city parishes of Botolph Aldgate and St. Botolph Bishopsgate, which Shakespeare would have known well since he seems to have lived in that part of the city for much of the 1590s.

Restraints against playing were published on June 23, 1592, when plays were suspended until Michaelmas because of the danger of plague and fear of civil unrest: Fear had stimulated an affray of apprentices ("a great disorder & tumult," in the words of the Privy Council minute) in Southwark a few days before. In such documents, especially those written by the city authorities, it is worth noting how the language used blurs the distinctions between the two threats to the city—large assemblies are held to have spread the "contagion" of unruly behavior, or to have brought down the plague as a divine punishment. In 1548 the Corporation of London had fired off a letter to the Privy Council attacking plays and players, in which they asserted: "To play in plague-time is to increase the plague by infection: to play out of plague-time is to draw the plague by offendings of God upon occasion of such plays." This time, the prohibition stretched on and on. The law sitting in Michaelmas Term was deferred twice, and then transferred to Hertford. In January 1593 a new, stronger prohibition was published, forbidding "all manner of concourse and public meetings of the people at plays, bear-baitings, bowlings, and other like assemblies for sports," and instructing local authorities to make sure "by special watch and observance" that no such gatherings ("preaching and divine service at churches excepted") took place within a seven-mile radius of the city.

The impact of these events on London was powerful. Those who could get away did so; shops, markets, water supplies, indeed the whole structure of metropolitan life provided endless opportunities for infection. And despite the practical steps taken to deal with the plague, conditions obtaining in the most densely populated neighborhoods of the city made survival a mere lottery. Dekker compared the silent watches of the plague nights in London to the experience

of being locked in an infinite charnel house, with decomposing
bodies at every turn:

> For he that durst in the dead hour of gloomy midnight have been
> so valiant as to have walked through the still and melancholy
> streets—what think you then should have been his music? Surely
> the loud groans of raving sick men, the struggling pangs of souls
> departing; in every house grief striking up an alarum—servants
> crying out for masters, wives for husbands, parents for children,
> children for their mothers. Here, he should have met some frantically
> running to knock up sextons; there, others fearfully sweating with
> coffins to steal forth dead bodies lest the fatal handwriting of Death
> should seal up their doors. And to make this dismal concert more
> full, round about him bells heavily tolling in one place or ringing
> out in another. The dreadfulness of such an hour is unutterable.

As already seen, the acting companies were compelled to seek
licenses to perform in the provinces, and their diminished companies traveled through the plague-torn country, viewed no doubt
by their potential audiences with a combination of fascination and
apprehension. Shakespeare was perhaps involved in the dismal,
ultimately abandoned tour by Pembroke's Men. But whereas his
companions returned to the city dejected and penniless, and forced
to sell off their assets to pay their daily bills, Shakespeare was
developing a powerful alternative string to his bow. Having been
a scriptwriter, the provider of texts for that insatiable, play-de-
vouring monster the public stage, he now showed himself to have
ambitions to be an author, a maker, a poet in his own right. And
that meant a shift from the free-enterprise world of the theater to
the feudal niceties of patronage, from the world whose insecurity
had been brutally brought home by the plague to one that promised
a more stable, if more conventional, career.

It may well be that he had already shown himself to be made of
different stuff—more hard-headed, more businesslike, more sure-
footed in his professional dealings—from his fellows. And many
scholars over the years have been attracted by the further possibility
that he had begun to cultivate his connection with the earl of Pembroke, who was later to stage shows with the King's Men at Wilton
House, and in time to be the dedicatee of the Shakespeare First
Folio.

But there is no element of doubt about the dedication that appears at the head of Shakespeare's first publication, *Venus and Adonis*, dedicated to the eighteen-year-old Henry Wriothesley, third earl of Southampton. The passage has been scrutinized for generations. What it reveals is a frank appeal for patronage, couched in the normal terms of such requests—perhaps even slightly less servile than most. In it, the poet offers his work as a nobleman's recreation to read, as it had been his own recreation to write it "in all idle hours"; he promises to follow up with something more substantial, something "graver," if this first morsel whets the aristocratic appetite:

> Right Honourable, I know not how I shall offend in dedicating my unpolished lines to your Lordship, nor how the world will censure me for choosing so strong a prop to support so weak a burden. Only if your Honour seem but pleased, I account myself highly praised, and vow to take advantage of all idle hours, till I have honoured you with some graver labour. But if the first heir of my invention prove deformed, I shall be sorry it had so noble a godfather, and never after ear so barren a land, for fear it yield me still so bad a harvest. I leave it to your honourable survey, and your Honour to your heart's content, which I wish may always answer your own wish, and the world's hopeful expectation.
>
> Your Honour's in all duty,
> WILLIAM SHAKESPEARE

Much about this passage is highly conventional. The image of the text as offspring, for instance, is standard Elizabethan usage; Sidney presented his *Arcadia* as "this child I am loth to father." Equally standard is the element of nonchalant self-deprecation, a quality much valued in the Renaissance, and given the Italian name *sprezzatura* after its appearance in Castiglione's *Book of the Courtier*. The tone is relatively formal, arguing no intimacy: It was quite common for such dedications to be speculative, fired off by writers in the hope of attracting support, to grandees of whose literary tastes and interests they may have known only through rumor.

Who was the young man? Henry Wriothesley succeeded to the title at the age of eight in 1581 on the death of his father. The second earl, a Catholic, had been implicated in the early intrigues surrounding Mary, Queen of Scots. Since his mother did not remarry for a number of years, Henry was made a ward of the lord treasurer, William Cecil, Lord Burghley, and was brought up with a group of similarly circumstanced nobles according to the most fashionable theories governing the upbringing and training of aristocrats. As guardian of these young people Cecil was able to influence their choice of marriage partners, and used them to further his own—and the queen's—political ends. The queen was notoriously anxious to ensure that matches had been officially approved: She was understandably nervous of rival dynasties. And Cecil's courtly academy was a very useful instrument of control—an instrument that was also personally profitable to the lord treasurer. Cecil tried, unsuccessfully, to marry the boy off to his own granddaughter, Lady Elizabeth Vere: Southampton was fined the huge sum of five thousand pounds when he came of age for his act of obstinacy in objecting to the match. The young Southampton went on to Cecil's Cambridge college, St. John's, and earned an M.A. in 1589. His early years at court were marked by the queen's favor (he accompanied her on her progress to Oxford in 1592), and by a developing friendship with the dashing Robert Devereux, earl of Essex, who had taken on Sir Philip Sidney's mantle as the paragon of Protestant chivalry. Sidney, dying of wounds during the Netherlands campaign in 1586, had bequeathed both his sword and his wife to Essex. And Essex saw himself as the leader of a generation of valiant aristocrats, increasingly held back by the dead, cautious hand of the older politicians whose hands pulled the levers of state. Southampton was one of many drawn to this fatally glittering star.

And it was to this culture—too nebulous at this stage to be called a "circle"—that Shakespeare himself was drawn. He was not the only one; other writers, too, saw in Southampton an actual or potential source of support. His Italian tutor, for instance, was the brilliant translator John Florio, later to create one of the age's greatest books, his translation of the *Essays* of Montaigne (published in 1603, but circulating in manuscript long before that). Thomas Nashe dedicated the first edition of his masterpiece *The Unfortunate Traveller* to the boy, with a veiled boast of his capacity to bestow immortality on any patron—"I am not altogether fame's outcast." The plea seems to have fallen on deaf ears, and it was not reprinted with later editions of the piece. Nashe's fiction is a very demanding work; even when it professes itself most conventional, most con-

sistent with accepted moral and aesthetic standards, it is shot
through with uncertainties and ambiguities. It pretends to be lighthearted, but is serious and disturbing in ways that are likely to
have perplexed or irritated the young courtier. Shakespeare's poem,
on the other hand, was much more acceptable. Here was epic
material, but not at epic length. Here were learning, sophistication,
eloquence, sex, and style, drawn from Ovid and Spenser.

When Shakespeare called *Venus and Adonis* the first heir of his
invention, it is unlikely that he meant he had written the poem as
a youth in Stratford and was now making it public. Rather it was
his first proper publication, and also, maybe, his first really substantial work. We have to remember the low status accorded to
play texts in this period, and recognize that Shakespeare, as a man
of his time, saw scripts as inescapably transient and collaborative
efforts; they were to be distinguished from a work of art, an altogether loftier enterprise and something grounded upon the idea,
the "foreconceit," the *concetto*, the "invention" of the poet.

With *Venus and Adonis* Shakespeare did two apparently contradictory things. He sought direct aristocratic patronage, as we have
seen; but he also entered the marketplace as a professional author.
He seems to have enjoyed a degree of success in the first of these
objectives. In the second, his triumph must have outstripped all
expectation. There were to be at least ten editions of the poem
during his lifetime, and a further six before 1636. We even have a
record of an individual sale of the book. On June 12, 1593 Richard
Stonely, an elderly civil servant who worked in the Exchequer,
took a stroll among the bookstalls of St. Paul's Churchyard. He
bought two books for a shilling, and entered the details into his
pocket book with all the meticulous care of his profession. One of
them, picked up from John Harrison's stall beneath the sign of the
White Greyhound, was *Suruay, or topographical description of France:
with a new mappe*, the other was *Venus and Adonis*. The entry runs:
"Books—for the Suruey off ffraunce with the Venus & Adhonay
pr Shakespear—xiid."

For his sixpence Stonely got a fine and elegantly printed book
with a text over which a great deal of care had been taken. It is
probable that the printer's copy was the poet's own manuscript,
and that Shakespeare had a chance to oversee proofs in much the
way that Spenser supervised the production of *The Faerie Queene*.

Most Renaissance authors wanted to have some say in their debut in print, and Shakespeare's printer, Richard Field, was both professionally accomplished and a Stratford neighbor.

Field was born in Stratford-upon-Avon in November 1561, so was three years older than Shakespeare. His father, Henry Field, worked as a tanner in Bridge Street, less than five minutes' walk from John Shakespeare's house in Henley Street. The two fathers, in similar lines of business, were clearly acquainted, and when the elder Field died in 1592 (just a year before the publication of *Venus and Adonis*) John Shakespeare helped to value his estate. Both men had seen their sons make their way in the new industries of the metropolis. Field's boy was apprenticed to Thomas Vautrollier, whose printing shop was in Blackfriars. When Vautrollier died in 1587 his widow married Richard, then aged twenty-seven and only recently out of his apprenticeship. Jacqueline Vautrollier, who had been, like so many women of her day (including Mary Arden and Anne Hathaway), a full and active partner in the business, perfectly capable of running the operation for extended periods, thereby took the most natural step to secure the continuance of her way of life. The firm had specialized to some extent in high-quality, often technically difficult work, including such books as Richard Mulcaster's *Elementarie* and North's *Plutarch* (the latter to be quarried endlessly by Shakespeare). *Venus and Adonis* is recognizably of a piece with their normal output. In 1591, for instance, they had printed the massive translation of Ariosto's epic romance *Orlando Furioso* by Sir John Harington (carefully supervised by the wealthy translator), and in 1598 they would produce the handsome folio *Arcadia* plus other collected works by Sidney, both works published by William Ponsonby. Field himself had begun to issue books under his own imprint as early as 1589, and his output included George Puttenham's *The Arte of English Poesie* and the 1596 edition of *The Faerie Queene*, as well as Spenser's *Daphnaida* and *Four Hymns*.

So Shakespeare's choice of printer indicates an ambition to associate himself with unambiguously high art productions, and on the title page he cites a text from Ovid's *Amores* (I,xv) that makes this point explicitly:

*Vilia miretur vulgus: mihi flavus Apollo
Pocula Castalia plena ministret aqua.*

A rough modern rendering might be: "Let worthless stuff excite
the admiration of the crowd: for me, let golden Apollo ply me with
full cups from the Castalian spring" (the spring of the Muses).
Marlowe's contemporary version was more imperious:

> Let base conceited wits admire vile things;
> Fair Phoebus lead me to the Muses' springs.

Such scorn of the base and vulgar may have been calculated to
appeal to the teenage Southampton. It was also immensely appealing to a sizeable slice of the reading public. Here, in the midst
of horror, disease, and death, Shakespeare was offering a glimpse
of a golden world; he was showing the delights of applying learning
rather than pointing out the obvious morals to be drawn from
classical authors when faced with catastrophe. While all around was
mortality, inescapable evidence of the vulnerability of human flesh,
Shakespeare's poem gave access to a different and more enthralling
world.

Venus and Adonis presents difficulties for academic critics; it was
probably meant to. From the outset it was addressed to the young
rather than to solemn explicators. Its mixture of tones, its combination of lightly borne learning and frank eroticism, its jumbling
of the jocular and the profound, all indicate both why it was so
popular and why it is so little studied today. In particular, it shows
an aspect of physical love that terrified more staid Elizabethans—
female desire. The poem is part of the vogue for the brief Ovidian
erotic poem, a genre sometimes known as the "epyllion" and which
includes pieces like Lodge's *Scilla's Metamorphosis* (1589); Marlowe's
Hero and Leander (published 1598, but circulating in manuscript
about 1590); and, from France, Ronsard's *Adonis* (1563). In 1590,
in Book III of the first part of *The Faerie Queene*, Spenser had given
an extended treatment of the Venus and Adonis story. And in 1591
John Clapham, one of Burleigh's secretaries, published a short Latin
poem called *Narcissus*, dedicated to Southampton—who was, of
course, Burleigh's ward and under pressure to conclude a marriage
agreement.

One of the features of this Ovidian movement was that it represented a sphere of writing in which women were not automatically
treated as idealized, distant, inaccessible icons, as they were in the

Petrarchan tradition. And it is notable that Shakespeare's Venus is described in exaggeratedly physical ways: her desire is compared to the hunger of a starved eagle, who

> Tires with her beak on feathers, flesh and bone,
> Shaking her wings, devouring all in haste,
> Till either gorge be stuffed or prey be gone.

At the same time, Shakespeare draws upon—usually playfully—ancient traditions of debate about the conflict between reason and passion, the nature of love, the relationship between physical desire and spiritual love, time and eternity, and so on. Venus describes her desire for Adonis in altruistic terms, saying that she is his way of becoming immortal and that she is helping the "law of nature" which obliges him to breed "That thine may live when thou thyself art dead." Whereas the sonnet tradition was built upon male frustration, on the blocking of male desire, *Venus and Adonis* is an account of the paradoxes and miseries of a woman who cannot possess what she longs for—in the narrator's succinct encapsulation, "She's love, she loves, and yet she is not loved." Venus is not on a pedestal—rather she is depicted "upon her back, deeply distressed."

The comic and absurd elements in the poem are obvious enough, but they do coexist with a more serious analysis of love and desire that parallels the investigations of the Sonnets and the comedies of the later 1590s. Like the early comedies, the poem offers moments of pathos alongside the eroticism—in this it is more like Marlowe than works such as Nashe's *Choice of Valentines*; and the poem's extraordinary commercial success indicates that its first readers were immediately drawn to this brilliant recreation of the spirit of Ovid.

Spenser's former tutor, the Cambridge don Gabriel Harvey, scribbled some comments in a notebook some time before the end of the century. He observed that "The younger sort takes much delight in Shakespeare's *Venus and Adonis*." And he was absolutely correct. In a student drama *The Return from Parnassus*, one of the so-called Parnassus Plays, staged at Southampton's old college, St. John's, Cambridge, the craze for this new literary marvel is the butt of a series of jokes. When the foolish slave (or "gull") to fashion, aptly named Gullio, appears, his fellows remark: "We shall have nothing but pure Shakespeare and shreds of poetry that he hath gathered at the theatres!" And so it proves. Gullio declares his love for the Bard, for "sweet Master Shakespeare," and declares: "I'll have his picture in my study at the court." He asks for verses in the styles of Chaucer, Gower, Spenser, and Shakespeare before repudiating the great artists of the past in favor of his hero—"Let this duncified world esteem of Spenser and Chaucer; I'll worship sweet Mr. Shakespeare, and to honour him will lay his *Venus and Adonis* under my pillow, as we read of one (I do not well remember his name, but I am sure he was a king) slept with Homer under his bed's head." Of course Gullio is a figure of fun—as his ignorance of the name of Alexander the Great suggests. But the play provides very striking evidence that students, and younger readers generally, found Shakespeare's poem more to their taste than more explicitly improving literature.

Nevertheless, Shakespeare had promised something rather more serious if his first effort pleased his patron. The subject of the next publication, *Lucrece*, again indicates that *Venus and Adonis* had been well received, and the tone of the dedication is different. It looks as though Shakespeare has come to know the young earl as more than a remote potential source of security. The dedication, printed by Field, seems warmer, as if indicating a new degree of closeness:

> The love I dedicate to your Lordship is without end: whereof this Pamphlet without beginning is but a superfluous moiety. The warrant I have of your honourable disposition, not the worth of my untutored lines, makes it assured of acceptance. What I have done is yours: what I have to do is yours: being part in all I have, devoted yours. Were my worth greater, my duty would show greater: meantime, as it is, it is bound to your Lordship, to whom I wish long life still lengthened with all happiness.
>
> Your Lordship's in all duty,
WILLIAM SHAKESPEARE

Gabriel Harvey was soon to observe that Shakespeare's "Lucrece, & his tragedy of Hamlet, Prince of Denmark, have it in them, to please the wiser sort." An index of the extent to which the "wiser sort" were pleased is the number of editions the poem went through—eight in all before 1640. The poem was cited in the Cambridge Parnassus plays, and is referred to in a bizarre and still impenetrable allegorical poem called *Willobie his Avisa*. This strange book contains, in its prefatory verses, an unambiguous reference to Shakespeare as poet ("Yet Tarquin plucked his glistering grape. And Shake-speare paints poor Lucrece' rape"). The date, 1594, makes this the earliest printed naming of Shakespeare as a writer.

Painting is precisely what Shakespeare does. Where *Venus and Adonis* had owed something to representations of the subject in Renaissance paintings, in *Lucrece* Shakespeare goes much further in creating what Sidney called "speaking pictures." Vivid and dramatic moments are depicted with a visual immediacy that makes this poem much more like the plays than its predecessor: "To see sad sights moves more than hear them told." Though both poems deal with desire and death, each occupies a different realm. Where the earlier poem evokes the world of Ovidian myth in the most ancient past, *Lucrece* is historical, and true in a different sense. Adonis achieves immortality through metamorphosis into a flower. Lucrece achieves it because of her exemplary degradation and self-destruction, Tarquin because his rape epitomizes a tyrannical kingly regime that was shortly to be replaced by a republic. The story was well known to Elizabethans as an example of tyrannical injustice, female heroism and a society's revenge on its oppressor. Lucrece was the beautiful and virtuous wife of Tarquinius Collatinus. Sextus, the son of Tarquin, king of Rome, conceived a passion for her and used violence and threats to rape her. Lucrece told her father, Lucretius, and her husband what had happened and then committed suicide to avoid further shame. Such was the horror of the Roman population that they drove their king permanently from the city.

As the action "freezes" into set-piece pictures, so the language condenses into epigrams and *sententiae*. But Shakespeare adds another dimension by furnishing Lucrece with soliloquies in which she analyzes her wretched lot. The contrast with the silent Lavinia in *Titus Andronicus* is instructive. Lucrece's suicide is depicted dramatically—it takes place before an audience of Collatine and his supporters, who are stricken with amazement—and without any sense of the Christian unease at suicide. She is shown "performing" her death, taking control of her life and reputation and intervening in the political process. For Lucrece, death is the only action available to her in an unjust and cruel world, as she makes clear:

What is the quality of my offence.
Being constrained with dreadful circumstance? . . .
The poisoned fountain clears itself again:
And why not I from this compelled stain?

The action of stabbing herself releases her soul from incarceration in the body Tarquin had defiled: "That blow did bail it from the deep unrest/Of that polluted prison where it breathed." And the poem ends in a double way: At one level it returns to history, to the expulsion of the Tarquins and the abolition of a system of rule that could countenance such abuse of power; at another, it shows Lucrece aspiring in her death to the status of Philomel and other wronged women, to move from the world of history to that of myth.

From the public reception of the two poems, from their numerous editions and the suggestion of some kind of response from the noble dedicatee, we can derive an impression of the popularity that Shakespeare had begun to enjoy. We might reflect on the vagaries of literary taste whereby the poems were regarded as his masterpieces and widely admired up to the eighteenth century, only to be relegated to the margins of the canon since that time. But a more interesting reflection might well be to ask what Shakespeare's contemporaries made of him. How did they react to the sudden appearance of this new phenomenon in the popular theater? Or to his apotheosis into a glittering star in the fashionable literary firmament? Since we lack reviews and press cuttings with which we are familiar today, it is hard to generalize with confidence. But there are some scraps of evidence.

If Shakespeare worked for the Queen's Men, as seems likely, he would have been aware of the writings, and presumably the colorful personality, of Robert Greene. Greene, formerly of St. John's, Cambridge (B.A. in 1580), was one of a generation of university-educated men who tried to make a living as writers. His attack on Shakespeare is well known. In a letter appended to the *Groatsworth of Wit,* the speaker, "R.G.," addresses three writers, Marlowe, Nashe, and George Peele, before proceeding:

Base minded men all three of you, if by my misery you be not warned. For unto none of you (like me) sought those burrs to cleave— those puppets (I mean) that spake from our mouths, those antics garnished in our colours. Is it not strange that I, to whom they all have been beholding: is it not like that you, to whom they have all been beholding, shall (were ye in that case as I am now) be both at once of them forsaken? Yes trust them not: for there is an upstart Crow, beautified with our feathers, that with his *Tiger's heart wrapped in a Player's hide*, supposes he is as well able to bombast out a blank verse as the best of you: and being an absolute *Johannes fac totum*, is in his own conceit the only Shake-scene in a country. O that I might entreat your rare wits to be employed in more profitable course, and let those Apes imitate your past excellence, and never more acquaint them with your admired inventions. I know the best husband of you all will never prove an Usurer, and the kindest of them all will never prove a kind nurse. . . . Trust not then (I beseech ye) to such weak stays: for they are as changeable in mind as in many attires.

Greene signals the chief target of his attack by punning on Shakespeare's name, and by parodying the duke of York's description of Queen Margaret at the battle of Wakefield in *Henry VI Part 3*, as a "tiger's heart wrapped in a woman's hide." But Shakespeare is cited as typical of a class of usurpers, of puppets, antics, dissemblers—in other words, actors, rather than university graduates—who, having mouthed others' words, now presume to write for themselves, stealing the finery ("beautified with our feathers") provided for them by their betters. This would be called in industrial contexts a demarcation dispute. Greene, a professional writer, is protesting that his specialized province has been invaded by untrained actors, whose scripts are shallow, showy, derivative, and (by implication, otherwise his tone would have been very different) popular with the undiscriminating groundlings.

So far, so good. But if we follow the lead of Professor Honigmann and restore Greene's words to their context, we may be able to sharpen the focus and see the point of the burned-out writer's attack on the new sensation. For Greene's volume does not end with the much-quoted letter. Instead, we are presented with an allegory, a fable of the ant and the grasshopper. It begins with each creature stating its position. To the grasshopper, the ant's "thrift" is no more than "theft," his prudence merely a killjoy's sourness. To the ant, it makes sense to make provision for the uncertain future—"Trust to thy self," he warns, because friends can be relied on for only "small hope in want." And so it proves. The feckless grasshopper finds himself unprovided for when winter comes. When he turns to the thrifty ant for help he is sent away hungry by the diminutive embodiment of the work ethic, who seems to rejoice in his distress. "Thou scorndst to toil, and now thou feelst the storm." So the dying grasshopper, like the dying Greene, passes on the wisdom he has learned from his miserable experience. The "world's trust," he declares, is "ruin without ruth . . . blest are they that like the toiling ant,/Provide in time gainst winter's woeful want." The text ends with Greene laboring his identification with the grasshopper ("Like him my self") and taking farewell of his reader and of his life.

Greene's book aims blows at several other writers, including Marlowe and Nashe, but it is the accusations against Shakespeare that are most significant. And in addition to the strictures in the letter, the fable paints a picture of the profligate genius (Greene) as the victim of the selfish heartlessness of the bourgeois, antlike, thrifty husbandman (Shakespeare). The passage is shot through with resentment: The speaker presents himself as an "old acquaintance" who is now (unconsciously prefiguring Falstaff's rejection by his former companion Prince Hal) spurned at a time of misfortune. And in such a light the reference to usury in the letter may be more explicable. Perhaps the improvident Greene had turned to Shakespeare for financial help and been refused. Perhaps he saw in the young actor-turned-dramatist even more disturbing qualities; for him Shakespeare was not just a "puppet" who had had the nerve to usurp the puppeter's role. Worse than that, he deemed himself their artistic superior ("in his own conceit the only Shake-scene in a country"), and gave himself unwarranted airs, capriciously exercising powers of patronage without the breeding or education of a lord.

This is quite strong stuff and, in the light of the fragmentary evidence we have about Shakespeare's personal and business life, an important contrary voice to the habitual references to him as "sweet" and "gentle." There can be no doubt, as we will see in a later chapter, that an anachronistic, wholly non-Elizabethan concept of the other-worldly poet, rapt in contemplation of eternal verities, has tended to edit out of the Shakespeare story material that mires him in the tangled webs of jealousy, intrigue, and hot-tempered litigiousness that characterized London life at the time. But that does not mean that Greene's testimony should be taken straight as the "real" story behind the myth, evidence that a brutal capitalist lurks behind the innocent facade of the Swan of Avon. To start with, it is by no means certain that Robert Greene wrote the pamphlet at all; there is at least one other very strong candidate for authorship. Further, the text of the *Groatsworth of Wit* oscillates between obscure fabling and blunt plain speaking, and is manifestly wrapped up with the fact that Greene had created for himself a distinctive and marketable pamphleteering persona. And the *Groatsworth* is certainly what he would have been expected to say by his public. The pamphlet, which is called his swansong, deals with his recognition of various truths about his reckless and wayward life, and listing lessons (such as "don't trust actors") as well as repenting his sins. If this were a detective story it would seem just too convenient, too neat, that these waspish criticisms of other writers so obviously came from the pen of a notorious sinner, liar, and maker of fictions, who could not be reprimanded or prosecuted because he had written on his deathbed. Suspicion would then naturally fall on one man, Henry Chettle.

In the Stationers' Register, the record of Greene's book entered the title "upon the peril [guarantee] of Henry Chettle" (the publisher's name nowhere to be seen). And though Chettle could argue that he was just doing a last duty for a friend by seeing his last words published, some scholars have, quite reasonably, questioned this. Some contemporaries even wondered if Nashe, with his genius for pastiche, might have been involved in the enterprise. Works by Chettle and Greene have been fed through computers to try to link the *Groatsworth* with other writings by Chettle. The findings may be statistically inconclusive, but Greene wrote in many styles, and Chettle, if he wrote the *Groatsworth*, would have been trying to imitate them. So we are not much further on.

But the barbs stung, and in a very short time an apology, almost a recantation, was forthcoming. The author was Henry Chettle. In the epistle dedicatory to his *Kind-Heart's Dream* (printed by William Wright, who had published Greene's pamphlet), he declared that he had been moved to take it upon himself to set the record straight, restoring the good name of the dying Greene's victims:

About three months since died M. Robert Greene, leaving many papers in sundry book sellers' hands, among other his *Groatsworth of Wit*, in which a letter written to divers play-makers, is offensively by one or two of them taken; and because on the dead they cannot be avenged, they wilfully forge in their conceits a living author: and after tossing it too and fro, no remedy, but it must light on me. How I have all the time of my conversing in printing hindered the bitter inveighing against schollers, it hath been very well known; and how in that I dealt, I can sufficiently prove. With neither of them that take offence was I acquainted, and with one of them I care not if I never be. The other, whom at that time I did not so much spare, as since I wish I had, for that as I have moderated the heat of living writers, and might have used my own discretion (especially in such a case) the author being dead, that I did not, I am as sorry as if the original fault had been my fault, because my self have seen his demeanour no less civil than he excellent in the quality he professes. Besides, divers of worship have reported his uprightness of dealing, which argues his honesty, and his facetious grace in writing, that approves his art.

Chettle's book was entered in the Stationers' Register on December 8, 1592, and probably appeared in the early months of 1593. The author protests (too strongly for suspicious minds) that he was not the author of the *Groatsworth*—"it was all Greene's, not mine, nor Master Nashe's, as some unjustly have affirmed." The writer he is delighted never to have met is presumably Marlowe. And while we can read into that part of the apology some kind of threat from Marlowe, we can also get a rare and fleeting glimpse of that extraordinary, tumultuous, brilliant personality that was shortly to be extinguished (maybe assassinated) in a tavern brawl on May 30, 1593.

Chettle's apology, whatever its context, is valuable for what it tells us, or at least what it implies, about Shakespeare at this obscure point of his career. We even get a fleeting sense of what he was like as a man. In response to the insinuations and criticisms in the *Groatsworth*, Chettle accepts responsibility for the offense caused— "I am as sorry as if the original fault had been my fault"—and vouches for Shakespeare's character quite fulsomely and on the basis of personal acquaintance—"my self have seen his demeanour no less civil than he excellent in the quality he professes." This compliment, I think, refers to the *Groatsworth*'s attack on Shakespeare's social and artistic pretensions: with "civil" suggesting education and refinement, and Shakespeare's professed "quality" being that of both a gentleman and an artist. The latter point is developed in the ensuing sentence, where Chettle concedes the good opinion held of Shakespeare by "divers of worship" (in the elaborately stratified language of address in Elizabethan England, this must mean gentlemen rather than nobles—aristocrats would have been referred to as "divers of honour"). The earlier attack on a swindling skinflint, a selfish hoarder, a derivative usurer, has clearly caused influential men to rally round and praise Shakespeare's "uprightness of dealing" and "honesty" (in writing and in business, presumably) as well as his "facetious grace" and "art" in composition. If the attack had been powerful, the defense is extraordinarily eloquent and testifies to the force of Shakespeare's personality among his friends and colleagues. We do well to bear this in mind. While the writings may be impersonal and yield little about Shakespeare's life, and while as a writer Shakespeare did not set out to create and market a personality in the way that Nashe, Greene, Jonson, and many others did, that does not mean that he was a gray cipher to those who knew him. All the indications—fragments though they be— are to the contrary, and the first of them come to light during these plague years.

The plague years were catastrophic for many people in countless ways. It was yet another of those constant reminders of the fragility of life which are an inseparable—though easily forgotten—component of Renaissance culture. Alongside our perspective, whence with hindsight we see the "success" of Elizabeth's reign and the overwhelming power of her propaganda, in which she was presented as the culmination of history, the masterpiece of providence, we need to remember that for many people an event such as the plague was a token of a world spinning out of control to its destruction. As far as the theater was concerned, the closure of the playhouses for such a long time put an end to the rapid expansion in the number of actors and companies. From now on, as we shall see, they were to be more tightly organized, more stable, and increasingly run by theatrical professionals with a stake in the business.

From this point of view, we can see these plague years as a turning point of another kind. With the death of Greene in 1592 and of

Marlowe in 1593 two of the age's most notable voices were silenced (though Greene was revived from the grave to "speak" several pamphlets published posthumously). With them, the dominance of the so-called university wits came to an end. In the place of such grasshoppers much more compliant ants, more professionally minded intellectuals such as Chettle and Anthony Munday wrote quite profitably for the stage; but neither cultivated the tabloid-style larger-than-life personality to which Greene had devoted so much attention. In that sense, the *Groatsworth* is a swansong both for Greene and for his generation. In the world that was to follow, the dominant voice was to be that of the "upstart crow."

It was with his poems that Shakespeare became known outside the theater. They were his first official publications, the first of his writings to appear with his name on the title page. Indeed, it was a further five years before he subscribed his name to the printed script of a play. In an age when dedications were part of the business of self-promotion, Shakespeare seems to have been unusually reticent—or perhaps unusually secure. Perhaps he did not need the sort of support for which the university wits were so habitually desperate. And this security could have derived from financial independence, or from a trustworthy patron, or from a combination of both. After the successful publication of the poems, Shakespeare's reputation was high and must have drawn more spectators to his plays. Yet, he seems not to have traded on the name for some time, and the implication must be that he did not need to do so.

Some (admittedly very faint) light may be shed on these years by an anecdote that has come down as part of the Shakespeare myth. In the first published biography of Shakespeare, in 1709, Nicholas Rowe, who tapped the reminiscences of older men who claimed some connection with Shakespeare, related a story (on the authority of William Davenant, "who was probably very well acquainted with his affairs") about Southampton's generosity. In Rowe's words, "my Lord Southampton, at one time, gave him a thousand pounds, to enable him to go through with a purchase which he heard he had a mind to." The scale of the alleged gift is inconceivably large, and needs to be put in context. First, Davenant, as a promoter and likely beneficiary of the Shakespeare cult (which included a serious attempt to pass himself off as Shakespeare's bastard son), and also as a writer himself, had an interest in setting before potential patrons of his own day the "going rate" for a genius. More prosaically, other accounts of Elizabethan court patronage from Davenant's period display similar ignorance of the Elizabethan economy. There are stories of Sidney giving Spenser advances for *The Faerie Queene* that, translated into modern terms, would compete easily with the sums paid for blockbusting popular fiction. And in these narratives, such moneys were usually conveniently at hand for disbursement to the impecunious author as the discerning patron instantly recognized the quality of his work. If, however, we look at Southampton's resources, we can see that the mid-1590s were not an easy time financially, and a gift of a thousand pounds would have been out of the question; the earl's total investments in property throughout his long life amounted to less than that. Nevertheless, there may be some truth in the report: It is certainly possible that it was with Southampton's help that Shakespeare was able to make his next major career move, by buying an interest in the Chamberlain's Men on their formation in 1594. But we should not forget the hints in the *Groatsworth* attack that Shakespeare was—largely through thrift and usury—comfortably off, and already dealing with writers as other proprietors and entrepreneurs did.

But let me end this chapter where I began, with the suggestion that the mists are about to clear, to reveal further details of Shakespeare's life as his career as a writer becomes more securely established. And even these plague years provide us with some images that we can hold on to. The theaters will open again, with slimmed-down companies—in one of which Shakespeare is to play a dominant role. We can see the deserted streets of a plague-ridden, fear-infested city; the silent theaters, the boarded-up houses, the tolling bells. We can see the dejected troupes of actors limping home to their lodgings after losing most of their assets on tour. We can conceive of the passions and jealousies among the writers as one generation gives way to another. And behind these shifting images, two faces: that of the writer, to whose defense as a man, business partner, and artist his friends rush; and that of the young earl of Southampton.

CHAPTER SEVEN

"Right Happy and Copious Industry"

In 1564, as an infant in Stratford-upon-Avon, Shakespeare had escaped the plague. Thirty years later, as life in London slowly returned to normal after another catastrophic epidemic, he was a good deal better placed than most to build a future for himself. When the theaters closed he had been an accomplished young writer, one among very many, supplying scripts for a variety of companies in a constantly changing theatrical world. Now he was more established, thanks to the poems, and was in position to play a central role in the new order.

According to the accounts in the exchequer office, we know that Shakespeare had become a householder in London by the mid-1590s. The property of all householders was regularly assessed for the purpose of taxation. If the value of your property had been assessed at ten pounds, and Parliament voted a subsidy to the Crown of two shillings in the pound, you would pay ten times two shillings. A significant administrative effort was put into the collection of this tax, and the exchequer, which employed its own petty collectors and commissioners to gather in most of the money, put the burden of chasing up defaulters on local authorities by ordering that county sheriffs should be able to account for any arrears in the course of presenting their annual accounts.

On November 15, 1597, the petty collectors of Bishopsgate ward made a list, parish by parish, of defaulters. The preamble states that the collectors

> . . . did say and affirm that the persons hereunder named are all dead, departed, and gone out of the said ward or their goods so eloigned or conveyed out of the same or in such a private or covert manner kept, whereby the several sums of money on them severally taxed and assessed toward the said second payment of the said last subsidy neither might nor could by any means by them the said petty collectors, or either of them, be levied of them, or any of them, to her Majesty's use.

Under St. Helen's Parish we read that William Shakespeare, assessed for five pounds, still owed the second instalment of five shillings. It must be assumed that he had paid the first some time before—the original assessment had been made in October 1596. Shakespeare was by no means alone—the numbers who failed to keep up with their payments were considerable—and this was not the last time his name would be recorded in such a context.

But this fragmentary record at least tells us the district where he was living. He was not one of the chief men of his parish: Seventy-three property owners were assessed and Shakespeare is well down the list, which is headed by Sir John Spencer, whose property was valued at three hundred pounds. Fortunately, the great antiquarian John Stow has left us detailed information on the Bishopsgate and St. Helen's area of London.

Now close to the Bank of England, in Shakespeare's day it was tucked inside the city wall (whose line is today marked by Camomile Street, Houndsditch, and London Wall). Bishopsgate Street was the main northerly thoroughfare. The district then was fairly well-to-do and the parish of St. Helen's boasted one substantial mansion, known as Crosby Place after its builder, Sir John Crosby, who died in 1475. Richard III lodged in the house when he was duke of Gloucester and lord protector. After that, the Tudors tended to accommodate visiting ambassadors there. In Shakespeare's day Sir John Spencer refurbished the place and built a great warehouse nearby. Stow's account of the rest of the parish includes descriptions of several water conduits, tokens of the prosperity, generosity, and public-spiritedness of the merchants who had lived there, as well as "divers fair and large built houses for merchants, and such like . . . many fair tenements, divers fair inns, large for receipt of travellers, and some houses for men of worship." Another substantial dwelling had belonged to Sir Thomas Gresham, founder of the Royal Exchange, but was soon to become a college designed to meet the practical needs of the merchant class. The center of the parish, inevitably, was the church, in which stood monuments to generations of parish notables—Gresham had offered to build a spire for the tower in recompense for the space taken up by his tomb, but by Stow's time the work had not been undertaken. There were some eight almshouses, provided through the estate of Alice Smith and administered by the Skinners' Company. The parish was part of the Bishopsgate ward, which was somewhat more varied in composition and not so uniformly well maintained and watered as this comfortable enclave. As Shakespeare walked north out of the city gate toward the Theatre or the Curtain he would have passed by less edifying sights, most notably the squalor of the town ditch and the imprisoned inmates of the Bethlehem Hospital, popularly known as Bedlam.

In 1597 a further subsidy was voted and Shakespeare was assessed again, this time as being liable for the whole amount of 13s. 4d. on property valued at £5. In the margin appears the abbreviation "Affid.," standing for "Affidavit," which indicates that the inspectors (Thomas Symons and Ferdinando Clutterbook) had verified this entry. The same officials also named Shakespeare in a document of 1598–9 prepared for the Exchequer, naming individuals who had defaulted but had, to the best knowledge of the inspectors, no property within the parish. Then, in an entry dated October 6, 1599, Shakespeare is again cited as a defaulter, but is noted to be now living in Surrey. Exactly a year later, on October 6, 1600, Shakespeare is noted once more as someone who stills owes his 13s. 4d. (which must have been a trivial sum to the leading actor/dramatist, shareholder in a large and profitable company, and recent owner of one of the biggest and grandest houses in Stratford); the matter is now referred to the bishop of Winchester.

The bishop, whose London residence was on Bankside close to

London bridge, was responsible for the area of land known as the Liberty of the Clink in Southwark (which lay outside the jurisdiction of the sheriff). The inference must be that Shakespeare was by that time a resident of this new suburb. And, as for his outstanding debt, it can be assumed that he paid up in the end. In the Subsidy Roll of 1601, the bishop accounted for monies given to him by persons whose cases had been referred to him by the sheriff. Though he gives no names, the fact that Shakespeare then disappears from these records suggests that the matter had been resolved.

What all these entries tell us is that Shakespeare, as we might have expected, lived in the mid-1590s within walking distance of his work in the two northern theaters, in the parish of St. Helen's, Bishopsgate. Then, at some point after the winter of 1596–7, and no later than the autumn of 1599, he moved across the river to live in the Liberty of the Clink in Southwark, even closer to his work in the newly constructed Globe.

After the plague, and after the winding-up of the Queen's Men in May 1594, the theatrical business was streamlined and its operations are easier to chart. The relaunched Admiral's Men, under the leadership of Alleyn until his retirement, took up residence at the Rose, presided over by Philip Henslowe (Alleyn's father-in-law). The Lord Chamberlain's Men, led by their chief tragic actor Richard Burbage and their star comedian William Kempe, played a short season with the Admiral's Men at Henslowe's Newington Butts playhouse in the first half of June 1594 before moving north of the river to the elder Burbage's playhouse, the Theatre. We can be pretty certain that Shakespeare was a member of the troupe at this time. On October 8, the lord chamberlain asked the lord mayor of London to permit his new company ("for the better exercise of their quality, and for the service of her Majesty if so need require") to rehearse and perform within the city precincts at the Cross Keys in "Gracious" (Gracechurch) Street. His letter goes on:

> These are to require and pray your Lordship (the time being such as, thanks be to God, there is now no danger of the sickness) to permit and suffer them so to do. The which I pray you the rather to do for that they have undertaken to me that, where heretofore

they began not their plays till toward four o'clock, they will now begin at two, and have done between four and five, and will not use any drums or trumpets at all for the calling of the people together, and shall be contributories to the poor of the parish where they play, according to their abilities.

Gracechurch Street would have given Shakespeare an even shorter walk to work from St. Helen's than the Theatre did. The Cross Keys was an inn on the western side of the street; its yard had been adapted for theatrical use and it had housed various spectacles, including a performing horse which aroused, according to a contemporary jest-book, the curiosity of Richard Tarleton, who himself had a nice line in animal acts. There had been unauthorized performances there in the past (as in November 1589, when Lord Strange's Men were the subject of a complaint by the lord mayor to Burghley), and this doubtless contributed to the conciliatory tone of Hunsdon's letter (Hunsdon was, we should recall, the queen's cousin as well as her lord chamberlain). It seems that this may have been the last occasion on which such permission was granted.

In the same winter season, the Chamberlain's Men performed at court on December 26 and then had to adapt to yet another new venue, the Hall of Gray's Inn, for their contribution to the Christmas Revels on Holy Innocents' Day (December 28)—*The Comedy of Errors*. In that play, Shakespeare showed his aficionados from the Inns of Court a further facet of his talent, a capacity to use staging, pathos, a theatrical occasion, with the same virtuosity he had shown in handling classical material in his poems and in *Titus Andronicus*.

The following March the Lord Chamberlain's Men performed for the queen at her palace at Greenwich. The accounts of the royal household for March 15 record payments to "William Kempe William Shakespeare & Richarde Burbage seruantes to the Lord Chamberlain." Here at last Shakespeare can be pinned down to a particular performance with a known company; the position of his name, sandwiched between two of the leading figures of the profession, argues his own prominence—probably as an actor. The other members of the company were veterans of the Admiral's-Strange's combination; many of their names—Thomas Pope, George Bryan, Kemp, Augustine Phillips, John Heminges, Richard Cowley, Burbage, William Sly, John Duke, and Robert Gough—appear on the plot of *The Seven Deadly Sins*. Many of them—including, probably, Shakespeare, Henry Condell, Alexander Cooke, and Christopher Beeston—seem to have been in Pembroke's company after that, where they had been joined by men like John Holland, John Sincler, and Nick Tooley.

In contrast with the fluidity of the theatrical world in the years before the plague, the new circumstances were remarkably stable. With one or two notable exceptions the following years were characterized by continuity, not least in the composition of the troupe. The implications are extremely important for Shakespeare's art. Even as a freelance, of course, he would have tailored his writing to the preferences and acting styles of the companies who took on his scripts. But now he was in a position to write parts—perhaps to write all a play's parts—with specific actors in mind, and he continued to do so for the rest of his career. The most notable relationship was with his chief actor, Richard Burbage, who with Shakespeare's writing was to achieve a status as tragic actor to equal Alleyn's; but the stability of this group of actors meant that, while their potential and limitations informed Shakespeare's compositions, so the demands he placed on them cultivated them into an ever more sensitive instrument for his talents.

The traditions from which the actors came encouraged versatility. Doubling was normal practice, especially on tour. John Sinkler played five parts in *The Seven Deadly Sins*, and no doubt his first years as a hired man for the Lord Chamberlain's Men involved equally energetic work. From contemporary allusions it appears that he was exceptionally thin, and writers like Webster, in the Induction to *The Malcontent* (1604), occasionally slip in jokes about his figure. Richard Cowley, Verges to Kemp's Dogberry in *Much Ado*, had played six parts in *The Seven Deadly Sins*, and may have specialized in "straight man" roles as a foil to clowns. Perhaps the most versatile member of the troupe, judging by the array of musical instruments and costumes he left behind, was Augustine Phillips.

Shakespeare was one of the "sharers" in the company—men who did not receive a wage but rather a share of the profits, in return for putting up a share of the capital. By 1596 the Lord Chamberlain's Men had eight sharers—Shakespeare, Burbage, Kemp,

Bryan, Pope, Phillips, Sly, and Heminges. These men usually
referred to each other as "Fellows':" in his will Shakespeare would
leave money to buy rings for "my Fellowes John Hemynge, Richard
Burbage, & Henry Cundall." In the years to come, Bryan would
leave in 1596, Kemp in 1599, while Pope was terminally ill by 1603;
their shares were taken over by Condell, Robert Armin, and Cowley. The number of sharers increased to twelve when the company
became the King's Men in 1603. But that day was far in the future
when Shakespeare began to write for the company, and it is to the
plays of these earlier years that I now turn.

King John is a strange, anomalous play. There has been endless
heated scholarly debate about its date, and its relation to an anonymous play published in two parts in 1591—*The Troublesome Reign
of John, King of England*. The second (1611) and third (1622) quarto
editions of *The Troublesome Reign* are attributed to "W.Sh." and to
"W. Shakespeare"; then, in 1623, the play we know as Shakespeare's
King John was published for the first time in the Folio. There is no
doubt that the two plays—though they exhibit many differences—
are related quite closely. The plots are almost identical, and names
and other verbal details correspond strikingly.

So what is the explanation? Adherents of the "early start" school
argue that Shakespeare had written his play before 1591 and that
the anonymous play is a "bad" quarto—that is, an unauthorized,
reported, text of the Shakespeare original. Adherents of the "late
start" school, on the other hand, hold that Shakespeare worked
with a copy of the quarto by his side, and that he embellished the
anonymous popular success for use by his new company. A more
radical view questions the concept of the "bad" quarto and proposes
that Shakespeare was indeed the author, alone or with others, of
The Troublesome Reign, and that *King John* represents his revision of
this earlier work.

Does it matter? The question of chronology, around which this
argument seems to rage, is interesting enough—there is a natural
curiosity to try to establish the sequence in which Shakespeare's
plays were composed in order to chart the growth of the poet's
mind. But there is another issue, more fittingly raised by this play
than by any of the others, and that issue is authority.

Until recently textual scholarship in English literature has tended to be based on the belief that it was the editor's duty to discover, on the basis of all available evidence, what the intentions of the author were, and to produce an ideal copy of the text. Thus misprints, illogicalities, and inconsistencies in a printed book could be replaced by readings which the editor believed to be consistent with the author's preferences or wishes, declared or undeclared. So in this case, the argument ran, there was an ideal *King John* which Shakespeare wrote, and which his excecutors published in the Folio after his death. Any problems posed by the Folio text inspired the editor to seek to reconstruct the Shakespearean original. In that endeavor, the mangled version preserved in *The Troublesome Reign* could be called in as a further witness in disputed or difficult passages, but a witness that was a less reliable, more "corrupted" guide to Shakespeare's intentions than the Folio. In recent years scholars have accepted that Shakespeare's intentions may not have been quite so fixed; he may well have adapted his plays for performance in different venues, with different actors; he may even have revised his plays quite substantially.

But it is understandable that a critique of the older idea of authorship may seem to be an attack on the idea of authority itself. Since Shakespeare is such a central component of British culture the suggestions that he might have had second thoughts about his writings, or that we might be unable to recover what he had in mind, or that he worked (as scriptwriters often do) collaboratively, have been either disturbing or exhilarating, depending on your point of view.

These questions are a useful way into *King John*. It is not just the textual and chronological problems that pose questions of authority; the action of the play does so as well. And it does so in ways that are strikingly different from the other early history plays. In *Richard III* and the *Henry VI* plays power, authority, rule—whether human or divine—had been presented as a kind of monolith, something to be identified, seized, or interpreted, but not to be questioned or shared. In those plays many voices are raised to the effect that division, discord, and dissent are ruinous both to the state and to the monarch, and the argument of the sequence is that there is a shape, a single governing order that fashions human affairs. We saw how these grand ideas derived both from Shakespeare's medieval predecessors and from contemporary attitudes to history, to the state, and to the monarch.

But *King John* reminds us (as indeed does *Love's Labour's Lost*) that there was a different way of looking at things. For a start, it is a "one-off" work outside the two great sequences. Then there is the figure of the King, whose role in his own play is much smaller than that of Richard III or of Marlowe's Edward II in theirs. The whole scale of the play is more human, less given to conflicts between abstractions, between angels and devils, saints and witches. The political and religious material it deals with is presented in a muted, almost reflective way. The play is written entirely in verse, and has about it the air of an examination, an investigation, rather than propaganda.

In popular memory, King John is probably remembered as the autocratic spendthrift forced to concede Magna Carta to his barons, or as the usurping tyrant of the Robin Hood legend or *Ivanhoe*. The Tudors saw him very differently, especially after the break with the Pope. in *The Troublesome Reign*, as in John Bale's hysterical *King Johan*, John is a patriot, a Protestant champion against the encroachments of Rome. He was a martyr for cause, who

set himself against the Man of Rome
Until base treason (by a damned wight)
Did all his former triumphs put to flight.

Shakespeare creates a more ambiguous, more complex picture.

In Marlowe's *Tamburlaine* the audience can sense the ultimate fragility of Tamburlaine's empire, its vulnerability to time, by the presentation of the leader's three sons. Each embodies a separate part of Tamburlaine's nature. It is as if his epic stature had been diluted, distributed in the next generation, with the inevitable consequence that the empire created and sustained by him will likewise disintegrate. In *King John* we are faced with the world from which another hero, Richard I, has departed. And the play provides us with three forms of kingship: the boy Arthur, legitimate heir but political pawn; John, the de facto king, forced to improvise a way through hostile foreign forces; and the Bastard Faulconbridge, who starts off as a stock Machiavellian villain ("Gain, be my lord, for I will worship thee") but discovers within himself the royal qualities of his father, Richard I, and eventually acts upon them.

The play was highly contemporary, whether it was written in 1589 or 1596 or anywhere in between. Elizabeth was a monarch whose claim to the throne had been denied. She faced the challenge of dealing with a rival claimant to the crown, Mary, Queen of Scots. She, too, faced the danger of foreign invasion. And no English audience in the 1590s can have failed to cheer the sentiments expressed by John to the papal legate:

> What earthy name to interrogatories
> Can taste the free breath of a sacred king?
> Thou canst not, Cardinal, devise a name
> So slight, unworthy, and ridiculous,
> To charge me to an answer, as the Pope.
> Tell him this tale, and from the mouth of England
> Add thus much more, that no Italian priest
> Shall tithe or toll in our dominions;
> But as we, under God, are supreme head,
> So under Him that great supremacy,
> Where we do reign, we will alone uphold
> Without the'assistance of a mortal hand.
> So tell the Pope, all reverence set apart
> To him and his usurp'd authority.

The play contains scenes of great theatrical spectacle: the challenges, sieges, and processions resemble those in the other English histories and in *Titus Andronicus;* the disposition of forces about the stage gives physical expression to the realities of military and political power. And yet the piece is full of surprises. It features rapid shifts in characterization: We see a king repeatedly contradicted by his courtiers; we see Machiavellianism confronted by pathos. Indeed, even the more static, processional element is a quality that creates a framework, not just for more intimate scenes, but also for the very consideration of ideas. It is as if Shakespeare is staging *quaestiones* again, but this time making it impossible to forget how the questions are mired in specific political circumstances, even if on occasions (as in the speech to the cardinal, or the references to the destruction of parts of the invading French fleet in a storm) explicit parallels exist with the here and now of the Elizabethan performance. And the last moments of the play are both sententious and polemical. The weak, dying king is brought on stage and pronounces the conclusion of his life:

> The tackle of my heart is crack'd and burn'd,
> And all the shrouds wherewith my life should sail
> And turned to one thread, one little hair . . .
> . . . all this thou seest is but a clod
> And module of confounded royalty.

These are the portentous tones of numerous speakers in that hugely popular anthology of tragic complaints, *A Mirror for Magistrates*. In death, John is assimilated to a venerable tradition, a kind of Valhalla of deceased monarchs. His cruelty, his indecisiveness, and his incompetence are all forgotten as the ritual of his passing is solemnly enacted. The action offers two simultaneous endings: While young Prince Henry draws the conventional kingly moral that, such as John is, so will he be in his turn, Faulconbridge sends the audience back into the fields and streets of Elizabethan London with a powerful call to arms ringing in their ears.

> O, let us pay the time but needful woe,
> Since it hath been beforehand with our griefs.
> This England never did, nor never shall,
> Lie at the proud foot of a conqueror,
> But when it first did help to wound itself.
> Now these her princes are come home again,
> Come the three corners of the world in arms,
> And we shall shock them. Nought shall make us rue,
> If England to herself do rest but true.

Questions of authority and authorship arise again in considering the remarkable document known as *The Book of Sir Thomas More*— "book" in this context means script. This fragile booklet contains the censored text of a collaborative play, part of which (the so-called Hand D) is commonly attributed to Shakespeare and is now thought to be in his own handwriting. Since the only other examples of his hand are six signatures, these 147 lines constitute a valuable piece of evidence for scholars. They preserve Shakespeare's own preferences for spelling and punctuation and show those idiosyncrasies in his hand, which might have been misread by men in the printing house. But it is also worth pausing for a moment over the play to which Shakespeare contributed this passage.

More reminds us of the essentially collaborative nature of Elizabethan dramatic art. The enterprise was no more author-centered than is the modern film industry. The position of the writer was not especially powerful. Texts were reshaped, rewritten, and revised to suit the requirements of the company or of the censoring authority, the Revels Office. In the case of *More*, we are dealing with the product of many minds and hands. In the first instance, probably in 1592–3, a play was put together by Anthony Munday (later to be praised as "our best plotter"), Henry Chettle, and Thomas Dekker, still only in his early twenties. Given the people involved, the size of the cast required, and the nature of the dominant central role of More, it is likely that the work was written with Edward Alleyn and Lord Strange's Men in mind.

The choice of subject is remarkable. More was remembered as a pious and learned man, and was held in affection by the citizens of London. But he had, in the eyes of many, died a Catholic martyr, and the writers faced the tricky problem of directing their audiences' attention to the personal qualities of the subject and to his human tragedy, without detailed reference to the political and religious context in which he operated. So there is a good deal of evasiveness about what the quarrel with the king is about, and there is no criticism of Henry VIII. When More goes off to his death at the end of the play, Surrey tries to wrap up the story and instruct the audience to go about its business:

A very learned worthy gentleman
Seals error with his blood. Come, we'll to court.
Let's sadly hence to perfect unknown fates,
Whilst he tends progress to the state of states.

Whose is the error? The king's or More's? The ambiguity, which survived the censor, is characteristic of the play's skirting around what in other treatments of the More story (like Robert Bolt's *A Man for All Seasons*) are central questions. But the censor did object to other aspects of the play, and ordered deletions and changes ranging from words and phrases to whole scenes. In particular, Edmund Tilney, the Master of the Revels, was made uneasy by

the early scenes depicting the so-called Ill May-Day riots when the
population attacked the French community in London. He evidently feared the consequences for public order of staging such an
event at a time of tension and hostility toward foreigners based on
fears of invasion. While apparently content to allow equivocal treatment of moral and political matters, he shared a common anxiety
of censors that dramatic shows had the potential to incite their
spectators to emulate what they saw. So Tilney instructed the
company in places that "This must be new written"; he made clear
that, instead of Frenchmen or foreigners, the text was to refer to
"Lombards"; and at the head of the script he wrote (spelling modernized): "Leave out the insurrection wholly and the cause thereof,
and begin with Sir Thomas More at the Mayor's Sessions, with a
report afterward of his good service done (being Sheriff of London)
upon a mutiny against the Lombards—only by a short report and
not otherwise. At your own perils. E. Tilney."

To have complied fully would have been to shed a massive
proportion of the play. At some point after this—whether as late
as 1603, as some editors think, or as early as 1594—several new
writers were brought in, evidently working very quickly to try to
produce a serviceable and acceptable play. Perhaps Tilney's severe
headnote was his reaction to those revisions, indicating that they
still fell far short of what was required. The Shakespearean passages
are of interest not least because his scene, in which More uses his
eloquence to quell the riot, recalls Shakespearean riot episodes in
the first sequence of history plays, and anticipates Menenius Agrippa's speech to the citizens in *Coriolanus*. Shakespeare makes More
argue for obedience to authority, because, he says, God

> . . . hath not only lent the King his figure,
> His throne and sword, but given him his own name,
> Calls him a god on earth. What do you then,
> Rising 'gainst him that God himself instals,
> But rise 'gainst God?

The impact on the crowd is powerful; the members of the turbulent
assembly say such things as: "Faith, 'a says true. Let's us do as we
may be done by. . . . We'll be rul'd by you, Master More. . . .
Before God, that's as true as the gospel," and so ask pardon for
their transgression. Later in the play, Shakespeare provides a so-

liloquy in which More ruminates on his rise. It would seem that the team of writers asked Shakespeare to furnish them with two of the staples of his art: the set-piece crowd scene with a formal speech at the center changing the minds of the participants; and a reflective soliloquy. In one part of it the statesman's reflection on his rapid advancement, and on the suddenness of the transformation of others' attitudes to him, is phrased in a way that seems disconcertingly close to Shakespeare's own circumstances. Certainly the speech echoes Shakespeare's life more closely than it does More's. More's father was not, after all, obscure or disgraced—he was a judge of the King's Bench. Alone at a great table, More notes some of the dangers that might make his head turn:

> That I from such an humble bench of birth
> Should step as 'twere up to my country's head
> And give the law out there—ay, in my father's life,
> To take prerogative and tithe of knees
> From elder kinsmen, and him bind by my place
> To give the smooth and dexter way to me
> That owe it him by nature, sure these things,
> Not physicked by respect, might turn our blood
> To much corruption.

Recent revivals and accessible new texts have rescued *More* from obscurity, and its powerful dramatic qualities have become apparent. It is an eloquent demonstration of what collaborative composition could achieve under the frantic conditions of censorship and the companies' insatiable need for new scripts. And it is understandable that posterity should revere the fragment in Shakespeare's hand as a kind of relic. We can all see in modern reproductions that it is free, easy, imprecise, unpunctuated, and notably fluent. It is the nearest we can ever get to Shakespeare at work, scrambling to meet a deadline and pouring out a torrent of words.

Love's Labour's Lost is one of Shakespeare's most brilliant, but also one of his most elusive, creations. Like so much of high Elizabethan art (*The Faerie Queene, Astrophil and Stella, Arcadia,* the comedies of John Lyly, Gascoigne's *Adventures of Master F.J.*), it constantly teases the modern reader or spectator to decode it. Elizabethan treatments of love almost invariably feature two elements: paradox and variety. For the former the authority, if one is needed, is Petrarch, with his antithetical formulations (ice and fire, war and peace, heaven and hell), depicting the contradictory lot of a frustrated lover. As for variety, we might remember Lyly's dictum that "in Love there is much variety." In *The Taming of the Shrew* Shakespeare shows a conflict between different ways of seeing and talking about the world, between on the one hand a humanist (often male) language of enquiry, discovery, and argument, and on the other a "courtly" (often female) language that is open-ended, playful, and mistrustful of simple explanations and easy generalizations. And this competition can be seen in *Love's Labour's Lost* too, as the title might lead us to expect.

With the publication of his poems, Shakespeare had staked a claim for some kind of reputation that would last beyond his own lifetime; so there is an obvious urgency about the way the play begins. The king of Navarre gathers his friends together in order to celebrate enlisting them in his scheme to retire from the world of action to that of contemplation. And the objective is not just enlightenment, it is also fame. He opens the action with high-sounding words:

Let fame, that all hunt after in their lives,
Live regist'red upon our brazen tombs,
And then grace us in the disgrace of death;
When spite of cormorant devouring Time,
Th'endeavour of this present breath may buy
That honour which shall bate his scythe's keen edge,
And make us heirs of all eternity.

And why? These men have vowed to make war on their own affections and live cloistered lives, "still and contemplative in living art," within a "little academe," for the space of three years. By winning their war against their own affections they will be hailed, the king assures them, as "conquerors." The external quests of chivalry are to be translated into the search for self-knowledge, for "philosophy."

The king's project is for a monastic separation from the world, a time of temperance and abstinence. This is a very strange opening for a comedy. Comedy tends to deal in celebration, feasting, trans-

actions between the sexes, with the ways in which society accom-
modates—or learns to accommodate—desire. But this play begins
with someone trying to impose a definite and arbitrary shape on
the unruly human condition. Throughout Shakespeare's writings,
when speakers seek to arrest time, to create an enclave of stillness
in the midst of the flux of existence, the wish to do so is shown to
spring from ignorance, folly, or worse.

The king opposes himself to time in two ways, First, he tries to
make time stand still by establishing his academy. Second, he tries
to overcome time by seeking to ensure that his fame will endure
forever. In so doing he denies two potent forces, love and death.
These forces are embodied in the two major interruptions of his
idyll, the first by the princesses, the second by the news of the
king's death, which concludes the action. If Shakespeare needed
models for his king of Navarre—leaving aside the suggestion that
his circle alludes to the group of intellectuals associated with Sir
Walter Ralegh, the so-called school of night—he could have found
them in such serio-comic figures as Basilius in Sidney's epic romance
Arcadia. Basilius, the king of Arcadia, reacts to an ambiguous prophecy by taking his family with him into a retreat, where events
ironically conspire to bring about the very consequences he sought
to avoid.

Interpreters have struggled with this play over the centuries. It
seems not just to defy interpretation, but to make fun of the very
enterprise. More disconcerting still, Shakespeare appears to go out
of his way to debunk most of the conventional explanations, jus-
tifications, and defenses of literature itself. Now from this play we
can have no idea what the historical Shakespeare thought on these
matters, but it might be useful to set *Love's Labour's Lost* in the
context of other works from this time whose tone has proved no
less elusive, in particular Sidney's *Defence of Poetry* and the plays of
John Lyly. In all these writings, the confident claims of learning
and scholarship are subjected to playful critique in ways that argue
for the importance of play, of sport, of recreation.

There used to be a tendency for critics to respond to the dazzling
surface gloss of the play's verbal texture by concluding that all this
display must be about something, that there must be some real
events and personalities encoded within the play. No doubt there
are numerous local allusions that will only be recovered by chance

discoveries, but I would argue that the play is emphatically not an allegory; it constitutes a challenge to simplistic interpretation.

In at least one respect, however, the play is of a piece with most of Shakespeare's romantic comedies. It stages a contest between two ways of looking at the world. One is based on books, the other on experience. In reply to the king's lofty proposals, Berowne responds wittily but pragmatically:

> . . . all delights are vain, but that most vain
> Which, with pain purchas'd, doth inherit pain:
> As, painfully to pore upon a book
> To seek the light of truth, while truth the while
> Doth falsely blind the eyesight of his look.
> Light, seeking light, doth light of light beguile;
> So ere you find where light in darkness lies,
> Your light grows dark by losing of your eyes.

These lines recall Sidney's image (in the *Defence of Poetry* and in *Astrophil and Stella*) of the philosopher who, looking at the stars, fell into a ditch. They may also conjure up the awful example of the great Italian writer Tasso, who ended his days as an exhibit, a tourist attraction in a ducal court; the deep, allegorizing searcher after truth reduced to a blind, mad warning of the terrible dangers of excessive intellectual enquiry.

The play as a whole resists trite conclusions, although many of its characters are addicted to them. The verbal combats that drive the plot—such as it is—derive their energy from the speakers' struggles to outdefine, to outqualify, each other. But where does it lead? How does Shakespeare manage the apparent tension between the preoccupations of the play—which are emphatically serious and potentially disturbing—and the seemingly endless flow of verbal invention, the sequence of word-playing duels which are its most striking feature?

The last major action in the play is the pageant of the Nine Worthies. Shakespeare, by modifying the traditional list, inevitably, though silently, qualifies the very idea of permanent, abiding fame which the king had articulated in Act I. He goes further. The Worthies are played by the five comic characters—the braggart Don Armado, the pedant Holofernes, the Clown, the curate Nathaniel, and the boy Moth. There is an onstage audience of the aristocrats, and much of the scene involves exchanges between the nobles and the Worthies. Scorn is repeatedly poured on the attempts to represent these heroes. The wit of the courtiers involves two strategies: They quibble with the words of the amateurish script the masquers have written for themselves, and they draw attention to the gulf separating the fiction they present from the natures of the actors.

As so often, however, the very act of staging provides an extra dimension to this episode. The inadequacies of the masquers are for the audience a source of pathos, not of scorn. The courtiers mock the surface, and yet see no further than that surface themselves. When Holofernes rebukes them, "This is not generous, not gentle, not humble," Boyet is oblivious to the criticism. He treats it as the first line of a couplet, which he tries to complete, saying, "A light for Monsieur Judas! It grows dark, he may stumble." In this exchange it is the courtier, not the pedant, who is naïve, trapped within a closed system. What is more, the courtiers' mockery of the country people takes no account either of the motivation, the goodwill, of the performers, nor indeed of the implications of the mockery for their own aspirations to fame. Through the self-consciously simple device of an improvised and chaotic piece of theater, Shakespeare shows how the acts of staging and of observing can expose ignorance and self-delusion. He also stages a kind of reversal in the sympathies of the wider audience, stirring compassion for the stumbling players through showing the shallowness of their observers.

It is through such strategies of reversal that Shakespeare makes his play something much more challenging than a glittering comedy of manners or a pantomimic version of Elizabethan court squabbles. The appearance of the women earlier in the play had set up an opposition between the king's inexperienced and self-absorbed "philosophy" and the more outgoing pursuit of love. Then, as the pageant comes to its end, the courtiers try to goad Armado (as Hector) to fight against Costard (as Pompey). The broad humor in the cowardice of the braggart feeds the desire to see his humiliation, but when he is forced to say why he will not strip off to his shirt to wrestle, his words strike a very different note:

The naked truth of it is, I have no shirt.
I go woolward for penance.

There is something distasteful about the revelation forced from
Armado: Such a private, intimate matter has been exposed merely
to gratify the spectator's wish for a good joke. Though Moth maintains that it is Armado's poverty that has been revealed, Armado's
resolution now to do penance for wronging Jacquenetta stands as
a powerful rebuke to the frivolity of the courtiers and creates a
moment of pathos—another one of Shakespeare's sudden, puncturing shocks to an audience's sense that it knows what is happening
onstage. It strips Armado bare, and he repents. It also strips bare
the action on the stage, as a messenger enters to announce the death
of the king of France.

In a flash the tone of the drama has changed: From watching a
joke pageant with a lighthearted mocking audience we have been
jolted into a realm of public humiliation, repentance, and death.
In this new atmosphere the playful courtship is put aside; the couples agree to separate for a year and a day, a period of mourning.
As Berowne self-consciously observes, "Our wooing doth not end
like an old play"; the conventional plot resolutions of romantic
comedy have been avoided. Instead of union, the play ends with
parting, as the men and women exit by different doors, and then
with contrasting songs by Spring and Winter. The last words are
spoken by the newly converted Armado: "The words of Mercury
are harsh after the songs of Apollo"—presumably contrasting Mar-
cade's announcement with the playful verbal sports of the courtiers
earlier in the play.

The play seems almost wilfully frustrating and incomplete. One
possible explanation is the idea that it represents half of a pair, and
that its lost companion, *Love's Labour's Won*, would have comple-
mented it decorously. But its combination of the lyric and the
dramatic, together with its eloquent display of the limits of eloquence, make it of a piece with Shakespeare's other plays of the
time. His concern with the value of art, with the relationships
between artifice and truth, surfaces constantly in the group of "lyrical" plays of the 1590s.

*   *   *

In recent years literary critics have taken a renewed interest in the shimmering artifice of Elizabethan court literature; and they have uncovered in countless texts a studied ambiguity, a resistance to interpretation, which they relate to the broader circumstances of patronage and censorship under which writers operated. Even if they touched on serious questions, or commented on contemporary politics, they had to be able to say they offered merely entertainment or a meditation on general matters. For instance, at the end of John Lyly's play *Sapho and Phao*, acted at the carnival time of Shrove Tuesday before Queen Elizabeth in 1584, an epilogue comes forward to apologize for dazzling and confusing the audience. He says, "We fear we have led you all this while in a Labyrinth of conceits. . . . There is nothing causeth such giddiness, as going in a wheel, neither can there any thing breed such tediousness, as hearing many words uttered in a small compass." So giddiness and confusion are only to be expected. And he wraps up his defense of "this dance of a fairy in a circle" by begging not to be overcarefully interpreted. In his words, "We wish every one of you a thread to lead you out of the doubts wherewith we leave you entangled: that nothing be mistaken by our rash oversights, nor misconstrued by your deep insights."

These words offer us some guidance as we look at Shakespeare's courtly performances of the 1590s. Like Lyly, he teases and confuses, illuminates and obfuscates as he balances the earnestness of recreation with the frivolity of seriousness. We might recall the ways in which Sidney teases his readers constantly with allusions to himself and to other identifiable—or almost identifiable—flesh-and-blood figures in his fictions. Shakespeare gives us the names of real Frenchmen—Henry of Navarre, the Duc de Longueville, the Duc de Biron, and so on. But their relation to the contemporaries who share their names is minimal. He hints at various matters, both literary and political, of current interest. The Muscovites recall revels at Gray's Inn, the "academe" the *Académie Française* of Pierre de la Primaudaye (translated into English in 1586). But Shakespeare does not write an allegory of his age, anymore than Lyly did. It was of the nature of his enterprise, which was called a "conceited comedy," to restage, replay, jumble its material in a dreamlike and elusive way. All his life Shakespeare would argue for the value of such an enterprise, for what he called in *Pericles* the "restorative" function of storytelling. And *Love's Labour's Lost* seems to have found responsive audiences way beyond its first performance. Evidence of revisions to the text indicates that it was still being worked on from time to time. We know that it was revived for Queen Anne, James I's consort, in January 1605 for performance at the earl of Southampton's house. A letter from Sir Walter Cope tells Robert Cecil that "Burbage is come, and says there is no new play that the Queen hath not seen, but they have revived an old one called *Love's Labour's Lost*, which for wit and mirth he says will please her exceedingly." A later edition of the play in 1631 confirms that it also received public performance, both at the Globe and at the Blackfriars.

The Prologue to Lyly's play, addressed specifically to the queen, asks her indulgence for the play. But he goes a stage further:

> Whatsoever we present, whether it be tedious (which we fear), or toyish (which we doubt), sweet or sour, absolute or imperfect, or whatsoever, in all humbleness we all, and I on knee for all, entreat that your Highness imagine your self to be in a deep dream, that staying the conclusion, in your rising your Majesty vouchsafe but to say, *And so you awaked*.

Such a passage, resembling the reverse created for Christopher Sly in *The Taming of the Shrew*, helps to create a sense of the world in which *Love's Labour's Lost* and *A Midsummer Night's Dream* were composed and performed, of the culture out of which the *Sonnets* were growing. Indeed, the title page of the first surviving edition of *Love's Labour's Lost* (1598) shows that it comes from rather similar circumstances to those in which *Sapho and Phao* was produced: The publisher proclaims that the play had been "performed last Christmas before the Queen."

A Midsummer Night's Dream also hovers between self-conscious inconsequence and brooding seriousness. One of its most striking features is its capacity to generate widely divergent, often contradictory, interpretations. Like the earlier play it has no single source, and has tantalized commentators with the possibility that it was commissioned for some specific aristocratic wedding. But unlike it, it has held the stage (in various manifestations) for centuries.

The fact that the piece has spoken to later generations in an unbroken sequence does not make it any less wholly Elizabethan. Its language and action can be paralleled in Sidney, Spenser, Lyly, and others too numerous to mention. Its self-conscious examination of the power of art, its preoccupation with love, and its constant shifts of identity make it a play that taps once again Shakespeare's favored repository of stories, Ovid's *Metamorphoses*.

The play deals with marriage and with the idea of union. Scholars have looked at a range of possible specific occasions for the play; few noble marriages in London during the 1590s have escaped their scrutiny. While it was common for wedding celebrations to include masques, the performance of a substantial drama requiring a very large cast would have been an innovation. This has proved no deterrent to those wishing to imagine a performance in the hall of a great house, before the queen and the wedding party. Clearly, if the queen were present, Oberon's story of Cupid and the "fair vestal throned by the west" would be a graceful allusion to her. To some, the very size of the cast strengthens the occasionalist argument—the forces required are greater than those available regularly on the public stage, and therefore suggest that the Lord Chamberlain's Men were augmented by other players, including several boy actors—for the one-shot performance. The enormous range of literary allusions identified over the centuries has made the task harder. For instance, the nuptials of the venerable courtier Sir Thomas Heneage to Mary, countess of Southampton (mother of the third earl) have had their supporters. But the celebration, on May 2, 1594, is impossible if one wishes to argue for the close affinities with Spenser's poem on his own marriage, the *Epithalamion* (published early in 1595). And the same consideration has moderated enthusiasm for another candidate, the wedding of William, earl of Derby, and Elizabeth Vere. The marriage took place on January 26, 1595, at Greenwich, where the court was at that time, and it is known that the queen attended festivities in Burghley's house in the Strand.

A more plausible suggestion, though we are a long way short of being able to prove it, is the marriage between Thomas, son of Henry, Lord Berkeley, and Elizabeth Carey, which took place at Blackfriars on February 19, 1596. The presence of the queen cannot be established—but the bride, like Elizabeth Vere, was her god-daughter. What is more, the bride's grandfather, Lord Hunsdon, was the lord chamberlain, and her father would in due course occupy the same position. If anyone could get the Lord Chamberlain's Men to perform at a private house, the lord chamberlain could, and his granddaughter's wedding would clearly be a suitable occasion.

There are two explanations of this scholarly quest. At one level, it is a response to the centrality of the idea of marriage in the play. But on another, it is a reaction to the quite extraordinary density of its literary texture. The argument is essentially that its language is so artful, its allusions so wide-ranging, its potential for opening up areas of philosophical speculation (especially neoplatonic speculation) so inexhaustible, that it cannot have been written primarily for the public stage. Only those steeped in the latest literature, in high culture, and in arcane thought, the argument runs, can possibly have been expected to respond intelligently to it.

The central concern of the play is the celebration of marriage as the embodiment and expression of union, between individuals and society, between individuals and other individuals, between the natural and the supernatural. And, just as in the marriage service the role of the witnesses, the representatives of the wider world, is crucial, so in this play the audience (whether it is the queen, or a bridal party, or the nut-cracking groundlings) plays a vital role. It is in their minds and hearts—and this is a Shakespearean commonplace—that all the elements of the play can exist. They become the medium in which the contradictory forces can all swim. They become the location of the union the play celebrates.

So of course there is a dark side, as well as a joyful one: Philosophical seriousness coexists with frivolity. Critics in their studies can abstract themes and identify motifs to illustrate countless propositions about the piece. But in performance, Shakespeare's first essay in what we would nowadays call "magic realism" marvelously comprehends a bewildering variety of tones, styles, and stories.

We do well not to forget how English the play is—and by that I do not simply mean its closeness to Chaucer and Spenser, whom Shakespeare would have seen as his great models, and to numerous contemporary writers. Alongside all the material from Ovid, Apuleius, and the rest, and the setting in the wood near Athens, the figure of Puck, Robin Goodfellow, represents a specifically English fairy tradition. It may well be that Shakespeare recognized that in the real world, the world of witch trials and demonic possession, Puck's day was almost over. Certainly Reginald Scott, in his *Discovery of Witchcraft* (1584), observed that in the past "Robin Goodfellow, and Hobgoblin were as terrible, and also as credible to the people, as hags and witches be now: and in time to come, a witch will be as much derided and contemned and as plainly perceived, as the illusion and knavery of Robin Goodfellow."

Whether such derision is justified is left open for the audience to judge. But we might remember how facile modern scorn of the currently unknown had been categorized as ignorance by Spenser in *The Faerie Queene*. At the opening of the second book of his epic, Spenser had declared that the parallel universe ruled over by Gloriana, the Fairy Queen, was not mere invention. It could be found by an explorer who could read "signs . . . set in sundry place." To claim it did not exist simply because it had not yet been discovered was to fly in the face of recent experience. In living memory, human investigation had brought to light such marvels as "the Indian Peru," and "Amazon's huge river," as well as that most resonant of miracles, "fruitfullest Virginia." Since all these things, which had been hidden from the wisest of the ancient philosophers, are "now found true," Spenser argues, it makes sense not to rush to dismiss things that may seem fantastic and improbable.

As in *Love's Labour's Lost*, Shakespeare draws many of the play's preoccupations together in the play-within-the-play. But here the preparations for the show have been shown to the audience; we share the experience of rehearsal and nervous anticipation. Through this exposure of its nuts and bolts, and the opening up of the players' inadequacies, the mechanicals' show is rendered somehow impervious to criticism, whether the supercilious sneering of the nobles or our sense of its patent absurdity. As history had been staged in *Love's Labour's Lost*, so tragedy is staged here—the plot of Pyramus and Thisbe is perilously close to that of *Romeo and Juliet*. Shakespeare takes a risk by burlesquing what is elsewhere presented "straight." But there is a pathos about Bottom, as there had been about Armado, which has a tendency to add an extra element to his absurdity and to load the dice against those who mock him or make sport of him.

A crucial moment in *A Midsummer Night's Dream* is Bottom's account of his dream. He speaks in the earth-bound idiom of prose:

> I have had a most rare vision. I have had a dream, past the wit of man to say what dream it was. Man is but an ass if he go about to expound this dream. Methought I was—there is no man can tell what. Methought I was—and methought I had—but man is but a patched fool if he will offer to say what methought I had. The eye of man hath not heard, the ear of man hath not seen, man's hand is not able to taste, his tongue to conceive, nor his heart to report what my dream was. I will get Peter Quince to write a ballad of this dream; it shall be called "Bottom's Dream," because it hath no bottom. . . .

The allusion is unambiguous enough. Bottom mangles the account in I Corinthians of the inexpressibility of the treasures laid up for the faithful by God. The text in the Bishop's Bible runs as follows (spelling modernized): "The eye of man hath not seen, and the ear hath not heard, neither have entered into the heart of man, the things which God hath prepared for them that love him. But God hath revealed them unto us by his spirit: for the spirit searcheth all things, yea the deep things of God!"

In a play so full of rhetorical display, the centrality of this jumbled vision and the well-intentioned stumblings of the mechanicals' pageant represents a very important counterbalance to the relentless pursuit of wit and eloquence by the fairies and the nobles. Bottom's dream is not a repudiation of Theseus's speech about imagination, nor is it somehow more profound because it is inarticulate. Rather it draws attention to two Shakespearean commonplaces: the inadequacy of all human discourse when faced with the supernatural, and the crucial role played by the motivation of the speaker or listener—the "goodwill" or "gentle patience" or "willing ears" that Shakespearean orators habitually crave.

The play is full of unresolved matters requiring the active engagement of an audience's interpretative response. What are we to make of Oberon's tricking Titania into an infatuation with a donkey, for instance? Is it a lighthearted game, in the spirit of a comedy of manners, to teach her a painless lesson? Or is it rather an exercise in humiliation and degradation, with the Queen of the Fairies set up to be abused by a lustful ass? In a play that creates a hierarchial series of plots—fairies, Athenians, mechanicals—what are we to make of the treatment of authority? When rulers act like Oberon and Egeus, how are we to respond to the conclusion of the play which leaves them still in power, and maintains the idea of hierarchy before our eyes?

Perhaps a key is to be found in Puck's last speech, in which he asks the audience:

> If we shadows have offended,
> Think but this, and all is mended:
> That you have but slumbered here
> While these visions did appear;
> And this weak and idle theme,
> No more yielding but a dream,
> Gentles, do not reprehend;
> If you pardon, we will mend. . . .
> Give me your hands, if we be friends,
> And Robin shall restore amends.

The perennial stage success of the *Dream*, its apparent capacity to be made and remade in each succeeding generation, seems to me to be bound up with the conscious incompleteness of the script. It is in many ways the least authoritarian of Shakespeare's plays. The audience is not steered to respond as it is in, say, *Richard III*. Even Bottom the weaver, Shakespeare's first great comic creation, represents a collaboration between the author and the celebrated clown William Kemp, who created the role. The play is realized and completed in each individual performance, in the mind of each individual spectator. And the idea of marriage, of union, that underlies the piece is more than just a celebration of a particular event or a hymn to romantic love. It is also a demonstration of the capacity of the mind to contain opposites, simultaneously to hold views that may seem contradictory, to recognize modes of truth that do not converge, to applaud and authorize parallel universes—the fantastic and the everyday.

Shakespeare's relationship to the Lord Chamberlain's Men seems to have involved the production of a couple of new plays every year. Broadly speaking, he provided them with a comedy and a tragedy or historical play for every season. The companion pieces to the two lyrical comedies are two no less lyrical tragedies, *Romeo and Juliet* and *Richard II*. While the detailed chronology of the four pieces is still unclear, it is generally agreed that they form a distinct group in Shakespeare's canon.

The title page of the first quarto edition of *Romeo and Juliet* (1597) describes the play as "An excellent conceited tragedy." Two years later, the Lord Chamberlain's Men released their "newly corrected, augmented, and amended" text, calling it a "most excellent and lamentable tragedy." These qualifying terms prepare us for much in the play. "Lamentable" had been the label fixed to *Titus Andronicus*, while "conceited" (that is, witty) connects the piece with *Love's Labour's Lost*—a play that also appeared in an "official" edition in 1599.

Romeo and Juliet is one of Shakespeare's most ambitious and unambiguous attempts to join the immortals, and as such seems at first blush very different from the demythologizing of *Love's Labour's Lost* and the openendedness of the *Dream*. It is introduced by a chorus, and wrapped up by a judgmental speech from a duke. And it sets out to transform its youthful lovers into mythical, "star-crossed" figures, fit to rank with all the celebrated pairs of tragic lovers throughout literary history. In particular, Shakespeare was seeking to join the company of English practitioners in this mode, most notably Chaucer, whose *Troilus and Criseyde* was then regarded as the finest poem yet written in the language, and Sidney, whose tragicomic *Astrophil and Stella* was beginning to rival the celebrity of Chaucer's creation.

But Shakespeare was to take a love tragedy and put it on a public stage; and it was to be a story that dealt not with lofty figures from the distant past or ancient epic, but with two adolescents in a recognizably modern city-state. Like Sidney's sequence, and like the two lyric comedies of these years, *Romeo and Juliet* hovers tantalizingly between fiction and actuality—in keeping with classical prescriptions, it is a tragedy based on a story that was believed to be true. In its ultimate Italian source, a novel by Masuccio Salernitano (published in 1476), the story of the lovers, Mariotto and Gianozza, is said to have taken place during the author's lifetime. When Luigi da Porta published his version in 1530, with the names changed to Romeo and Giulietta, and their families identified as the Montecchi and Capelletti, he claimed that his tale was verifiable fact (although the historical Capelletti came from Cremona, and da Porta's coupling of them was based on a very literal reading of a line in Dante.) Corte, in his history of Verona (1594) accepted da Porta's word and told the story as an illustration of the civil dissent of the time. To this day, tourists to Verona are directed to the major sites featured in the tragic story.

In addition, Shakespeare's play may well have glanced at circumstances in the life of his patron and his family—or at least, the world he created in his play bore some fleeting resemblances to events in Elizabethan England. It would be rash to suppose, for instance, that feuds, vendettas, murders, concealments, and the rest were the exclusive province of hot-blooded Mediterraneans. In 1594 the Danvers brothers, Sir Charles and Sir Henry, were imbroiled in a dispute with Sir Walter Long and his family. When a fight broke out in a tavern, Sir Charles was wounded by Henry Long's sword: Sir Henry drew his pistol and shot Long dead. Both brothers then made their escape and hid in the house of none other than the earl of Southampton, who on October 6 went ahead with the lavish celebrations of his coming of age while concealing the runaways in his house at Titchfield in Hampshire.

A less barbaric connection with Southampton, but one hardly more accessible to the playgoing public, is provided by George Gascoigne's masque of 1575. The piece was written to celebrate a double marriage in the Montague family, involving Southampton's mother, the dowager countess. The cast included a boy actor who wore a bonnet bearing the badge of the "Mountacutes of Italie." He explained to the assembly that the "Mountacutes" were a revered and ancient Italian house, who wore their emblem in order to distinguish themselves from their hated rivals, the "Capels," "for ancient grudge which long ago 'twene these two houses was."

But what I want to stress is that the story would have been seen as both modern and true. For example, the setting is not ancient Troy but a modern city-state, and the difficulties the young lovers face, and the chief matter of the play, can be seen to belong firmly in the Renaissance. After all, a love-tragedy was a novelty—plenty of figures in tragic stories had been lovers (Pyramus and Thisbe showed that clearly enough), but the love-narratives were habitually only parts of much bigger events. And its novelty is connected with

the abiding concern of so many writers and other people in the
Renaissance—love, what it was, what its obligations might be, what
effect it had on individuals and states. In this play we see very
clearly a conflict that surfaces in other texts of the time—that between love and duty. And it is important to set this clash in its
historical context. All of Shakespeare's works spring from a world
in which the individual's quest for selfhood coincides with the
centralizing impulse of the early modern state, and we can see this
relationship in countless of his plays. And often in those plays love
is a means whereby individuals come to know and define themselves, whether by finding their "other half" or by finding their
identity within a community.

In *Romeo and Juliet*, Shakespeare addresses anxieties about love
that are staples of Elizabethan songs, where it is normal for lovers
to ask what love is, to wonder if it is an illision or delusion, and to
muse on how they can tell the genuine article from lesser forces
such as infatuation. At the play's outset, Romeo typifies the melancholic lover of Petrarchan tradition. He claims to love one Ros-
aline, and when he comes upon the debris of the street fighting
sees it as an emblem of his inner state:

> Here's much to do with hate, but more with love.
> Why then, O brawling love, O loving hate,
> O anything of nothing first create!
> O heavy lightness, serious vanity,
> Misshapen chaos of well-seeming forms!
> Feather of lead, bright smoke, cold fire, sick health,
> Still-walking sleep that is not what it is!

The expression of this antithetical love involves exile, exclusion,
spending time (like the Athenian lovers of *A Midsummer Night's
Dream*) in wild, uncultivated woods. Clearly this state is meant to
seem absurd, inauthentic, and narcissistic. Its opposite, the mutual
love of Romeo and Juliet, is presented to us in starkly different
terms. Instead of roaming unbuttoned, undisciplined through an
uncultivated (and not enclosed) wilderness, Romeo meets Juliet at
a masked ball. Such an event involves disguise, not self-revelation.
The movements of the dancers are highly patterned, as they weave
the intricate shapes of court dances. And the language in which
the two lovers address each other is markedly formal and artificial.

Their exchange of pleasantries that ends with a kiss is in the form of a sonnet, which they speak—and which they seem to invent, collaboratively. The couplet is rounded off with an embrace, the closure of the poetic form being mirrored in the actions and sentiments of the lovers.

The implication is that this series of paradoxes—that the truest poetry is the most feigning, that the most profoundly personal utterance is also the most artful—is somehow superior to those that Romeo had uttered earlier in the play. The truest love, the argument seems to run, is not one that evades difficulties but rather one that embraces and transcends them. So it is with the balcony scene, for example, where instead of bursting out of the confines of the city into the wilderness Romeo climbs into that triumph of art over nature, a formal garden, from which further strenuous efforts will release him. Later, when his access to the mausoleum is blocked, he has to fight his way through to the door and then use a crowbar to break in. The final union of the lovers is in the form of two statues erected as a permanent monument to their love and an abiding warning of the perils of civil strife. And that episode generates further paradoxes: Though separate, they are joined forever; though slain by civil dissent, their example quells it; and so on.

In marked contrast with *Love's Labour's Lost*, the play seems to deal with the consolations that art might offer. Indeed, the highly formal structure of the piece, with its clearly marked acts (reminiscent of the structure of Chaucer's *Troilus*) and its use of a chorus who reminds us of the overall shape of the narrative, is in itself an illustration of the way in which art can shape narrative into an instructive and (to Renaissance eyes) consoling symmetry. The tragedy is somehow modified by its artfulness. The lovers do not rise from the dead, but their statues confer a species of immortality on them.

The duke's final words to the assembly onstage serve as a concluding caption, summing up the stage action, as well as an indication of what the future will hold.

A glooming peace this morning with it brings;
The sun for sorrow will not show his head.
Go hence, to have more talk of these sad things;
Some shall be pardoned, and some punished:

For never was a story of more woe
Than this of Juliet and her Romeo.

This six-line stanza shows the play ending with the same formality that had been apparent at crucial stages in the story—a formality that creates the sense of pattern, of shape, in the tragic story of the lovers. And yet the lines look outward to the future—"some shall be pardoned, and some punished"—in a way that does not simply gloss over the terrible events we have witnessed, and which the Friar has explained to the citizens. Shakespeare took the word *glooming* from the first canto of the first book of *The Faerie Queene*. In Spenser's romance, the virtuous but inexperienced Redcrosse Knight makes his way into the dark cave of the monster Error, encouraged by the exhortation that "Virtue gives her self light, in darkness for to wade." As he proceeds, his armor gives off "a little glooming light, much like a shade . . . by which he saw the monster," and by which he was able to win the ensuing fight. This small verbal echo of a feeble light that nevertheless reveals error to human sight epitomizes the movement in the play toward consolation and resolution.

In the previous comedies Shakespeare had conducted a witty critique of some of the claims traditionally made for art, and had shown the fallibility and inadequacy of human invention when it failed to take adequate account of forces and facts such as love and death. In *Romeo and Juliet*, the transforming potential of love is first portrayed and then shown to be in opposition both to the squabbling, factional world of politics and to the worlds of cynical wit (exemplified by Mercutio) and earthy, no-nonsense, worldly wisdom (exemplified by the Nurse). By distancing his tale through the use of the chorus and other devices which accentuate its formality, Shakespeare massages, but cannot altogether remove, our sense of loss, our recognition that the transformation is wrought on the survivors rather than on the tragic lovers.

The play was, and has remained, popular. Its combination of elements, its mixture of the lofty and the bawdy (we know that Kemp played the part of the Nurse's man Peter), has proved perenially attractive. To Elizabethans, it constituted an important redefinition of what tragedy was, and of the kinds of subjects appropriate to the form. It did so by incorporating material and styles from Chaucer, Sidney, Spenser, and other authorities, and by feeding the audience's desire for verbal wit and for physical spectacle and pathos. From an epigram by John Marston we know that the play received some successful performances at the Curtain, and that its verbal felicities had passed into the language of fashionable gentlemen. He addresses a gallant:

> *Luscus*, what's played today? faith now I know
> I set thy lips abroach, from whence doth flow
> Naught but pure *Juliat and Romio*.

The Curtain was also the home of professional fencing exhibitions. The street brawl with which the play opens typifies the way that Shakespeare habitually exploited the resources of his playing spaces and the specific expectations of his audiences, while at the same time producing a piece of self-consciously high art.

With the new security of a stable company, Shakespeare was in a position to plan. If his first tetralogy had been improvised and had grown piecemeal from the original two-part conception of *Henry VI*, his second seems to have been from the outset altogether more deliberately structured. And here the model of *Romeo and Juliet* was instructive: He had created a powerful sense of structure, a scaffolding, to support the story and to enable him to tell it poetically, while at the same time directing attention to the personal predicaments of his protagonists. The oscillation between close-up and panorama is now managed with a new sure-footedness.

Every age is an era of transition. But the Renaissance was a period especially marked by an extraordinary sense of change, and of the challenges posed for societies and for individuals by those changes. Shakespeare's second tetralogy indicates that the attitudes to history which underpinned the first sequence of plays were now being challenged. A providential interpretation of history was now having to compete with a more scholarly, evidence-based approach, and the evolution of the second tetralogy illustrates aspects of the relationship between the two. In particular, and wholly in keeping with Shakespeare's work in other genres, the plays show just what an elusive thing truth is, how fallible are human interpretations, and how precipitate are human judgments.

Richard II also shows changing attitudes to tragedy. When Richard is, in his self-dramatizing attitudes to tragedy, preparing his entourage for his deposition after the news of the execution of Bushy, Bagot, and Green at Bristol, he asks his fellows not to speak of comfort. He begins a little aria on the life of man and the brevity of earthly glory. In the course of it he says:

> For God's sake let us sit upon the ground
> And tell sad stories of the death of kings,
> How some have been deposed, some slain in war,
> Some haunted by the ghosts they have deposed,
> Some poisoned by their wives, some sleeping killed,
> All murdered. For within the hollow crown
> That rounds the mortal temples of a king
> Keeps Death his court, and there the antic sits
> Scoffing his state and grinning at his pomp,
> Allowing him a breath, a little scene
> To monarchise.

What he is actually inviting them to do is to draw on their memories of works like *A Mirror for Magistrates*, and Lydgate's *Fall of Princes*, works that consist of laments by people who, having fallen from greatness, have learned the lesson that greatness precedes decline. This is the tradition of medieval tragedy, from which lessons were derived about the state of mankind in general. It is to this pattern that Richard repeatedly seeks to make his own story conform, as when he spectacularly descends ("Down, down I come, like glistering Phaethon") from the walls of Flint Castle to meet the silent Bolingbroke. Richard's other favored mode of self-presentation is to liken himself to Christ—with specific reference to the events surrounding his betrayal, humiliation, and crucifixion.

But Shakespeare provides us with another model. In the prison scene in Act V, Richard is shown to us in a position that everybody in that day would have recognized as the epitome of the human condition. They rejoiced in the metaphor of human life as a prison, of the body as the prison holding the soul captive. Richard delivers himself of an extraordinarily introspective speech, one of the turning points in Shakespeare's writing. Like so many of his meditations on the human condition, it is cast in dramatic terms. But unlike the earlier model, its point is not to show this king's life fitting into a common pattern; it aims, rather, to demonstrate this individual human being attempting to come to terms with his own identity, to understand his life, to know himself. He opens, not in the declarative, self-posturing mode of earlier scenes, but in an almost scholarly vein, declaring that he has been "studying" how to "compare/This prison where I live unto the world." He finds in the course of his speculation that he is no single person—"thus play I in one person many people." He encounters and proclaims ambiguities and identifies apparent contradictions. His understanding of the multiplicities of interpretation is expressed by setting two scriptural texts, "Come, little ones" and "It is as hard to come as for a camel to thread the postern of a small needle's eye," against each other.

In this speech, the language of self-knowledge is the language of acting; the techniques of impersonation those of self-discovery. Shakespeare has taken into the most private sphere the paradoxes he has used elsewhere to talk about love and art. Just as the truest poetry is the most feigning, so the understanding of the self is bound up with a recognition of the competing voices within it. Where Henry VI and Richard III had been confronted by representatives of warring facets of their natures, Richard contains these conflicts within himself and is sufficiently self-conscious to be able to describe the process.

The beginning and end of the play demonstrate the chasm separating performance from actuality in political rituals, but the demonstration is available only to the audience and its implications are left for them to carry with them into the sequel. The action, after all, opens with a bogus trial, a pretense at justice. Richard, having connived at the death of his uncle the duke of Gloucester, permits a trial of his agent Mowbray to proceed at the instigation of Bolingbroke. But the king's involvement is suppressed. He banishes both men, and specifically condemns Mowbray to a silent exile where he will be deprived of the power to communicate. Then, at the end of the play, Bolingbroke banishes Exton. In a chilling echo of earlier events, the blame for Richard's death is heaped on the head of an agent, condemned to wander like Cain "thorough shades of night":

Though I did wish him dead,
I hate the murderer, love him murdered.
The guilt of conscience take thou for thy labour,
But neither my good word nor princely favour . . .

The repetition, the pattern, is there for us to see.

Richard II is written entirely in verse. It is dominated by certain images—the sun, images of rising and falling, of enclosure—and features a remarkable formality of language in moments like the confrontation between Mowbray and Bolingbroke, where there is extensive use of rhyme. As in *Romeo and Juliet*, but also as in the comedies of the time, the capacity of artful language to reveal as well as to conceal is constantly manifest—sometimes couplets indicate a speaker's settled certainty, at other times complacency or self-delusion or a desperate attempt to impose order on unruly events.

Critics have identified the play's use of the imagery of the four elements—earth, air, fire, and water—and of the garden, with its assocation with Eden and the Fall. Taken together, they contribute to the creation of a nostalgic vision of a world about to be torn apart, a realm in which the harmony of elements is fragile and the effort to cultivate gardens is about to be abandoned. This constitutes both a recollection of the first tetralogy, where the Wars of the Roses began with the symbolic plucking of roses in the Temple garden, and more obviously an echo of the Fall, an episode traditionally accorded a prime position in the mystery cycles. The effect is to generalize the events we see. Richard becomes an Everyman, and his England a metaphor for the human condition. At times these metaphorical correspondences and analogies, in which Elizabethans delighted, are made very explicit; never more so than in the "Garden" scene, where the application of the gardener's words to the nation as a whole is made explicit. When the gardener asks the servant to prune uncontrolled and unruly growth in the garden, the servant replies:

Why should we, in the compass of a pale,
Keep law and form and due proportion,
Showing as in a model our firm estate,
While our sea-walled garden, the whole land,
Is full of weeds, her fairest flowers choked up,

Her fruit trees all unpruned, her hedges ruined,
Her knots disordered and her wholesome herbs
Swarming with caterpillars?

There is, then, a mythologizing impulse in the play—or rather, there are several such impulses. The king seeks to fit his life to the patterns of Christ's life, while the story of the Fall provides a governing conceit for the whole and thereby the sequence which it inaugurates. But there are other elements at work. In the relationship between Richard and Bolingbroke we see an early example of a Shakespearean staple—a conflict between a man of words and a man of pragmatic action. *Richard II* stages in a stark form a contrast between an anointed, childless, indecisive monarch unfit to govern and a talented subject in armed opposition to him. And though the sympathetic presentation of Bolingbroke is related to his being the ancestor of the Tudors, Elizabeth herself found a different parallel in the play: In 1600, speaking to William Lambarde, she remarked, "I am Richard II, know ye not that?"—and the play was used as propaganda by the supporters of Essex's coup attempt in the following year.

The play was probably written in 1595, in the wake of the publication of Samuel Daniel's *The Civil Wars*, though its major source was Holinshed's *Chronicle*. It has attracted speculation that it received private performance. There is an enigmatic reference in a letter of December 7, 1595, to Lord Burghley by Sir Edward Hoby, inviting the chief minister to dine with him and see a new spectacle. He writes (spelling modernized):

Finding that you were not conveniently to be in London tomorrow night I am bold to send to know whether Tuesday may be any more in your Grace to visit poor Cannon Row, where, as late as it shall please you, a gate for your supper shall be open, and King Richard present himself to your view. Pardon my boldness that ever love to be honoured with your presence. . .

The evidence suggests that the play was popular on the public stage, and it is tempting to imagine that a private show was arranged for the great statesman's benefit. We might speculate that the reference to King Richard "presenting himself" may allude to the introspection, the self-revelation, especially of the latter part of the play. More particularly, the possibility of a private showing may perhaps shed some light on the question of the "Deposition Scene," that politically sensitive passage in Act IV which was not included in any printed version of the play before 1608. It may be that, though not permitted on the public stage, it was available for show in private houses, and that it formed the centerpiece of the Essex rebels' staging of the play. With *Richard II* Shakespeare completed his quartet of poetic dramas; he wrote with the confidence of a man with a secure toehold on Parnassus, who flourished under the admiring gaze of spectators high and low. With such security, he was able to start putting right some ancient wrongs.

It takes little more than a cursory reading of Shakespeare's works to note the importance placed—and not just by royalty or aristocrats—on honor, reputation, the good name of individuals, and of families. And ever since his adolescence Shakespeare must have been conscious of, and maybe driven by, his father's fall. His plays abound with instances of public humiliation, where characters either experience or describe the mockery of those who had once shown respect. It is determination to avoid such public shaming that motivates Cleopatra's suicide. But others are forced to endure the double disgrace of fortune and men's eyes. Shakespeare would have been aware, and would have known that the people of Stratford still remembered, that at some point after 1568 his father had made an attempt to persuade the College of Heralds to grant him the coat of arms to which his official rank in Stratford entitled him. Before the matter could be resolved, John Shakespeare had plummeted to an enforced retirement, and no more came of the application.

By the mid-1590s William was in a position to rebuild his father's standing, even if only at a symbolic level. He was prosperous, famous, and beginning to move in circles where pressure could be applied to the ponderous and mandarin workings of the College of Heralds. What is more, by restoring his father's name in such a public way he was also doing himself and his family, notably his eldest son Hamnet, a good turn. A coat of arms would be likely to stifle the possibility of any more sneering attacks like Greene's.

Shakespeare's efforts met with both success and unexpected failure. As the bureaucratic wheels ground slowly, that of fortune swung suddenly and unpredictably. The bare record of Holy Trinity tells us that Hamnet, Judith's twin, was buried in Stratford-upon-Avon on August 11, 1596 at the age of eleven. No more is said. When Ben Jonson's eldest son, also called Benjamin, died of the plague in 1603 at the age of seven, his father wrote a brief and touching lament for him:

> Farewell, thou child of my right hand, and joy;
> My sin was too much hope of thee, loved boy.
> Seven years thou wert lent me, and I thee pay,
> Exacted by thy fate, on the just day.
> Oh, could I lose all father now! For why
> Will man lament the state he should envy?
> To have so soon 'scaped world's and flesh's rage,
> And, if no other misery, yet age?
> Rest in soft peace, and, asked, say here doth lie
> Ben Jonson his best piece of poetry;
> For whose sake, henceforth, all his vows be such,
> As what he loves may never like too much.

These lines, published more than a dozen years later in the *Epigrams*, afford a rare glimpse into private grief—which we are not granted in the case of Shakespeare.

But the application for arms was successful. The archives preserve two drafts of a document written by the Garter King of Arms, Sir William Dethick, dated October 20, 1596. A scribbled note indicates that Dethick had decided to bring the matter to a rapid conclusion. He wrote that "This John" had presented a "pattern hereof under Clarent Crooke's hand . . . xx years past," and then summarized the case:

> A Justice of peace And was Baylue The Q officer & cheff of the towne of Stratford vppon Avon xv or xvi years past.
> That he hath Landes & tenementes of good wealth, & substance 500li.
> That he married a daughter and heyre of Arden, a gent. of worship.

Dethick cites both John Shakespeare's marriage and the rewards given to his ancestors by Henry VII to justify the grant. The device

is "Gold, on a bend sables, a spear of the first steeled argent, and
for his crest or cognizance a falcon, his wings displayed argent,
standing on a wreath of his colours, supporting a spear gold, steeled
as aforesaid, set upon a helmet with mantles and tassles as hath
been accustomed . . . " One copy has three versions of what may
be a motto: NON SANZ DROICT (Not without right). There is no
indication either that it was officially the Shakespeare motto or that
he or his family ever used it.

John Shakespeare appears in the Stratford records as a simple
yeoman on January 26, 1597, but it is likely that the grant had
gone through by then. A later document, from 1599, is primarily
concerned with giving permission to the Shakespeares to include
the Arden arms on their own. But the question did surface again
three years later. Dethick was accused of slackness of various kinds
by the York herald, Ralph Brokesmouth. In particular, it was alleged that Dethick had been too liberal in granting coats of arms
to persons not properly entitled to bear them, and that some devices
he authorized were already in use. In a schedule of problem cases
prepared by Brokesmouth, Shakespeare appears as number four.
The grant is attacked on two fronts. Not only were the arms said
to be insufficiently differentiated from those of Lord Mauley, but
there was also the question of status, exemplified in the contemp-
tuous note that Brokesmouth wrote underneath his sketch of the
coat of arms: "Shakespeare ye Player by Garter." The complaint,
essentially a byproduct of personal rivalries and animosities within
the Heralds' Office, was not upheld. The reply, jointly by Garter
and Clarenceux, argues that there is sufficient distinctiveness in the
coat of arms, and that, as for the recipient: " . . . the man was A
magestrat in Stratford vpon Avon. A Justice of peace he maryed
A daughter and heyre of Ardern, and was of good substance and
habelité."

So the coat of arms was secured in the latter part of 1596. Perhaps
Hamnet's funeral in August that year is one occasion when Shakespeare was in his hometown. But we cannot know for certain; nor
can we know if he came home to celebrate with his father. John
Aubrey's version has it that he spent part of each year with his
family. It may be that at this time he made the journey more often;
things were changing in Stratford for the Shakespeares, despite

their recent bereavement. And their new standing was about to be given physical expression by the purchase of a substantial property, the house at the corner of Chapel Lane and Chapel Street known as New Place.

Visitors to Stratford today can see the foundations of this house and walk in a garden on the site of Shakespeare's own plot. But even though it requires an effort of imagination to recreate the building (singled out by Leland, the traveling antiquary, in 1540, long before Shakespeare's birth, as "a pretty house of brick and timber"), notwithstanding the survival of a sketch from 1737, its location can still be appreciated. The house was built by Sir Hugh Clopton and stood next to the Gild Chapel, where Clopton funded refurbishments and left money to pay for prayers for his soul. So the associations of the house for the townsfolk would have been with the ideas of benefaction, of the local manifestation of success in the wider world, of the conjunction of wealth, success, and the preservation of a good name.

But these are abstract notions. In the real world, the house had passed out of the hands of the Cloptons in a state of serious disrepair in the year before Shakespeare's birth. The new owner was the notorious William Bott, who may have been a murderer, and was manifestly a difficult and irascible man. Bott was expelled from his position as alderman in 1565, and replaced by John Shakespeare. Bott sold New Place in the same year to a lawyer named William Underhill, clerk of assizes at Warwick. It was Underhill's son, also William, who sold the property to William Shakespeare on May 4, 1597. The sum involved was small, merely sixty pounds in silver. And even though the house was in bad repair, it must have seemed a bargain to the Shakespeares. Here was an expression of the father's rehabilitation, of the fulfillment of the father's dreams for his son, and for the family in general. The hopes so cruelly dashed in the 1570s were now set to be realized. The "merry cheeked old man" could once again walk the streets of Stratford with the confidence of his youth, and could live out his last days as a gentleman. We can imagine his satisfaction when in 1598, during the course of the repair work to New Place and the garden, he (or his son) sold off a load of stone to the corporation to use for the repair of the Clopton bridge.

The people of Stratford seem to have acknowledged this revival
in the Shakespeare fortunes. While the rehabilitation must have
had a lot to do with William's successes in London, they would
presumably have paid more attention to what was before their eyes,
to the local management of the estates, and have seen in that sphere
evidence of sound judgment, reliability, and influence with the
powers that be.

Shakespeare might well have been the hoarding, cautious ant to
Greene's profligate grasshopper; he may well have refused to help
improvident fellow dramatists. Perhaps the kind of loan Greene
had in mind was a gentlemanly guise for a gift. If so, Shakespeare,
like his father, was unlikely to be attracted by the notion. Both
men were happy to lend if the security was good, and John Shakespeare's fall had probably taught his son a lesson or two about
whom to trust.

William Shakespeare was now involved in the life of his hometown more fully than for many years. During one of the official
attempts to regulate private stores of corn, barley, and malt during
the sequence of bad harvests, he was recorded in February 1598 as
having a store of ten quarters of malt—one of the larger hoards in
the town, but nothing on the scale of some dealers. Shakespeare
was a man whom his father's cronies could do business with, especially as it now seemed to them that he had come into a lot of
money fairly suddenly and might be looking for an investment
opportunity. John Shakespeare's friend and neighbor Adrian Quiney suggested to Abraham Sturley—an educated man, a former
student of Queens' in Cambridge, and recent bailiff of Stratford—
that the younger Shakespeare might be interested in buying some
land, in particular some tithes, to add to his present holdings. So
on January 24, 1598, Sturley wrote to Quiney's son Richard, then
in London, and included this advice:

> This is one special remembrance from your father's motion. It
> seemeth by him that our countryman Master Shaksper, is willing
> to disburse some money upon some odd yardland or other at Shot-
> tery or near about us; he thinketh it a very fit pattern to move him
> to deal in the matter of our tithes. By the instructions you can give
> him thereof, and by the friends he can make therefore, we think it
> a fair mark for him to shoot at, and not unpossible to hit. It obtained
> would advance him in deed, and would do us much good. . . .

As far as is known, nothing came of this first approach. Later in the same year Quiney was sent to London on official business, to request special treatment for Stratford in the aftermath of two serious fires which had aggravated the crisis caused by chronic bad weather. Quiney hung about in London for several months, bemoaning the law's delays and incurring ever greater expenses. Eventually on October 25, he addressed a letter "To my Loveinge good ffrend & contreymann Mr. Wm. Shackespere" from his lodgings, the Bell Inn, in Carter Lane. The letter is a request for a loan of thirty pounds to tide him over. Quiney, who was to die in Stratford a few years later after being accidentally wounded when he tried to stop a skirmish involving some of Greville's men, writes like a man at the end of his tether. Cooling his heels in the big city, cooped up in an inn with Greville's henchmen, cannot have been an ideal way for a sober (possibly puritan) burgher to spend the autumn months. He finishes the note by declaring he is off to the court again to see if he can achieve anything.

The letter has survived because it was never sent, but wound up instead among Quiney's papers in Stratford. Nevertheless, it is the only surviving letter addressed to Shakespeare by someone who knew him, so I give it in full (spelling modernized):

> Loving Countryman, I am bold of you as of a Friend, craving your help with xxx li. upon Mr Bushell's and my security or Mr Mytton's with me. Mr Rosswell is not come to London as yet and I have especial cause. You shall Friend me much in helping me out of all the debts I owe in London, I thank God, and much quiet my mind which would not be indebted. I am now toward the Court in hope of answer for the dispatch of my Business. You shall neither lose credit nor money by me, the Lord willing, and now but persuade yourself so as I hope and you shall not need to fear but with all hearty thankfulness I will hold my time and content your Friend, and if we Bargain farther you shall be the paymaster yourself. My time bids me hasten to an end and so I commit this [to] your care and hope of your help. I fear I shall not be back this night from the Court. Haste. The Lord be with you and with us all Amen. From the Bell in Carter Lane the 25 October 1598. Yours in all kindness. Ryc. Quyney.

It could well be that the letter was not sent because Shakespeare turned up in person; or perhaps Quiney decided to make his approach directly. The older Quiney had already written to Richard and assumed that there would be no trouble in borrowing quite a substantial sum. The ancient mercer advises, "If you bargain with Mr Sha., or receive money therefore, bring your money home if you maye, I see how knit stockings are sold, there is great buying of them at Evesham"—in other words, anything left over after settling the expenses was to be used to stock up their shop with stockings from Evesham market. In the old man's words—"I think you may do good, if you can have money." Quite so.

On November 4 Sturley wrote to Quiney, replying to a letter clearly written later on the same day as the letter to Shakespeare. It looks as though Shakespeare had verbally promised to help Quiney, and then Quiney wrote to reassure his partner. Sturley's reply starts by expressing a wish for hard cash and some real figures rather than a personal assurance as described in Quiney's letter " . . . which imported . . . that our countryman Mr Wm. Shak. would procure us money, which I will like of as I shall hear when, and where, and how." But he then goes on to resurrect the idea of persuading their wealthy neighbor to consider an investment back home—there must have been some bargains available in the depressed borough: "I pray you let not go that occasion if it may sort to any indifferent conditions."

The story ended happily enough. Stratford's suit to Queen Elizabeth was successful, and Quiney's expenses were met by the exchequer.

This world of business, negotiation, and commerce provides a context for the next group of plays. All of them, even the comedies, are physically and imaginatively rooted in an altogether more pragmatic universe than that of their predecessors.

Compared to *Richard II*, the two *Henry IV* plays display an extraordinary mixture of styles and modes, combining tragedy and farce, pathos and slapstick, religiosity and buffoonery. Where the universe of the earlier play had been lyrical, with the entire text in verse, the different levels of style and language make the world of the *Henry IV* plays more compartmentalized and more confusing.

The earliest surviving complete edition (a slender fragment, a mere eight pages, is all that remains of a predecessor) is entitled *The History of Henrie the Fourth; With the battell at Shrewsburie, betweene the King and Lord Henry Percy, surnamed Henrie Hotspur of the North. With the humorous conceits of Sir John Falstaffe*. It appeared in 1598. The publication of two editions within a year, and then of five further editions before the 1623 Folio, testifies to the popularity of the play—a popularity matched only by *Richard III*. And the detail of the first title page suggests the diversity of the attractions that it held for Elizabethan and Jacobean readers and playgoers.

Falstaff was an immediate hit and courtiers and literary men began to quote him. By 1598 Tobie Mathew was able to write ironically of Sir Francis Vere and other officers that "Honour pricks them on," and Meres, ever with a ready eye for a quotation, cited in his *Palladis Tamia*, "There is nothing but roguery to be found in villainous man." But it was not as "Falstaff" that he made his first great impression. It looks as though the first performances (probably in 1596) featured a character named Sir John Oldcastle as the comic lead—played by William Kemp.

Historically, Oldcastle had been a Wycliffite, executed for heresy—including condemning the pope as Antichrist—in the reign of Henry V. As a result he became a hero to Protestant hagiographers—even modern editors refer to him as a martyr—and there were several accounts of his life and death presenting him as a precursor of the Reformation, including one in Foxe's *Actes and Monumentes* of 1563. There was, as might be expected, an alternative view. To Catholic sympathizers, Oldcastle cut an altogether less heroic dash. The Catholic writer Robert Parsons, in his scathing attack on the new Protestant saints, described Oldcastle as "a ruffian-knight as all England knoweth, and commonly brought in by comedians on their stages: he was put to death for robberies and rebellions." Parsons's attack is more than a little Jesuitical—among the several texts that had by 1604 glorified Oldcastle as a Protestant hero were pieces like John Bale's *Brief Chronicle concerning the Examination and Death of the Blessed Martyr of Christ Sir John Oldcastle* (1544) and the Lord Admiral's Men's play *I John Oldcastle* (by Drayton, Munday, Robert Wilson, and Richard Hathway), performed in 1599. This latter had declared in its prologue that its version of the hero was "no pampered glutton . . . Nor aged counsellor to youthful sin."

But the real problem was that Shakespeare, for whatever reason, had failed to take account of the sensitivities of Oldcastle's descendants. They were the prominent and influential Brooke family, one of whose chief members, William Brooke, Lord Cobham, served briefly as Lord Chamberlain to the Queen from August 1596 to his death in the spring of 1597. And that meant that he was not just an "aged counsellor"—he was also the patron of Shakespeare's company.

So the name was changed for the printed edition and for public performance. In a cavalier modification of chronology, Shakespeare plucked the name of the cowardly knight Falstaff from *Henry VI* (possibly with a self-deprecatory glance at his own name in mind). He also sanitized the names of Oldcastle's henchmen Harvey and Russell to Bardolph and Peto. The former might have been thought to glance at Sir William Harvey, who was about to marry the countess of Southampton, and the latter might have offended the Bedfords, whose family name was Russell. Doubtless Shakespeare hoped the embarrassing matter would rest there. In the Epilogue to the sequel, *Henry IV Part 2*, the speaker looks forward to the French wars of Henry V and says, " . . . for anything I know, Falstaff shall die of a sweat, unless already 'a be killed with your hard opinions; for Oldcastle died martyr, and this is not the man." But there are intriguing hints that the original name may have surfaced again from time to time (as when the lord chamberlain entertained the Burgundian ambassador with his company's *Sir John Old Castell*). And the name-changing was such an abiding part of the Shakespeare story throughout the seventeenth century that the 1644 Shakespeare folio includes the rival play as his.

The controversy suggests that the importance of Falstaff in the play was chiefly a matter of local, topical satire. It is, of course, much greater than that. He plays a crucial role in the conception and design of the two-part play. At one level he is an alternative father for Prince Hal, at another a figure of misrule. In a play which, like *Twelfth Night* or *As You Like It*, shows identity to be a problematical issue, and which stages competing sets of values, Falstaff's words and actions are inseparable from all the main concerns of the piece.

Henry IV Part 2 has all the hallmarks of a sequel: Its fragmentary nature seems to be a conscious demonstration of how events work themselves out; it shows consequences, a series of conclusions and results, based on what had been more discursively developed in the first part. The title page of the first edition (1600) again indicates the centrality of Falstaff. It reads: "The Second part of Henrie the fourth, continuing to his death, and coronation of Henrie the fifth. With the humours of sir John Falstaffe, and swaggering Pistol." Taking the plays as a pair, we can see that they deal with interlocking subjects: a battle for the control of the kingdom; Henry Bolingbroke's struggle to atone personally for the deposition of Richard; and the struggle over the soul of Prince Hal.

The first of these is the most straightforward in political terms, but it is inseparable from the others. Henry IV's opening words, which acknowledge his failure to fulfill the promise with which he had ended the previous play, are:

I'll make a voyage to the Holy Land,
To wash this blood from off my guilty hand.

And the king's journey, which structures the plays, is at one level a voyage from disillusionment to bathos. The plays are full of prophecies and predictions, most of which come to pass. But Henry does not die after seeing Jerusalem. Instead, he breathes his last in a chamber in Westminster known as Jerusalem. The dying king, on learning of the name, recalls the predictions:

It hath been prophesied to me, many years,
I should not die but in Jerusalem,
Which vainly I supposed the Holy Land.
Bear me to that chamber, there I'll lie:
In that Jerusalem shall Harry die.

The irony teeters on the edge of comedy, before revealing the sorrow of Henry's recognition that he must settle for the name of Jerusalem rather than the place itself. His acceptance of such an end brings to an end a career that has assumed tragic dimensions, and which has shown Henry's life after his deposition of Richard as a series of misunderstandings and misreadings—of his son, of his nation, of his friends and foes, and, ultimately, of himself.

We see that a consequence of rebellion is a universe that is be-

wildering and indecipherable. People, events, speeches, relationships proliferate, duplicate, and ramify in perplexing confusion.
Falstaff is a version of the king, as too are those lookalikes who are
stationed in the royal army to confuse the opposition. The king
sees Hal as another Richard, sees Hotspur as a better Hal, an image
of himself; so it goes on. It is Hal who keeps his counsel, while
revealing an inner self to the audience; and yet around that self
swirl suggestions, advice, interpretations. Hal in many ways takes
us back to the world of the morality play (with Falstaff as the Vice,
striving to lead the virtuous innocent youth astray), and the humanist fascination for education, for the institution of a Christian
prince, and for treatises on statecraft. The story of Henry's tragedy
runs alongside the narrative of Hal's upbringing, and the play as a
whole feeds into a discussion that has not yet become irrelevant—
does a ruler need to be virtuous in order to be effective?

The play's educational focus also relates to Shakespeare's exploration of the "advice to a young man" topic in the *Sonnets*. We might
go further, and see the preoccupation with father-son relationships
in both the plays and the sequence of poems as responses to the
loss of Hamnet in 1596. We might find a great personal poignancy
in the failures and limitations of communication between the flawed
mentors and their charges, subject as they all are to the ravening
tooth of time.

Hal is shown to be fully aware of the role of display, of theatricality, in royal behavior, as well as of the inner resources required
of a governor. Queen Elizabeth herself remarked that "we princes
are set on stages, in the sight and view of all the world." If Richard
had been all show and no substance, and Bolingbroke blunt, tac-
iturn, and undemonstrative, Hal is shown to combine their qualities in ways that his father cannot comprehend. And Shakespeare
lets us in the audience view the inner self of Hal on a number of
occasions, so that his eventual performance, his banishment of Falstaff and so forth, has been prepared for.

The most crucial moment, and I regard it as the hinge on which
the sequence turns, is the battle of Shrewsbury at the end of Part
I. It is notable for a combination of the theatrical and the personal,
and for challenging the audience to find absurd something that is
clearly of great significance. It is at the battle, while facsimiles of
his father stalk the field, that Hal comes face to face with his alter

ego Hotspur, and they announce themselves to each other and to the audience in formal language that transforms a chance encounter in the turmoil of conflict into a duel. Where other comic plays had staged pageants before an aristocratic audience, in this piece Shakespeare provides an onstage audience in the massive shape of Falstaff, who throughout the combat is pretending to be dead. The two princes fight, and Hotspur is killed. Faced with two corpses (one genuine, one bogus), Hal delivers two contrasting eulogies.

Hal completes the connection with his rival when he takes his own tabard and places it on Hotspur's face:

> But let my colours hide thy mangled face;
> And, even in thy behalf, I'll thank myself
> For doing these fair rites of tenderness.
> Adieu, and take thy praise with thee to heaven!

Already the audience has been given an opportunity to deflate this heroic and courteous behavior. When Hal says to the corpse of Hotspur:

> This earth that bears thee dead
> Bears not alive so stout a gentleman.

The temptation for the actor playing Falstaff to open his eyes is considerable. And when Hal turns to the cowardly knight his words are in marked contrast, concentrating on his old friend's flesh rather than his spirit:

> I could have better spared a better man.
> O, I should have a heavy miss of thee
> If I were much in love with vanity . . .
> Embowelled will I see thee by and by.
> Till then, in blood by noble Percy lie.

Hal's view of Falstaff's place in the world, and in his own life, is starkly articulated in these lines. The whole episode shows the young prince destroying a rival whose qualities he then assimilates, and showing how fragile are the ties that bind him to the fat knight.

The event sets the second half of the play in motion. Again, Shakespeare challenges us to find it ridiculous. As Hal leaves, Falstaff rises up with the word "Embowelled!" on his lips. It is a powerful comic moment, as the tension is released. But beyond that we are asked to consider the consequences: If, for example, Falstaff is not dead, are both of Hal's laments devalued? Indeed, there may be a sense that Hal's words over Falstaff have a truth which is impervious to the objection that they are based on a factual inaccuracy. They articulate truths about the prince's relationship with his surrogate father that had been expressed more obliquely before. So there is a pathos about Falstaff's carrying on much as before—we now know that his days of favor are numbered. And when he picks up and wounds the corpse of Hotspur and claims to have killed him, his cowardice and exaggeration suddenly seem to have taken on a new shade of mendacity and meanness after Hal's premature obituary. As so often in these plays, Shakespeare uses the metaphors of disguise, theatricality, and performance to explore questions of inwardness and identity, and he does so through the constant engagement of the audience in the dramatic process.

As the 1590s came to an end, Shakespeare's art was developing in distinctive ways. His writing was showing a capacity to combine profundity and surprise with familiarity. He drew his material from well-known sources—chronicles, popular novels, folktales, school texts, and so on. But he made the experience of watching these stories, the very activity of being a spectator, a crucial part of the events he staged. As time passed, he also seems to have aspired to the status of an author, and to have his scripts published as if they were serious works of art. But it was with the transforming, miraculous qualities of the theatrical that he had been preoccupied, displaying a concern with the immediate that would lead some to find his plays sentimental, to see them as tangential to the loftier purposes that some defenders of poetry had claimed were the poet's responsibility.

These general reflections are intended as a prelude to consideration of a very specific case of Shakespeare's concern with the immediate. *The Merry Wives of Windsor* is one of the few plays which academics have, albeit grudgingly, come to accept as having started life as a work that grew out of specific events and people in a particular time and place. Particular occasions for several of the plays have been advanced, with varying degrees of plausibility; and there seems to me a strong argument that Shakespeare was trying to create in some of them the sense that his fiction was woven on the basis of some actual events. But it is with *The Merry Wives of Windsor* that there has been least scholarly resistance to identifying correspondences with happenings in Elizabethan England.

In his earliest comedies, Shakespeare had shown the ability to work in a variety of comic styles. In *The Two Gentlemen of Verona*, for instance, he had created a part in Tarleton's style (Launce with his dog, Crab), as well as the almost surreal verbal quibbles and puns of Speed, aping the manner of Lyly. He had produced versions of older comic traditions, as well as of ancient comedy and fashionable Italianate humor. As the century drew to its close a new kind of comedy arose; it was practiced by a new generation of writers, most notably Ben Jonson, born in 1572, and George Chapman, who was four years older than Shakespeare but had only recently turned to writing plays. This new style, the so-called Comedy of Humors, is connected with that other genre, the "City Comedy," that was to be so successful in the coming decades.

The allusions to the latest comic vogues are not especially deft; indeed, there is an almost willful obviousness about them. Shakespeare illustrates in the person of Falstaff's sidekick Nym the dangers of a little learning. For him, the theory of humors explains everything, and colors his every utterance: "The anchor is deep. Will that humour pass? . . . I have operations which be humours of revenge. . . . My humour will not cool." The whole play is crammed with stereotypes and familiar plot devices. Falstaff and his troupe would already have been recognizable to the audience from their appearance in *Henry IV*, and would have brought their previous histories with them on to the stage. Other aspects of the piece are similarly part of the traditional stock of comedy material: There is a comic doctor with a strange foreign accent; a comic schoolmaster who has the additional hilarity of being Welsh; and the action features cuckoldry, disguise, concealment, and most of the usual ingredients of farce.

It is now thought that Shakespeare interrupted work on *Henry IV Part 2* in order to write it, perhaps to a specific commission. From the eighteenth century comes a report (in John Dennis's 1702 adaptation of the play, as *The Comical Gallant* [1702]) that Shakespeare wrote it in two short weeks in response to Queen Elizabeth's express wish to see Falstaff in love. And there is one moment—usually omitted in performance and, strictly speaking, superfluous to the dramatic action—which stands out as a highly specific reference to the queen. It occurs in the last scene of *Merry Wives*, when Mistress Quickly enters, disguised as the Queen of the Fairies:

> . . . About, about!
> Search Windsor Castle, elves, within and out.
> Strew good luck, oafs, on every sacred room,
> That it may stand till the perpetual doom
> In state as wholesome as in state 'tis fit,
> Worthy the owner and the owner it.
> The several chairs of order look you scour
> With juice of balm and every precious flower.
> Each fair instalment, coat, and several crest,
> With loyal blazon, evermore be blest!
> And nightly, meadow-fairies, look you sing,
> Like to the Garter's compass, in a ring.
> Th'expressure that it bears, green let it be,
> More fertile-fresh than all the field to see;
> And *honi soit qui mal y pense* write
> In em'rald tufts, flowers purple, blue, and white
> Like sapphire, pearl, and rich embroidery,
> Buckled below fair knighthood's bending knee.
> Fairies use flowers for their charactery.

This passage, which, though not included in the 1602 Quarto edition, is in the Folio text, is plainly a reference to the ceremonies associated with the installation of Knights of the Garter, and in particular with the annual Garter Feast on April 23. It is now thought likely that the play was commissioned for the Garter Feast in 1597, and that it was performed before the queen and all the Knights of the Order, probably that evening. One of the knights due to be newly installed was the company's patron, the new lord chamberlain—George Carey, second Baron Hunsdon. He was formally made lord chamberlain on April 17, but had been expected to take the post once it became clear that the present incumbent, Lord Cobham, was dying (he died on March 5, 1597). Carey's father, Henry, first Baron Hunsdon, had been lord chamberlain between 1583 and 1596, and he had also repeatedly nominated his son—by then in his late forties—as a candidate for the Garter. Lord Cobham's family name, Brooke, is the name taken by the comic jealous husband, Master Ford. Shakespeare makes sure that we take special note of the name, and that we recognize its significance. Bardolph tells Falstaff, "there's one Master Brook below would fain speak with you, and be acquainted with you . . . "; Falstaff replies, "Brook is his name?" and then observes that "Such Brooks are welcome to me, that o'er flows such liquor."

Perhaps in these moments Shakespeare, under the protective gaze of both the queen and his new patron, Lord Hunsdon, was getting his revenge for the trouble that had been caused not long before, when Cobham (or perhaps his son) had taken exception to the use of Oldcastle's name for the character renamed Falstaff. Further topicality is suggested by the fact that another candidate for the Order of the Garter—elected *in absentia*—was Frederick, Count Mompelgard, Duke of Württemberg, who may be the "duke de Jarmany" of whom Caius speaks in Act IV of *The Merry Wives of Windsor*.

The title page of the 1602 Quarto explains that the text is of the play "As it hath been divers times acted by the Right Honourable the Lord Chamberlain's Servants. Both before her Majesty, and elsewhere." So an important selling point was its royal connection. But there is another sense in which the play's court performance gives significant clues to its unusual (for Shakespeare) dramatic qualities. It suggests that the text's meaning was vitally connected with the circumstances of its performances—in particular, that its enactment had occurred before the queen. Thus, for instance, the bogus Fairy Queen was acting in front of the "real" one, and the collision of bourgeois values and debased chivalry was acted out before knights whose order was based on a cult of self-control, discipline, and high moral ideals. In other words the play, unlike the romantic comedies, was limited in the range it could represent. It could not cover the spectrum of human and supernatural types depicted in *A Midsummer Night's Dream*, for instance. Its hierarchies are to be completed by the presence of particular observers—as was to be the case in Jonson's *Bartholomew Fair* in 1614. In that play, the anarchy and chaos of the fair are in the end held to make sense in the unique sight of the observing monarch. In Jonson's words to King James:

> Your majesty hath seen the play, and you
> Can best allow it, from your ear and view.

So what we see is a play in a middle-class, emphatically English world that is itself anomalous. The elements of romance, notably the Herne the Hunter episode, stand out in contrast, say, to those in the *Dream* as stage-managed human illusions. Their magic depends on the skill of their enactment and the gullibility of their victim, rather than on any other-worldly force.

And while in the court such a show provided a manifest contrast to the highly mythologized, iconic self-presentation of Gloriana and her courtiers, on the public stage the values that triumph are not so much those of the court but those of the rising urban middle class. It is the force of bourgeois marriage that withstands and subdues Sir John. Even Fenton, though he speaks in eloquent, courtly verse that contrasts with the vigorous prose of most of the play, is assimilated at the end. His eloquence is in a sense tamed; the power of his tongue to persuade is used not for seduction but for a proposal of marriage. We see a young, chivalric, romantic hero accommodated to the values of the middle class; we see a middle-class girl marrying into the gentry (as Shakespeare's own granddaughter would—she was born Elizabeth Hall, but died as Lady Barnard). So the final moments of the play, removed from the specific occasion of their Windsor performance, are in their cozy way a hymn to the triumph of bourgeois values. After Page has finally given his blessing to the union ('What cannot be eschewed must be embraced') his wife gathers the company—even the humiliated Falstaff—together:

> Well, I will muse no further. Master Fenton,
> Heaven give you many, many merry days!
> Good husband, let us every one go home,
> And laugh this sport o'er by a country fire,
> Sir John and all.

When in the summer of 1598, the Lord Chamberlain's Men sought to block the unauthorized publication of a successful comedy, the entry in the Stationers' Register referred to "a booke of the Marchaunte of Venyce or otherwise called the Jewe of Venyce." The alternative title suggests that, as in the Henry IV plays, the theatrical prominence of one of the characters had enabled that figure to take on a life independent of—and perhaps in opposition to—the play which spawned it. And that independence, that tendency of Shylock to be viewed separately from the original circumstances of his creation, has created problems, especially in this century. While it has proved possible to provide a feminist interpretation of *The Taming of the Shrew*, what many regard as the manifest anti-Semitism of *The Merchant* has not been so easily argued away.

In performance, as in performances of Marlowe's remarkable *The Jew of Malta*, considerable sympathy is aroused for the Jewish figures—though only after they have been shown to conform to crude and hostile stereotypes. In each of the plays, by the end the real focus of attack is the hypocrisy and complacency of the professed Christians. Indeed, the degradation and defeat of the Jew is a spectacle that shows the onstage audience in a distinctly unfavorable light in a way that recalls the endings of the two earlier romantic comedies *Love's Labour's Lost* and *A Midsummer Night's Dream*.

The play brings together material from his earliest comedies—stories from Italian novellas, topics from humanist debate such as the relationship between Justice and Mercy—with techniques and themes from the romantic comedies and the histories. Its juxtaposition of worlds, its collocation of systems of values, as well as its creation of the huge and memorable part of Shylock for Kemp, creator of Falstaff and Dogberry, to play, locate the script firmly enough in this phase of Shakespeare's writing career. The role played by money is very considerable. Money is woven into the texture of the romance-story of ships and storms, and it is the stuff of which the wooing in the play is made. We are made fully aware of Portia's status as an object, a prize, a commodity. The retreat from the world of business to that of love and retirement in the two earlier comedies has been reversed. If *Henry IV* had examined the place of honor, of chivalry, in the harsh world of politics, *The Merchant* places a series of ideals—love, truth, justice—in the potentially hostile environment of the marketplace.

The play mingles the immediate and the faraway, the fairytale with the commercial. Its connection with the world around it is easily demonstrated. It draws upon, for instance, the popular hostility to Jews that had been whipped up in 1594 by the earl of Essex and his supporters in prosecuting a Portuguese Jew called Lopez for treason. Lopez was a physician who had been in the service of the earl of Leicester before being taken on by the queen herself. He became involved in political conspiracy, especially after the arrival in London in 1592 of Don Antonio, a claimant to the Portuguese throne. But Essex sought to use him in his own intrigues, as a means of cultivating a source of intelligence about Spain and Portugal not available to his gray-bearded colleagues on the Privy Council. Lopez went along with this, but made sure the queen was informed of any new developments before Essex was. This gave rise to bad feeling between the men, and eventually Essex denounced him as a traitor, plotting to poison both Don Antonio and the queen. At first Essex was laughed to scorn and went off to sulk in his chamber. But he came back with new accusations, with more substantial evidence, and stirred up popular anxiety about possible plots and assassinations. In February Lopez was tried and found guilty of plotting the queen's death, and several accomplices were also convicted.

In May Marlowe's *Jew of Malta*, revived for performance at the Rose, appeared in a printed edition. And in June Lopez and his associates were executed, protesting their innocence to the last. The convicted men were taken on a long last journey: by water across the Thames from Westminster to Southwark—we know that Marlowe's play and *Titus Andronicus* were playing that week at Newington Butts, not far away—and then on hurdles over London Bridge and through the crowds up Leadenhall Street and out along what is now Oxford Street to the gibbet at Tyburn. Lopez caused mirth in the crowd at Tyburn by crying out that he loved the queen as much as he loved Jesus Christ. He was then hanged, drawn, and quartered.

The wretched Lopez became a focus for the anxieties of a population encouraged to be afraid of traitors, of cunning fifth columnists in their midst who would stop at nothing to achieve their diabolical ends. And the continuing success of Marlowe's play in revivals after 1594 kept the image—in a distorted, mythologized form—fresh in the minds of citizens.

But while Shakespeare may have recalled the Lopez case, and while he obviously drew upon Marlowe's play, the earlier piece was not the occasion or spur for the composition of *The Merchant*. There are several other points of intersection with people and events of the 1590s. The queen's musicians, for instance, included no fewer than eight members of the Bassani family, and there were in Elizabethan London numerous contacts with Venice and the Venetians. It is now usually accepted that *The Merchant* alludes to events much later than 1594. The most obvious instance is the allusion to Essex's capture of two great Spanish galleons off Cadiz in June 1596. One of the ships, the *San Andres*, renamed the *Andrew*, came to stand in the popular mind as the archetypal treasure ship. Its name is used in this way by Salarino in the opening scene of the play:

I should not see the sandy hourglass run
But I should think of shallows and of flats,
And see my wealthy Andrew docked in sand,
Vailing her high top lower than her ribs
To kiss her burial. . . .

Even from its early days, British imperialism always had a powerful mercantile element. In proposals for new ventures, whether for expeditions to far-off lands or for more domestic enterprises such as enclosures, investors are promised both honor and profit. The world of the *Merchant* corresponds in many ways to that of Elizabethan London, and the competing social and economic forces are shown in their complex interrelationships; and we saw earlier that usury was something with which Shakespeare himself was familiar enough. He was happy to go to court to recover debts, as we shall see. His father had been involved in legal action, and had perhaps lost his fortune, as a result of the confused ways in which Elizabethans tried to reconcile their need to borrow money with their scripture-based conviction that it was an undesirable activity. The play mirrors the contradictions and equivocations in Elizabethan practice, and the presentation of Shylock indicates the deep unease and hostility aroused by the emerging economic system.

This set of problems of tone is connected with the play's variety of styles and diversity of genres. Formally, the play eventually submits to the dictates of the comic form, but it strains at the leash considerably. And some features, notably Shylock himself, almost succeed in taking over the piece and leading it in quite different directions. The problems the audience faces in recognizing the sort of performance being staged for it, and adjusting its expectations accordingly, are related to the moral and interpretative problems that the play addresses. So we can perhaps see *The Merchant*, along with *Much Ado*, as Shakespeare's first "problem plays."

The play deals with the problematic relationship between justice and equity, or between the letter and the spirit of the law. This was a topic with which Elizabethans, a most litigious people, were very concerned, as the fifth books of Sidney's *Arcadia* and of Spenser's *The Faerie Queene* illustrate. To complicate matters, Shakespeare fills *The Merchant* with biblical language, and it might be thought at first glance that he is staging a conflict between Old Testament literalism championed by Shylock and the new dispensation of Christ as championed by Portia. In an odd and surprising way, the roles are reversed in the trial scene. It is Shylock who keeps to the spirit of the bond, while Portia quibbles about the text of the agreement in a most literal-minded fashion. And, at a broader level, the behavior of the Christians as the play proceeds is—to put it at its mildest—such as to open up a gulf between ideal and practice.

The Merchant is a disturbing play, and it may also reflect anxiety and unease on the part of its author. For although he was building a play from elements he had used before—novella story, gender-reversal, fairytale, and so on—some of them are given a new twist here. An example is the treatment of Portia. Her role may well have been a troubling one for Elizabethans. They had got used to the idea of a female monarch, and in principle were in favor of female education. But Portia takes on the job of a professional at the very moment when the legal profession was establishing, codifying, regulating itself. The situation anticipates the way Helena in *All's Well That Ends Well* joins that other "male" profession, medicine. And it may be that the bawdy exchanges in which Portia is involved in Act V are more than just a comic relief from the tensions of the trial scene, more than a playful use of the same quibbling intelligence that had resolved the crisis. Perhaps Shakespeare shared the nervousness of many of his contemporaries when faced with a woman doing a man's job, and so creates for her a vein of coarseness, of verbal licentiousness, wholly out of keeping with what we have seen before but typifying the male Elizabethan's edgy response to the power of an active and learned woman.

For whatever reason, the play seems to have had a relatively short period of popularity; there are no records of productions between 1605 and the 1740s. After that, it was a different story. Only *Hamlet* has been as frequently performed over the centuries. In the Romantic period *The Merchant* was Shylock's play; like the parts of Hamlet and Richard III, that of Shylock became a central role in the repertoire of the great celebrity actors, with productions habitually built around his melancholy tale. But that is another matter. The Elizabethan *Merchant* was a play of delicate and subtle ensemble writing, where balance, juxtaposition, and shades of comparison combined to create a theatrical experience of marked ambiguity. And these ambiguities seem to have been both deliberate and unconscious. For not only was Shakespeare creating a play of ideas, a challenging problematical work of mixed genre; he was also at some level restaging the situation of parts of his own life and career at the time. Some of the uncertainties are Shakespeare's own.

By the time of *The Merchant* Shakespeare was in a sense suspended between Stratford and London, between the city and the country, between the court and the city, between the rising generation of politicians and their elderly predecessors. He was restoring his family's fortunes both materially and less tangibly with the coat of arms. And it was perhaps just beginning to dawn on him after the death of Hamnet that his hopes of defeating time, of speaking to posterity, could be focused as much on his occupation as a scriptwriter as upon his reassembling of estates in Stratford.

An abiding feature of the Elizabethan publishing trade is the popularity of collections of maxims, proverbs, and axioms on various improving subjects. They were the printed equivalents of the commonplace books that humanist educators recommended their charges should compile, and their chief model was Erasmus. Like his works, these anthologies were designed to cultivate eloquence. In 1597 Nicholas Ling brought out *Politeuphuia: Wit's Common-*

wealth, a work which contains selections from modern writers such as Sidney alongside classical models. In 1598 Francis Meres brought out a successor, entitled *Palladis Tamia: Wit's Treasury. Being the Second Part of Wit's Commonwealth.* Tucked away among the comparisons and rhetorical models is a short account of modern English letters, in which the excellence of the present generation of writers is demonstrated in terms of their similarity to the classics. Now that Shakespeare had been published—two poems and perhaps as many as eight plays—Meres felt able to launch into an extended praise of his writing:

> As the soul of Euphorbus was thought to live in Pythagoras: so the sweet witty soul of Ovid lives in mellifluous and honey-tongued Shakespeare, witness his *Venus and Adonis*, his *Lucrece*, his sugared *Sonnets* among his private friends, etc.
>
> As Plautus and Seneca are accounted the best for Comedy and Tragedy among the Latins: so Shakespeare among the English is the most excellent in both kinds for the stage; for Comedy, witness his *Gentlemen of Verona*, his *Errors*, his *Love's Labour's Lost*, his *Love's Labour's Won*, his *Midsummer Night's Dream*, and his *Merchant of Venice*: for Tragedy his *Richard the 2*, *Richard the 3*, *Henry the 4*, *King John*, *Titus Andronicus* and his *Romeo and Juliet*.
>
> As Epius Stolo said, that the Muses would speak with Plautus tongue if they would speak Latin: so I say that the Muses would speak with Shakespeare's fine filed phrase, if they would speak English.

For a conventionally trained rhetorician of serous inclination—he ended his days as the parish priest and schoolmaster of Wing in the county of Rutland—Meres appears not just well informed but also genuinely enthusiastic about the most modern literature. It is easy to scorn Meres as a critic, not least because some (though not many) of the names he praises along with the giants of the age have been forgotten by posterity. But as a rhetorician he was especially sensitive to eloquence, to the augmentation of the resources of the English language: "The English tongue is mightily enriched," he wrote, "and gorgeously invested in rare ornaments and resplendent habiliments by Sir Philip Sidney, Spenser, Daniel, Drayton, Warner, Shakespeare, Marlowe and Chapman." He seems particularly to have admired versatility, exemplified by Spenser ("who excelleth in all kinds") and Shakespeare ("excellent in both kinds for the stage"). And it is clear that the praise of "mellifluous and honey-tongued" Shakespeare with his "fine filed phrase" was designed to be read in 1598 as something more precise than a vague compliment.

The chief focus of attention has been on the list of plays as a guide to Shakespeare's chronology—a guide now taken to be fairly reliable rather than authoritative (he forgets, or does not know about, the *Henry VI* plays, *The Taming of the Shrew*, and the recent sensation *Henry IV Part 2*). Numerous scholarly studies have attempted to explain the reference to *Love's Labour's Won*. Some have taken it to indicate a lost play of that title, others that it was an alternative title belonging to some other Shakespeare play; yet others have said it is Meres's mistake. In 1953 the title surfaced in a bookseller's list of 1603, and it is usually taken to refer to a lost play, performed before 1598 and in print before 1603 but not included in later editions.

Round about the time that Shakespeare's standing as a writer was being so strongly supported, he seems to have taken steps to present himself to the public in a more prominent way. Before 1598, no published text of any of his plays had featured the author's name. The narrative poems in 1593 and 1594 had done so, but they were recognizably part of an established and self-consciously literary culture. As remarked earlier, the literary status of scripts and the market value of scriptwriters were low.

But in 1598 new editions of Shakespeare's three successful tragedies, *Richard III*, *Richard II*, and *Romeo and Juliet*, were published with Shakespeare's name on the title page of the first two. Their gravity and artfulness perhaps made them a suitably serious debut, and a demonstration that this writer could excel in a tragic vein as well as in the mode of the classical poems. An edition of *Love's Labour's Lost* above Shakespeare's name in the same year also showed to the literate classes that his range encompassed eloquent, courtly comedy. A further stimulus was the appearance of two new writers possessed of formidable talent, substantial learning, and massive conceit. The new comedies of Jonson and Chapman, in which the humanist classicism Shakespeare himself had deployed in *The Comedy of Errors* and *The Taming of the Shrew* was augmented by the theory of "humors," had begun to attract large audiences. And when Jonson published his scripts, there was to be no doubt in the reader's mind as to the identity of the author; nor was the reader allowed to ignore the author's claim to intellectual and moral superiority. As this new generation began to construct both a profession and a literary "image" for themselves through plays rather than through more conventional publications, Shakespeare's decision to acknowledge three of his most serious works is rather more explicable. And intellectuals duly took note. Gabriel Harvey, a prominent Cambridge don and the former tutor of Spenser, seems to confirm the establishment of Shakespeare's reputation as an artist with the comment from around this time that his tragedies and classical works had it in them "to please the wiser sort."

Shakespeare was still acting—his name appears in the list of actors who took part in Jonson's *Every Man in His Humour*, a minor but significant source for *Othello*—in 1598. We do not know what part he played, but we can be certain of his continued active daily involvement in his company, and of this participation in its business ventures as well as its theatrical productions. And the years 1597–8 were exciting times for the Lord Chamberlain's Man.

It is easy with hindsight to see the great flowering of English drama in this period as following a smooth upward trajectory, but to do so would be to ignore the numerous difficulties the new industry faced. After the plague, and alongside the unabated hostility of the civic authorities, further threats to their livelihood kept cropping up. One of the problems faced by the Lord Chamberlain's Men was that their relations with their landlord, Giles Allen, were never easy. Allen and James Burbage had signed a lease for twenty-one years back in 1576, and for some time both parties had explored possible future arrangements for the site. Burbage was keen to negotiate a new lease in accordance with the provisions of the old one. But Allen held back. In 1585 and then in 1591 Burbage brought in expert craftsmen to draw up plans of the site to show the nature and extent of the improvements he had carried out, and to support his claim that he had spent in excess of two hundred pounds on the property. As the lease drew to a close, Burbage was happy to settle for an increase in rent. But Allen wanted to include a provision that would enable him to take possession of the site after five years in order to convert the buildings to some other use. Negotiations came to a standstill.

Burbage, perhaps expecting support from the aristocratic aficionados of the stage, decided to try to move into the city. For the substantial sum of six hundred pounds he acquired part of the large complex of buildings of the former Blackfriars monastery—where, as it happened, the lord chamberlain was living. An obvious attraction was that the site was not within the jurisdiction of the city authorities. He put more money into creating a theatrical space there, but opposition to the conversion from the influential residents meant that the Privy Council stalled Burbage's ambitious plans. it would be ten years before Shakespeare and his company could stage plays there.

So Burbage was faced with serious problems, having sunk money into a new site that might not be available for a long time, and having reached an impasse with his present landlord. He did not live to resolve the crisis. By the end of January 1597 James Burbage, the "First Builder of Theatres," the man to whose industrious energy and foresight the stage owed so much, the mediocre carpenter who constructed a venue in which some of the most remarkable artistic achievements of the European Renaissance were created, was dead.

His business was carried on by his son Cuthbert, but no new lease was signed, and the antitheatrical forces were growing stronger by the day. on July 28, 1598, the Privy Council received the annual letter of complaint from the lord mayor and the Court of Aldermen, in which the council was, as usual, alerted to the depravity, dis-order, and scurrility of the public theaters and urged to close them down. This year they added an aesthetic item—that the plays presented on the stage were "Contrary to the rules and art prescribed for the making of Comedies even among the Heathen." Perhaps they calculated that blanket condemnation of the theater was not getting them anywhere. But even so they probably expected the usual bland official brush-off. The Privy Council had already been angered by what it saw as the unpatriotic failure of the city to raise troops for the current action against the Spanish. So the brief meeting ended, and since the lord mayor's party did not expect a reply they adjourned for a month.

But for once they found a receptive audience—indeed, the Privy Council had already acted more savagely than the alderman's most crazed destructive fantasies could have anticipated. On the same day—and presumably before its members had considered the lord

mayor's letter—the Privy Council expressed a hitherto unprecedented hostility to the stage. A prohibition in the summer to reduce
the risk of plague was one thing. Yet for some reason now, in 1598,
they ordered the playhouses to be "plucked down" because of the
"lewd matters that are handled on the stages" and the "very great
disorders" resulting from the "resort and confluence of bad people."
Their proclamation went into some detail, naming the playhouses
so to be plucked, and urging how and when and by whom the
plucking was to be done.

Richard Topcliffe, the government's most assiduous pursuer and
interrogator of Jesuits and a man with a well-earned reputation as
a torturer, joined in the open season that seemed to have been
declared on the theaters. Just a few days after the council's decree,
he reported to Elizabeth's chief minister, Cecil, that information
had come his way of "a lewd play that was played in one of the
playhouses on the Bankside, containing very seditious and slan-
derous matter." As a result several members of the company were
imprisoned, "whereof one of them was not only an actor but a
maker of part of the said play"—that unfortunate individual was
Ben Jonson. His coauthor, Thomas Nashe, had wisely fled the city.
So Cecil instructed Topcliffe to round up as many of the company
as he could and interrogate them systematically, and also to conduct
a minute inspection of papers found in Nashe's lodgings.

The play that became the subject of the enquiry is now—hardly
surprisingly—lost. Faced with the prospect of a conversation with
the brutal and ingenious Topcliffe, the players were doubtless anxious to destroy any scraps of text that might be twisted against
them. Nashe, who knew all about the way Thomas Kyd had been
treated during the investigation into the murky circumstances surrounding Marlowe's death, evidently had a clear sense of the risks
he would have run if he stayed in London. The piece that caused
all this fuss was a satire called *The Isle of Dogs* performed by the
newly formed Pembroke's Men at the Swan Theatre. From the
title we can imagine that it was an anticourt satire. The Isle of
Dogs is just across the river from the royal palace of Greenwich,
and was used to house the hounds kept by the royal household.
Presumably parallels were suggested between the queen's animal
subjects and her human courtiers, alternately cooling their heels
and dancing attendance on Gloriana. Further, the notion of mordant

or "biting" satire was presumably meant to be conjured by the title.
But not even Topcliffe could make the charge of sedition stick
effectively, and early in October Jonson was released, as were the
two actors originally apprehended, Gabriel Spencer and Robert
Shaw. The playhouses were not plucked down, and the two great
companies continued to provide entertainment for court festivals
in the winter of 1598–9.

The main victims of this peculiar episode were Pembroke's Men,
and Francis Langley, proprietor of the Swan. The Privy Council
had earlier been suspicious of Langley's business dealings and was
probably anxious to restrict the number of theatrical enterprises to
two. It is possible, therefore, that the council's vehement words of
July were really directed to those ends, and that it was expedient
to be able to show that the company was under arrest for performing
a seditious play. Once the company folded and its men drifted back
to the other groups (mainly to the Admiral's Men), the immediate
danger to the public theaters subsided.

Whatever else might be said about this rush of blood to the
corporate head of the Privy Council, it cannot have helped the Lord
Chamberlain's Men. Their patron seemed to have turned against
them. After all, he had signed the document of July 28. Their
landlord must have been gratified at the prospect that the vogue
for public playhouses was now to end. He and others must have
relished the harsh words for the theater from those very men who
had so often protected it from the censure of the godly. So what
was Burbage to do?

He was not in a strong position. At Allen's request, the Chamberlain's Men moved out of the Theatre after a short season and
set up operations at the Curtain. The deserted amphitheater became
a byword for solitary desolation ("One like the deserted Thea-
tre/Walks in dark silence, and vast solitude," wrote the satirist
Edward Guilpin in his *Skialetheia* of 1598), and Burbage's company
now had to face the future without a permanent home. Late in
1598 he reluctantly acceded to new terms in discussions that were
held with Allen at the George Inn in Shoreditch. He regarded the
new arrangements as excessive and exorbitant, but felt there was
no alternative if the company was to continue on its previous footing. He named his actor brother Richard—already a considerable
celebrity—as security. But Allen refused to accept this, and, having

exhausted his patience with the players, he declared that he was now resolved to demolish the Theatre and "convert the wood and timber thereof to some better use." He then left town on business.

News of his decision galvanized the Burbages and their friends to take drastic action. Under the watchful eye of their mother, the brothers assembled a party (including the master carpenter Peter Street, with a dozen workmen, and their business partner William Smith) to take advantage of a covenant in the original lease. Under this the tenants were entitled, under certain conditions, to dismantle the amphitheater. The group gathered on December 28, 1598.

A vivid account of the ensuing events was delivered by Allen himself a couple of years later, when he sued Burbage for eight hundred pounds damages (seven hundred pounds representing his valuation of the Theatre). In his words, the brothers, their mother, their carpenter, their banker, and their laborers riotously assembled themselves

> . . . and then and there armed themselves with divers and many unlawful and offensive weapons, as, namely, swords, daggers, bills, axes, and such like, and so armed did then repair unto the said Theatre. And then and there, armed as aforesaid, in very riotous, outrageous, and forcible, manner, and contrary to the laws of your Highness' realm, attempted to pull down the said Theatre, whereupon divers of your subjects, servants, and farmers, then going about in peaceable manner to procure them to desist from that their unlawful enterprise, they (the said riotous persons aforesaid) notwithstanding procured then therein with great violence, not only then and there forcibly and riotously resisting your subjects, servants, and farmer, but also then and there pulling, breaking, and throwing down the said Theatre in very outrageous, violent, and riotous sort, to the great disturbance and terrifying not only of your subjects, said servants, and farmers, but of divers others of your Majesty's loving subjects there near inhabiting.

The timbers were unlikely to have been treated so roughly. A valuable asset, they were carried carefully through the city's wintry streets, ferried across the river, and brought to a plot of vacant land in the shadow of St. Mary Overy in Southwark. There they were used in the construction of the most famous of all English theaters. And this building, this immense and solid affirmation of the company's will to continue, was given a name that captured in a word the metaphor whereby these men justified their existence. That metaphor—that all the world's a stage—was encapsulated in the flag which flew above the new theater, showing Atlas bearing the entire world on his shoulders. The new playhouse was to be known as the Globe.

The structure grew rapidly, to the amazement of some and the dismay of others. By May of 1599 it was referred to as *"de novo edificata"* (newly built), and it was said to be *"in occupacione Willielmi Shakespeare et aliorum"* (in the possession of William Shakespeare and others). But the site was about halfway between Henslowe's house and his theater, the Rose; he quickly became alert to the threat to his own business. The Rose had not been well maintained, it was built on wet land, and it was going to look very unappealing once Burbage's operation got under way. The records of takings in the spring of 1599 show that, despite some better days, the Rose had lost a substantial part of its audience to the Lord Chamberlain's Men within a very short time of their transfer.

Alleyn and Henslowe acted rapidly to improve the situation: They leased land in Finsbury—higher, drier, and in an area (like Southwark) to which Londoners were accustomed to resort for recreation. Like the sites of the Theatre and the Curtain this land lay outside the city's jurisdiction, half a mile to the east. There the two men built a theater called the Fortune, between Golden Lane and Whitecross Street—there is still a Fortune Street on the site—and were open to paying customers in late 1600. Burbage's carpenter, Peter Street, worked to specifications that have survived to this day, constituting a valuable guide to the archaeology of the London stage in its greatest days. Meanwhile, the Rose was to fall from prominence, being shut for long periods, and not very profitable when reopened. The Lord Chamberlain's Men were a rival attraction so powerful that attempting to compete with them would have been pointless.

The Burbages and their associates were a strong and united group, convinced of the justice of their bold initiative against Allen (and the failure of Allen's repeated legal actions shows that their confidence was not misplaced). They leased the land for the Globe from Nicholas Brend. Half of the lease belonged to the Burbages; the other half was split among five sharers in the company, William Kemp, Augustine Phillips, Thomas Pope, John Heminges, and

Shakespeare himself. So each of these men had a 10 percent stake in the business, and they took steps now to make sure their families and heirs could profit from the new enterprise. The partnership was changed from a "joint tenancy" (in which a departing shareholder left his share to be divided among those remaining, until in time only one remained) into a "tenancy in common" (whereby a tenant could pass on his tenancy to his heirs).

The company's preeminence was now unarguable. In addition to their domination of the public theater, they performed at court during the Christmas seasons of 1598–9 (at the same time as they were moving the timbers of the Theatre across the river!), 1599–1600, 1600–1, and 1601–2, and they were also commissioned to perform at great houses, at the inns of court, and elsewhere.

Much Ado is not mentioned in Francis Meres's list of Shakespeare's plays in his *Palladis Tamia* of 1598. Its title appears in a list of plays dating from 1600. In the Quarto and Folio text, the first editions of the play, some of Dogberry's speeches are attributed to "Kempe" and those of Verges to "Cowley," so William Kemp and his sidekick Richard Cowley evidently created these comic roles in the aftermath of their success in the *Henry IV* plays. Since Kemp left the Lord Chamberlain's Men early in 1599, we can be fairly confident that the play dates from between the summer of 1598 and the spring of 1599.

The first, and only, quarto edition of the play appeared in 1600, as "*Much adoe about Nothing. As it hath been sundrie times publikely acted by the right honourable the Lord Chamberlaine his servants. Written by William Shakespeare.*" We should note the stress on public performance, and the unambiguous attribution to Shakespeare—the latter a relatively recent development. But records of the early performances have not survived. It is possible that it remained in the company's repertoire from then onward; certainly it was performed twice early in 1613, when the King's Men gave twenty court performances as part of the celebrations for the wedding of King James's daughter Princess Elizabeth. The play's abiding popularity, and the renown of its two leading comic characters, is attested by some lines in the poem that Leonard Digges prefaced to the 1640 edition of Shakespeare's *Poems*:

. . . let but Beatrice
And Benedick be seen, lo in a trice
The Cockpit, galleries, boxes, all are full.

In his copy of the 1632 Second Folio, King Charles I (who as a boy of twelve probably saw the performances at his sister's wedding) wrote "Benedik and Betrice" next to the title of the play.

The play continues to enjoy immense popularity on the stage, judging by the frequency of its revival—and that (refreshingly and instructively) despite the struggles that generations of critics have had to reconcile the apparent tension between the "festive" and "dark" elements in the play.

The year 1598 had seen the publication of the major, authorized edition of Sidney's *Arcadia*, alongside his other chief works, including the *Defence of Poetry* and *Astrophil and Stella*. This was a significant moment in English literature. Sidney was the first modern vernacular writer to be treated as an "author," with all the respect that the term implied in the Renaissance. As much because of his reputation as an exemplary Christian knight as for his literary gifts, Sidney, in contemporary eyes, dignified the profession of letters—even though it was a profession he himself had sought to avoid. Several writers, most notably Jonson, were inspired by Sidney's model and aspired to a similar dignity and status. Shakespeare seems to have been affected by the event in a different way. His writing was immediately and profoundly influenced by what he found in the handsome folio "collected works."

I do not simply mean that he recognized the *Arcadia* right away as an inexhaustible quarry for potential dramatic subjects. That, as the evidence of his own plays and those of countless other dramatists over the following forty years suggests, goes without saying. Nor indeed that he seems immediately to have been drawn to imitate Sidney's patterned eloquence and the way that social hierarchies in *Arcadia* are expressed through clearly distinguished levels of style—though such features are readily apparent in *Much Ado*, *As You Like It*, and *Twelfth Night*.

The most formally innovative quality about the *Arcadia* as Shakespeare read it is its genre. It is a genuine tragicomedy, a truly hybrid mixture of literary modes. The *Arcadia* that he read was much more of a mixed bag than Sidney had intended. It consisted

of the three books of the revised epic romance *Arcadia* which had
been left unfinished at Sidney's death, with the addition of the final
two books of an earlier version (known as the *Old Arcadia*, and not
published in full until this century). The three books of epic romance are rounded off with the plot reversals of a complicated tragicomedy to produce a work of disconcertingly mixed genre. Given
Sidney's literary reputation, his example authorized others to make
similar experiments.

From *Arcadia* comes the major reversal in Shakespeare's plot, the
apparent resurrection of Hero. In *Arcadia* Basilius, the king who is
supposed to be dead, wakes up during the trial of those accused of
killing him—potential tragedy turned in an instant into reconciliation by way of farce. From the same source come Dogberry and
Verges; Sidney uses a comically stupid shepherd, Dametas, to uncover the web of deceptions that had confused all the other characters. Beyond these two major debts to Sidney, playgoers familiar
with Sidney might have found more general reminiscences of *Arcadia* in the mixture of genre, combats of eloquence, the presence
of active evil (Don Pedro echoing Sidney's Cecropia), the concern
with reputation, and the use of such devices as reversal, resurrection, trials of virtue, disguise, and proxy wooing.

In this experimental tragicomedy, Shakespeare shows, within
the confines of a single play, the qualities that led Meres to praise
him as "the most excellent in both kinds for the stage." But as so
often, especially in his later plays, tragicomedy exists alongside
another mixed form, romance. By this I mean that the play represents a view of the world and of human beings that resists pigeon-
holing into the conventional categories of comedy and tragedy; an
implication is that a writer who seeks to imitate nature is obliged
to find a form that does justice to nature's contradictions, variety,
and amplitude. We will see later that in his romances Shakespeare
was to develop a vision of the human condition that was inescapably
double, both happy and sad, both noble and degrading. And *Much
Ado* embodies this view in embryo.

Shakespeare took the Claudio/Hero story, as he took so many
others, from Italian tradition—in this case from the fifth canto of
Ariosto's *Orlando Furioso*, which tells the tale of Ariodante and
Genevra. But there were two modern versions of it that he clearly
knew. One was in Sir John Harington's translation of Ariosto's

epic. The other was in Spenser's *Faerie Queene*—the story of Claribell, killed by her lover Phedon, who had been duped by his friend Philemon into thinking her unfaithful. There are numerous versions of the story, including ones by authors to whom Shakespeare turned regularly, such as Belleforest and Bandello, and a lost play performed by Merchant Taylor's schoolboys in 1583. But the most significant consideration is that while Ariosto makes his story a comedy, in which the lovers are united after coming very close to death, Spenser makes his a tragedy; the same material could be developed in two generically contradictory ways. So it was open to Shakespeare to take either route. In the end, he took both.

Throughout the play, Shakespeare exploits (as he would in *As You Like It*) the uncertain border between comedy and tragedy by making it hard to distinguish jokes from seriousness, game from earnest. This confuses some critics, and poses a particular problem for directors—less so perhaps for actors and audiences. An instance of this is the play's use of names. Some are very elevated, such as Hero and Beatrice, conjuring images of ideal women from ancient and modern times; likewise with Benedick, whose name includes the ideas of blessing and eloquence. But Dogberry, Verges, and Borachio are names from altogether less idealistic literary realms.

This matter of classification—and how it is approached—is inseparable from the play's broader concerns. One example is the play's treatment of relations between the sexes. Critics have recognized for a long time that Shakespeare presents us with a world divided into two realms: one female, the other male. The differences between their values, their attitudes, and their behavior are the source of both comic and potentially tragic components of the plot of *Much Ado*. A central preoccupation of *Much Ado*, as of *Troilus and Cressida*, is the perceived correspondence of relations between the sexes and warfare. Something that is normally and conventionally simply a metaphor is presented directly to us onstage. So in *Much Ado*, the "merry war" between Beatrice and Benedick takes place during an interval in a real war—and Hero is set to be a real enough casualty.

The differences between the sexes are also embodied in the distinct literary worlds the sexes inhabit: The men are associated not just with war and chivalry, but also with the simpler plot devices associated with tragedy and comedy. The women, on the other hand, are connected with the forms of tragicomedy, and, more especially, of romance. One of the chief qualities of romance is that its plot does not have the neat closure of classical tragedy or comedy. And throughout the Renaissance romance is a form associated with women, with female qualities and virtues.

When women wrote or spoke within this tradition, the aim was not to proceed to a conclusion or a proof, but rather to arrive at a truth that was multiple, comprehensive, open-ended. Renaissance history and fiction yield countless examples of courtly conversations involving, and often presided over by, women. Often their discourses are set in a time of rest after a war or a plague. This became the conventional setting for courtly games, for witty exchanges between men and women, and the play gives us several instances of this procedure. It was recognized as a distinctively female way of talking and arguing, and the rhetoric of such courtly language was crucially different from the humanist, schoolroom, or courtroom rhetoric in which men were trained. In addition, these women's games were often associated not just with rest but with recreation and healing.

We can see here, perhaps, parts of the context of *Much Ado*—and also, incidentally, of the exclusively and disastrously male debates in *Troilus*. In *Much Ado*, it is men who leap to conclusions. One of the play's many paradoxes is that in a piece so full of ostentatious eloquence it is the least eloquent characters, the constables with their absurd malapropisms ("comparisons are odorous"), who uncover truth, rather than the men who claim control of people and events.

While for the most part men and women constitute separate realms, speak distinct languages, and have their own characteristic rules, loyalties, and conventions, there are important qualifications to such a simple dichotomy. Shakespeare takes pains to construct a densely populated society, a teeming world for the action of the play to develop in. In such an environment it becomes evident, as in *Arcadia*, that it is impossible for events to be sealed off from their consequences. In addition, our attention is drawn to the social and familial forces that define and shape individual identity.

And change is possible, at least in one case. A crucial moment in the play comes when Benedick is given a searching test by Beatrice, in the shape of an injunction to defect from the world of men. She instructs him to "Kill Claudio." Beatrice cuts through the layers of verbal and gestural artifice and pretense. She shows that she recognizes the implications of Hero's disgrace. She is able to demonstrate conclusively to Benedick that Hero is a victim of men's attitudes to women.

The title of the play might be glossed in a cheerful way as "much ado about a foolish trifle" or "a great controversy about a woman's honor." Shakespeare himself in his sonnets used the conceit of a woman's sexuality as "nothing" compared to the male "something." Both men and women are involved in telling stories, making up fictions, making something out of "nothing." And both sexes are also involved in decoding, interpreting, "nothing."

The play abounds with pretense. Borachio, Don John, Claudio, Hero, and many others engage in a variety of deceptions—each makes a fiction, makes something out of nothing. And that is precisely what Shakespeare himself is doing, of course. *Much Ado* is a highly self-conscious play, in which Shakespeare holds up for our inspection both the act of pretending, of making fictions, and the act of observing, judging or interpreting. By heaping up these different pretenses and fictions Shakespeare demonstrates how difficult it is to read, interpret, and judge. Some of the examples are broadly positive—Don Pedro plays at love in order to generate love between Beatrice and Benedick, but also to stir love between Hero and Claudio. But most are negative, as when we see the way Claudio and Don John are so easily tricked. Above all, Claudio stage-manages an essentially theatrical event in his denunciation of Hero at the wedding. And Hero's revival, which prefigures the resurrections of the later plays, is also in its own way theatrical, manipulative, coercive.

We are presented with numerous fictions and supposes and invited to distinguish between them. As so often in Shakespeare, the crucial factor to be determined before constructing an interpretation is the will or disposition or motivation of the performer and the observer. It is therefore fitting that the last words, spoken as a kind of blessing, are given to Benedick, whose career in the play goes from eloquence (well-saying) to blessing (benediction). His story is figured as a beneficent process of education, under the guidance of Beatrice and the pressure of potentially tragic events, out of self-love into self-knowledge and integration with his "other" and with society more generally. Whether the rest of the male hierarchy learns very much from its experience—where only accidents and the goodwill of others have prevented a savage injustice—is a matter that is much harder to determine, and the play is wrapped up before the question can be raised.

So in the few years just before the turn of the century Shakespeare experienced some major changes of fortune, which included having to face the prospect of the suppression of the theaters and/or the financial ruin of his company. But he came out of this period with his personal status as a writer enhanced, his financial position secure beyond what he might have imagined even a few months before the lease was signed on February 21, 1599, and with the prospect of working with an outstanding group of actors in a venue that was immune from the city's threats. It was a challenge to which he would rise in the most astonishing fashion.

CHAPTER EIGHT

Art and Politics

Two political matters color everything produced for the stage in the last years of the sixteenth century. The first is the rise, rebellion, and subsequent fall of the earl of Essex. The second is the physical and mental decline of the queen and the uncertainty about what political arrangements would follow her imminent death. As a writer for the Lord Chamberlain's Men, Shakespeare had regular opportunities to observe the mood of the court and of the capital; as a professional, he had to assess the disposition of his audience. Further, as a protégé (since the poems) of the earl of Southampton he was personally close to a faction that was drawn over the precipice of a doomed attempt at a coup d'état. Newly installed in the Globe, and able to write for a company that had developed into one of the marvels of the age, Shakespeare, having arrived at the height of his powers, had to learn to walk a political tightrope.

The story of Henry V was familiar to Elizabethan theatergoers. In 1594, a play called *The Famous Victories of Henry the Fifth* was entered in the Stationers' Register—it was published in 1598, but may well date from 1588. In 1592, just four years after the defeat of the

Spanish Armada, Thomas Nashe (in *Pierce Penniless*) exclaimed that it was "a glorious thing" to have "Henry the Fifth represented on stage, leading the French King prisoner." There was a new play on the subject playing at Henslowe's Rose during the 1595–6 season, and the king's costume was listed in the inventory of properties held by the Admiral's Men in 1598.

So why did Shakespeare feel the need to add another play on the subject? On one level, the move to the Globe might well have encouraged an attempt at a new version of a "South Bank" theme: Shakespeare and Burbage might well have wished to show themselves the superiors of Alleyn and his scriptwriters. They also responded to the implications of the Globe's proud name, and the story of Henry V had the grandeur and epic sweep, as well as the imperial connotations, of *Julius Caesar*, on which Shakespeare was also working during 1599.

A more immediate stimulus was the short-lived tide of patriotic optimism associated with the preparations made by the earl of Essex for his campaign in Ireland. From November 1598 until Essex's departure in late March 1599, expectations were aroused of a final punitive strike against the Irish rebels led by the earl of Tyrone. Then, in late September, as *Julius Caesar* was playing to packed houses at the Globe, Essex came back to London unexpectedly. After an initially friendly reception by the queen on the twenty-eighth, the next day Essex was placed under arrest at the house of the lord keeper as word began to spread of the dismal failure of the expedition. Factions formed, gossip raged, and the court seethed with plots, intrigues, and rumors. A powerful political grouping at court was warmly receptive to news and speculation about the troubles of the campaign, and about possible treachery by its commander. As early as June it had become evident that Essex could not possibly win a decisive victory, and to the glee of his opponents was added the disappointment of many of his supporters.

Thus, when we hear the chorus introduce Act V in the following words, it is pretty certain that they were composed either before the army left or in the early days of the expedition. Only then could a comparison between the triumphant return of Henry V from his French victories and that of Essex be entertained:

As, by a lower but high-loving likelihood,
Were now the General of our gracious Empress—
As in good time he may—from Ireland coming,
Bringing rebellion broached on his sword,
How many would the peaceful city quit
To welcome him! . . .

So we can date the play more exactly than most. But it can be misleading to place too much emphasis on the contemporary context—to suppose that the play's strangeness can be somehow explained away by relating it to popular enthusiasm for war or to Shakespeare's attempt to provide a suitable script for the new playhouse. What we see and hear challenges such simple ideas of how events connect with each other, and makes us alert to the ease with which interpretation can become a species of self-delusion.

The strangeness referred to above may require some explanation. We may be used to thinking of the play as the epic culmination of Shakespeare's sequence of historical dramas, as a triumphal display celebrating a king who managed to excel both as a ruler and as a man; and we may remember the patriotic speeches and victories. But if we look carefully at the piece it becomes clear that Shakespeare has created a very striking hybrid. Take the play's language, for example. There are whole scenes in French, as well as extensive passages in approximations to Scottish, Irish, and Welsh dialects. Then there are the contrasts between the language of courtiers and that of the low-life figures, between the legalistic words of the bishops and the bombast of the French nobility, and so on. As for the action of the play, Shakespeare uses a chorus as he had done in *Romeo and Juliet*, and oscillates between narrative and dramatic modes of presentation, between telling and showing. Attention is thereby directed to the art of the piece; we are aware that the scenes we see have been chosen carefully from a much more ample store of historical material, and that our view is being guided. And the scenes that appear are as diverse as the play's language. We see debates, battles, tricks, wooing, low comedy, pathos, spectacle, and so on.

And how are we to make some sense or order out of such multifariousness? The king's stirring "Once more unto the breach, dear

friends," for instance, is immediately followed by the absurd spectacle of Pistol crying out: "On, on, on, on, on! To the breach, to
the breach!" Shakespeare seems to be challenging us to refrain from
seeing the latter as a parody of the former, as something which
undermines its forces. He seems to want us to hold two things
simultaneously in our minds: to find the king's words impressive
and Pistol's ludicrous. At the start of the play the chorus directly
asks the audience, "Piece out our imperfections with your
thoughts," and we seem to be required to make the connections
between events, to leap across the sea and across time, to engage
very fully with that we see and hear. But the earlier history plays
had shown what human beings are notably fallible interpreters of
history. The tragic story of Henry IV had demonstrated the folly
of jumping to conclusions about the shape of historical events. And
in *Henry V* Shakespeare gives us a spectacular negative example of
how not to do it.

Just after the king's order to kill the prisoners and noncombatants
has been carried out, the two Welsh officers, Fluellen and Gower,
provide their own commentary on events. Gower is content to
praise the king in terms of the present—"the King, most worthily,
hath caus'd every soldier to cut his prisoner's throat. O, 'tis a gallant
king!" But Fluellen wants to put this in a proper historical context,
and ascertains that Alexander the great ("Alexander the Pig") had
been born in Macedon. Then he solemnly develops a comparison
between Henry and Alexander. (Shakespeare's joke springs from a
heavy-handed spoof of the Welsh accent, reflected in the odd spelling.)

> I think it is in Macedon where Alexander is porn. I tell you, captain,
> if you look in the maps of the orld, you sall find, in the comparisons
> between Macedon and Monmouth, that the situations, look you, is
> both alike. There is a river in Macedon, and there is also moreover
> a river at Monmouth. It is called Wye at Monmouth; but it is out
> of my prains what is the name of the other river; but 'tis all one,
> 'tis alike as my fingers is to my fingers, and there is salmons in both.
> If you mark Alexander's life well, Harry of Monmouth's life is come
> after it indifferent well, for there is figures in all things. Alexander,
> God knows, and you know, in his rages, and his furies, and his
> wraths, and his cholers, and his moods, and his displeasures, and
> his indignations, and also being a little intoxicates in his prains, did,

in his ales and his angers, look you, kill his best friend, Clytus. . . . I
speak but in the figures and comparisons of it: as Alexander kill'd
his friend Clytus, being in his ales and his cups; so also Harry
Monmouth, being in his right wits and his good judgements, turn'd
away the fat knight with the great belly doublet . . . I'll tell you
there is good men porn at Monmouth.

Odorous comparisons indeed. While there may be points of similarity between Alexander and Henry, the basis of Fluellen's dis-
quisition—that there is a river in Macedon as well as a river in
Monmouth—draws attention to a common feature of historical
comparison: its unavoidable selectiveness. It is a characteristically
bold move from Shakespeare—who is himself writing an interpretation of history—to furnish us with so memorable and vivid an
illustration of the limitations of the subject. The move is even more
surprising in that it seems to parody the method of Plutarch, whose
Lives were organized in parallel in order to illustrate correspondences between Greeks and Romans. What is more, Shakespeare
was at this very moment reading Plutarch's life of Caesar (the source
of *Julius Caesar*, which he was to write immediately after *Henry V*);
and Plutarch's parallel life to Caesar's was that of Alexander the
Great. But we do also have a more positive, less compromised
version of the reading of history.

While everyone else in the play participates in the human capacity for self-delusion and wishful thinking, only Henry takes a
broader view. In such a noisy play, a play so wordy and busy, so
full of acting and disembling and public exchanges, the king's soliloquy stands out as a moment of stillness and clarity—though
even that is delivered in disguise and under cover of darkness.

On the night before the battle, the king passes in disguise through
his army and falls into argument and discussion, much of it highly
critical of his policy. When left alone, he speaks at length in terms
that recall his father's nocturnal meditations:

What infinite heart's ease
Must kings neglect, that private men enjoy!

leading to the conclusion that he bears all the responsibility for his
people so that they may sleep safely in their beds:

The slave, a member of the country's peace,
Enjoys it; but in gross brain little wots
What watch the King keeps to maintain the peace,
Whose hours the peasant best advantages.

But he does not stop there. He frankly acknowledges the sin of
rebellion that led to his inheriting the throne, and to appeal for
mercy. Specifically he asks God to hold back his judgment on him
at least for the duration of hostilities. He pleads:

Not to-day, O Lord,
O, not to-day, think not upon the fault
My father made in compassing the crown!

And he records the various pious strategies he has deployed to try
to make up for his father's seizing the throne:

I Richard's body have interred new,
And on it have bestowed more contrite tears,
Than from it issued forced drops of blood.
Five hundred poor I have in yearly pay,
Who twice a day their wither'd hands hold up
Toward heaven, to pardon blood: and I have built
Two chantries, where the sad and solemn priests
Sing still for Richard's soul. More will I do;
Though all that I can do is nothing worth,
Since that my penitence comes after all,
Imploring pardon.

The audience at the Globe knew that nobody sang still for Richard's
soul. All the chantries had been closed down sixty years earlier.
They also knew that Henry's victory in France had proved unsus-
tainable, and that his years of glory were followed by decades of
brutal civil war. But nevertheless this soliloquy, placed at the core
of the play, stands as a moment of plainness, clarity, and understanding. In a way that recalls Henry VI on his molehill, it is
surrounded by deceptions, fictions, and the turmoil of battle. But
this latter speech is the reverse of self-indulgent self-dramatization;
the king, unlike his son in the earlier play, adopts a priestly role
and displays a profound recognition of the limits of his own powers.
The speech makes the marvelous military triumph of Agincourt

seem more clearly the work of the Almighty, a providential sweeping away of the enemy that prefigures the Armada.

The soliloquy is the very center of the presentation of Henry, but he appears in numerous manifestations in the course of the play. If it were not for this guarantee that he had a core to his nature, there could hardly be a monarch who was—on the surface— more removed from the motto Elizabeth gave herself—*Semper eadem*, or "always the same." His performance recalls another facet of the queen, epitomized in her famous remark that "we princes are set on stages, in the sight of all the world duly observed." To survive, the implication seems to be, a monarch needs to possess both a firm sense of self and personal integrity and at the same time a grasp of the theatricality of the arts of power. As the play unfolds, this is the disconcertingly Machiavellian lesson taught by the successful career of this great soldier-prince.

Just as Spenser celebrated Elizabeth in paradoxical terms—paradoxes typified by her colony in "fruitfullest *Virginia*"—so did Shakespeare with *Henry V*. And just as Spenser defended the scale and variety of his epic romance by saying that its multifariousness was the only way of approximating to the variety of his queen's gifts, so Shakespeare defends his own art in the theater by showing that theatricality is not necessarily the opposite of truth or virtue. He also rides a favorite hobbyhorse in the play, contrasting Henry's protean pragmatism with the nostalgic idealism and chivalry of Fluellen, Pistol, and the French court.

The fact that Shakespeare's Henry is shown to be both a hero and a pragmatist has repeatedly disturbed commentators and has given rise to a variety of theatrical and critical readings. Indeed, the play has been hijacked to support contradictory ideological positions, now conservative, now radical. Most would agree that to conclude that the king is either a paragon or a Machiavel is to oversimplify a delicate, and, I would argue, deliberately unresolved matter. For the relationship between honor (whether personal or military) and expediency was a highly charged question in the politics of the late 1590s, and it constituted an area of debate between Essex and his followers (who saw themselves as embodiments of chivalric honor) and the political establishment (easily stereotyped as soulless pragmatists). That the play should to this day resist unequivocal identification with either camp is a mark of the

skill with which Shakespeare—like his contemporaries—had to negotiate a path between powerful opposing forces. More positively,
by furnishing Henry with a moment of privacy in which he can
talk undisguisedly and with a degree of self-knowledge, he provides
an underpinning for the king's shape-shifting theatricality. On a
broader level the tremendous stylistic, linguistic, generic, national,
and representational variety of the play is an extended metaphor
for the concept of *e pluribus unum*, an articulation of national integrity.

As seen in the case of *More*, this was an age when writers could
face real problems with the censoring authorities. When in Book 5
of *The Faerie Queene* Spenser depicted the exemplary silencing of
the poet Mal Font, whose tongue was nailed to a post, he was close
to the world in which writers faced the prospect of mutilation,
imprisonment, and disgrace. Yet Shakespeare seems to have been
able to deal with politically sensitive material without suffering any
obvious penalty. No less notable, perhaps, is his failure to become
involved in the literary squabbles that were such a feature of these
years.

When John Marston's satires were publicly burned in 1599, his
vituperative energies were diverted from attacks upon fellow Inns
of Court intellectuals to other targets, and he switched genres from
verse satire to satirical drama. He seized upon Jonson as an object
for scorn, and the two men then embarked upon a public quarrel
that involved several other writers and filled not a few theaters
during the next two years, generating plays such as *The Player
Whipt, Poetaster, The Untrussing of the Humourous Poet*, and Dekker's
Satiromastix. With the exception of a few lines in *Hamlet*, and one
or two allusions in *Troilus and Cressida*, Shakespeare kept out of the
affair, known to posterity as the "war of the theaters." But where
he managed to tiptoe his way through the minefield of court performance with a high degree of nimbleness, others did not always
display the same tact.

Jonson was still seeking a more elevated role in the cultural and
political life of the court. Irritated and humiliated by the low status
accorded to scriptwriters, he aspired to the status of those gentlemen
playwrights whose works were staged by the boys' companies,
usually more responsive to an author's wishes. But he botched his
opportunity. He was desperate to be involved in the "solemn revels"

being prepared at court for the winter season of 1600–1, and he chose a subject that in his view represented the current political situation very clearly.

Essex had fallen into disgrace, not least because, on his return from the failed expedition to Ireland, he had burst unannounced into the queen's chamber. On a parallel with the story of Diana and Actaeon, Jonson constructed his play *Cynthia's Revels*, with the anti-Essex alternative title *The Fountain of Self-Love*. The plot ends with a victory for a young poet, Criticus (a scarcely disguised version of Jonson himself), who is rewarded by the patronage and protection of the queen.

In the real world, Jonson's fate was very different from this fantasy. The play did not secure royal patronage; worse, it seems to have irritated many of the watching courtiers. So Jonson had to carry on squabbling with other writers, and his chance of being appointed official scourge of vice and hypocrisy was lost. Meanwhile, Shakespeare treated politics in a contrasting, much more oblique and indirect way. And he enjoyed marked success.

We can be confident about dating *Julius Caesar*, since we know it was being performed in the newly built Globe in the autumn of 1599. In the audience on September 21 was a Swiss traveler named Thomas Platter, a doctor from Basle, and he recorded the experience in his diary:

> On September 21st after dinner, about two o'clock, I and my party went across the water, and there in the house with the straw thatched roof we witnessed the tragedy of the first Emperor Julius Caesar, very excellently performed, with about fifteen characters. When the play ended they danced admirably and most gracefully together, as their custom is, two dressed as men and two as women.

Platter's reference to the straw thatch may indicate that the Globe's bright new straw stood out from the vermin-infested thatch of neighboring buildings, and from the tiles of the large structures on the south bank. The dance—the jig with which many theatrical performances closed—is a reminder of how distant our experience of Elizabethan drama is from what playgoers saw then. It was common to conclude plays, including tragedies, with a jig—a lively, sometimes farcical afterpiece, and Shakespeare had ended *Part 2 Henry IV* with one, presumably performed by Kemp. Not surprisingly, serious dramatists (including Shakespeare and Jonson) complained that the less sophisticated members of the audience tended to be impatient for the drama to end so that they could enjoy the broad humor of the jig. But the fashion proved resilient on the public stages.

That Platter should have seen a play on Julius Caesar is not unusual—there were numerous treatments of the theme—but that he saw it on a public stage is significant. Other Caesar plays had been the products of academic environments, such as *Caesar Interfectus*, presented at Oxford in 1582. The tradition includes the Senecan tragedies by Muret (1553) and by Grévin (1561), as well as Kyd's *Cornelia* (1594—translated from Robert Garnier's *Cornélie*), the anonymous *Caesar's Revenge*, and Sir William Alexander's *Tragedy of Julius Caesar* (1604).

Shakespeare writes with an eye on this tradition, but with a clear sense of how different the public stages are from so-called "closet" drama that is, drama for the study rather than the stage. As in *Macbeth* and *Antony and Cleopatra*, his drama stands in relation to academic plays as films do to stage plays. He removes the walls of the closet and broadens the sweep of his treatment, encompassing scenes and events that were beyond the range of the academic drama.

In particular, he was writing for actors who had developed an unprecedented degree of sophistication in character portrayal. And in this play he stretched his leading players to new limits. The earliest classical historians had written about the great men of their day in terms of contrasts and antitheses. Thus Caesar was possessed of virtues (an able general, a distinguished orator, a public benefactor) as well as failings (he was ambitious and ruthless). And while Brutus slew his patron and misread the tide of history, he was at the same time a sincere patriot. Later traditions, as they would have been available to Shakespeare, amplified these contrasts. To a medieval tradition condemning the conspirators as traitors was added a Renaissance admiration for republican virtues. For Montaigne Caesar was spoiled by his vanity and ambition:

> This only vice . . . lost, and overthrew in him the fairest natural
> and richest ingenuity that ever was; and hath made his memory

abominable to all honest minds, insomuch as by the ruin of his country, and subversion of the mightiest state and most flourishing Commonwealth that ever the world shall see, he went about to procure his glory.

Such contradictions are meat and drink to a scholar in the privacy of his study. For an actor they pose a professional challenge, and Shakespeare seems to go out of his way to make each of the major actors in the play ambiguous or problematical in some way, extending the equivocal presentation of Henry V to a large group of characters. He required Burbage and his troupe to embody the contradictions that commentators had identified in these men; the dry reflections of moralized history were to come alive under the afternoon sun on the Bankside.

Similarly, Shakespeare included material that would have been familiar from schooldays, much as he had in the earliest comedies. There are several set-piece debates and formal speeches that recall the schoolroom. Perhaps the most obvious instance is the contrasting orations delivered by Brutus and Mark Antony over the body of Caesar. But there are many others—such as Cassius's "temptation" of Brutus early in the action. Again, these staples of a much drier tradition are animated by their context, by the act of performance at the Globe.

The familiarity of the story, and of the problems it could throw up, may in some measure account for the play's brevity—the audience would not need to have the implications of the action spelled out. As in *Henry V*, Shakespeare could direct their attention to particular points in the narrative; and here the material was so well known that no chorus was needed. Like its predecessor, this is also a generically various work, hovering between history and tragedy (and if it is a tragedy, whose tragedy is it—Caesar's or Brutus's?) and furnishing us with a wide range of dramatic set-pieces. We have day scenes, night scenes, mobs, conspiracies, omens, pageants, battles, debates, soliloquies, and ghosts.

As so often in Shakespeare's more learned plays (*Antony and Cleopatra* and *Troilus and Cressida* are other examples), the audience's expectations are central to the conception of the work. What can Thomas Platter have thought when he went to see the tragedy (in his words) of the first emperor, only to find that the great soldier was presented as a vain, frail, deaf old man, and that he was in any case dead halfway through the action? Spectators on the Bankside would not have found Shakespeare's Ancient Rome an austere and lofty world, far removed from the present, but rather a prefiguring of the contemporary situation, where Essex and the Council staged a competition between idealism and pragmatism, and also a relation to the popular dramatic form of the revenge play. And although they would have grasped, as in the other historical plays, that the patterns to be discerned in human affairs correspond to the operations of providence rather than to the schemes of mortals, they would also have been directed time after time toward the internal conflicts tormenting the protagonists, to see human beings struggling to know themselves and to read their times.

As much as in the comedies of this period, Shakespeare constructs hierarchies of language, ranging from oracles through the formally impersonal to the tumultuously colloquial—a variety established in the very first scene, with its punning rebels and its nobles who speak one language in public and another among their own kind. And Shakespeare directs the audience to be sensitive to evasiveness and self-deception. So when Cassius tempts Brutus a little later, the measured and reserved syntax of the superficially dispassionate response nevertheless conveys a clear sense of the way Brutus will resolve the war within himself:

> That you do love me, I am nothing jealous;
> What you would work me to, I have some aim.
> How I have thought of this, and of these times,
> I shall recount hereafter. For this present,
> I would not (so with love I might entreat you)
> Be any further mov'd. What you have said
> I will consider; what you have to say
> I will with patience hear, and find a time
> Both meet to hear and answer such high things.

Through such speeches the audience is prepared to see beneath the surface of the rhetoric politicians use—most notably in the scene in the forum after Caesar's death. Just after that we are shown, in a very brief scene, an event that epitomizes the savagery of the forces unleashed both by the assassination and by the manipulation of the Roman crowd. The mob crowds in on Cinna the poet and quizzes him roughly:

Cinna: I am going to Caesar's funeral.
1. Pleb.: As a friend or an enemy?
Cinna: As a friend. . . .
3. Pleb.: Your name, sir, truly.
Cinna: Truly, my name is Cinna.
1. Pleb.: Tear him to pieces, he's a conspirator.
Cinna: I am Cinna the poet, I am Cinna the poet.
4. Pleb.: Tear him for his bad verses, tear him for his bad verses.
Cinna: I am not Cinna the conspirator.
4. Pleb.: It is no matter, his name's Cinna. Pluck but his name from his heart, and turn him going. . . .

This horrific scene is a moment of unjust brutality; it is also an instance of deliberate misreading, of a conscious suppression of evidence. On a more self-conscious level, Shakespeare was providing an instance of the vulnerability of art—Cinna, after all, was the author of a celebrated epic poem, of which only a few fragmentary lines have survived—to the caprices and vagaries of political fortunes.

The play is full of such moments, where an immediate dramatic incident is shaped in such a way as to prompt broader reflections. Shakespeare's reading—in particular, Montaigne's *Essays* and Plutarch's *Lives*—encouraged him to take a wider, more philosophical view.

But at the same time the whole play seems designed to make an issue of the very fact of its own existence and particular qualities. The first audiences were not reading a treatise in political philosophy; nor were they participating in an academic debate or university play; nor were they witnessing the standard fare offered at the nearby Rose. Shakespeare's retelling of the Caesar story is entrusted to actors, whose skill reanimates and depicts the ethical dilemmas and contradictions of the men they impersonate. And the theatrical event, the very act of staging the story, is presented as an activity that can actually recreate incidents lost in the mists of time, making them happen again now as we watch them.

Just after the death of Caesar, the conspirators lock the doors of the chamber (though they cannot exclude us, the audience) and try to prepare their presentation of their action to the Roman people. They do so by inventing a ceremony in which they wash their hands in the blood of their victim. And the exchange between Brutus and Cassius collapses the distance between ancient Rome and modern London:

> Brutus: Stoop, Romans, stoop,
> And let us bathe our hands in Caesar's blood,
> Up to the elbows, and besmear our swords;
> Then walk we forth, even to the market-place,
> And waving our red weapons o'er our heads,
> Let's all cry, "peace, freedom, and liberty!"
> Cassius: Stoop then, and wash. How many ages hence
> Shall this our lofty scene be acted over
> In states unborn and accents yet unknown!
> Brutus: How many times shall Caesar bleed in sport,
> That now on Pompey's basis lies along
> No worthier than the dust!

It is as if Shakespeare is challenging us to imagine we are eavesdropping on a turning point in world history, on the participants imaging how they will be seen by us. After all, in a literal sense, the Caesar we see is bleeding "in sport" and the actors, from a state then unborn, are speaking English. But Brutus says Caesar is dead "now," and in so doing asserts an authenticity that in an odd way is strengthened by the theatrical self-consciousness. Shakespeare stakes the entire illusion of his play on that word "now," on the immediacy of the theatrical event that connects Caesar's Rome with Elizabethan London.

All the evidence suggests that *Julius Caesar* was as popular in its own day as it has been ever since. Allusions to it spring up instantly: phrases and incidents in the writings of Jonson, Michael Drayton, John Weever, and others are tokens of the play's impact. Though it was not published until the Folio, it enjoyed a high reputation from its stage performances. And with its combination of gravity and theatricality, of ethical seriousness and dense characterization, it marked a new beginning in Shakespeare's art. It also probably coincided with a major development in the composition of the Lord Chamberlain's Men.

William Kemp had been the last of the great Elizabethan clowns, and his departure signaled the end of a tradition. Kemp's talent as a clown—a profession in which he saw himself as Tarleton's heir—had been to produce and perform in the jigs, dances, and other diversions that were part of the whole experience of performance on the public stages. And when he left the company, it was to embark on a marathon dance to Norwich after which he became the first "Nine-Days' Wonder" as a result of the publicity he generated by this escapade.

Yet he must also have been a considerable actor. His range included the conventional clowning of Peter in *Romeo and Juliet* and the memorable comedy and pathos of both Dogberry and Falstaff. His skill seems to have developed in two rather different directions: one the off-the-cuff exchange of repartee with an audience, and the other a specialization in playing blustering, bogus authority figures. In one of the Parnassus plays, Kemp appears as himself, and teaches an undergraduate how to set about playing the part of a "foolish mayor or a foolish justice of the peace." Such a range suggests that he was able to adapt to the new sophistication of the stage and to submit himself—reluctantly—to the novel discipline of scripts that left few openings for extempore digressions and jigs.

After Kemp's departure early in 1599, Shakespeare's comic writing understandably reflects the loss of one of his major performers. But Kemp was replaced by another remarkable figure, Robert Armin, whose distinctive, innovative style gave the company and its chief dramatist possibilities hitherto undreamed of. Armin was to create Touchstone in *As You Like It*, Feste in *Twelfth Night*, and then, at the height of his powers, the Fool in *King Lear*. Not for him the pomposity and malapropisms of Kemp; his style was to quibble with words, to twist their sense, to play the role of the professional fool whose task was to invert conventional categories, to prove the wise to be fools and reveal the wisdom of his own apparent folly.

A notable feature of Shakespeare's writing in mid-career is his choice of extremely familiar material on which to construct his plays, and this applies as much to *As You Like It* as to the histories and tragedies written at the same time, 1600; the play was entered in the Stationers' Register on August 4 of that year. Shakespeare based his play—whose throwaway title links it to *Twelfth Night, Or What You Will*—on Thomas Lodge's hugely popular prose romance *Rosalynde* (1590). While Lodge's fiction claims close kinship with the courtly romances of John Lyly, *Rosalynde* is more obviously middle class and more explicitly a vehicle for moral instruction. Lodge tells his readers that he deploys "precepts that shall leade you unto vertue," and they are urged to "read it . . . to profit by it." He structures his tale on the basis of discussions and debates on such questions as "whether Fortune or Nature were more prodigall." There is a great deal of psychological self-questioning, too, and he depicts his speakers' inner debates, weighing love against duty, love of virtue against love of wealth. And unlike Lyly's fictions, which are open-ended and resist narrative closure, *Rosalynde* comes to a definite ending with the marriage of the leading characters.

Most Renaissance treatments of love emphasized its multifariousness, its variety. *As You Like It* recalls Spenser's observation in *The Faerie Queene:*

> Wonder it is to see, in diuerse minds,
> How diuersly loue doth his pageants play,
> And shewes his powre in variable kinds:

The play provides numerous demonstrations of love's diversity, the most striking of which is the group marriage at the end (four couples—the largest number Shakespeare was ever to show onstage), with its procession of different kinds of lovers (like the animals rushing for Noah's Ark, as Jaques jibes). And the play itself is a compilation of the "variable kinds"—comedy, satire, epic, tragedy, and so on. It was also conventional to find within this variety of love a series of paradoxes, and in *As You Like It* we are constantly presented with proverbial wisdom couched in conundrums, riddles, and paradoxes ("the truest poetry is the most feigning"; "the fool doth think he is wide, but the wise man knows himself to be a fool").

Some critics have called *As You Like It* plotless. In fact, it is as elaborately plotted as any formal Renaissance garden. And like such a garden, it is a space in which art confronts nature, combats it, and seeks to outdo it. The play's basic structure, like that of a garden, is simple: the conventional pastoral pattern of banishment, exile, and return. Within that framework contrasts abound: court and country, youth and age, innocence and experience, nature and nurture, judgment and forgiveness. But throughout, Shakespeare sets up expectations only to show how unreliable they are.

There are passages that contribute to the sense of escapism, of retreat, of action set in a forest where normal rules do not seem to apply. We might think of Orlando's words, "There's no clock in the forest," or those of the exiled Duke Senior—"Here feel we not the penalty of Adam." The word *tomorrow* occurs thirteen times in the play: three times in the first scene, and then ten in the last act. It is as if the middle of the play is set in a suspended time, when there is no awareness of a future.

But that is only part of the story. The situation in Arden is very different: Rosalind, Celia, and Touchstone survive in the forest because Celia wisely made provision before they left—"Let's get our jewels and our plate together"—so that they could buy their way into the pastoral economy (and she seems to have brought a traveling clock—Elizabethan high technology—as well). For others, the conditions are harsher. Corin remarks:

> I am shepherd to another man
> And do not shear the fleeces that I graze.
> My master is of churlish disposition.

And when Adam, poor though he is, offers to give all his savings to help Orlando, the young man's praise is directed out to an audience of his own time, to the world of enclosures, the beginnings of a wage economy:

> O good old man, how well in thee appears
> The constant service of the antique world,
> When service sweat for duty, not for meed.
> Thou art not for the fashion of these times . . .

Of course the play contains idyllic moments, and features play, sport, recreation—but the context is the world of death, betrayal, and power, of work, of wages. And Shakespeare reminds us that even the "sports" (wrestling, hunting, wooing) have painful con-

sequences (broken limbs, bleeding carcasses, cuckold's horns). The
pastoral world we see is populated by more than a group of noble
exiles in philosophical retreat. There is hunting, poverty, winter.
The reiterated exhortations to be patient would sound more at home
in a tragedy. At one point an army is said to be on its way, though
Shakespeare stops short of depicting the more extreme violence of
Rosalynde, which had featured pitched battles. The hunting horn,
the antlers of the stag, are celebrated as signs of victory, but they
are also badges of cuckoldry, of betrayal, and humiliation. When
Corin asks Touchstone, "How like you this shepherd's life?" his
simple question is misconstrued. The courtly fool Touchstone
thinks the shepherd is embarking on the courtly pastoral pursuit
of the eclogue, the literary dialogue in which fictional shepherds
lamented their lofty passions turn and turn about (in Virgil's phrase,
"Alternate song is what the Muses love"). But to Corin, their exchange is stupid; his wisdom is acquired by experience rather than
from books. Sheep are his livelihood, not an opportunity to follow
the promptings of a visiting gentleman to conform to fashionable
literary stereotype. He says:

> You have too courtly a wit for me. . . . Sir, I am a true labourer: I
> earn that I eat, get that I wear, owe no man hate, envy no man's
> happiness, glad of other men's good, content with my harm, and
> the greatest of my pride is to see my ewes graze and my lambs suck.

In this play, melancholy is embodied in the punningly named
Jaques (*Jakes* equals *privy*). Melancholy was said in those days to
arise from an excess of black bile in the system, and scholars from
Aristotle onward had observed that when black bile was heated it
gave off vapors which could inspire the subject to great insight or
bravery. The presiding deity of melancholy was Saturn—crafty,
secretive, inimical to love, unforgiving.

More generally, the study of melancholy was one of the ways
in which the Elizabethans tried to make sense of the inner workings
of the human mind—*Hamlet* provides the fullest instance. A professional melancholic like Jaques was someone who declared impa-
tience at human pretense and scorn of mortal folly. Like the fool,
he had a license to speak plainly to his lord, to offer satire and
criticism directly where other courtiers had to be more oblique.

Duke Senior keeps Jaques by him for the "matter" that flows from him in his "sullen fits."

Experience eventually leads most characters in the play toward love, forgiveness, and companionship. Most find that the certainties with which they had approached their time in Arden, or the proverbs with which their education had equipped them to combat the blows of fortune, do not survive the pastoral world. For the melancholy Jaques, however, his profit from experience is a sense of separation, isolation, and removal from the procreative impulse. Like Malvolio, he is excluded from the unions that end the play, though his exclusion is presented as a conscious choice to be separate. The verbal battle between Jaques and Orlando, "Monsieur Melancholy" versus "Signior Love," is finally resolved when Jaques is proved to be a fool, someone absorbed in himself, gazing on his own image. Love is figured in the play as the opposite of narcissism, as union with the other, as a force that drives individuals out from themselves to discover their identity in society and in their loved ones. Jaques, like Touchstone, is part of the material that Shakespeare added to his source, furnishing new layers of contrast, commentary, and context for the two central love stories.

In *As You Like It*, as in most of his comedies, Shakespeare challenges conventional assumptions about literary categories, about the distinctions between "serious" and "comic" writing, between instruction and entertainment. The text's apparent self-consciousness focuses attention on its own literariness and playfulness, its own status as fiction. There are major set-pieces such as the wrestling, the Seven Ages of Man speech, the scattering of poems in the forest, the definition of the lie, the appearance of Hymen, and so forth. And there are plenty of moments where we are reminded of the play's implausibility; most of the major characters ask "Is it possible?" or words to that effect.

In addition, the play calls upon a surprisingly elevated sphere of literary allusion. For example, Orlando's name conjures up both the French *Chanson de Roland* and the great Italian epic *Orlando Furioso*. And at times Shakespeare's Orlando (wrestler, swordsman, lover, champion of the oppressed) is as mad in love, as bold and headstrong as his Italian counterpart. We might also recall that Roland's close friend was Oliver, and as a pair they were as celebrated as David and Jonathan. And yet *As You Like It* begins with

Orlando and Oliver fighting; the brothers' squabble suggests the disruption of a proverbially intense friendship, as well as family stability. Later, when Orlando carries Adam, he recreates the scene from Virgil's *Aeneid* where Aeneas carries Anchises from the flaming ruins of Troy (an allusion supported by Adam's warning that Oliver intends to burn down Orlando's lodgings). There are also plenty of biblical echoes: to Adam, to Cain and Abel, to Noah's Ark, to the prodigal son, to the Sermon on the Mount. Meanwhile, the play draws on the Robin Hood legends, with both Rosalind and Orlando sharing Robin's characteristics of boldness, ingenuity, and dedication to restoring ancient rights illegally taken away.

The cumulative effect of these allusions (and the others, to Ovid, to Rabelais, to Sidney, to Marlowe, to Greene) is to suggest that the events played out before us have a meaning, that they touch on questions much larger than a lighthearted escapist romance. And through these suggestions and implications other categories are questioned, too.

"If I were a woman, I would kiss as many of you as had beards that pleas'd me": Rosalind's epilogue would have had a special resonance in Shakespeare's theater, where, of course, it was spoken by a boy. Throughout the play Rosalind floats freely between male and female identities, and her control over events in Arden depends partly on her ability to fit her gender to the predicaments she faces. At one level, her actions are a version of the ways in which Queen Elizabeth had based her political strategies on a fluid sexual identity—now austere and virginal, now flirtatious, now majestic. At another, Shakespeare seems to be participating in the widespread anxiety of the late 1590s caused by the so-called "masterless women": women (from any social class) who lived independently, who were free to choose not to live within the traditionally male-dominated household. And that, perhaps, is why the play ends with the boy actor reminding us that he is a boy: The audience has observed an inversion of normal social conventions, has seen "women on top," and perhaps needs to be reassured that it was all a dream, a game, a carnival.

The play is literary, as I have suggested, in a very self-conscious way. But it also subjects to scrutiny the claims that literature has traditionally made for itself, and in places echoes the words of Sidney's *Defence of Poetry*. Right at the end, there is a moment where conventional notions of plausibility have to be jettisoned, when a god—Hymen, the god of marriage—appears onstage to bless the unions established primarily through Rosalind's endeavors, but also through a general access of goodwill.

Shakespeare prepares the ground for this bizarre episode, this flight into a new realm that we would call "magic realism" today, in Touchstone's speech about kinds of lying. The speech clearly refers at some level to that kind of lying discourse to which fiction belongs. Sidney had defended poets against the ancient charge that they are liars by declaring that "The poet nothing affirms, and therefore never lyeth." Shakespeare's defense is similar. Touchstone ends his anatomy of mendacity by declaring that "your 'if' is the only peacemaker. Much virtue in 'if.' " The audience is invited to imagine that what is staged at the end really takes place, to agree to an "if," to suppose that the fiction is true. By giving its assent to the "if," the audience is somehow involved in the harmony of the resolution, implicated in the "suppose," in the suspension of disbelief which crowns the end.

It is as if, when all is over, Hymen's words to the assembly are addressed to us: "Feed your selves with questioning,/That Reason wonder may diminish." We seem able to choose whether we prefer our reason to explain away our wonder or our wonder to conquer our reason. As in *The Tempest*, it is for the audience to decide the fate of the play (in a way that recalls Spenser's words, "Such ones ill judge of love that cannot love,/Nor in their frosen harts feel kindly flame.") Shakespeare relies on us to grant the play an existence outside the mind of its maker. The alternative is an eternity of silence. As Touchstone says, in an oblique and moving reference to the "Dead Shepherd" Marlowe: "When a man's verses cannot be understood, nor a man's good wit seconded with the forward child, understanding, it strikes a man more dead than a great reckoning in a little room."

With these words the play makes its claim on posterity, and it is a claim that chimes in with similar moments in the other works from this anxious time. In fact, although the play has been enduringly popular, there is no hard evidence of performances during Shakespeare's lifetime. It is generally supposed that it was one of the plays staged for the king in 1603, when he was staying at Wilton House near Salisbury, and it is known that Shakespeare's troupe, the King's Men, was in attendance. In the nineteenth century the scholar William Cory wrote of a visit to Wilton in which he was told by Lady Herbert: "We have a letter, never printed, from Lady Pembroke to her son, telling him to bring James I from Salisbury to see *As You Like It;* 'we have the man Shakespeare with us.' She wanted to cajole the King in Ralegh's behalf—he came." Cory did not see the letter himself, and it has not surfaced since. If it were true, it would give rise to any number of interpretative possibilities, not least because Wilton was where *Arcadia* had been written for Sidney's sister, the countess of Pembroke.

In the late 1580's Robert Devereux, second earl of Essex, had assumed the mantle of Elizabeth's favorite during the decline and final illness of his predecessor—and stepfather—Robert Dudley, earl of Leicester. For the next dozen years he conducted an extraordinary, ultimately doomed, courtship of the queen. He professed total and abject devotion, but was also driven in quest of honor and military glory; he chafed at his monarch's reluctance to place him at the head of her armies. The queen oscillated between her habitual caution and the behavior of a jealous teenager, screaming at court ladies who paid too much attention to the dashing, quixotic earl. Around Essex grew up a cult of the new Achilles, England's hero, and to some this represented a challenge to Elizabeth's dominant image. To his side flocked a generation of young men who could identify with his sense of frustration, men who saw their lofty ambitions thwarted by an entrenched, gerontocratic establishment.

After years of agonizing and sulking and complaining, and after having come close on several occasions to going far beyond what was tolerable in the relationship of a nobleman to his monarch, Essex eventually made the last, and most quixotic, move of his doomed career early in 1601. He failed to attend the Privy Council on Saturday, February 7, and sent word from his house on the Strand that he was ill; when the secretary came to him, Essex protested that he feared for his life and would not stir from his house. Early the next morning, four members of the Council were sent to speak to the earl. They were admitted—minus their attendants—and found a large assembly of knights, gentlemen, and others. Essex, still claiming that there were plots against his life, took the party into a private room and had them locked in. Their arrival had disrupted his plan, which had been to confront the queen directly. He gathered a group of some two hundred men and set off instead toward the city, where he hoped to enlist the support of the mayor and sheriffs.

His failure was total. He was met by a silent city, and as the minutes passed, loyal forces blocked the roads around him, closing the net ever tighter. He found the road home sealed off with a chain near St. Paul's, and after a skirmish he took a boat to return to his hostages at Essex House. When he got there he found the councillors gone, and began despairingly to prepare for a siege. In the end he and his chief ally, Shakespeare's patron the earl of Southampton, were persuaded to surrender. Because it was dark, and because the tide did not permit passage under London bridge, they were imprisoned not in the Tower but in Lambeth Palace.

From that point, events unfold like the denouement of a drama. The half dozen chief conspirators were condemned by proclamation, tried and executed—all except Southampton, whose mother interceded eloquently on his behalf. Though condemned to death, Southampton spent the brief rest of Elizabeth's life in the Tower, with his black-and-white cat for a companion. There were some frantic efforts to revive the possibility of a coup or to rescue Essex— a Captain Lee was arrested attempting to kidnap the queen and force her to sign papers releasing the earl—but the machinery of the state survived this crisis essentially intact, and the queen's placid demeanor throughout was held up as an example to all.

In the course of the extensive investigations into the rebellion, the Lord Chamberlain's Men became involved more closely than they can have wished. Attention was directed to a production of *Richard II* at the Globe on the afternoon before the insurrection. The instigator of the show was Sir Gelly Merrick, who approached the players and offered them forty shillings above their normal fee to stage "the play of the deposing and killing of King Richard the Second." Shakespeare's colleague Augustine Phillips testified that he and his fellow players "were determined to have played some other play, holding that play of King Richard to be so old and so long out of use that they should have small or no company at it," but the conspirators reinforced their insistence with hard cash.

Other witnesses reported that the audience for the play included almost all the plotters and their adherents. Francis Bacon's book *The Declaration of the Practices and Treasons . . . by Robert Late Earl of Essex* says of Merrick: "So earnest he was to satisfy his eyes with the sight of that tragedy which he thought soon after his Lord should bring from the stage to the state, but that God turned it upon their own heads."

What is surprising is that the players suffered so little; in fact they were performing again at court on February 24, the night before Essex was executed. So it is clear that Phillips was believed, and that the blame for the uprising was concentrated on a small central group.

Essex's lengthy, doomed public courtship of the queen had been fed, like Orsino's love, by music. The practical impossibility of the relationship made it a natural vehicle for the disdain, despair, and frustration so conventional in Elizabethan love poetry. A notable example is Dowland's song "Can She Excuse My Wrongs with Virtue's Cloak?" (from his *First Book of Songs* of 1597), where the lover complains:

> Cold love is like to words written on sand,
> Or to bubbles which on the water swim.

The piece was popularly known as The Earl of Essex's Galliard, and its sentiments are close to those of a dejected sonnet attributed to the earl and set to music by Sidney's former page Daniel Batchelar. It appears in Robert Dowland's *Musical Banquet* of 1610:

> To plead my faith, where faith hath no reward;
> To move remorse, where favour is not born;
> To heap complaints, where she doth not regard,
> Were fruitless, bootless, vain and yield but scorn.
> I loved her whom all the world admired.
> I was refused of her that can love none;
> And my vain hope, which far too high aspired,
> Is dead and buried and for ever gone.
> Forget my name, since you have scorned my love,
> And womanlike do not too late lament;
> Since for your sake I do all mischief prove,
> I none accuse nor nothing do repent.

I was as fond as ever she was fair
  Yet loved I not more than I now despair.

Melancholy had been a badge of political disaffection; the cult of
the malcontent had been part of the coalition of postures Essex had
gathered around him. Its signs were unmistakable enough: distrac-
tion, alienation, clothes unbuttoned, broad-brimmed hat, arms
crossed, gaze shifting from side to side but directed downward,
and a passion for the music of John Dowland ("*Semper Dowland,
semper dolens*" "ever Dowland, ever mourning"—as the punning tag
had it). Yet the vogue did not expire with its champion. Indeed his
was the kind of fall that invested failure with a kind of glamour.
And Shakespeare's next two plays took melancholy as a starting
point.

In *Twelfth Night*, the world of melancholy finds itself in competition with the realm of romance. The action of the play is framed
by the great surges of the sea, a huge force that is shown as destroyer
(and the embodiment of time), as well as preserver and worker of
miracles. From the sea come Sebastian and Viola, just like countless
conventional heroes of romance, such as the shipwrecked princes
in Sidney's *Arcadia*. They find themselves deploying a variety of
strategies (including transvestite disguise) to put right the situations
they encounter. What they find in Illyria is a world dressed in
black, a melancholy society whose leaders (Olivia, Orsino, and
Malvolio) seem to be dressed to express their heightened self-ab-
sorption. Shakespeare presents the fluidity of Sebastian and Viola,
and Feste's motley coat, as alternative models of identity.

Into this static world of self-indulgent gloom come the forces of
romance and regeneration. Structurally, it is a familiar process, one
which Shakespeare was elsewhere to treat very seriously. But here
he sets a casual, almost throwaway tone with the play's very title—
Twelfth Night, Or, What You Will. The first part arouses expectation
of epiphany, of showing forth, as well as of ritual festivity and
carnival; the other establishes a strand of apparent arbitrariness. In
performance, it is worth noting how frequently the characters seem
to deprecate what they have just been so busily doing, with phrases
like "Well, let it be," "All's one," "This is so," and the rest. The
play hovers between game and earnest, between magic and trivi-
ality.

In some ways it recalls the earliest comedies, especially *The Comedy of Errors*, but it also draws heavily on the prose romances of the 1590s, in particular on Barnabe Riche's *Farewell to Military Profession* (1581, reprinted 1594). Riche draws upon material from the popular anthologies of European romance stories by Bandello and Belleforest throughout this collection of tales, as in the immediate source of Shakespeare's play, the story of Appolonius and Silla. Riche's version of the story is more turbulent, with violent reversals and brutal acts, and mistaken identities leading to pregnancy. In the eyes of at least one contemporary witness, however, the play's similarity to the earliest comedies was most noticeable. After a performance of the play at the Middle Temple on the Feast of the Purification (Candlemas), February 2, 1602, a lawyer, John Manningham, recorded the event in his diary:

> At our feast we had a play called "Twelve night, or what you will"; much like *The Comedy of Errors* or *Menaechmi* in Plautus, but most like and near to that in Italian called *Inganni*.
>
> A good practice in it to make the steward believe his Lady widow was in love with him, by counterfeiting a letter, as from his Lady, in general terms, telling him what she liked best in him, and prescribing his gesture in smiling, his apparel, etc., and then when he came to practice, making him believe they took him to be mad.

Manningham wrote, but then crossed out, "Mid . . . " as the title of the play—which suggests he had probably seen *A Midsummer Night's Dream* on some earlier occasion. His connection of the play with Plautus and Italian Renaissance comedy explains why the tricking of Malvolio sticks in his mind. He clearly associated Shakespeare with such droll japes, too. Later in the diary he recorded an anecdote he had heard from his distinguished fellow lawyer William Towse:

> Upon a time when Burbage played Rich 3. there was a Citizen grew so far in liking of him, that before she went from the play she appointed him to come that night unto her by the name of Ri the 3. Shakespeare, overhearing their conclusion, went before, was entertained, and at his game ere Burbage came. Then message being brought that Richard the 3d was at the door, Shakespeare caused

return to be made that William the Conqueror was before Rich the 3.

Manningham helpfully notes "Shakespeare's name William." Whatever the basis for the anecdote, it at least indicates that the "bed-trick," a staple of stage comedy and of comic tales at the time, was believed to be possible in everyday life. So when Shakespeare uses the device in *Measure for Measure* and *All's Well that Ends Well* we should beware of dismissing it as an improbable fiction, nothing more than a comic convention.

Like most of Shakespeare's romantic comedies, *Twelfth Night* combines the fairytale with the everyday. Some have wished to see the play as having been commissioned for a performance on January 6, 1601, as part of the entertainment of the duke of Bracciano, Don Virgilio Orsino. If it was, Shakespeare and his company must have worked at astonishing speed, since the duke's visit was only announced on December 26. More likely Shakespeare wrote after the event, and incorporated the name of the celebrated visitor as part of the blending of the ideal and the actual that characterises the play. Further, he establishes a somber and serious element, especially in the action involving Malvolio; Olivia's steward is tormented in a fictional "hell" onstage and ends the play vowing revenge on the "whole pack" (his choice of term encompasses both the playfulness of cards and the savagery of hunting) of the reconciled company onstage.

One of the most remarkable features of the play is Shakespeare's control over it. *Julius Caesar* ended with a jig, and no doubt that play, like most others, emerged out of some other entertainment. But in *Twelfth Night* Shakespeare opens the action with Orsino's response to atmospheric music being played onstage ("If music be the food of love, play on . . . "), and he closes it with a conventional epilogue ("We'll strive to please you every day") in the form of a song by the company's clown. Similarly, the role of Feste is deeply integrated in a novel way. It is Feste's function to "prove" the folly of those used to thinking themselves sane. He does so by means of a series of set-piece interrogations, starting with his exchange with Olivia, "Good madonna, give me leave to prove you a fool," and proceeding through a conversation with Orsino to the destabilizing

of the imprisoned Malvolio by Feste in the guise of Sir Topas the
curate. These interrogations go along with the play's apparent
unease about its own genre; there are elements of humanist comedy,
romance, city comedy, and, in the resolution of the Malvolio plot,
more than a hint of tragedy and revenge.

Shakespeare weaves this sense of instability into the play's psychological concerns, its treatment of individuality, identity, and
love, as he was to do in *Hamlet*. And the play acts out, much as
Romeo and Juliet had, the conventions of romantic love, but it proceeds through inversion and travesty. Thus we see that Orsino,
the focus of his court, has himself to court Olivia. In an odd way,
he embodies some of the paradoxes and contradictions that were
thought to be inherent in Queen Elizabeth. Shakespeare wittily
invests Orsino with many of the qualities that the prejudices of the
time labeled as exclusively feminine—he is indecisive, changeable,
governed by his feelings rather than by reason. In contrast Olivia,
at least initially, is shown to be in charge of a household, and
apparently in control over herself. Shakespeare blends the treatment
of identity and difference with an examination of sexual desire,
most clearly in the Olivia/Viola story. Orsino, of course, asks Viola
to impersonate him: "Surprise her with discourse of my dear faith;
It shall become thee well to act my woes"; and the play abounds
with remarks like "I am not that I play"; "What I am, and what I
would, are as secret as maidenhead; to your ears divinity, to any
others, profanation." We might recall Sidney's Astrophil begging
Stella, "I am not I, pity the tale of me." In Sebastian's words, "This
may be some error, but no madness."

Transvestism constitutes another part of a process of education
through inversion, and is related to the evolving notions of the
individual—especially to the developing notions of masculine identity in that period. The "suppose" is that after the inversion, recognition generates stability. The question is complicated by the
fact that on the Elizabethan stage all the parts were played by males,
with boys acting the roles of women and old men. At the end Viola
is still Cesario—we do not see the union, nor the change of dress.
What is more, in the world outside the play, after the performance
the boy playing Viola disguised as Cesario will resume his maleness.

The near-miracle with which the play concludes makes the whole process of self-discovery seem magical and strange. But the result, as in *As You Like It*, puts a limit to the magic and amazement, and reassures the audience that what they have experienced is a play, something that can be taken or left as they will. Yet Malvolio resists that closure, and represents the stubbornness of human existence, its tendency to resist compartmentalization. The play may seem to push us toward a view that individuals are incomplete in themselves and need to find themselves in their "other half" and in society, and that games and role-playing can provide an experience of otherness which is essential to a sense of self. But the incompleteness of the ending—Viola still dressed as Cesario, and Malvolio refusing to join in—enters a reservation about this fundamental basis of Shakespearean romantic comedy. And he was never to return to the form again.

The image of Shakespeare that emerges from outside the printed canon confirms the picture Ben Jonson painted, of an easy and felicitous grace in composition, and a generous and witty nature. Some years after Shakespeare's death, Ben Jonson jotted down an explanation of his well-known criticism that "Shakespeare wanted art," and his scorn of the players' compliment that Shakespeare never blotted a line in his scripts:

> My answer hath been, would he had blotted a thousand. Which they thought a malevolent speech. I had not told posterity this, but for their ignorance, who choose that circumstances to commend their friend by, wherein he most faulted. And to justify mine own candour (for I loved the man, and do honour his memory (on this side idolatry) as much as any). He was (indeed) honest, and of an open, and free nature: had an excellent *Fancy;* brave notions, and gentle expressions: wherein he flowed with that facility, that sometimes it was necessary he should be stopped: *Sufflaminandus erat;* as Augustus said of *Haterius*. His wit was in his own power; would the rule of it had been so too. Many times he fell into those things, could not escape laughter: As when he said in the person of Caesar, one speaking to him: *Caesar thou dost me wrong.* Hee replied: *Caesar never did wrong, but with just cause* and such like: which were ridiculous. But he redeemed his vices, with his virtues. There was ever more to be praised, than to be pardoned.

The mocking epitaph of his Stratford friend John Combe (see p. 395) may be an instance of extempore wit. The manuscript tradition preserves a couple of versions of lines on Jonson himself. A commonplace book, which includes a variant on the Combe poem, also has this:

> Being Merrye att a
> Tauern, mr Jonson haueing begune this for his Epitaph
> Here lies Ben Johnson that was once one
> he gives ytt to mr Shakspear to make vpp who presently
> wrightes
> Who while hee liu'de was a sloe thinge
> and now being dead is Nothinge.

The long love lyric "Shall I die?" which survives in at least two manuscripts, once attributed to Shakespeare, may—if it is authentic—come from this kind of extemporizing event. The highly charged sentiments expressed by the speaker are of the sort usually guyed in the plays (Orsino is the obvious example), and the occasionally faltering control of the difficult stanza form may be designed to undermine the soulful speaker and inject a note of absurdity into the enterprise. The element of parody, of gentle mockery of a characterized speaker, may make the poem more of a piece both in date and culture with the other poems in the manuscripts.

Some other poems, preserved in much more abiding form, have been attributed to Shakespeare over the centuries. In 1664 the antiquary William Dugdale recorded the inscriptions on the Stanley family tomb, at Tong in Shropshire, as "verses . . . made by William Shakespeare, the late famous tragedian." There are two epitaphs, one on the east, the other on the west end of the monument:

> [EAST]
> Ask who lies here, but do not weep;
> He is not dead, he doth but sleep.
> This stony register is for his bones,
> His fame is more perpetual than these stones;
> And his own goodness, with himself being gone,
> Shall live when earthly monument is none.
> [WEST]
> Not monumental stone preserves our fame,

Nor sky-aspiring pyramids our name;
The memory of him for whom this stands
Shall outlive marble and defacers' hands:
When all to Time's consumption shall be given,
Stanley, for whom this stands, shall stand in heaven.

Tombs were frequently designed, often even constructed, long before their intended occupant was dead. These verses seem to have been written for Sir Thomas Stanley and his son Sir Edward, who was two years older than Shakespeare and died in 1632. They were probably written between 1600 and 1603, when Edward was knighted. If authentic, they reinforce the suggestion that Shakespeare had been associated with Lord Strange's Men (Lord Strange was Sir Thomas's nephew, Sir Edward's cousin).

A much more important, and almost impenetrably enigmatic, product of Shakespeare's connections with the Stanley family is the extraordinary poem *The Phoenix and Turtle*. The piece was published in 1601 in an anthology called *Love's Martyr*, compiled by a journeyman poet named Robert Chester as a compliment to Sir John Salusbury, a distant Welsh relation of Queen Elizabeth's. Salusbury was knighted in 1601, and the publication perhaps celebrated that event. Chester's own contribution is a lengthy poem entitled "*Loves Martyr*, or Rosalins complaint. Allegorically shadowing the truth of Love in the constant Fate of the Phoenix and Turtle," to which was added a group of poems by some of the most celebrated poets of the day—Jonson, Marston, Chapman, perhaps Donne, and Shakespeare himself. In December 1586 Salusbury married Ursula Stanley, the acknowledged illegitimate daughter of the fourth earl of Derby (therefore, Lord Strange's half-sister). The date of the individual poems in the anthology cannot be conclusively established. It may well be that Chester's, a dense allegory whose key is lost, but which seems to be at least in part about sexual ecstasy, is from the time of the marriage—though there have been plenty of attempts to read into it a series of political events in Elizabeth's court. Perhaps Shakespeare's poem was a youthful compliment by the young actor-schoolmaster to the newly married couple.

Whatever the truth may be, it is instructive that two completely different ways of reading this poem have developed in parallel. On the one hand there are those who seek to crack its codes, to ground

its allegory in the circumstances of Elizabethan England, and in
particular to help to locate Shakespeare within networks of patronage and influence. On the other, there is a school of interpretation that treats the poem as "pure poetry," as verbal music, a
play of ideas wholly cut off from mundane conditions. Renaissance
writers (including Shakespeare) frequently defended themselves
against the charge that they were criticizing or subverting authority
by claiming that what they wrote was merely a trifle, a toy, or a
dream.

The poem is an important text to consider as part of Shakespeare's
treatment of love and of the relationship between desire and identity. In particular, the "anthem" chanted before the grave of the
two birds is suggestively close to both the *Sonnets* and the comedies
of the turn of the century:

> Love and constancy is dead;
> Phoenix and the turtle fled
> In a mutual flame from hence.
>
> So they loved, as love in twain
> Had the essence but in one:
> Two distincts, division none:
> Number there in love was slain.
>
> Hearts remote, yet not asunder,
> Distance, and no space was seen
> 'Twixt this turtle and his queen:
> But in them it were a wonder.
>
> So between them love did shine,
> That the turtle saw his right
> Flaming in the phoenix' sight;
> Either was the other's mine.

The dense, metaphorical suggestiveness of the whole poem is
epitomized by that last word, *mine*, which combines the notion that
distinctions between the lovers are annihilated with the potentially
contradictory idea that each sees the other as a source of wealth
and treasure. Where the *Sonnets* examine two contrasting relationships, one of love without sex, the other of sex without love, this
intense and dramatic piece aspires to depict the marvel of their
simultaneous presence.

*   *   *

Hamlet, the man and the play, have been staples of western European culture for a couple of centuries; ignorance of this play is conclusive proof of philistinism. Thus in David Lodge's *Changing Places*, in a great set-piece at the University of Euphoria State, there is a party game called Humiliation, in which points are awarded for humiliating admissions by the players. One young professor, a very narrow English literature specialist, is intensely ambitious. A decision about his tenure is pending, and he is ambitious for that; but he is also desperate to win the game. By admitting he has not read *Hamlet* he scoops the board but loses his job.

The play has become part of common currency, so that when the cautious Pope Paul VI was described as *amletico* ("Hamlet-like") it was a widely comprehensible shorthand that suggested a tendency to delay action, to brood over possibilities, perhaps to be paralyzed into indecision. At such a level it would be easy to argue for its universality, at least in Europe and in the European traditions, on the basis of its abiding presence within cultural life. And we can all recognize, no doubt, the forces that led the distinguished critic Harry Levin to declare that "*Hamlet* is the most problematic play ever written by Shakespeare or any other playwright."

Let's look at the text from the perspective of the time of its first composition and appearance. I'll start by looking at the connections that have been perceived between Shakespeare's play and the events in the world from which it sprang.

First there is the name, which has often seemed suggestively close to that of Shakespeare's son, Hamnet (named for Hamnet Sadler of Stratford), who had been christened with his twin sister Judith on February 2, 1583, and who was buried in Stratford on August 11, 1596. Then there is the reference to the boy actors, to the "little eyases" who "berattle the common stage" and are now "the fashion." This is an unmistakable allusion to the instant popularity of the boy actors who began to perform at the Blackfriars in the last months of 1600. In the same passage reference is made to the way the tragedians have been silenced, prevented from performing since "the late innovation," which reads as an allusion to the restrictions placed on public displays in the wake of Essex's failed coup d'état in February 1601.

There is, unfortunately, no consensus about the play's date.

Some would hold that it was being acted from late 1599, and that later topical allusions were added during its theatrical life and prior to publication. If a later date is accepted, the external event that would have pressed most strongly on the text is the death of Shakespeare's father. John Shakespeare, the Holy Trinity record says, was buried on September 8, 1601.

William Shakespeare had already had to accommodate himself to new responsibilities during his father's declining years. After the old man's death there were further obligations that would now need to be discharged in Stratford, alongside the duties he performed in London in connection with the growing business of the newly built Globe. While his profitable and fashionable city existence was taking him close—at times perilously close—to the vertiginously unstable world of court politics, his father's death brought him back to earth. He was suddenly presented with final responsiblity for property, tenants, business interests, and dependants far away in the town of his birth, and the fixed points of the commercial and agricultural calendar were not going to wait for him. Perhaps it was a relief to get away from London to deal with the estate, to escape involvement with the jockeying for power, the recriminations and executions, and the imprisonment of his patron Southampton.

After 1601, the merry-cheeked old man was no more. There may have been in Shakespeare's mind as he approached his play—or as he returned to revise it—a powerful sense of obligation to his father, to see that his memory was properly served, that his inheritance was well looked after, that the responsibilities passed on to the next generation were duly carried out. Certainly an important set of impulses in the figure of Hamlet—the wish that his father should lie peacefully in his grave, that his kingdom should be cared for as he would have wished, and that his name should not be erased— can be connected in some ways to the intimate circumstances of Shakespeare's life. And they do not depend on narrow chronology, since they are of a piece with his gradually increasing involvement in the life of Stratford and with his restoration of his family's fortune and social standing.

In any case, John Shakespeare was not murdered, and William was not sworn to avenge him; nor did Mary Shakespeare remarry. Yet there may be an element that can be related to more human

promptings. Hamlet's revulsion at the revelation of carnality implicit in his mother's remarriage has been extensively discussed over
the years. But there is also, I think, a tangential relationship with
that bizarre courtship of the proverbially virgin queen by the vol-
atile, mercurial, melancholic, unstable earl of Essex. Just as Essex
wrestled with twin formulations, with parallel views of the queen
(then in her sixties)—one minute she was an austere and chaste
Diana, the next a mistress to whom he would pour out the most
passionate words and act out the most extreme courtship display
behavior—so too Hamlet wrestles with the familiar and not dis-
similar problems of coming to terms with his mother's sexuality,
with the resultant rage, despair, disquiet, and confusion. In other
words, the political life of the nation had witnessed the acting out
of an inner drama, a clash between idealization and revulsion, on
a stage much grander than the Globe but with an end no less brutal.

If Hamlet recalls Essex, he also recalls Brutus. *Julius Caesar* had
shown some of the ways in which an intellectual can be tormented
by political action. And Hamlet's sense of himself is wrapped up
with his self-consciousness about the literary fictions to which he
seems to be conforming. The crudity of the revenge tradition can
be overstated. It was a genre which could address serious questions
about justice and morality; but it was unquestionably a popular
rather than an intellectual form, and sophisticated writers (like John
Marston in his *Antonio's Revenge*) created versions that depended for
their effect upon the audience's awareness of the conventions that
were being elegantly rehearsed for them. So Hamlet finds himself
living out the sort of play any fashionable intellectual would have
been shamefaced to admit going to see except as a joke.

But then there is no single revenge. The play is, in effect, as
much about revenge drama as about revenge itself or about Hamlet.
As there had been multiple marriages in *As You Like It*, so in *Hamlet*
there are three interlocking revenge stories—Hamlet avenging the
death of his father Old Hamlet by killing Claudius; Laertes avenging
the death of his father Polonius by killing Hamlet; and Fortinbras
avenging the death of his father Old Fortinbras at the hands of Old
Hamlet by taking over Old Hamlet's kingdom from his successors.

The commission given to Hamlet by his father's ghost is a profoundly allusive, literary act—indeed, there was a popular Hamlet
play on the Elizabethan stage, of which all we know is that a ghost

called out "Hamlet, Revenge!" But Hamlet, like Sidney's Astrophil and most lovers in sonnet sequences, is determined to hold on to a self that is not confined to a stereotype. Of course, that is itself a conventional pose. And Hamlet exhibits the qualities of several literary stereotypes, the most notable being that of the melancholic. After first showing symptoms of melancholy, thereafter he appears as disillusioned scholar, satirist, misogynist, political malcontent, melancholy lover, madman, revenger—all characteristic poses of the melancholic. Likewise, he conforms to some visual conventions of melancholy, appearing with a book, dressed in black, carrying a skull, and frequenting graveyards. His changeableness recalls Feste's words to Orsino in *Twelfth Night*:

> Now the melancholy god protect thee, and the tailor make thy doublet of changeable taffeta, for thy mind is a very opal. I would have men of such constancy put to sea, that their business might be everything and their intent every where, for that's it that always makes a good voyage of nothing.

In contrast with the movements in *Twelfth Night*, where individual identity is wrapped up with others and with society, *Hamlet* provides us with numerous soliloquies in which the protagonist can speak of, and to, himself. The convention of the soliloquy as a form of introspection parallels the contemporary vogue for the sonnet. The very structure of the soliloquies mirrors the variety in Hamlet's personality that other speakers comment on: their drama—a voice speaking to itself, challenging its own assertions, calling back and qualifying what it proposes—is typical of the way the Elizabethans conceived of the interior life as a debate between competing voices. The sonnet, the soliloquy, and the cult of melancholy were significant Elizabethan modes of introspection, and played a role in the construction of a notion of the private person, of the individual. They were fascinated by it, and the persons in *Hamlet*, like good Elizabethans, are connoisseurs of Hamlet's condition, especially after he announces he can tell nobody about it—"But break, my heart, for I must hold my tongue." After that, others are free with their advice and analysis. Thus in Act III Claudius tells of cures; Polonius gives a conventional analysis of Love/Melancholy; and then, equally conventionally, Rosencrantz urges Hamlet to share his troubles.

One of the devices that Hamlet employs in his attempt to secure generic control over the events through which he has been called to live is to try to transform the tragedy—for a tragic situation it most emphatically is—into some other form, such as satire or comedy. So he adopts the posture of the malcontent satirist in his outburst to Polonius in Act IV—"Your worm is your only emperor for diet: we fat all creatures else to fat us, and we fat ourselves for maggots; your fat king and your lean beggar is but variable service, two dishes, but at one table—that's the end." The same happens with his staging of the Gonzago play, which he conceives of as an illustration of the educational, or revelatory, potential of art. When, in the course of that episode, Hamlet recalls lines from an almost identical moment in Kyd's *The Spanish Tragedy* ("And if the world like not this tragedy/Hard is the hap of old Hieronimo"), his recollection seems to suppress the tragic context of the original. As he says: "For if the King like not this comedy,/Why then belike he likes it not, perdy." It is as if he is seeking to reverse the moment in Kyd's play where Hieronimo, who had been asked to arrange for a comedy to be played, had instead staged a tragedy.

At other points in the same scene, Hamlet shifts between the throwaway strategies of *Twelfth Night* ("What should a man do but be merry") and a much graver mode. Take, for example, his bizarre comment, "the croaking raven doth bellow for revenge," which conflates a couple of lines from a speech in the anonymous play *The True Tragedy of Richard III*. The allusion points to parallels between the situations—Richard married the widow of one of his victims, usurped the throne, and, it was believed, murdered his nephew—it's as if, through an apparent joke, Hamlet employs a historical precedent to classify his duty for revenge as an act in accordance with divine providence and justice.

In the end, however, Hamlet's delay is set aside and he acts (though even his resolve may be seen as an attempt to convince himself as much as anything else). In his words in the graveyard scene: "We must speak by the card or equivocation will undo us," and from there onward it seems that Hamlet's uncertainties are largely resolved, and that he will act the part of the avenger. The movement toward revenge, like that toward marriage in *As You Like*

It and *Twelfth Night*, is formally a movement toward closure, toward resolution; and, as in those other plays, the play's process of self-definition is wrapped up with the protagonist's quest for self-knowledge. In all cases it seems that the discovery of a self involves an assimilation into some larger entity, that the problem of how to act virtuously can only be solved by engaging with the world.

Shakespeare was making new bricks with old straw. While the form of the play, the revenge tragedy, was a familiar and popular feature of Elizabethan culture, the use to which it was put was novel in the extreme. It was so novel, in fact, that the English language of his day had not developed names for two of *Hamlet's* most striking characteristics: It did not include the words *aside* or *soliloquy*. Right at the outset of the play Hamlet directs our attention to an idea that may seem commonplace to us, but which was then novel, controversial, radical—the notion of an interior life that can never be accurately represented by word or deed; an interior self with an existence of its own. He says:

'Tis not alone my inky cloak, good mother,
Nor customary suits of solemn black
Nor windy suspiration of forc'd breath,
No, nor the fruitful river in the eye,
Nor the dejected haviour of the visage,
Together with all forms, moods, shapes of grief,
That can denote me truly. These indeed seem,
For they are actions that a man might play,
But I have that within, which passes show;
These but the trappings and the suits of woe.

Shakespeare takes a risk in these lines—the melancholy behavior, after all, was a part that Richard Burbage was playing as he spoke the lines. In the *Sonnets* Shakespeare explored this new subjectivity, and seems to have tried to find a language to express it. As the play ends, Hamlet is concerned that his behavior should be fully explained, and asks Horatio (whose name puns on *oratio* [speech] and *ratio* [reason]) to tell his story. It is as if his final attempt at a generic shift is from the closure of tragedy to the more open-ended narrative of history—*Othello* was to end in a similar way. Or, to put it differently, we might think that the play ends with a paradox of sorts; that posterity's knowledge of the triumph of good over evil, justice over injustice, providence over chaos—to which Hamlet in a sense sacrifices his own freedom of choice—derives from, and may even depend upon, the truthful retelling (restaging) of Hamlet's story.

The relationship between the great sweep of history and personal tragedy, as well as the connections between identity, love, and reputation, are woven into the fabric of *Troilus and Cressida* as into that of *Hamlet*. But where the former play builds toward a climax, albeit a paradoxical one, and toward an acceptance, at least on the surface, of the generic imperative of tragedy, its successor shies clear of such a resolution. Partly Shakespeare can do that because he knows the story is so familiar to his audience that they can supply the narrative he leaves out. After all, Londoners fondly believed themselves to be the inhabitants of Troy Novant or New Troy, the descendants of the Trojan royal house (as Spenser wrote in *The Faerie Queene*, "for noble *Britons* sprong from *Troians* bold/ And *Troynovant* was built of old *Troyes* ashes cold"); and Chaucer's *Troilus and Criseyde* was acknowledged as the greatest literary masterpiece written in English. But that hardly solves the problem, since the outlines of *Hamlet* and *Henry V* were themselves hardly mysteries to the playgoers.

Then again, everything about *Troilus and Cressida* is decidedly quirky. It poses some very basic questions. What is its title? When and where was it written and performed? What sort of play is it? All these have proved intractable for generations of commentators. *Troilus and Cressida* was entered in the Stationers' Register in February 1603, where it is said to have been acted by the Lord Chamberlain's Men. This entry was probably made to prevent someone publishing a pirated text of the play, which suggests it was popular in 1601–2, though there is no evidence of performance. The first edition was eventually published in 1609, with two different title pages. One claims it was acted at the Globe, the other that it has never been "stal'd with the stage, never clapper-clawed with the palms of the vulgar."

Like *Julius Caesar*, *Troilus and Cressida* is unquestionably a title that fits in with the new surge in artistic ambition that followed the move to the Globe. And each play generates expectations only to frustrate them—what we actually see in Julius Caesar is not a great general, but rather an infirm old man driven by vanity—and he is dead halfway through. Likewise in *Troilus and Cressida*, not only do the lovers play a comparatively small part in the play (if they dominate the first half, the second is really Hector's tragedy— or maybe Achilles' triumph), but the world that is shown to us is far from idealized and heroic. Indeed, a spectator who came to see Shakespeare's play with any of his major sources in mind, whether Chaucer or Homer, would have been surprised. The play combines a systematic debunking of mythic and heroic sterotypes with a disconcerting oscillation between then and now, between a remote past and contemporary England.

Some parts would be familiar enough. As in some of the earliest plays, Shakespeare reminded his audience of their schooldays. He included the formal debates they enjoyed, one set in the Greek camp, the other in the Trojan council. The spectator would have relished the way each speaker is characterized by a distinct oratorical style. And yet, as the play develops, it becomes clear that many of these great set speeches are actually directed to some very narrow and specific end: When Ulysses debates reputation and honor with Achilles, he is in fact manipulating the petulant soldier rather than swapping general statements with him. The episode recalls the similar scene in *Julius Caesar* where Cassius tempts Brutus to take action against Caesar.

Much of the play's topicality is irretrievably lost, but some can be recaptured. To start with the first moments of the play, "Enter the prologue, armed," this was no token display of antiquarianism— quite the reverse. It was Shakespeare's joking allusion to the so-called war of the theaters—Ben Jonson had used an armed prologue in his *Poetaster* (1601) to indicate his own embattled position. It is possible that both the prologue and the bombastic figure of Ajax are versions of Jonson himself.

Even the treatment of heroic, epic virtues was charged with significance at this time. As we have seen, the idea of the heroic, of classical virtues and of lofty chivalry, were part of contemporary political discourse. They had become a code through which the earl of Essex, and what he represented, could be discussed. The doomed earl, with his weakness for the quixotic gesture and his tendency to sulk in his tent, was often identified at the time with

Achilles—not least by Chapman, who dedicated his translation of Homer to Essex in 1598. There is little doubt that Essex and his followers, including Southampton, were driven by self-consciously archaic notions of honor that many have seen embodied in the presentation of both Achilles and Hector. We might note how these lofty and prickly individuals are manipulated—as so frequently in Shakespeare—by more pragmatic, more political figures.

As in *Much Ado*, honor and virtue, love and war are closely related. And a context for thinking about them is provided by the stories of Cressida and Helen, women whose status shifts from being an icon, to being a piece of merchandise, to being a strumpet. We see them shaped and used by the entirely masculine environment in which they exist, and they speak to us only in the silence which is forced on them. Shakespeare did not enjoy Chaucer's advantage of employing a narrative voice to speak up for Criseyde, to temper the automatic male hostility to her deserting Troilus for Diomed. And no boy actor could carry soliloquies on the *Hamlet* scale: Cressida's plight has to speak for itself, as in the cavalier way her departure for the Greek camp is treated by the Trojan nobles. We are told nothing and shown little of what goes on inside her mind. Troilus is presented as a naïve and idealistic figure, with a touching faith in the veracity of speech; almost alone among the speakers, he is shown to mean what he says. For him the language of love is not merely a set of clichés. Like Hamlet, he expresses horror at the hypocrisy with which he finds himself surrounded, and he does so in Hamlet-like terms when he complains at "words, words, mere words; no matter for the heart."

Much of the dynamism in this play is invested in its numerous commentators, in particular Pandarus and Thersites. On his first appearance Thersites may seem to be little more than a comic routine, automatically spraying vituperative abuse over every person and everything he encounters. But Shakespeare's device of giving him the last word has the effect of turning him into a commentator whose authority increases as the major actors live down to his snarling assessments of them. To Thersites, Troilus and Diomed are "the wenching rogues," the Greek and Trojan armies are "all incontinent varlets," and he sees the world around him as "Lechery, lechery, still wars and lechery, nothing else holds fashion." His invective against Menelaus is a comic but nonetheless

powerful reminder that the war is not just about military honor; it
is also about jealousy and degradation. Thersites' words open up
what is unsaid for much of the play. At the core of this great epic
struggle is the anxiety about cuckoldry that was a staple of city
comedy (brilliantly depicted in plays such as Jonson's *Every Man
in His Humour*). Menelaus may be a prince, and he may be an actor
in an epic story, but he is treated with the habitual scorn that
Elizabethans accorded cuckolds. The movements of armies and
navies, the invocations of gods and goddesses, strip him of his
privacy; everybody involved in the Trojan wars knows what has
happened to him, and the implication is that his humiliation will
endure throughout history. In Thersites' words:

> To be a dog, a mule, a cat, a fitchew, a toad, a lizard, an owl, a
> puttock, or a herring without a roe, I would not care: but to be
> Menelaus, I would conspire against destiny! I care not to be the
> louse of a lazar, so I were not Menelaus!

The structure of the play is disconcerting. In the first half the
action follows recognizable patterns, and events are brought to a
conclusion with a scene of almost heartbreaking pathos between
Pandarus and the two lovers. The moment is dense and charged
with a dramatic irony that depends on the audience's foreknowledge
of the tragedy.

> **Troilus**: True swains in love shall in the world to come
> Approve their truth by Troilus.
> **Cressida**: If I be false . . . let memory
> From false to false among false maids in love,
> Unbraid my falsehood.
> **Pandarus**: I'll be the witness. Here I hold your hand, here my cousin's.
> If ever you prove false to one another, since I have taken
> such pain to bring you together, let all pitiful goers-between
> be called to the world's end after my name; call them all
> Pandars. Let all constant men be Troiluses, all false women
> Cressids, and all brokers between Pandars! Say Amen.

We might expect the second half to consist of the working out
of the irony. Not a bit of it. What we see is fragmentary and chaotic
in the extreme, with the story of the lovers relegated to the margins

of events, while the major forces on both sides are involved in savage slaughter. The focus is shifted to Hector and Achilles. But the quickfire sequence of scenes is furnished with a series of commentators to sum up, to judge, to interpret what is happening. The first half of the play, with its set-piece debates and formal exchanges, had been relatively static. The second half is driven by action, by lust and anger, and our attention is directed away from specific incidents and toward what they might tell us cumulatively about the human condition. Shakespeare seems to be representing these qualities of human existence as intractable, as resisting the symmetries and forms of conventional dramatic structure.

The ever-increasing and chaotic abundance of the play's language and its exceptional range of styles contrast markedly with the high point of the final act, the slaying of Hector. This scene, which is the most prominent episode in the second half, parallels the Troilus/Cressida/Pandarus tableau. Not only is the incident charged with meaning in contrast with the turmoil all around it, but it also sounds different from what surrounds it. Almost the entire scene is written in rhymed couplets—stressing, perhaps, the formal, inevitable, almost ritual quality of Hector's death. And this moment of specifically poetic savagery reminds us that the language of *Troilus* seems very deliberately poetic. Pitted against the tendency to chaotic fragmentation of actions and savage language is a consistency in the use of certain central images. It is as if the play is held together by ideas and concepts (in particular by images of time, of eating and of animals), and by the audience's experience of isolated moments, rather than by an overarching architectural structure.

In other words, if the play makes sense, it does so in the eyes and hearts of the inhabitants of New Troy, the descendants of the people represented onstage. It recalls the moment in Book III of *The Faerie Queene* where the heroine Britomart, champion of the Angles and destined to be the mother of the line of British kings, is moved to tears by an account of the fall of Troy. In Spenser's narrative, her lament is a sign that she is beginning to glimpse her own identity and destiny as she looks at the chaos and destruction of the high towers on the windy plain:

O lamentable fall of famous towne,
Which raignd so many yeares victorious,

And of all *Asie* bore the soueraigne crowne,
In one sad night consumd, and throwen downe:
What stony hart, that heares thy haplesse fate,
Is not empearst with deepe compassiowne,
And makes ensample of mans wretched state,
That floures so fresh at morne, and fades at euening late?

Shakespeare had reached the height of his powers at a time when, in the opinion of many, the world was declining to its end, when many were convinced that the times themselves had become corrupt and degenerate. He seems to have resisted the kinds of nostalgia that could be stimulated by such reflection. These plays from the turn of the century are characterized by a scepticism about such prevailing views. The ancient world we see in them is not noticeably better than Elizabethan London. From our modern perspective we can see that a significant event had been the publication in 1598 of a new translation of Tacitus' *Annals*, a book that took the account of Roman history forward to the time of Nero. In so doing it showed how idealism led to tyranny, how power corrupts, and how it is harder to identify progress in history than to see endless cycles of futile rising and falling.

These plays also display a burgeoning scepticism about much of the received wisdom about art; it is as if, perhaps prompted by his reading of Montaigne, Shakespeare was coming to a view of the human condition as something that resisted conventional pigeon-holes. I am reminded of Montaigne's self-deflating dictum that dogmatism and certainty are infallible signs of stupidity; and also Sidney's summing up of events in *Arcadia*—"So uncertain are mortal judgments, the same person most famous, and most infamous, and neither justly." In the words of Thersites: "A plague of opinion! A man may wear it on both sides, like a leather jerkin."

CHAPTER NINE

"The Arte and Faculty of Playinge," 1603–6

The Lord Chamberlain's Men performed before Queen Elizabeth in Whitehall on December 26, 1602, and then for the last time at Richmond on the feast of Candlemas, February 2, 1603. Her death on March 24, though long expected, left London stunned. There is a moving evocation in the pages of the lawyer John Manningham's diary:

> This morning at about 3 o'clock her Majesty departed this life, mildly like a lamb, easily like a ripe apple from a tree. . . . About 10 o'clock the Council and divers noblemen, having been a while in consultation, proclaimed James the 6, King of Scots, the King of England, France, and Ireland. . . .
>
> The proclamation was heard with . . . silent joy, no great shouting. I think the sorrow for her Majesty's departure was so deep in many hearts they could not so suddenly show any great joy, though it could not be less than exceeding great for the succession of so worthy a King. And at night they showed it by bonfires, and ringing. . . .
>
> No tumult, no contradiction, no disorder in the city; every man went about his business, as readily, as peaceably, as securely, as

though there had been no change, nor any news ever heard of competitors. God be thanked, our King hath his right.

With the stability of the government apparently assured, and with the carriages and horses of the nobility clogging the roads as they scrambled northward to greet him, King James could afford to take his time. He crossed the border at Berwick on April 6, and arrived in London early in May. Soon, so did the plague.

The 1603 visitation was one of the most severe; as ever, its effect was concentrated on the less sanitary, more densely populated parts of London. In St. Giles, Cripplegate, out of a population of three thousand only six hundred were left alive. Among those who died was Ben Jonson's first son, his "best piece of poetry." Public assemblies were prohibited; the people were kept away from the king's coronation in July, and the great procession was postponed. The king's entry pageant did not take place until almost a year after his accession, on March 15, 1604.

In his treaties on kingship, *Basilikon Doron*, James observed that "those people were blest, where a philosopher rules, and where the Ruler plays the Philosopher." Readers in England were soon able to ponder this, for within days of Elizabeth's death the presses in London buzzed with activity, as printers toiled to satisfy the public's curiosity about their new ruler. James was a formidably learned man, brought up by some of the greatest scholars of his time. He had also been king of Scotland from infancy, and had used those thirty-six years to reflect on his experience. He chose to present himself to his new subjects as a new Solomon, a second Augustus, and announced the inauguration of a new age, the establishment of a new dynasty; he brought with him two sons and a daughter.

In this new age learning was to flourish under the guidance of James's "kingly pen." He had already published volumes of poetry (and had let his hostility to "harshe verses after the English fashion" become known), as well as treatises such as *Basilikon Doron* and *Demonology* (on witchcraft). English writers welcomed his accession, though in varying degrees of fullsomeness. Like the citizens of London, they were torn between lament for the dead queen and praise of her successor, and it was a difficult balance to strike. Michael Drayton plunged headlong into his *Panegyric Gratulatory* to James, while saying next to nothing about Elizabeth; he was widely thought to have breached decorum, and in his later years observed that he had "suffered shipwrack" because of his "forward pen."

James was naturally concerned to show that he had his own ideas and principles of kingship, and that they were to be distinguished from those of his enigmatic predecessor. Elizabeth had faced the problems involved with being a female ruler, and had cast around for role models in ancient and biblical times; she had declared herself to be wedded to the kingdom, a mystical concept expressed through allegory and obliquity. In his speech to Parliament published in 1604 James proclaimed a new order, in which the monarch was plain and direct rather than inscrutable:

> It becometh a King, in my opinion, to use no other eloquence than plainness and sincerity. By plainness I mean, that his speeches should be so clear and void of all ambiguity, that he may not be thrown, nor rent asunder in contrary senses like the old oracles of the pagan gods. And by sincerity, I understand that uprightness and honesty which ought to be in a King's whole speeches and actions; that as far as a King is in honour erected above any of his subjects, so far should he strive in sincerity to be above them all, and that his tongue should be ever the true messenger of his heart. And this sort of eloquence may you ever assuredly look for at my hands.

But James was also capable of behaving allegorically, or deploying indirection and shows, at least as well as his predecessor. On his progress through England to London, he staged one or two displays of the theatricality of power that might almost have been taken from *Henry V*. At Newark he provided two exemplary instances of retribution and clemency. The British Solomon first astonished the onlookers when, on hearing that a pickpocket had been captured red-handed in the crowd, he ordered him to be instantly hanged. Then, just before he left the town, he freed all the prisoners held in the castle.

James was soon to make such theatricality a staple of his rule. His entry into London, under triumphal arches decorated with words by Jonson, Daniel, and other writers, was a massive public display of those august personal qualities to which he aspired, as well as of his royal authority. He operated on a less grandiose scale as well, keeping his people and his officials on their toes. The repeated postponement of Ralegh's execution, for instance (he lived in the Tower, under sentence of death, from 1603 to 1613), was merely the most extreme case of his artful manipulation of his subjects' anxiety. The senior participants in the so-called Bye plot had to watch as one by one their associates were publicly tortured and executed. They were then led to the scaffold themselves, only to be told they had been granted a two-hour reprieve. The confused prisoners were then asked if they believed their sentences were just; when they agreed that they were, the sheriff announced that the king had spared their lives. Dudley Carleton, describing this episode in a letter, wrote that the three men stood in amazement, "together on the stage as use is at the end of the play." The king's stage management of the show typifies his sense of the need for power to be displayed persuasively to the general populace and to those courtiers rash enough to question it.

In the private sphere of the court, James sponsored the masque as a form designed to express what he held to be certain fundamental truths about himself and his position. It became both a vehicle for articulating specific policies and an elaborate and allegorical way of representing James's view of the way God had organized society— with the king as the father, the earthly deity, placed incontestably above the rest of creation.

Such interests disposed James to play a more direct role in the patronage of drama than Elizabeth had, and Shakespeare and his fellows were the immediate beneficiaries. Only ten days after his arrival in London, James instructed Cecil to publish letters patent appointing the Lord Chamberlain's Men the king's own troupe of players:

> Know ye that we of our Special grace, certain knowledge, and mere motion, have licensed and authorised . . . these our servants Lawrence Fletcher, William Shakespeare, Richard Burbage, Augustine Phillips, John Hemings, Henry Condell, William Sly, Robert Armin, Richard Cowley, and the rest of their Associates freely to use and exercise the art and faculty of playing comedies, tragedies, histories, interludes, morals, pastorals, stage-plays, and such others like as they have already studied or hereafter shall use or study, as well for the recreation of our loving subjects, as for our solace and pleasure when we shall think good to see them, during our pleasure. . . .

The patent goes on to exhort local authorities to allow performances by these men, and to "be aiding and assisting them, if any
wrong be to them offered." During the rest of the plague year the
company—armed with their new patent—traveled widely, playing
at Bath, Coventry, Shrewsbury, perhaps Ipswich, Oxford, and
Cambridge. The company were at Mortlake on December 2, 1603,
when they received the royal summons to play before the king and
the earl of Pembroke at Wilton. In the list of players pride of place
is given to Lawrence Fletcher, not recorded elsewhere as a member
of the company. It seems he was already known to the king, having
led a group of English actors to perform in Scotland, where he was
referred to as "comedian to his majesty." He played no role in the
company after 1605, and it may be that his chief task was to assist
in the establishment and organization of the company on its new
basis, which perhaps also helps to explain the prominence of Shakespeare's name on the list. From this time forward the named actors
were members of the royal household, with the rank of Grooms of
the Chamber. They would probably have marched, clad in scarlet
livery, in the king's processional entry in May 1604, and on other
great occasions; in the wardrobe records, Shakespeare's name heads
the list of players receiving scarlet cloth.

Other dramatic companies also came under the patronage of the
royal family: the Admiral's became Prince Henry's Men, and
Worcester's became Queen Anne's Men. But there is plenty of
evidence, most obviously the records of court performances, to
testify to the preeminence of Shakespeare's company. During the
final years of Elizabeth's reign, the Chamberlain's Men had averaged
three appearances at court per year; after the accession of James,
however, the picture changed markedly, and not merely because
the king was especially fond of dramatic shows. In the first ten
years of his reign—the last ten of Shakespeare's active career—the
King's Men performed at court a dozen or so times every year—
more than all the other troupes put together. In each of those last
two seasons, 1611–12 and 1612–13, they were to give some twenty
performances. And Shakespeare was without question the writer
whose works were most numerously and regularly performed. In
1604–5, for instance, the company appeared on eleven occasions,
mostly in plays by Shakespeare (*Love's Labour's Lost*, *The Comedy of
Errors*, *The Merry Wives of Windsor*, *The Merchant of Venice* [twice],

Othello and *Measure for Measure*). The actors were also involved in other forms of court display: In the summer of 1604 they were attached to the household of the newly arrived Spanish Ambassador, Velasco, for three weeks during the peace negotiations between England and Spain.

James, his wife, and many of their leading courtiers were also interested in other forms of drama, the most distinctive of which was the court masque. In 1604 Samuel Daniel's show *The Vision of the Twelve Goddesses* was staged at Hampton Court with Queen Anne performing. The following year, the partnership between the great architect and theater designer Inigo Jones and Ben Jonson created the *Masque of Blackness*, and from then on the tradition was established.

In these entertainments the roles played by the royal and noble participants were usually mute, while professional actors, singers, and musicians performed around them. Shakespeare, who never wrote a royal masque himself, incorporated material from the new genre in his plays. He was also influenced by the so-called closet drama that had recently become fashionable. These were plays written for private study or declamation, and they tended to treat subjects in political history and theory from a high-minded, almost distinterested, point of view. One of the king's closest friends, his literary collaborator Sir William Alexander, wrote in 1604 a series of plays called the *Monarchic Tragedies*—on Alexander, Darius, Croesus, and Julius Caesar. Fulke Greville, the countess of Pembroke, Elizabeth Carey, and Daniel were others who developed the form.

Writers responded in different ways to the challenge posed by a new king who was a ruler and a political theorist as well as a poet and a thinker about literature. They were writing under the eye of a practitioner and a theorist, a man whose personal contradictions were too numerous to list but which included an apparently irreconcilable combination of unquestioning authoritarianism and relish for debate and argument. Shakespeare—perhaps as much because he was never at the center of the court and never had to rely on patronage, as for any reason of temperament—managed to negotiate these years as skillfully as he had the last days of Queen Elizabeth.

It seems that he had moved to new lodgings in London by this time. On the basis of evidence he himself gave in a court case heard in 1612, we know that in 1604—and perhaps from as early as 1602, for Shakespeare's own memory was unclear when he testified—he was living in Cripplegate ward, just inside the city walls, in the household of Christopher Mountjoy, a French Huguenot "tire-maker" (a maker of decorative headdresses for women). The house, with its shop underneath, was at the corner of Silver Street and Monkwell Street. Nearby, in Wood Street, lived his Stratford neighbor Richard Field; and Field's wife Jacqueline is certain to have known Madame Mountjoy, since they both attended the same French church. Other neighbors in the adjacent parish of St. Mary's Aldermanbury were his colleagues Heminges and Condell. The antiquary Stow and others describe this area as featuring substantial dwellings, halls belonging to livery companies, and well-maintained churches and almshouses. But Shakespeare's parish church, St. Olave's Silver Street, is given short shrift in Stow's description: "a small thing, and without any noteworthy monuments."

But at the same period, if rumor is to be believed, Shakespeare was a regular and valued guest of the Davenant family, who were wine merchants in Cornmarket Street, Oxford. This was a natural stopover on his journeys between the capital and Stratford. In all probability he knew the Davenants from London, where they had all been employed by the queen's court and its members. And John Davenant seems to have been an enthusiast for the drama throughout the 1590s before he moved to Oxford. Sir William Davenant encouraged the belief that he was the illegitimate offspring of Shakespeare, whose godson he also claimed to be. If Shakespeare was indeed the godfather of the future poet laureate, he would have been in Oxford for the christening at St. Martin's, Carfax, on March 3, 1606.

Othello is almost the definitive Jacobean tragedy, set in a world where heroic and spiritual values are undermined by diabolic intrigue and jealousy, and where the quality of heroic patience is exemplified by a suffering woman. It is also especially Jacobean because it draws on a variety of the king's known preoccupations. That is not to say that it was written specifically for the king— rather that the king's publicized interests and concerns constitute an important part of the play's context. These factors would have been most apparent when the "Kings Majesty's Players" gave the play, entitled "The Moor of Venice," at the Banqueting House in Whitehall on November 1, 1604.

The king had, as was well known, written a poem to celebrate the Christian victory over the Turks at Lepanto in 1571; and there were plenty of people keen to advocate a crusade against the Turks (whose conquests now stretched as far as Austria)—though they soon transferred their energies to Prince Henry when the king's pacific disposition became recognized. Shakespeare clearly knew and used Richard Knolles's recent book *A Generall Historie of the Turkes* (1603). James was also fascinated by evil, and especially by witchcraft, on which he regarded himself as an expert; he was in addition—understandably, given the circumstances of his earliest years—exceptionally wary of intrigues and plots. The inscrutable figure of Iago would have given him plenty to think about. The careers of Othello, Iago, and Cassio would have been of interest at a time when the new administration was busy filling all the posts that had fallen vacant on the queen's death. In the words of Sir Anthony Weldon, James was believed to have a policy of promoting "mean men" to "great places . . . that when he turned them out again, they should have no friend to bandy with them; And besides, they were so hated by being raised from a mean estate, to overtop all men, that every one held it a petty recreation to have them often turned out." To these might be added the interest aroused by the recent visit of the Commedia dell'Arte from Venice, and the continuing general fascination with Venice and its democratic system of government among those interested in modern political organization.

As in *Romeo and Juliet*, Shakespeare derived much of the material from the Italian novel tradition, to which he habitually turned for comic and romantic stories. The story of Desdemona and the (unnamed) Moorish captain came from Giraldo Cinthio's *Gli Hecatommithi;* and Shakespeare also drew once more on Geoffrey Fenton's translation of Bandello, *Certain tragicall discourses* (1567).

The oscillation between the comic and tragic, between the domestic and the heroic, disturbs preconceived distinctions between comic and serious events. The setting of the play takes the action from the world of Italianate political intrigue in Venice to the exotic, amorous island of Cyprus, associated with the queen of Sheba and Venus. The place of trial surrounded by the turbulent sea is a common romance motif. At one level the setting is indeed epic and heroic, derived from the political and religious conflicts of the age, spiced with connections with romantic epic—Othello resembles many figures of romance, notably Orlando in *Orlando Furioso* and Amphialus in Sidney's *Arcadia*. Amphialus, like many heroes of love tragedies, is an especially notable model for Othello and Antony because of his tendency to ruin what he loves, to find tragedy and destruction where he seeks love and contentment.

At another level the setting is domestic and recalls the world of domestic tragedy, exemplified by plays such as Thomas Heywood's *A Woman Killed with Kindness* (performed by Worcester's Men at the Rose in March 1603). It also suggests the world of domestic comedy, the domain of Shakespeare's own *Merry Wives of Windsor*, in which much depends upon the conceit that cuckoldry enjoyed the status of a national pastime, and which is recalled on several occasions during the Cyprus scenes of *Othello*. Shakespeare's play was revived for a court performance on November 4, 1604. There are also numerous echoes in *Othello* of Jonson's *Every Man in His Humour*. Jonson's play was published in two versions: that in the Folio of 1616 is set in London, and the jealous husband is called Kitely. In the first version, from 1601, a version in which Shakespeare probably acted, the jealous husband is called Thorello (the play also includes a Prospero and a Stephano). *Every Man in His Humour* was revived by the King's Men for a performance at court on February 2, 1605.

In the course of the play, the status of Othello veers between these realms, and indeed the same is true of many other figures and situations within the play. For instance, there is a clear debt to the Commedia dell'Arte, which visited London on several occasions, and from which the relationship between a bombastic soldier and his cunning, self-conscious, audience-wooing servant could have been derived. Similar material might have been gleaned from the Spanish picaresque tales beginning to be read in England. On the other hand, there may well be a more "heroic" register. An example, pointed out by Barbara Everett, is Iago's name. It is, after all, Spanish rather than Italian. In Spanish Santiago Matamoros—St. James the Moor-slayer—is accorded special reverence and associated with the defense of Christendom against pagan Moors. This peculiar mixture—Othello's name recalling a foolish, jealous husband, Iago's a great defender of the Church against the Moors—is just part of the way this disconcerting play foxes and confuses, even when it seems most direct.

Shakespeare could easily have created a narrative solely out of the events in Cyprus; and had he done so it might have conformed to the canons of neoclassical tragedy, displaying unity of time, place, and action. The way Shakespeare truncated the long drawn-out conclusion of the source shows that he was quite capable of paring down the material for dramatic economy. But he also added the lengthy beginning in Venice, which indicates that his decision not to write a neoclassical tragedy was quite deliberate.

The first scenes are strikingly similar to *Much Ado About Nothing*: They occur during an interlude in a war, and involve a plan to spread slander. The schemes of the wicked Don John are thwarted by Dogberry and Verges—who in their foolish way embody the social infrastructure of Messina; that society seems well enough organized to cope with slander. At the outset of *Othello*, Venice seems similarly equipped. In the Council scene, the interests of the state in the end take precedence over private concerns stirred up by Iago's artfulness. The duke, after all, starts by promising that Brabantio can do what he will with the abductor of his daughter; but on learning that Othello is the accused, he protests, "To vouch this is no proof," insists that his general be heard, and concludes after Othello's speech: "I think this tale would win my daughter too." It is a combination of the Moor's eloquence and value to the state that dismisses Brabantio's protest. The stage is then filled with the sort of event more normal at the end of a comedy, where the union between Desdemona and Othello receives the sanction of Venetian society—though Brabantio's speech, the words of a man excluded from the Council and from the revelry, includes overtones of something less joyful. Clearly Desdemona, like Helena in *All's Well that Ends Well*, arouses male insecurities because of her independence. In her father's words:

Look to her, Moor, if thou hast eyes to see.
She has deceiv'd her father, and may thee.

Othello describes how Brabantio invited him to tell the story of his life, and how Desdemona fell in love with him, in the usual way of romances, through the intermediate step of pity. He says of his narrative:

I ran it through, even from my boyish days,
To the very moment that he bade me tell it.

What is arresting about these words is that Othello's life at that stage makes sense for him—he is able to tell his story right up to the present. This faculty remains with him until he is removed from the infrastructure and values of Venetian society to the storm-battered island of Cyprus. When he first arrives he is still able to make an artistic shape out of his life story:

If it were now to die,
'Twere now to be most happy; for I fear
My soul hath her content so absolute
That not another comfort like to this
Succeeds in unknown fate.

Events prove him to be correct. Thereafter, deprived of his social self, removed from the Venetian framework, Othello can't make sense of the world. His *raison d'être*—the Turkish force—is blown away by a tempest. He misreads evidence, and veers toward the panic-stricken cuckold status of Jonson's Thorello. We can see a powerful contrast with the confident game-playing of Desdemona, as in her exchange of wit with Iago while waiting for Othello to arrive:

I am not merry, but I do beguile
The thing I am by seeming otherwise.

As feminist critics have pointed out, however, the presentation of Desdemona exemplifies the difficulty faced by so many Jacobean dramatists—that of depicting virtue, and especially female virtue, in language and action. The usual solution was to extol essentially static qualities such as constancy and patience. The alternative, deeds or eloquence, seems to have generated alarm, mistrust, and anxiety on the part of male spectators, terrified by the spectacle of female freedoms. In *Othello*, Iago recognizes and exploits his society's nervousness in trying to distinguish female liberty from depravity; Desdemona can only speak persuasively of her nature to Othello when she has been stifled.

The conclusion of the play visually recalls the Venetian scene. Then, the bridal couple had been attended by a large party of Venetians; the next time such an assembly appears is when Othello, having just killed his wife, is confronted by the Venetians who have been sent to Cyprus. The "tragic loading of the bed" is a final, grotesque version of comic tradition. The spectacle causes Othello to return to his story-telling mode. His final speech is an attempt to transform his tragedy into part of a bigger narrative, to have it assimilated within the broader context of Venetian history. It is as if he is attempting to dictate to Lodovico the terms of his official report to be delivered to the Venetian senate. And, like the story of his life in Brabantio's house, again it is told to the very moment of its delivery:

> I pray you in your letters,
> When you shall these unlucky deeds relate,
> Speak of me as I am: nothing extenuate,
> Nor set down aught in malice. Then must you speak
> Of one that loved not wisely but too well;
> Of one not easily jealous, but, being wrought,
> Perplexed in the extreme: of one whose hand
> (Like the base Indian) threw a pearl away
> Richer than all his tribe: of one whose subdued eyes,
> Albeit unused to the melting mood,
> Drops tears as fast as the Arabian trees
> Their medicinable gum. Set you down this;
> And say besides, that in Aleppo once,
> Where a malignant and a turban'd Turk
> Beat a Venetian and traduc'd the state,
> I took by th' throat the circumcised dog,
> And smote him—thus.

Othello's last words follow:

> I kissed thee ere I killed thee. No way but this,
> Killing myself, to die upon a kiss.

These words evoke the familiar conceits and paradoxes of love poetry. But here they are literalized in a most harrrowing way.

The play is troubled, disturbing, and ambiguous. Perhaps Othello himself is to be imagined as believing that a noble death could put right all that had gone before, and dies putting his case to the court of posterity. In the words of Montaigne's essay, "That we should not judge of our happiness, until after our death":

> . . . the same good fortune of our life, which dependeth of the tranquillity and contentment of a well-borne mind, and of the resolution and assurance of a well-ordered soul, should never be ascribed unto man, until he have been seen play the last act of his comedy, and without doubt the hardest. In all the rest there may be some mask . . . But when that last part of death, and of our selves comes to be acted, then no dissembling will avail, then is it high time to speak plain English, and put off all vizards: then whatsoever the pot containeth must be shown, be it good or bad, foul or clean, wine or water. . . . Lo here, why at this last cast, all our life's other actions must be tried and touched. It is the master-day, the day that judgeth all others: it is the day, sayeth an ancient writer, that must judge of all my forepassed years. To death do I refer the essay of my study's fruit. There shall we see whether my discourse proceed from my heart, or from my mouth. I have seen divers, by their death, either in good or evil, give reputation to all their forepassed life. . . . When I judge of other men's lives, I ever respect, how they have behaved themselves in their end; and my chiefest study is, I may well demean [comport] my self at my last gasp, that is to say, quietly, and constantly.

King James I, it is commonplace to observe, was a mass of contradictions: questioning yet authoritarian; intellectual yet coarsely physical. He was a committed patron and cultivator of drama, and believed strongly in his own role as speaker and writer. Yet personally he was deeply antipathetic to crowds, and had none of the famous multilingual grace that his predecessor had so readily displayed. Sir Anthony Weldon, later to be a strident supporter of Parliament in the Civil War, provides the following sobering account of the king, whom he describes as being "naturally of a timorous disposition," wearing padded doublet and breeches to deflect the assassin's knife:

His beard was very thin: his tongue too longe for his mouth, which ever made him to speak full in the mouth, and made him drink very uncomely, as if eating his drink, which came out into the cup on each side of his mouth . . . his legs were very weak, having had (as was thought) some foul play in his youth, or rather before he was born, that he was not able to stand at seven years, that weakness made him ever leaning on other mens' shoulders; his walk was ever circular, his fingers ever in that walk fidling about with his cod-piece.

Of all Shakespeare's Jacobean plays *Measure for Measure* has been the one most frequently and closely related to the king himself. The Revels accounts for the winter of 1604–5 record the perform-ance "On St Stephen's Night in the Hall" of "A play called Mesur for Mesur" by "Shaxberd." And in that play Shakespeare presents us with a ruler who seems to share some of James's qualities. In particular, he displays the same uneasiness about crowds. Accord-ing to a contemporary work, *The Time Triumphant* (1604), James, faced with a tumultuous crowd on a visit to the Royal Exchange, "discommended the rudeness of the multitude, who, regardless of time or place or person will be so troublesome." The author asks the population: "Will you in love press upon your sovereign thereby to offend him, your sovereign perchance mistake your love, and punish it as an offence?" This episode may lie behind Angelo's reference to the way in which:

The general subject to a well-wish'd king
Quit their own part, and in obsequious fondness
Crowd to his presence, where their untaught love
Must needs appear offence.

And the Duke's words of explanation for his disappearance may similarly have their origin in the historical James:

I love the people,
But do not like to stage me in their eyes;
Though it do well, I do not relish well
Their loud applause and *aves* vehement;
Nor do I think the man of safe discretion
That does affect it.

But there is no evidence that the play was specifically written for court performance in the presence of the king on St. Stephen's Day. It is much more likely to date from the previous summer, and was probably performed at the Globe. The political situation in the Vienna of the play seems to recall the peace negotiations with Spain that were taking place in August 1604, when the King's Men spent three weeks attached to the Spanish Ambassador's household. So while the new king is a vital part of the play's context, his Christmas celebration was not its occasion.

More relevant is the contemporary vogue for plays featuring disguised rulers who conduct experiments on their former subjects. Setting to one side the disguise episode in *Henry V*, Shakespeare was a relative late comer to this new genre, which started in the private theaters with their companies of boys. On February 20, 1604, the Paul's boys acted, in the king's presence, Middleton's play *The Phoenix*, in which a prince, having feigned departure, adopts a disguise in order to seek out wrongs and put them right. John Marston's *The Malcontent* and *The Fawne*, with very similar plots, were put on by the Blackfriars boys in 1603 and 1604 respectively.

The new genre is perhaps as closely related to the appearance of Montaigne's *Essays* in 1603 (cited on almost every page of *The Fawne*, for example) as to the king's anxieties. Shakespeare's play opens with the identification of two ways of looking at the world and authority. The duke's words in the opening scene are first to Escalus, "Of government the properties to unfold . . . " and then to Angelo:

> There is a kind of character in thy life,
> That to th'observer doth thy history
> Fully unfold. . . .

These words contrast markedly with Angelo's response to his commission:

> Now, good my lord,
> Let there be some more test made of my mettle
> Before so noble and so great a figure
> Be stamp'd upon it.

The play develops into a competition between these two views—the duke representing an investigative strategy of unfolding and seeing beneath the surface, while Angelo declares adherence to the letter of the law, to an idea of authority as immutable. Here we see a struggle between defining and exploring. For the consideration of the relationship between justice and equity Shakespeare draws on many Renaissance commonplaces—which were conveniently rehearsed for him in both the *Arcadia* and *The Faerie Queene*. A particular example is the use of the empty judgment seat, which in performance exercises a powerful silent influence over several scenes. Indeed the play proclaims its connection with some staples of humanist treatment of the human condition. The best example is the setting of scenes in prison, where the duke's counsel to Claudio not to set too much trust in the things of this world is reinforced by the way the episodes visually express the common humanist view of human life as a period of imprisonment, during which the soul is incarcerated within the body.

Through such staging, and the consistent deployment of biblical language, Shakespeare heightens the sense of the play's seriousness, of its preoccupation with ideas. There are scenes that are set up almost as set-piece formal debates, in particular the two private exchanges between Angelo and Isabella in the second act, and the duke's persuasion of Claudio to accept death, as well as the lofty, semireligious language of the duke's soliloquy:

> He who the sword of heaven will bear
> Should be as holy as severe.

But this elevated material coexists with the exuberant semianarchy of the low-life scenes and the intense pragmatism of the "bed-trick" with which Angelo is to be duped into sleeping with his abandoned betrothed. In addition, the play includes, as *Othello* had, a powerful element of romance, exemplified by the very self-conscious fictionality and artificiality of the conclusion and, more obviously, by the fact that the resolution of the plot depends upon sheer good fortune, washed up from the sea—in the duke's words, "an accident that heaven provides."

So no matter how assiduous a stage manager the duke may be, the success of his project depends crucially on a *deus ex machina*, on an intervention by a power beyond his control. And the play abounds in such apparent contradictions. After all, if the duke represents "unfolding," he does so by shrouding himself in a cowl for much of the action. And while the duke may initially be presented as the representative of an experimental rather than an absolutist view of existence and authority, in contrast to the comparative rigidity of both Angelo and Isabella, by the end he finds himself reasserting his authority in distinctly hierarchical terms. After announcing to each of the figures onstage the decision he has made about their future, he tells the company:

> So bring us to our palace, where we'll show
> What's yet behind, that's meet you all should know.

Here he breaks with Shakespeare's comic convention—normally such retirements at the end of comedies are for the purpose of sharing experiences and reestablishing a sense of community. In the duke's words, the concept of sharing has been silenced in favor of a plan to dispense information that is "meet you all should know." It is to be less a pooling of experiences and more a kind of selective briefing.

So it is possible that the thrust of the play is away from experiment, away from asserting the social values of self-knowledge and love, toward something much more authoritarian. Perhaps we are to conceive of the duke as learning something by his experiments, but also eventually returning to a more traditional model of rule. One of the lessons he seems to learn, in fact, is the need to "stage" himself in the eyes of his people, to grasp the essential theatricality of power. Though he may claim, as Feste had in *Twelfth Night*, that *cucullus non facit monachum* ("a cowl does not make a monk"), his disguise has been very effective: It has gained him special and privileged access to Claudio, and has given him the sort of free-floating social role that the cross-dressed heroines of the romantic comedies conventionally perform.

The most extended demonstration of the duke's use of theatricality is in the final scene. Like James with the Bye conspirators, the duke goes out of his way to arouse anxiety, especially by letting Isabella believe that her brother has been executed and by watching her as she pleads for Angelo's life. King James comes to mind; he had a theatrical streak and clearly relished the comic and theatrical possibilities that his position gave. He had, for instance, as well as a weakness for hearty practical jokes, a deadpan sense of humor. In Weldon's words: "He was very witty, and had as many ready witty jests as any man living, at which he would not smile himself, but deliver them in a grave and serious manner." The result of the duke's deception is to marry off Angelo, and to instruct Isabella to marry him. Accordingly, if Isabella is dressed in religious garb and if the duke has removed only his cowl and not his cloak, the betrothal procession at the end is led by what looks like a monk and a nun.

The play seems much less wedded to individualism than is Shakespeare's wont. Indeed we might speculate that in the duke's view— as in the view of some thinkers of the time and since—identity properly consists of participating in the state, and authority includes the right to dispose of the bodies of its subjects in marriage. At this point a broader political consideration emerges, not least from the heroine's name (Spanish for Elizabeth). It is as if the resolute defense of chastity is to be conceived of as worthy and noble, but ultimately less than the active engagement with one's self and one's state that marriage confirms. In other words, there is a sense in which the play exacts some facets of the transition from the values and the mythology of Elizabeth's reign to those of the new monarch.

But if the play treats—at some level—political material, and is thus a problem play because it addresses ideas, it is also a problem play in a simpler sense. It poses especially acute problems of classificiation, and Shakespeare seems to have gone out of his way to send confusing generic signals. We see this most obviously at the end of the play, where we are not sure how it will resolve itself, and where the wrapping up of the plot is made problematical, uncertain, almost perfunctory.

I would argue that the play's connection with the world from which it sprang is very strong, but that we can also see in it a continuation of some features of Shakespeare's art and the further treatment of some developing preoccupations. Of course James was a variable, contradictory, and paradoxical figure, and so is the duke (as a kind of walking oxymoron, the discoverer covered up); but the real development is in Shakespeare's continuing dissatisfaction with the literary forms he had inherited. He seems to have become increasingly persuaded that the attempt to imitate life required a recognition that the human condition was not assimilable to the ancient forms of comedy and tragedy. Indeed, the unease with which playgoers and readers have responded to *Measure for Measure* over the centuries may well indicate that there is something ultimately unsatisfactory about it. And Shakespeare would never again present a figure of authority in such a way.

For want of conclusive external evidence, *All's Well that Ends Well* is usually dated, on the basis of internal signals, to roughly the same period as *Measure for Measure*. And these two pieces, with their challengingly proverbial titles, are often bracketed together as "problem comedies," since they seem to stretch the conventions of comedy beyond limits established elsewhere. In particular, the situations in which the characters find themselves are more authentically life-threatening, and more morally extreme, than those in any of the earlier comedies. If the title of *Measure for Measure* had aroused expectations of a treatment of justice, reciprocity, retribution, this play's title suggests an interest in the process of ending. Of course both of these plays examine this topic, but in *All's Well* there is almost an obsessiveness with which the idea of an ending is interrogated.

Shakespeare had used the title phrase earlier. In *Henry VI Part 2* he had given Clifford the dying words, *"La fin couronne les oeuvres"*; then in *Troilus and Cressida* another heroic figure, Hector, had announced:

The end crowns all,
And that old common arbitrator, Time
Will one day end it.

If *Measure for Measure* shows the strain of returning to a form that Shakespeare had artistically outgrown, *All's Well* is his first attempt at the genre that was ultimately to engross him in his later years— romance. In that respect, it seems generically less of a problem play than many of those which precede it.

One of the staples of romance stories is the way in which apparent endings turn out to be beginnings, how events unfold in ways unimagined by their instigators. And that, I would propose, is a way of looking at the ceaseless probing of the idea of ending within the play, a probing that grows from a technical problem in managing narrative into an attempt to depict the intractable confusions and contradictions of the human condition.

All's Well opens and closes in the manner of a fairytale—indeed the cure of the king early in the play is taken by the courtiers as a marvel that refutes modern wisdom—"They say miracles are past." Shakespeare took his material from Boccaccio, probably via William Painter's *Palace of Pleasure*. In adapting the story he compressed the early episodes and modified the presentation of the central pair, with the effect of making Bertram seem a good deal less appealing, and arousing more sympathy for Helena's predicament. In addition, Shakespeare widens the social gulf between Helena and Bertram. In his source, the woman Giletta was well-to-do, had several admirers, and was supported by her kinfolk. By removing all this Shakespeare shows that Helena had only her personal virtues to commend her.

While the play may in some ways resemble a fairytale, it is also notable for reversing some of the basic components of traditional love stories. Most obviously, there is no opposition to the match from the older generation; quite the reverse. And Helena's name (Shakespeare's choice) might be seen a deliberate evocation of the story of the Trojan war, involving a similarly disconcerting set of inversions (such as the way her choice of husband—which is made in Paris—is a version of the choice of Paris).

The play embraces within its romance framework a great variety of modes, and slides readily from the fantastic to the naturalistic, giving expression through its plot to two common metaphors for love—as warfare and as pilgrimage or quest. There are moments of city comedy, debates, magic, satire and so on, while the play also invokes the conventional antithesis between the court and the country that had been treated in *As You Like It*. These varied settings provide a context in which Shakespeare explores, as he had in the plays from the turn of the century, the concepts of honor and truth.

Bertram's repudiation of Helena is based on two counts: the first that she is not someone he had chosen for himself; the second that she is from a lower social class—"A poor physician's daughter my wife! Disdain rather corrupt me ever!" The king's response to the first is to reassert his authority; to the second, that he could exalt Helena to any rank he wished—" 'Tis only title thou disdains't in her, the which I can build up." What follows from him is a short essay on the relationship between words and things:

Good alone
Is good, without a name, vileness is so:
The property by which it is should go,
Not by the title. She is young, wise, fair,
In these to nature she's immediate heir;
And these breed honour.

He goes further, as do most representatives of the older generation in the play, to say that the outward signs of honor, the titles and monuments, are habitually deceptive. In his words:

The mere word's a slave
Debosh'd on every tomb, on every grave
A lying trophy.

But if that were all, the play would be much simpler than it is, and would involve teaching Bertram the lesson that, in Spenser's words,

Vertues seat is deepe within the mynd,
And not in outward shows, but inward thoughts defynd.

In fact the play, just as much as *Hamlet* or *Troilus and Cressida*, moves out from a commonplace situation into a more thoroughgoing investigation of all manner of human and artistic categories. The very name of Parolles keeps constantly before our minds the difference between "mere words" and the "word" or troth that is so regularly given in the play, while the play's repeated use of proverbial and sententious phrases invites comparison of experience with received wisdom.

The play soon shows how facile it would be to stress Helena's simplicity on the basis of her early, Hamlet-like remark, "I do affect a sorrow indeed, but I have it too." She turns out to be just as paradoxical as the duke in *Measure for Measure*. While she is held up as a model of integrity, of the coincidence of inner virtues and outward excellence, she also, like Spenser's Britomart (or indeed like Queen Elizabeth), is inseparable from riddles, ambiguities, and mysteries, in both her actions and words:

> . . . with the word the time will bring on summer,
> When briers shall have leaves as well as thorns,
> And be as sweet as sharp. We must away:
> Our waggon is prepar'd, and time revives us.
> All's well that ends well! still the fine's the crown:
> Whate'er the course, the end is the renown.

In interpreting these riddling, oracular words, much hinged on belief and trust, as Helena makes clear at the outset. She invites the king to place his faith not in her medical skills alone, but in God—"Of heaven, not me, make an experiment." It is clear that the idea of a female doctor arouses all kinds of anxieties which need to be soothed (as had been the case when Portia took on the "professional" role of a lawyer in *The Merchant of Venice*—performed before James twice during the 1604–5 season). First of all, her skill is presented as her inheritance from her father. Then it is said to be a channel for God's will. Finally, Helena equates it specifically with her honor as a woman. If she fails in her treatment, she tells the king, she will expect:

> Tax of impudence,
> A strumpet's boldness, a divulged shame,
> Traduc'd by odious ballads: my maiden's name
> Sear'd otherwise . . .

Inevitably, then, for the audience, Helena acquires a special status after the king has been healed. This apparently divine intervention and token of favor recalls the "accident that heaven provides" with which *Measure for Measure* had been resolved, and the appearance of Hymen at the end of *As You Like It*. As in the later romances, there is a coincidence of such supernatural elements and more explicitly human ones.

The Parolles story, crammed as it is with dissimulation, disguise, deliberately mangled language, self-deception, false honor, false courage, and the rest, moves toward the crushing of its victim through forcing him to behold his folly and to recognize that he is known to be a fraud. But then Parolles is given words that speak directly to the audience, puncturing our sense of superiority. He asks, "Who cannot be crushed by a plot?" and then speaks a powerful soliloquy that transforms the tone of the whole play from riotous comedy to the more elevated mode of the semiritualized ending:

> Yet am I thankful. If my heart were great,
> 'Twould burst at this. Captain I'll be no more,
> But I will eat and drink, and sleep as soft
> As captain shall. Simply the thing I am
> Shall make me live. Who knows himself a braggart
> Let him fear this; for it will come to pass
> That every braggart shall be found an ass.
> Rust sword, cool blushes, and, Parolles, live
> Safest in shame!

But it is magic, or apparent magic, together with faith and redemption that dominate the play's ending. The movement toward the conclusion is announced in Helena's statement of the play's title at the end of the fourth act. After that, as the last scene unfolds, we see a seemingly endless series of revelations, each of which shows that previous attempts to make sense of events were premature. The king repeatedly falls for the power of novelty, and his assertion, right at the start of the scene, that "All is whole" needs constantly to be revised in the light of unfolding experience. We see the predominantly male world of judgment, definition, decision, and external shows of honor swept aside by the female modes of indirection, multiplicity, and interior integrity. Diana (whose name, like Helena's, is rich in associative force) offers an explanation that is beyond her listeners: "he's guilty, and he is not guilty." She goes on to introduce Helena in disguise, saying "there's my riddle: one that's dead is quick—and now behold the meaning."

In Boccaccio, when the jilted wife appears she brings with her two children with whom to confront her husband. In Shakespeare's retelling, it is for Bertram and the king—and for us in the audience—to believe that she is pregnant, to "suppose" that what we are told is so. Helena merely reports that the challenge she was set has been met; she declares simply that "This is done."

The conclusion, as we might expect, is postponed. Bertram,

following Touchstone's advice, thinks but of an "If," when he tells
the king:

> If she, my liege, can make me know this clearly,
> I'll love her dearly ever, ever, dearly.

Likewise with the king's last words: "All yet seems well. . . ." As
in the later romances, the company on stage are invited by the king
to pool experiences, to explain the miraculous events that have led
to this riddling conclusion. But the crucial role in all this is to be
played by the audience; it is for us to imagine, to suppose, that all
will indeed end well.

And what guidance can one offer to an audience? How might
Shakespeare have expected to be understood? In the course of Montaigne's great essay "Of Experience," he writes:

> There is no end in our inquisitions. Our end is in the other world.
> It is a sign his wits grow short, when he is pleased; or a sign of
> weariness. No generous spirit stays and relies upon himself. He ever
> pretendeth and goeth beyond his strength. He hath some vagaries
> beyond his effects. If he advance not himself, press, settle, shock,
> turn, wind, and front himself, he is but half alive; his pursuits are
> termless and formless. His nourishment is admiration, questing, and
> ambiguity.

Those final words might almost have been written with *All's Well*
in mind, for the play supplies precisely such nourishment for the
generous spirit. And the words of the king in the epilogue make it
clear that the final responsibility for the fulfillment of the story
rests with the audience and depends upon its generosity of spirit:

> All is well ended, if this suit be won,
> That you express content.

As in *The Tempest*, the act of applauding, which usually marks the
end of a play, becomes instead a moment of active participation in
it and a guarantee of its continuation.

The play has not been short of detractors over the centuries.
However, scholarly interest has revived, and in recent years there
have been some distinguished productions that have brought out

the play's strange power to disturb. They have shown that Shakespeare's first romance is a work which, even if it is in many ways experimental, can still move and astonish and perplex.

Everybody knew that King James was terrified of violent death. Given the fate of his parents, and indeed that of his son Charles I, his ambition to die peacefully in his bed was understandable, and many contemporaries found in this personal preoccupation an explanation for the king's constant advocacy of peace and diplomacy in international relations. The king's anxiety was also fed by a series of plots against him, some more substantial than others.

One particular set of events was deliberately kept in the public's mind. On the morning of August 5, 1600, the king was hunting near Falkland Palace in Scotland; he then rode with Alexander, the master of Ruthven (and younger brother of the earl of Gowrie), to Gowrie House in Perth, where they joined Gowrie for dinner. After dinner, when James and the master were separate from the rest of the party, an altercation developed, as a result of which James's attendants killed both brothers. James then staged in Edinburgh elaborate demonstrations both of his innocence and of the loyalty of his supporters in the clergy. The many who doubted his version of events, and who suspected him of murdering the two young noblemen, were banished for life. The bodies of the young men were quartered and exposed throughout the country. For information beyond that we have to rely on the extraordinary publications that followed it. James rushed into print, his own official account, *The Earl of Gowries conspiracie against the King of Scotland*; it appeared in London within a month, early in September 1600. It was then reprinted as soon as James succeeded to the English throne in 1603. In addition, James declared August 5 a day of thanksgiving in perpetuity, confirmed by the publication in 1603 of *A form of prayer with thanksgiving, to be used every year the fifth of August, being the day of his highness's happy deliverance from the bloody attempt of the Earl of Gowrie.*

In the wider world, reactions ranged from raised eyebrows to frank disbelief, not least because James produced a story that reads more like a fantastic romance than a sober explanation of violent events. The narrative features a mysterious stranger with a pot of gold, and has the brothers pressing James to come and see this phenomenon. On going with Ruthven to the tower where the stranger was to be, James found instead a man in armor carrying a dagger. Ruthven seized the dagger and threatened the king. The king used eloquence to persuade his assailant to go and consult his brother. In his absence, more royal oratory persuaded the armed man to open the window, so that when Ruthven returned to kill the king, help could be summoned. After a struggle in which the king comported himself heroically and wholly defensively, the two brothers were found to be dead, having received wounds in the back.

The dramatic and commercial possibilities of this story were not lost on the King's Men. After all, if the king had deemed it necessary to publicize these events so aggressively and in such a specifically literary way, might it not both amuse him and suit his wider purposes to have the narrative staged before the general populace? So they took the exceptional step of writing a play on a contemporary event. A letter of December 18, 1604 from John Chamberlain runs:

> The Tragedy of *Gowrie*, with all the Action and Actors hath been twice represented by the King's Players, with exceeding Concourse of all sorts of People. But whether the matter be not well handled, or that it be thought unfit that Princes should be played on the Stage in their Life-time, I hear that some great Councillors are much displeased with it, and so 'tis thought shall be forbidden.

So it was, and not a trace has survived. But the episode indicates both the temptation of staging the king and his known interests and values and also the limits of such representation. It is a useful caution against the excessive literalism that sometimes occurs in interpretations of plays from this period. The line was drawn at *Gowrie*, at direct representation of the king in an unmediated, unambiguous form. To be granted permission to perform in public plays which touched the king closely, the King's Men would have to adopt a more oblique, suggestive approach. They would need always to be able to defend themselves against charges of excessive directness, and it seems clear that a play like *Measure for Measure* has built-in defenses against such criticisms.

King Lear survives in two substantive texts, a Quarto edition of 1608, entitled *The History of King Lear*, and the very different text printed in the First Folio of 1623, known as *The Tragedy of King Lear*. It is now held that the 1608 edition is *King Lear* as Shakespeare first wrote it in about 1605; he then returned to the material some two or three years later and extensively revised the play—possibly to accommodate it to some specific theatrical requirements.

Like *Gowrie*, this play had first been performed in the king's presence; but this time both publication and advertisement of public performance were permitted. The Stationers' Register records on November 26, 1607 "A book called, Master William Shakespeare his history of King Lear, as it was played before the King's majesty at Whitehall upon Saint Stephen's night at Christmas Last, by his majesty's servants playing usually at the Globe on the Bankside," and the title page of the Quarto repeats the information. However significant the royal performance, the play is unlikely to have been written specifically for such an event. It seems to have been designed to fit the circumstances both of intimate, indoor staging and of large-scale public performance at the Globe, and to appeal both to a "private" audience of courtiers and politicians and to the undifferentiated mass of theatergoers.

The scholarly collections of sources indicate the remarkable fact that many of *King Lear*'s antecedents are not tragic at all, but are found in comedy, legendary history and romance. In particular, the play can be related to Sidney's *Arcadia* and to the anonymous play *King Leir* (performed in the early 1590s and published in 1605—whether in response to the success of Shakespeare's play or as a stimulus to Shakespeare's imagination is not known). In the sources and models, as in the Book of Job, the Lear figure is an expression of patience rewarded: *King Leir* has a happy and patriotic ending, as the restored company onstage resolve to invade France. The king's last speech reflects this mood of resolution:

Ah, my *Cordella*, now I call to mind,
The modest answere, which I tooke vnkind:
But now I see, I am no whit beguild,
Thou louedst me dearly, and as ought a child.
. . . Come, sonne and daughter, who did me aduaunce,
Repose with me awhile, and then for Fraunce.
    Sound Drummes and Trumpets, Exeunt.

In Nahum Tate's adaptation, which held the stage from 1687 to
the revival of Shakespeare's play in 1843, the happy resolution was
restored. But Shakespeare chose to work against the grain of many
of his sources, and translate this material into a tragic mode. It is
as if he creates a world in which the potential for redemption, for
resolution, is constantly left unfulfilled. In such a context the play's
allusiveness, its very literariness, become tokens of its bleakness.
An example is its manifest closeness to the form of the pastoral—
and especially to that of *As You Like It*. Structurally, for instance,
Lear features a tragic version of the normal pastoral pattern of exile,
re-creation, and return. Then the king himself provides some versions of pastoral staples like the pathetic fallacy—it is his inner
condition which seems to determine the weather, the state of the
kingdom, the health of his subjects, and so forth. And in this
pseudopastoral structure, dialogues and debates become versions
of the pastoral eclogue. But the heath is not Arcadia.

Superficially the play appears to be constructed on the basis of
plot and counterplot, with the subplot as a reflection or repetition
of the main plot. But the relationship of the two turns out to be
much more complex. As in *Measure for Measure*, Shakespeare inter-
rogates the very principles and methods of contrast and analogy at
the same time as he exploits them. Partly this is a way of handling
politically sensitive material, of oscillating between the general and
the particular. The play makes parallels and contrasts hard to develop into interpretation or application. Thus Albany becomes an
absurd figure through his endlessly sententious utterances, his
ceaseless attempts to assimilate the events he witnesses into the
realm of sentenious, proverbial lore, to make unruly experience fit
neatly into the matrix of truisms. Indeed, it is arguable that the
play's structure, with its proliferation of short scenes, mimes disintegration, not counterpoint.

Like the problem plays, *Lear* shows the influence of Montaigne,
with Shakespeare seeming to become increasingly uncertain, sceptical, and questioning. As in *Measure for Measure*, he deploys a great
deal of biblical and proverbial language in the play, but stresses its
anachronism. He takes pains to emphasize how ancient, how pagan
his Britain is. And it is for us to consider whether the events of
the play undermine religious faith or support it. Is the fragmentation
and obscurity of language a sign of grotesque darkness or of glim-

mering light? Lear's Britain is a place from which the supernatural is absent. Tom O'Bedlam is a fake, and by implication all the rituals in the play are based on illusion, fraud, and self-deception. The contrast is with a play like *The Comedy of Errors*, where the demons and sorcery were real enough, but so was the sense that they were to be vanquished by the new Christian revelation. If we take a particularly bleak view of the play, we might see it as offering a critique also of drama as an activity that had no truth, no substance.

Shakespeare returns yet again in this play to the question of identity and self-knowledge, matters wrapped up in the Renaissance mind with consideration of the relationships between show and substance, name and thing, clothes and bodies. A conventional image for truth was a naked body, to be clothed in the garments of language, and it is an image that plays a central role in the play, alongside the other concept of the king's two bodies, one royal and one personal. The play recalls an extraordinary episode in an Italian novella (by Giovanni Sercambi):

> A furrier from Lucca went to a public bath, and took off all his clothes. He was horrified at the thought that he might not know who he was. So he put a straw cross on his shoulder, in order to mark his identity. Unfortunately, a neighbour in the bath-house seized the straw cross, and said to the furrier, "Now I am you; begone, you are dead." The furrier lost his wits, convinced that he was dead.

Parallel to the revelation of a world deserted by the supernatural is a process whereby the metaphorical resources of language are emptied out. Lear is a version of Midas, and the granting of his wish for unambiguous truth, for an end to dissimulation, is as paradoxical and fatal to him as was Midas's wish to transform all he touched into gold. The most harrowing instance is surely the blinding of Gloucester, where the king's metaphorical blindness is translated into appalling actuality on the body of his follower.

Yet there are moments when Shakespeare uses visual, emblematic puns to indicate a realm of meaning which exists for the audience even if it is inaccessible to the speakers in their fallen, unredeemed world. On the heath, just after Lear has started to tear off his clothes, the Fool observes, "Prithee, nuncle, be contented, 'tis a naughty night to swim in. Now a little fire in a wild field were like an old lecher's heart, a small spark, all the rest on's body cold. Look here comes a walking fire." Immediately Gloucester enters, bearing a torch, almost as if he had been conjured by the words, or gives concrete expression to them. In the previous act, Kent falls asleep in the stocks after remarking that "Nothing almost sees miracles/But misery":

> All weary and o'er watch'd
> Take vantage, heavy eyes, not to behold
> This shameful lodging.
> Fortune, good night: smile once more, turn thy wheel.

What follows is the stage direction *Enter Edgar* and Edgar's first words, "I heard myself proclaim'd . . ." This is the first real suggestion—accessible only to the audience—that the wheel of fortune might eventually relent, and the first identification of Edgar with a future beyond the tragedy.

Lear is a love story between generations. Like many love stories it deals with the inexpressibility of love and the impossibility of ever knowing if love is true or if it is reciprocated. At the beginning and end of the play the relationship between love, truth, and words is central. And as the play concludes, Shakespeare once more uses a visual device to communicate beyond the script.

One of the few emblems that we can be certain Shakespeare knew was *Veritas filia temporis*—"Truth the Daughter of Time"— which he could have seen in Whitney's *Choice of Emblems* (1587). He used it at the end of *As You Like It* and in *The Winter's Tale*. Whitney's emblem shows a cave, from which a young woman (Truth) is being led by a bearded old man (Time). The end of *Lear* is closely related. We see the old man Lear bearing Cordelia in his arms as they emerge from the prison cell. But the thing about emblems is that they were meant to be indivisible, that the components of the emblem, the words and the picture, were as inseparable as body and soul: to try to part them was held to be fatal. Here the "meaning"—that truth is revealed in time—is at one level a castigation of Lear's initial treatment of Cordelia; more generally it stands as a token that such a thing as meaning or truth might exist. But that sense is not available to those onstage. It is for the audience to apprehend the role of time in assuaging the pain of tragedies, in forging historical structures and patterns that lead to the present.

In the same way, the concepts of patience and pity have been insinuated into our consciousness as the play has proceeded. Patience is in the foreground in the first half of the play, with several scenes and the whole Gloucester plot recalling those accumulating sequences of horror and grief in *Titus Andronicus*. Patience (both waiting and enduring) is the alternative to Revenge, the quality with which virtuous men and women can oppose the vicissitudes of Fortune. As Lear says, though far too late, "I will be the pattern of all patience. I will say nothing." After the middle of the third act, however, references to pity become numerous, and they are associated with the visual element, the spectacle of the play, traditionally the aspect designed to arouse compassion. And it is through pity, initially, that Shakespeare is able to draw the audience in to the events he depicts, and then make them a crucial element in the resolution. And such involvement is wrapped up, as so often in his plays, with a display of what the very act of staging, of dramatic representation, can magically do.

Anyone watching *King Lear* in the years 1605–6 would have recognized that the ancient British ruler was not so much a version of their new monarch as his mirror image. James built his cult on his Solomonic dispensing of justice, his peaceable nature, his ability to guarantee a dynasty through his two sons, and his unification of the whole island of Britain. Indeed, at the time of the play the question of uniting the kingdoms of Britain was a matter of urgent political interest. As the audience understood history, the last time the island had been united had been in the reign of King Lear. So when Lear is shown mismanaging and mistreating his family, behaving in a strikingly unjust way, and above all dividing the kingdom, he is the polar opposite of King James.

So little wonder the world of the play is marked by discord and chaos. Like the antimasques that prefaced the great royal shows, it depicts a riotous chaos which the presence of the authentic shape of government will in time dispel. No doubt the contemporary resonances at the performance at Whitehall on St. Stephen's Day would have been greater. It may well be, for instance, that the discourtesy and repudiation of generosity that is such a feature of the play, starting with Lear's treatment of Cordelia and Kent, is meant to jar with the tradition that St. Stephen's Day—Boxing Day—is a time for giving presents, especially to servants. There may have been jokes that were acceptable in private but had to be removed for the Globe. Thus in the Quarto version, after the direction "Enter Lear mad," the king says, "No they cannot touch me for coyning, I am the king himselfe." This probably alludes to the way James, in his writings and speeches on the royal prerogative, repeatedly referred to his absolute and indivisible authority to coin money. And such a joke was probably tolerable within the festival context of Christmas, which often featured ritualized inversion of the social order. In the Globe text, the king does not enter "mad"—he just enters. And what he says is made much more general: "No, they cannot touch me for crying. I am the king himself." Likewise the exchange between Lear and the Fool: "Dost thou call me fool, boy?—All thy other titles thou hast given away, that thou wast born with," is only in the Quarto version.

But the King's Men had learned their lesson with *Gowrie*, and Shakespeare shows in *King Lear* that he could be both popular and arcane, that he could address several audiences at once. And he did so with a combination of directness and obliqueness that none of his contemporaries was able to match. Jonson, for instance, found himself in prison in 1605 for presenting in *Eastward Ho* a man with a thick Scottish accent who referred to "my thirty-pound knights," and was then hauled before the Privy Council to answer charges that his tragedy *Sejanus* was seditious and Popish.

It is normal to date *Macbeth* to 1606. Some scholars claim that it was the play staged when the King's Men performed before the king of Denmark at Hampton Court in August that year; but there is no evidence to prove that it was performed anywhere other than at the Globe, where it was seen in April 1611 by Simon Forman. But even if *Macbeth* cannot be proved to be a court play, traces of contemporary events (in particular the aftermath of the Gunpowder Plot, discovered in November 1605) and the perceived personality and interests of the king can be plausibly identified.

The circumstances of the Gunpowder Plot were almost as murky and confusing as those of the Gowrie conspiracy, and James certainly encouraged the view that the two events were similar. Each, he claimed, was an instance of divine intervention that had saved him for his providential task of ruling the kingdom. The recently imprisoned Ben Jonson, who was known to have dined with two of the conspirators some weeks previously, was asked by the Council to prove his loyalty by finding a priest who was supposed to have been involved in the plot. He failed, but made strenuous efforts on behalf of the investigation, writing to Cecil, "I do not only with all readiness offer my service, but will perform it with as much integrity, as your particular favour, or his Majesty's right in any subject that he hath, can exact." Shakespeare had already shown an ability to deal with politically sensitive material in an indirect way. He had no need to go out of his way to display his loyalty; nevertheless his play can be seen to touch on the atmosphere of 1606 in a couple of places.

The most notable is the otherwise incomprehensible speech of the Porter: "Faith, here's an equivocator, that could swear in both the scales against either scale, who committed treason enough for God's sake, yet could not equivocate to Heaven: O come in, equivocator." Equivocation had become a vogue word in 1606, especially during and after the trial of Father Henry Garnet, a Jesuit implicated in the conspiracy. Cecil wrote a pamphlet, *Answer to Certain Scandalous Papers*, on the subject, and James himself became obsessed by it, so much so that he continued to debate with Garnet's defenders long after the wretched man had been tried and executed on May 3. Not long afterward, the scholar Isaac Casaubon wrote wearily of the king that "Hardly a day passes on which some new pamphlet is not brought in, mostly written by Jesuits, on the martyrdom of Saint Garnet, the sufferings of English Catholics, or matters of that description. All these things I have to read and give my opinion upon." It is evident that many loyal Catholics were shocked—as they were no doubt meant to be—by the reports of Garnet's equivocation. And *Macbeth* reflects these concerns. Throughout the play Macbeth equivocates with his own conscience, and so do many other speakers: The witches constantly speak in the gnomic, obscure language that James had specifically repudiated in his speech to Parliament; similarly Lady Macbeth; and then Malcolm in his dealings with Macduff. Equivocation may also partly account for the frequency with which the language of antithesis and opposition ("fair is fowl, and fowl is fair," and so on) is employed in *Macbeth:* "Such welcome and unwelcome things at once 'Tis hard to reconcile."

Shakespeare was evidently thinking about history again in the first years of the new reign, and was back once more to Holinshed and Plutarch, working more or less simultaneously on both *Macbeth* and *Antony and Cleopatra*. There are many points of similarity between the plays. In particular there are many correspondences between the final acts, as in the treatment of Macbeth's arming, or the moment where he asks, "Why should I play the Roman fool, and die on mine own sword?"; and each play features prophecies, dreams, and oracles, which are related to history, politics, and illustrate the vagaries of individual interpretations of events and signs. The play presents equivocation of utterance; but it also, like the English history plays, demonstrates the difficulties posed by historical interpretation. As the action develops, most judgments expressed in the play are seen to be inescapably flawed, partial, self-interested, or ignorant. Yet even to recognize that is shown not to be a guarantee against relying upon erroneous impressions. Thus, when Duncan comments on Malcolm's report of the way Cawdor had behaved at his execution for treason, his words seem to acknowledge how difficult it is, especially for a ruler surrounded by flatterers, to read the heart from external signs:

> There's no art
> To find the mind's construction in the face;
> He was a gentleman on whom I built
> An absolute trust.

But immediately Macbeth enters, to be welcomed and showered with thanks. The moment is closely related to the constant examination in Jacobean literature—including the king's own writings, *Measure for Measure*, and *All's Well*—of the problems that people in authority face in interpreting the words and actions of those who serve them. The difficulty was not so much the words themselves as the motivation behind them. Even plain speaking, as James and others recognized, could be a cloak for something else.

If the king's anxieties were aroused by inscrutable courtiers, they were also fed by his well-known fascination with witchcraft and his curiosity about methods of identifying witches. Just a few years after *Macbeth* the judicial slaughter of the Pendle witches in Lancashire would inaugurate another spate of witch-hunting in England, and the contrasting responses of Macbeth and Banquo to the weird sisters are part of the contemporary interest in the matter. But then, interpreters are everywhere in the play. In performance, particular weight is thrown on the chorus-like moments in the first half of the play, such as the exchange between Ross and the mysterious, anonymous "Old Man" at the end of Act II, and the similar commentary on events by Lennox and an unnamed "Lord" which concludes the third act. All these interpreters and interpretations help to foreground the challenge—illustrated in all Shakespeare's historical plays—of trying to decipher providence, to read one's fortune.

Macbeth presents us with a world of darkness, chaos, and blood; treason and rebellion are staged in ways apparently designed to evoke the intense horror with which many writers in the early years of King James outlined the consequences of regicide and rebellion. But the play's art, and the audience's growing awareness of its shape, stand as metaphors for providence. *Macbeth*'s very brevity and elegance are part of its meaning; it is consolingly well proportioned.

Shakespeare takes pains to distinguish his play from neoclassical and "closet" drama as well as from other popular genres. And he does this partly by reproducing the form he is avoiding; the artistic debate between Shakespeare and Jonson was not one-sided. Thus the captain's description of Macbeth's fight is just that, a report of offstage events we do not see. The scenes surrounding the murder of Duncan take place—in accordance with neoclassical convention—in an antechamber. Yet the banquet scene with its ghost evokes a feature of the more popular mode of revenge drama. No less explicitly, the pageants and apparitions in Act IV, Scene I relate the action to epic, to history, and to the masque.

Competing with this diversity, however, are forces, such as the constant stress of psychological inwardness which draw the play's elements together, making it one of Shakespeare's densest, most singly focused works. The play deploys a small number of powerful central images—blood is the most obvious—which have the effect of generating an imaginative coherence; and the numerous descriptions are especially rich in metaphorical and visual material (like Duncan's "silver skin laced with his golden blood").

The story of Macbeth was an even stronger part of the Jacobean myth than that of King Lear. King James traced the Stuart line back to Banquo, and liked to imagine that it would continue forever, which is implicit in Macbeth's vision of Banquo's successors when he sees "the line stretch out to the crack of doom." In the pageant of eight kings, the last bears a glass in his hand in which he shows Macbeth "some . . . That two-fold balls, and treble sceptres carry"—evidently an allusion to James himself as unifier of Britain. The looking glass was one of the king's favorite properties. When, many years later, John Donne was giving advice in a sermon to the new King Charles, he urged him:

> . . . make your selfe as a *Glasse*, (when the *Sun* it selfe is the *Gospell of Christ Jesus*) to reflect, and cast them upon your *Subjects*. It was a *Metaphor* in which, your *Majesties Blessed Father* seemed to delight; for in the name of a *Mirroir, a Looking Glasse*, he sometimes presented *Himselfe*, in his publique declarations and speeches to his *People*.

Donne's words support the view that *Macbeth* does not depend exclusively, as a masque would, on the particular circumstances of a specific royal event. We might wish to imagine a performance in which the actor playing the pageant king turned his looking glass out to King James in the audience. Occasionalist readings of this play do not take into account its implicit assertion of the superiority of public over private dramatic forms. The positive examples of kingship in the play all acknowledge the role of display—the most notable example is Malcolm's adroitly deceitful and ambiguous use of the theatrical arts of power. One of the most remarkable features of Macbeth—a feature it shares with its Elizabethan counterpart *Richard III*—is that the force of the dynastic compliment depends crucially upon the power and grandeur of the hero-villain. Thus, when Malcolm dismisses Macbeth and his wife as "this dead butcher, and his fiend-like Queen," his words, when placed in the context of the Globe in 1606, fall far short of being an adequate or satisfying summary of the man whose death we have witnessed. As with the ending of *King Lear*, the audience is sent away to experience the fruits of their privileged perspective (under which Macbeth is both heroic and a monster, both treacherous and the ignorant instrument of providence), those fruits being, to return to Montaigne, "admiration, questing, and ambiguity."

Of Shakespeare himself at this high summer of his art, next to nothing is known. But what little there is serves as a reminder, as the next chapter will show, of the importance he attached to building up his estates in Stratford and securing his family's material resources.

CHAPTER TEN

Three Classical Plays

The timing of Shakespeare's visits to his family in Stratford-on-Avon cannot be established very accurately, although he does feature in the local records with reasonable frequency. We can assume that he was in the town for such events as the funeral of his son Hamnet in August 1596, and later for the burial of his father in September 1601 and his mother in September 1608. And the likelihood is that he spent part of most summers among his family as the diarist Aubrey reported.

Once installed as the master of New Place, Shakespeare was in a stronger position to set about restoring his family's damaged fortunes. By a series of purchases of land, and through engaging in business with the leading men of the town, he reinforced the new status conferred by the grant of arms, his national fame, and his financial stability. But he was concerned, especially after his father's death, to show he was no soft touch. He shared his contemporaries' willingness to go to law to seek redress, and was persistent in trying to settle matters—not least, perhaps, because of the misfortunes heaped upon his father's head in such cases.

An example is the case of Philip Rogers, an apothecary licensed to sell ale, tobacco, and drugs. In common with many households.

in the town, the Shakespeares brewed their own ale. If they followed the same pattern as others of their class, Anne Shakespeare would have supervised her maidservants once a month in brewing the household's supply. The stock of malt kept at New Place was sometimes substantially greater than was needed for domestic use, and the surplus was occasionally sold off. Between March and May 1604, Philip Rogers bought some twenty bushels of malt from the Shakespeares, and on June 25 borrowed two shillings from them. Of this total debt of some two pounds he later repaid only six shillings, so Shakespeare sued him in the fortnightly Court of Record under the presidency of the bailiff. He wanted his money, and demanded a further ten shillings in damages. Since no more is heard of the matter, it may be that Rogers paid up. In the summer of 1608, Shakespeare tried to recover a debt of six pounds from John Addenbrooke, a gentleman. The case dragged on from August 1608 to June 7, 1609. Addenbrooke was arrested but freed on the guarantee of Thomas Hornby, a blacksmith who operated an ale-house in Henley Street. By the time the court found in Shakespeare's favor, awarding him his debt plus costs plus damages, Addenbrooke had made himself scarce.

What is clear from this is that Shakespeare shared the tendency of his age and class to turn readily to the law for redress, even over quite minor matters. We can see in many of his plays—*The Merchant of Venice* being a particularly vivid example—how questions of debt, obligation, honor, and family shame could occupy his mind. That *The Merchant* dates from the very time when Shakespeare was reestablishing his family's finances, and rehabilitating them as figures in the Stratford community, may be more than coincidence. Shakespeare's relentless legal pursuit of Philip Rogers is contemporary with his much loftier examination of the law and government and the relationships between private and public morality in *Measure for Measure*.

In October 1608 Shakespeare stood as godfather for William, the son of Henry Walker, who was bailiff of Stratford in 1607–8. It is possible that Walker was distantly related to Shakespeare, through a remote branch of Shakespeares in Solihull. But what is known is that he had a mercer's shop in High Street, was an alderman, and served as bailiff also in 1624 and 1635. During his first term as bailiff Walker authorized a payment to players—in fact the only payment to players made at Stratford during the years 1597–1618. His son was to be a beneficiary of Shakespeare's will, and went on to be called a gentleman and to play his part in the life of the town, being elected bailiff in 1649. He died, one of the last direct contacts with Shakespeare, in 1680.

The early years of the new century saw Shakespeare adding substantially to his estates in and around Stratford. The first major transaction occurred on May 1, 1602, and involved the considerable sum of three hundred twenty pounds. This was the price William Shakespeare of Stratford-upon-Avon, gentleman, had to pay to William Combe of Warwick, esquire, and John Combe of Old Stratford, gentleman, for:

> All and singuler those errable landes, with thappurtenances, con-teyning by estymacion fowre yarde lande of errable lande, scytuate, lyinge and beinge within the parrishe, feildes or towne of Olde Stretford . . . in the saide countie of Warrwick, conteyninge by es-timacion one hundred and seaven acres, be they more or lesse.

This parcel of land (which later records show also included an additional twenty acres of pasture) lay in "Old Stratford," an area to the north of the borough which the Combes had leased to Thomas and Lewis Hiccox. It is not clear whether they continued to farm the land after the ownership changed hands, although in the fol-lowing year a Lewis Hiccox (who may have been the same person) was running an inn in Henley Street, possibly even the inn (later named the Maidenhead) that operated in the eastern part of what is now known as the Birthplace. It is conceivable that they followed a common local work pattern with Lewis Hiccox continuing to work in the fields while his wife Alice brewed and sold ale (and fell, according to the records, into quarrels with her rival landla-dies). The deed tells us that Shakespeare did not attend the signing of the legal documents. The deed was handed over to his younger brother Gilbert, "to the use of the within named William Shake-speare, in the presence of Anthony Nashe, William Sheldon, Hum-phrey Mainwaring, Richard Mason, and John Nashe."

On September 28, that year Shakespeare bought a small plot of land behind New Place. It was about a quarter of an acre in extent, on the south side of Chapel Lane, and it included a cottage which faced on to the garden of New Place. Shakespeare's continued ownership is recorded in 1604 and 1606; it passed into the hands of his daughter Susanna in 1617.

In the summer of 1605 part of Shakespeare's mind was doubtless occupied with the fate of Lear, a king who foolishly divided his kingdom. Another part was engaged in some empire-building. On July 24, he purchased, for the large sum of four hundred forty pounds, a half-share in the tithes of "corn, grain, blade and hay" from Old Stratford, Welcombe, and Bishopton, and of the tithes of "wool, lamb and other small and privy tithes" within the parish of Stratford itself. The vendor was Ralph Hubaud of Ipsley. As a result of this investment Shakespeare would have received, even after paying the rents, some sixty pounds per annum from the tithes. The management of these tithes—a complicated and time-consuming business—was entrusted to Anthony Nashe (who had signed the earlier deed); Thomas, Nashe's son, would in due course marry Shakespeare's granddaughter Elizabeth.

After the death of Hamnet in 1596 Shakespeare had no son to carry on the family name or to succeed him in any of his professions. But we have seen how powerful was his drive to create an estate that would last beyond his lifetime, and we can assume that he took care to try to make good matches for his daughters Judith and Susanna. With the latter, he seems to have been fortunate, at least in material terms.

As with her grandfather and her great-uncle, Susanna Shakespeare first appears as an adult in the Stratford records in a disciplinary context. Not for her an unauthorized dunghill or proscribed headgear, however. In the spring of 1606, when she was twenty-three years old, her name appears on a list of persons who had failed to take communion during the Easter season. There was a good deal of anti-Catholic feeling in the country in the aftermath of the Gun-powder Plot of 1605, and the Church authorities had intensified their vigilance in supervising adherence to Church discipline and regulations. The Stratford list of twenty-one undoubtedly includes the names of several Catholics, and of some who were related to recusant families; but others named had failed in their duties for less significant reasons. Such people could escape heavy fines and punishments by taking communion: at least ten of them did so, and the word *dismissa* next to Susanna Shakespeare's name indicates that she was one of them.

She married just a year later, on June 5, 1607. Her husband was unambiguously Protestant; he was John Hall, and was about eight years older than his wife. Hall had settled in Stratford at the turn of the century, and within a short time had established a practice and a glowing reputation as a physician. His father, who styled himself gentleman, as his son would, had been a successful doctor in Middlesex, and had provided a good education for his son. The young man had earned a B.A. (1594) and M.A. (1597) from Queens' College in Cambridge, and had presumably carried on with his medical studies (perhaps in Europe) before settling in Stratford.

Hall was a dedicated physician, a man who turned down local office and national advancement (in the shape of a knighthood) out of a combination of professional single-mindedness and puritan scorn of earthly glory. In later years he became decidedly prickly, and was expelled from the Council for repeatedly disturbing their business. His patients over the years came from far and wide, and represented most rungs of the Jacobean and Caroline social ladder; at one point he attended Shakespeare's exact contemporary, the distinguished poet Michael Drayton, who spent most of his summers with Sir Henry Rainsford and his wife Anne (the *Idea* of Drayton's sonnet sequence) at their house in Clifford Chambers, a couple of miles outside Stratford. As the years went by, Hall compiled masses of case notes, some of which were eventually published as *Select Observations on English Bodies* (1657).

John Hall died when he was about sixty, and was buried on November 26, 1635; the parish record notes the burial of "Johannes Hall, *medicus peritissimus*" (most skilled physician); he had lived at New Place from 1616 (or maybe earlier) until his death. Of his wife, who survived him by some fourteen years, we know very little. Hall's monument refers to her eulogistically as "*fidissima conjux*"—most faithful wife. We know they had one child, baptized Elizabeth on February 21, 1608. We cannot be certain that Susanna could read—at least when James Cooke, Lord Brooke's doctor from Warwick, showed her Hall's medical manuscripts he felt obliged to point out that they were in her husband's hand. It may simply be, of course, that Hall's professional jottings (in Latin) proved incomprehensible to her. And she was also praised in her epitaph as being "witty above her sex" and "wise to salvation." In these respects it was said that she possessed "something of Shakespeare" in her personality.

During these years of getting and spending, of consolidating his estates and securing a future for his children, Shakespeare's writing seemed to be on a wholly different plane as he took on three great classical subjects. But they too are concerned with some matters that must have been at the forefront of his mind—the relationship between private fortune and the wider world, the competition between excess, greatness, liberality, and prudent thrift, and above all, perhaps, how reputation is constructed, how humans are remembered by those who outlive them.

Timon of Athens clearly comes from the period when Shakespeare was rereading Plutarch and working on *Antony and Cleopatra*, *Macbeth*, and *Coriolanus*. *Timon* combines elements of tragedy and problem play; or, to put it differently, it can be seen as "tragedy of ideas" comparable to contemporary works like *The Revenger's Tragedy*. The focus in such plays is less on the fate of the protagonist than on the questions raised, and dilemmas posed, by the story. It may be useful to remember as well that the same period saw some remarkable comedies in which there was a similar "problematic" thrust. The most outstanding example is probably Jonson's *Volpone* of 1607. What these plays have in common is that they are set in a world from which idealism has been purged; they are the reverse of utopian pastorals. But having created their bleak landscapes, the writers then address the question of what Sidney called "well doing"—how a person can behave virtuously when surrounded by expediency, opportunism, and greed. Broadly speaking, their answer comes in two forms: the active (exemplified by Vindice in *The Revenger's Tragedy* and by Volpone); and the static (exemplified by the Lady in the anonymous *Second Maiden's Tragedy*, and by Timon)—and each course generates its own problems.

Timon is no less bizarre than *Troilus and Cressida*, and its survival is wrapped up with that of the earlier play. Detailed inspection of the First Folio has shown that *Troilus and Cressida* was suddenly pulled out of the volume, but not before three pages had already been printed. It is assumed that there was a dispute between the editors of the Folio and the publishers of the 1609 Quarto of *Troilus*. So the gap was filled with *Timon*. Only when the Folio project was nearing completion was a manuscript of *Troilus* obtained—which meant that the editors did not have to rely on the Quarto text—so *Troilus* scraped into the volume between *Henry VIII* and *Coriolanus* (though not on to the table of contents) and *Timon* survived (sandwiched between *Romeo and Juliet* and *Julius Caesar*) to perplex scholars and move its many devotees, ranging from Hazlitt to Karl Marx.

As with his other classical plays, Shakespeare's *Timon* owes much to Plutarch, where the story of Timon of Athens is included as part of the narrative of the life of Mark Antony (the source of *Antony and Cleopatra*). From Plutarch came the main elements of the tale, that Timon's self-exile and misanthropy resulted from the ingratitude of his former friends, that he hated the Athenians, and that his only companions were Apemantus and Alcibiades (whose Life in Plutarch is the parallel to that of Coriolanus, which Shakespeare knew closely). In Renaissance eyes, however, Timon was better known through the satirical dialogue on the subject by Lucian.

Lucian was a great favorite in the Renaissance, at least with those who could read Greek. It is possible that Shakespeare had been exposed to Erasmus's translation (first published in 1528) while still a schoolboy—the text was studied at some Elizabethan schools. The first full English version, Thomas Heywood's *Misanthropos*, was published only in 1637, but the evidence from contemporary references to Timon in the works of countless Elizabethan and Jacobean writers suggest that the story was sufficiently well known for Timon's misanthropy to have become proverbial. What is more, there were many other treatments that Shakespeare might have known, including Italian versions and, most important, a pedantic, academic drama that has been plausibly argued to be an Inns of Court play from around 1602–3 (and slightly less plausibly attributed to Middleton).

The end of the latter play features not Timon's death but a final savage attack on flatterers, as in Lucian's version. And Timon's last speech is unambiguous in its repudiation of mankind:

I protest,
And all the Gods to witnesse invocate,

I doe abhorre the titles of a friende,
Of father, or companion, I curse
The Ayre yee breathe. I lothe to breathe that Aire.
I grieve that these mine eyes should see that Sunne.
My feete treade on that earthe yee treade upon.
I first will meete Jove thundering in the clouds,
Or in the wide devouring Scylla's gulfe
Or in Charybdis I will drowne myself,
Before Ile shew humanity to man.
[*He beates them with his spade.*]

The context of this railing is the festive world of misrule, of in-version, and Timon's spectacular display of wrath is immediately followed by a reassuring, deflationary metamorphosis as he speaks the epilogue:

What's this? I feele throughout
A sodeine change: my fury does abate,
My heart grows milde, and laies aside its hate.
. . . Timon doffs Timon, and with bended knee
Thus craves a favour . . .

And he, wholly conventionally, asks for the audience's applause in the midst of a series of protestations that the tale's harsh fiction was only that, and that it is now over. Given that Shakespeare was so fond of epilogues, and of retirements for exchange of experience, it is immediately noticeable that, if he knew Lucian or this learnedly hilarious Lucianic play, he chose to adopt a very different strategy. Not only does Timon die, but his death is presented with an unusual degree of finality, and is of course expressed in the two contrasting epitaphs which Alcibiades reads to the audience at the end.

This unambiguous move toward finality accounts in large mea-sure for the way the play's narrative is organized. The action of the second half matches that of the first, and so illustrates the consequences of Timon's change of fortunes. The play tends to be unified by ideas rather than by psychological continuities. And the end result is to draw a border round the story, to make Timon seem exemplary, to hold him up as a phenomenon. Critics have often likened the episodic, illustrative pattern to the tradition of the Morality play, and to later examples of the mode such as Marlowe's *Doctor Faustus*. But *Timon*, like the other Jacobean tragedies, is also held together by its images, by its poetry. Indeed, some of the most commitedly appreciative criticism of *Timon* has been based on a view of the text as an extended dramatic lyric. Like *The Phoenix and the Turtle*, it has been seen by some as a marvelous epitome of Shakespeare's most profound preoccupations.

Yet the two halves of the play are more alike than they may seem, in that there is as frantic a lack of discrimination and self-control about Timon's generosity as about his misanthropy; what is more, Timon operates throughout on the basis of an abstract view of human nature that inevitably jars with our experience in the theater, as *The Merchant of Venice* had demonstrated. In his isolation in the second half of the play Timon seems to acquire a new stature, to expand from the realm of the recognizably human. He swells into either a god or a grotesque.

In its absence of women, *Timon* resembles *Coriolanus* more than *Lear* or the romances. It has been called an "abortive romance" that was left unfinished because it could not be developed in such a way as to accommodate the redemptive female principle that Marina and Thaisa would represent in *Pericles*. The only women in the play are Alcibiades' whores—to whom Timon gives gold and whom he incites to destroy male sexuality—and the female figures in the masque of Amazons. It is clear that Timon's misanthropy includes misogyny, and each is a facet of his professed self-sufficiency. It is not simply that he repudiates other people—he conceives of himself as somehow containing or including them. And likewise with women—his loathing coexists with some remarkable moments where he seems to take on female characteristics, to include and assimilate a female principle within himself. Thus in the first scene the poet describes Timon's generosity in terms that suggest a mother feeding her offspring:

> His large fortune,
> Upon his good and gracious nature hanging,
> Subdues and properties to his love and tendance
> All sorts of hearts.

But Timon's feeding others was more costly than he supposed. As with Coriolanus, his assertions of self-sufficiency are shown—

at least in a material sense—to be unfounded. In their absolutism, both men walk a tightrope between dignity and absurdity, between self-knowledge and blind ignorance.

Shakespeare created a world reminiscent of countless other satirical portraits of his own age, notably in its treatment of money, justice, and honor. He surrounded Timon with figures who, like Alcibiades, corresponded closely to stereotypes of Jacobean court life. And in Timon he made one of those unassimilable, prickly figures so often found in drama of these years—as well as Coriolanus, Chapman's Bussy d'Ambois can stand as a representative example. Like Don Quixote, such individuals are both absurd and noble. And Timon's contradictions are left with us as the action ends. Alcibiades reads out an epitaph which combines the two contradictory inscriptions recorded in Plutarch, the second couplet written by Callimachus:

> Here lie I, Timon, who, alive, all living men did hate;
> Pass by and curse thy fill, but pass and stay not here thy gait. . . .

And the other by Timon himself:

> Here lies a wretched corse, of wretched soul bereft:
> Seek not my name, a plague consume you, wicked caitiffs left!

Most scholars have felt that Shakespeare intended to return to this passage and iron out the contradiction. But it is equally possible that he meant to leave us with the final unresolved image of Timon's tomb, washed around by the turbulent sea.

Like many other Shakespeare plays, *Coriolanus* has over the years been revived, rewritten, adapted, and revised to suit particular local purposes and to meet specific demands. On several occasions in England it has been revived in a political context of anxiety at the possibility of rebellion. In 1681, in the time of the Popish Plot, Nahum Tate's adaptation, *The Ingratitude of a Common Weale*, was explicitly slanted to encourage obedience to lawful authority. There were productions in the aftermath of the 1715 rebellion and after the 1745. Then in February 1789, on the eve of the French Revolution, John Philip Kemble's adaptation was first performed. Kemble (who cut out Menenius's fable of the belly) presented Coriolanus as a noble patrician hero dragged down and destroyed by a cruel, mean-spirited mob; his version held the stage for more than twenty years. Coriolanus as defender of the *ancien régime* was succeeded in 1820 by Edmund Kean's neurotic, tortured hero, in a production (admired by Hazlitt) that tried to evoke sympathy for the Roman populace.

On the Continent the play, understood as a contest between democratic and aristocratic, militaristic values, seemed to have a special relevance for Germany in the early years of the century. Later French and German productions in the 1930s seem to have embodied a fascist admiration for both militaristic heroism and self-abnegating nationalism. Olivier's celebrated performance, presenting Coriolanus as a massively arrogant patrician, was staged at the Old Vic in 1938. Since the Second World War the play has continued to arouse controversy. In occupied Germany performances were forbidden by the American authorities during the immediate postwar period. Bertolt Brecht rewrote the text with the particular circumstances of the emerging East Germany of 1952–3 in mind, and brought aggressively to the fore both the plebians and their representatives, the tribunes. In response, a dozen years leater Günter Grass produced an adaptation designed to counter Brecht, to display what he saw as the play's inescapably antidemocratic thrust, and to point to contradictions in Brecht's own position.

We know that Shakespeare took the story of Caius Martius Coriolanus directly from Thomas North's translation of Plutarch, published in 1579 as *The Lives of the Noble Grecians and Romans*. North's Plutarch, as already noted, presents lives in parallel. Thus the stories of Alexander and Julius Caesar, for instance, are placed together, and followed by a short essay comparing and contrasting their careers—a procedure invoked and gently mocked in Fluellen's comparison of Alexander and Harry of Monmouth in *Henry V*. In Plutarch's sequence Coriolanus is paired with Alcibiades, the Spartan who led an Athenian army against his own state, and who plays an important role in *Timon*. Plutarch's comparison highlights the irony that whereas Alcibiades, though licentious and corrupt, brought success to his adopted army, the upright Coriolanus, despite his "notable abstinence from bribes," failed because he lacked both political and military judgment. The main thrust of Plutarch is biographical ("of all his misfortune and ill happe, the austeritie of his nature, and his hawtie obstinate minde, was the onely cause"); its focus is on the natures and achievements of great men, and it implicitly accepts that history is formed by them.

But the story of Coriolanus obviously held other kinds of interest for Jacobean England. At the most basic level, as we have already seen, the notions of personal identity which inform Plutarch's account were not those of Shakespeare's day, the age of reformation, of new learning, of new attitudes to the individual and to individuality. Coriolanus himself dramatizes many of the anxieties that such matters generated in Renaissance England. In the play he is torn by various competing impulses—he tries to wrest a personal identity from his various roles as Roman, as general, as politician, as husband, as father and, most of all, as son.

At the same time, the way people thought about the state was changing. And the centralizing impulse characteristic of most Renaissance states meant that the individual person's quest for identity and for autonomy ran up against the state's impersonal need to ensure its survival. In *Coriolanus* the state is figured as a person, persons as states and kingdoms. The relation between the two is made explicit in the reiterated image of the body, most obviously in the great fable of the nation as a body, whose members are mutually interdependent, with which Menenius Agrippa quells the riot in Act I. But the play is full of references to organs of the body: The leader of the citizens is the "great toe" of the assembly; the commons are the state's "bosom," or a "multitudinous tongue"; the wars touch "the navel of the state"; and to disease—the tribunes call Coriolanus "a disease that must be cut away"—he calls the people "scabs" and "measles." Coriolanus himself is impelled to act out the Renaissance ideal of self-creation, "as if a man were author of himself, and knew no other kin." And this drive, which has obvious parallels with the story of *Timon*, causes Coriolanus to be protective of his physical self; it makes him reluctant to show himself to the crowd, to speak before them. It is as if his sense of physical propriety and modesty involves locating the ideas of wholeness and integrity literally in his body.

This unusual defensiveness, this protectiveness, lends special pathos to the paradox that the very moment he is most himself, when he recognizes his relationship to his twin mothers, Volumnia and Rome, is the moment when his personal autonomy is swallowed up by the relentless, mechanical march of Roman history. Such a recognition is implicit in his show-stopping words to his mother at the climax of what is perhaps Shakespeare's most dramatically arresting scene, when, to quote the extraordinary stage direction, "*He holds her by the hand silent*":

> O mother, mother!
> What have you done? Behold, the heavens do ope,
> The gods look down, and this unnatural scene
> They laugh at. O my mother, mother! O!
> You have won a happy victory to Rome;
> But for your son, believe it—O, believe it—
> Most dangerously you have with him prevail'd,
> If not most mortal to him. But let it come. . . .

Or to put it more literally, his self-integration coincides with the moment when he is torn limb from limb.

Plutarch was not the only source, and Shakespeare clearly did not conceive—in this play or in any other, for that matter—of history solely in terms of the actions of great men. From Livy, and maybe (as Anne Barton has suggested) from Machiavelli's commentaries on Livy, Shakespeare would have learned to think of the Coriolanus story in terms both of the development of the Roman state and of political history and values more generally. At the simplest level, we can see Aufidius standing for a clear-sighted, at times cynical, pragmatism popularly associated with Machiavelli. He contrasts with Coriolanus's political naïveté ("What his breast forges, that his tongue must vent"), and his anguished attempt to be true to a self he comes to know only when it is too late. Even more strongly than in *Timon of Athens*, we are reminded in *Coriolanus* once again of the ambiguities inherent in that frequently staged competition between political expediency and "heroic," aristocratic values.

The tone in which the matter is handled has changed since the years of the rise and catastrophic fall of Essex. Alongside the stress of writers such as Chapman on ideas of unassimilable "greatness" in a debased world, there are countless other treatments that approach the subject with an apparent consciousness of its absurdity, such as in *Don Quixote*, or Francis Beaumont's hilarious Blackfriars play *The Knight of the Burning Pestle* of 1607. Whether comic or tragic, there often seems to be the implication that epic valor has become an anachronism, perhaps even a somewhat self-indulgent folly, in a world shaped by practical functionaries and by the overriding needs of the state. What, for instance, is the tone of Aufidius's comment—"I was moved withal"—in response to Coriolanus's reconciliation with his mother?

So, though the action represents the ancient world, it stages controversies that were of urgent concern in Jacobean London—most obviously the clash between aristocratic values and those of the city, between absolutism and negotiation, breeding and business. And Shakespeare had a foot in each camp; he was both a royal servant and a businessman.

The realities of censorship and patronage meant that a Jacobean playwright, especially if he was writing for the King's Men, could only treat politics obliquely. Common sense dictated that he could only voice any reservations about the current policy indirectly, through allegory. The safest strategy—and Shakespeare followed this in most of his Jacobean tragedies—was to present a play as a study of a general problem in political theory. This procedure relied upon James's self-image as a philosopher-king who liked to suppose he was engaged in serious dialogue with other thinkers on statecraft and government. In such a context, Rome was a good subject—respectable, intellectual, and safely in the past; it posed few of the problems Chapman had to wrestle with when he chose to set his *Byron* plays in the contemporary French wars of religion. Writers could always invoke in their defense the fact that events from Roman history were regularly set at school as topics for debate and analysis. Some decidedly pointed treatments of Jacobean court politics (notably Jonson's *Sejanus*, and, to a lesser extent, his *Catiline*) treat Roman subjects.

Coriolanus is set at a time (494 B.C.) when the nascent Roman state was struggling for its existence, battling against competitors on the Italian peninsula. So the audience would have watched the events onstage unfold against the backdrop of their knowledge of the future long history of Roman triumph, expansion, and eventual decline. And they would have seen the play performed by the King's Men, by the company owing direct loyalty to the man who saw himself as a new Augustus, turning the kingdoms of Great Britain into an empire.

On the other hand, *Coriolanus* may well seem to us a strange dish for Shakespeare to have set before his king. It is hardly a piece of unambiguous propaganda for absolutist, imperialist values. It is set at that time in Roman history when the city-state had just rid itself of tyrannical monarchs and was constructing a new social order. Indeed, the Rome Shakespeare presents was developing the institutions necessary to function as a republic while also striving for military preeminence.

At the same time, the audience would have been aware that he was addressing the terror of the mob, of rebellion, that had been stirred up by the food riots in the Midlands, including disturbances at Hampton-in-Arden, not far from his own farmlands in Stratford, in 1607. The disputes, which have for generations been recognized as a crucial part of the context of *Coriolanus*, initially concerned the enclosure of common land, a practice in which Shakespeare himself was later to become involved. But while the men of Hampton complained about "these devouring encroachers," they and others seem to have connected enclosures with food shortages and price rises—such as those in the price of wheat in 1608 and of barley in 1609. And the troubles surfaced in the city, too, where food shortages were exacerbated by a customs dispute between the city and court officials, which disrupted supplies. In parliamentary debates of 1610, parallels with Rome were made, and politicians from King James down deployed the metaphors of Menenius's belly fable. The king's use was the least ambiguous, when asking Parliament for money: "The head hath the power of directing all the members of the body to that use which the judgement in the head thinkes most convenient. It may apply sharpe cures, or cut off corrupt members, let blood in what proportion it thinks fit. . . ."

Where did Shakespeare stand? The short answer is that we do not know. We can appreciate that he was constrained by the circumstances under which he wrote, and we might expect that a landowner and a member of the royal household would inevitably be hostile to the mob. But the strange thing is that he seems not to have been. For instance, in Plutarch the famine is attributed to peasant idleness; in *Coriolanus*, as in Jacobean England, to less controllable factors—to the disastrous weather and to the gods. Fur-

ther, the processes of government, the elections, and arguments in
the play about the people and their "voices" would have struck a
chord with Jacobean audiences at a time when the size and composition of the electorate, and the principles governing parliamentary elections, were questions of moment and urgency. In
particular, Shakespeare's unusually generous treatment of the people in the play may reflect sympathy with the contemporary belief
that Rome owed much of its dynamism and greatness to the insti-
tutionalized tensions between its classes, rather than to ideas of
unity, stability, or fixed hierarchies. After all, some political the-
orists were beginning to suggest (following Machiavelli) that men
with a stake, with a "voice" in their government, would defend that
state more vigorously than disenfranchised soldiers or mercenaries.

The question of how art relates—or should relate—to politics
continues to divide us. Should it acknowledge its participation in
its own age, or aspire to an ideal of timelessness? Is art of its very
nature subversive or conservative? Shakespeare stages one answer
to these questions at the start of the play, when Menenius Agrippa
calms the starving population by "feeding" the crowd with a story,
a parable, a work of art (Timon had fed his guests with stones
painted to look like food). But if we take the play as a whole, it
offers in its own right another way of looking at the matter. Coriolanus's folly, we hear, is to act:

> As if a man were author of himself
> And knew no other kin . . .

And he is ultimately compelled to acknowledge that, however un-
congenial it may be to him, his identity is inseparable from his
family and his nation. Once that is understood, of course, it follows
that every act, however remote, oblique, or ambiguous—and that
certainly includes the act of writing a play—cannot help but participate in the politics of its time.

Given the circumstances under which he worked, Shakespeare
was compelled to be ambiguous even when he seemed most direct.
In the play he holds up for examination serious and abiding questions about the state, about idealism, about pragmatism and honor,
in the context of a personal tragedy of pathos, terror, and humanity.
Coriolanus does not, as Coleridge argued, display "marvellous phil-

osophical impartiality"; it is not the product of olympian or patrician detachment from the world. Rather it is a genuinely open-ended play, in which Shakespeare managed to stage the birth-pangs of a republic in the reign of a monarch who believed in the Divine Right of Kings. It was a political play when it was first written. It still is.

The story of Antony and Cleopatra held considerable fascination for writers in the Renaissance. In England, Sir Philip Sidney's sister the Countess of Pembroke had published in 1592 her *Tragedy of Antonie*, a translation of Robert Garnier's *Marc Antoine*. In 1594 Samuel Daniel's *The Tragedy of Cleopatra* had appeared; it was to be published in 1607 in a second, revised, edition which some scholars believe shows the influence of Shakespeare's play. These are Senecan closet dramas, texts for the study, for reflection, tragedies to be performed in the mind and therefore, in their philosophical elevation, part of the most elitist strand of humanism. These plays show the lovers facing inevitable death with calm resolve, as they recognize the punishment their passion will exact from an implacable fate. And the chorus at the end poses a series of questions to the gods ("Are these the bounds y'have given/Th'untranspassable barres,/That limit Pride so short," and so on), as if to open the action out for further debate and discussion.

So while Shakespeare based much of the play closely on Plutarch (the invention of Enobarbus is perhaps Shakespeare's most notable addition), he was also able to draw upon a lengthy and various tradition of commentary on the story. And this tradition furnished him with contrasting views of each character and situation that he then depicted—whereas Plutarch's view of the lovers is censorious, essentially "Roman" in its orientation, condemning them for excess. Shakespeare knew accounts of these events that presented Octavius as both model ruler and coldhearted schemer, Antony as both diminished and ennobled by love, Cleopatra as both unchaste and royally heroic.

Clearly, *Antony and Cleopatra* is not a historical treatise. What is more, it is ostentatiously not a closet drama. It is a play in which Shakespeare seems to go out of his way to exploit the resources of public staging. Shakespeare's tragedy constitutes an extraordinary demonstration of the liberating scope of Renaissance tragedy when set alongside either its ancient models or its modish contemporary imitations. The offstage murder of Duncan in *Macbeth* had shown that Shakespeare was capable of reproducing the methods of neo-classical tragedy as a prelude to moving far beyond its confines. So it is in *Antony and Cleopatra*. Instead of concentrating on a brief period in a single place, Shakespeare boldly stages great gaps of time and shifts in location.

The extraordinary proliferation of scenes generates the sense of movement, space, urgency, and even more complicated contrasts that had been similarly effected in the early acts of *King Lear*. In this play, at least initially, the variety seems designed to reinforce the notion of two opposed world-views—one Roman, one Egyptian. At the end, of course, the hectic scene-shifting ends with a grand and operatic finale in the lengthy climax of Act V, Scene II, which consists of some 366 lines.

He also writes with a strong awareness of the antitheatricality that was part of Renaissance culture. Indeed, he challenges his audience on a couple of occasions to find the very process of dramatic representation absurd. The most striking example is the speech in which Cleopatra explains that her reluctance to surrender stems in large measure from her apprehension about her reception in Rome:

> Now Iras, what think'st thou?
> Thou, an Egyptian puppet, shall be shown
> In Rome, as well as I. Mechanic slaves
> With greasy aprons, rules, and hammers shall
> Uplift us to the view. In their thick breaths,
> Rank of gross diet, shall we be enclouded,
> And forc'd to drink their vapour. . . .
> . . . saucy lictors
> Will catch at us like strumpets, and scald rhymers
> Ballad's out a'tune. The quick comedians
> Extemporally will stage us, and present
> Our Alexandrian revels: Antony
> Shall be brought drunken forth, and I shall see
> Some squeaking Cleopatra boy my greatness
> I'th'posture of a whore.

This remark is in its way breathtaking, because it is exactly what is taking place before our eyes and has been for two hours. We have seen the Alexandrian revels, and Antony drunk. And our "squeaking Cleopatra"—played by a boy—was presented to us in the opening scene as a "strumpet." And Cleopatra's scorn of the Roman audience, with its unwholesome breath, matches in almost every detail conventional complaints about the theater audiences of Jacobean London. Of course these words come close to the end of the play, after numerous passages in which dissembling, acting, and performing have been accorded both praise and blame. And the play will end with Cleopatra's theatrical staging of her own death, an action which concludes the repeated series of comparisons between her art and the art of her creator, in a tragic version of the extreme artistic self-consciousness of the lyrical comedies of a decade earlier.

Throughout the play behavior—not just Cleopatra's behavior—is figured as a conscious performance, as in Octavius's description of the coronation of Antony and Cleopatra. Or when Antony repudiates himself as a stereotypical melancholic lover:

> Eros,
> Wouldst thou be window'd in great Rome, and see
> Thy master thus with pleach'd arms, bending down
> His corrigible neck, his face subdued
> To penetrative shame . . .

Cleopatra's scorn of Caesar seems to be based on her sense that he does not possess her capacity to control and shape events theatrically:

> 'Tis paltry to be Caesar.
> Not being Fortune, he's but Fortune's knave,
> A minister of her will: and it is great
> To do that thing that ends all other deeds,
> Which shackles accidents, and bolts up change . . .

In her view, and it echoes Richard II as well as Queen Elizabeth, it is part of a monarch's function—even responsibility—to play in one person many people. As she puts it in Act V, Scene II:

> . . . we, the greatest, are misthought
> For things that others do; and, when we fall,
> We answer others' merits in our name . . .

After she describes possible reworkings of her story on the Roman popular stage, she seeks to close them off by dying, by providing a conclusion to the narrative of her life. Where Othello and Hamlet try to turn their personal tragedies into histories, she tries the reverse, seeking to escape the censure of history through the aesthetic approval of tragedy.

Despite its operatic sweep, the models of sexual behavior the play presents are very stereotypical: Cleopatra conforms to the stereotype of female variety and insatiability; Antony to the stereotype of the male lover torn by powerful and irreconcilable forces, duty, and desire. And, though not always in these words, such is the estimate of the large number of commentators in the play. Shakespeare gives none of them—with the exception of Enobarbus for a brief period—any special authority. But the message that emerges from the numerous asides and observations is that this aging roué and his shrill strumpet are a good deal less unusual than they imagine they are. Not only the observers take this line: Octavius, too, articulates throughout a chilling pragmatism that scorns the hedonism of the lovers. When Antony urges him to join in the drinking at the summit conference, to "Be a child o'th'time," Octavius replies, as the representative of the new age, "possess it."

Like all Shakespeare's love stories, this play is built around a series of oppositions: Rome and Egypt, love and duty, honor and pragmatism, and so on. Shakespeare constructs for the audience two contrasting experiences: one of juxtaposition, paradox, fragmentation; the other of unity, coherence, wholeness. And the wholeness is an imaginative wholeness or continuity, a consistency of specifically poetic effects. The verse of the play—which has never wanted admirers for its richness and suppleness—features a series of reiterated images (fortune, poison, games, images of Roman restrictions opposed to those of flowing Egyptian sensuousness). *Antony and Cleopatra* is shot through with those staples of the Elizabethan sonnet-sequence: neoplatonism and Petrarchism. The former shows itself primarily in the idea of the apotheosis of the lovers in death, the suggestion of a "higher" reality beyond the merely political. And Cleopatra is more often associated with it, as she is with the notion of theatricality. The latter shows itself, as so often, in paradoxes and contradictions, and it is especially associated with Antony: "a Roman by a Roman valiantly vanquish'd."

The lovers, like Romeo and Juliet, aspire to an apotheosis in death. But it takes them a while to get there, as if Shakespeare had in mind that they needed somehow to "earn" the status to which they aspired by learning its difficulty. Cleopatra fakes her death, Antony bungles his. And an allegorical dimension is suggested by the presence of two sorts of love, Eros and Philo, as attendants on Antony. It is only when Eros has self-destructed that Antony can do so; note the explicitly erotic language: "I will be a bridegroom in my death, and run into't/As to a lover's bed. . . ." Only then does he learn that Cleopatra is not in fact dead, which leads to his being lifted up to the monument. Where the fleshliness of Antony is stressed by his struggle to die, and by the effort involved in elevating his bulk, Cleopatra at this point is described in altogether new and different terms, as a queen, as "Egypt." Indeed, she dies as the queen we had not seen before, as the queen whom history will know. The ending recalls their many attempts to locate themselves in the realm of myth during life: Antony, for instance, associates himself with Hercules, Mars, and Aeneas.

Shakespeare adds, however, an extra complication where the political victory of Octavius is poetically upstaged by the imaginative triumph of the (literally) elevated lovers. When Cleopatra spoke of Octavius's lack of control of events, she repeated a staple of Christian thought. As Augustus, he might have been praised for founding the Roman imperial line and claiming to rule the world; but his real function was to act as God's agent, creating a moment of relative stability in the world into which Christ could be born, and Shakespeare drops several hints as the action proceeds. There are three references to King Herod, for example, (including an oblique prophetic allusion to the massacre of the innocents). And when Octavius declares, "The time of universal peace is near," his words ironically foreshadow a major shift in human history, the transition from a pagan to a Christian world, but that shift takes place far from the great pageant over which he presides, far from the twilight of the pagan gods which has been acted out before our eyes.

In 1596 James Burbage had tried to gain a foothold in the city of London by paying six hundred pounds for a substantial building within the Blackfriars complex. The site, though within the walls, fell outside the city's jurisdiction; but the residents had objected to the construction of a playhouse, Burbage had died, and the matter rested for a while. It seems that the local residents, who had been happy enough for children to perform at Blackfriars, were apprehensive about the noise, spectacle, and crowds associated with the adult companies.

Within a few years, indeed, there was a major revival of playing by boys' companies, and in the years around the turn of the century they attracted the services of some of the age's most distinguished writers—preeminently Jonson, Marston, and Chapman. As *Hamlet* testifies, they enjoyed considerable popular success, and became immensely fashionable. The repertoire tended to be satirical or tragic, or a mixture of the two, and plays tended to feature exceptional self-consciousness—prologues, epilogues, asides, parodies, and so forth. The boys' companies were always sailing close to the wind, even by their very existence, which was against the spirit of the Privy Council's theatrical legislation (which aimed to keep the number of companies down to two). And their subject matter and style were always getting them, their proprietors, and their authors into trouble.

Their vogue was short-lived, but their legacy was significant. For one thing, they accorded a different status to writers. Whereas in the adult troupes writers were essentially the providers of raw material for the company to use, the tradition in the boys' companies was different. Writers followed on in the footsteps of generations of humanist pedagogues, in full control of the performances by their youthful changes. And the published prologues and epilogues, as well as the so-called "war of the theaters," all show the writers communicating directly to other adults outside the specific circumstances of the performance by the children. At the most basic level, they show writers in control of their texts in ways that were foreign to their practices on the public stage.

Shakespeare was affected by, and responded to, the new dramatists of the children's companies. They based their performances on slightly out-of-date but very well-known staples of the public theater. Shakespeare's own relish for reworking well-known material, and his developing sense of artistic self-awareness and control, which were derived in large measure from his special status as actor and sharer, gave him an affinity to his new generation of rivals. And there are times when he seems to go out of his way to take on this new wave of sceptical intellectuals, in whose writings scepticism, parody, and debunking are endemic.

The chief proprietor of children's plays at the Blackfriars was a man called Henry Evans, a scrivener by trade, and a former colleague of the greatest writer of the first generation of the boys' companies, John Lyly. Evans was involved in a great number of complicated deals, some of them distinctly shady, and his financial position seems always to have been insecure. In 1603 he discussed the possibility of giving up the twenty-one-year lease which he had from the Burbages, but in the end carried on with his various enterprises until, in March 1608, they finally went too far. The French ambassador, La Boderie, was, unsurprisingly, deeply offended at Chapman's treatment of contemporary French politics in the *Conspiracy and Tragedy of Charles, Duke of Byron*. King James himself ordered that the company be dissolved, and had several of them, including Marston, imprisoned. Chapman made himself scarce. Such royal disfavor tended to dissipate fairly quickly—in fact the company played at court the following Christmas—but Evans saw that his enterprise was doomed and rapidly resumed negotiations with the Burbages. As a result the King's Men took on the lease of the Blackfriars in August 1608.

The lease names seven "housekeepers"—the Burbage brothers, one Thomas Evans (a relative of Henry?), Hemings, Condell, Sly, and William Shakespeare. Each partner was to pay a seventh of the annual rent of forty pounds, a share that was to increase to a sixth within the death of Sly a few days later. Six weeks later, on September 20, the long-awaited charter for London was promulgated. One of its provisions was to extend the city's jurisdiction to include Blackfriars—though in the event, no trouble arose in Shakespeare's lifetime from this new arrangement. The investment was a good one; in the 1630s a Blackfriars share was worth ninety pounds per annum, whereas a Globe share brought in only about twenty-five pounds.

The Blackfriars was smaller than the public playhouses. It was a distinguished and imposing chamber, once used to house Parliament, and held about seven hundred spectators in a paved auditorium furnished with benches. Contemporary accounts assert that it was 656 feet (about 20 metres) from north to south, and some 46 feet (14 metres) from east to west. The stage was probably built against the shorter side, with the tiring house (dressing room) extending the width of the chamber. At stage level it was flanked by boxes or lords' rooms; this means that the stage area must have been substantially smaller than at the Globe, whose stage was some 40 feet (13 metres) wide. And gallants could sit on the stage in front of the boxes, which could lead to noisy disputes, not least during the period when large hats and ostentatious feathers were part of fashionable male attire, and when it was considered chic to engage in the conspicuous consumption of tobacco by surrounding oneself in an expensive cloud. Above these boxes were spaces which could be used to house distinguished spectators, as well as for music and for action set above the stage. A consequence of the constricted playing area was a more cautious approach to fights onstage; there was simply not enough room available for swashbuckling displays of swordsmanship.

Apart from that, the stage conditions resembled those of the public stages pretty closely, although there seem not to have been stage posts. There was a trapdoor, and there was machinery, in the "heaven" above, to facilitate flying; there were windows in the upper acting area, and two doors to the tiring house with a curtained discovery space (or perhaps a third door) between them, to represent a room beyond the stage.

The differences were important, too. Blackfriars plays were staged in conditions of greater intimacy, within a culture of less constricted artistic experiment. The use of artificial light opened a whole range of possibilities in the construction of illusions, and in demonstrating both human uncertainties and moments of recognition and magic. Above all, perhaps, the more prominent status accorded to the author in the private theaters gave Shakespeare further encouragement, if he needed it, in continuing with the experiments that had characterized his art from the start. To an even greater extent than with the move to the Globe, the acquisition of the Blackfriars meant that the King's Men's writers could now legitimately consider themselves authors rather than journeymen.

In the years immediately before the acquisition of the Blackfriars, the King's Men continued to give numerous and regular performances at court, and though the names of the pieces they gave are rarely recorded, we can be certain that Shakespeare's plays formed the core of their repertoire. They were also seen in other towns and cities—Oxford, Barnstaple, and Dunwich in 1607, and Marlborough and Coventry in 1608—as well as at the Globe. The most remarkable record, however, is of an amateur performance far from these islands. In September 1607, three ships of the East India Company were anchored off the coast of Sierra Leone in West Africa. The journal of William Keeling, captain of the *Dragon*, contains an entry concerning the reception given to an ambassador from the local king. Keeling wrote how on September 5 he "sent the interpreter, according to his desire, aboard the *Hector*, where he broke fast, and after came aboard me, and we gave the tragedy of Hamlet." On the thirtieth of the same month he records, "Captain Hawkins [of the *Hector*] dined with me, where my companions acted King Richard the Second"; then the following March, he described how "I invited Captain Hawkins to a fish dinner, and had *Hamlet* acted aboard me; which I permit to keep my people from idleness and unlawful games, or sleep." And it is with this strange record of a shipboard performance of *Hamlet* off the coast of Africa that we turn to the even more extraordinary world of the romances.

CHAPTER ELEVEN

"A World Ransom'd, or One Destroy'd": The Romances

On June 5, 1607, Shakespeare's daughter Susanna was married to John Hall in Stratford. Two months later the poet's young nephew Edward, the "base-born," illegitimate son of his brother Edmund, was buried in the cemetery of St. Giles without Cripplegate. Before the year was out the child's father was himself buried in St. Mary Overy (now Southwark Cathedral). He was buried with all solemnity, with the great bell tolling; we can safely assume that the expenses were met by Shakespeare, and that he arranged for the interment of his youngest brother to take place in the morning so that the King's Men could attend before they had to return to their duties. They had given court performances on December 26, 27, and 28, and were to return on January 2, on Twelfth Night, and on a series of subsequent days in the winter season. As the frosts of that harsh winter dragged on, with the Thames and other rivers frozen solid, Shakespeare's first grandchild was born: Elizabeth Hall was christened at Holy Trinity in Stratford on February 21, 1608. Later in that same year, as the plague closed the London theaters and forced the King's Men to return to touring, Mary Shakespeare died in Stratford and was buried on September 9, 1608. Within just a few months Shakespeare had become a grandfather and lost his mother.

Shakespeare's status as an author, as we have seen, was steadily rising; his was a name that could attract customers. His name, and a clutch of his poems, had been used to promote the anthology *The Passionate Pilgrim* in 1599. As well as pirated editions of Shakespeare plays, there were also instances of plays being spuriously attributed to him as a means of stimulating sales—in 1605 there had appeared a play called *The London Prodigal*, attributed to Shakespeare. It was followed by *A Yorkshire Tragedy*, entered in the Stationers' Register on May 2, 1608.

He himself seems to have taken a renewed interest in bringing out texts of his plays—partly in response to the actions of unscrupulous publishers, and partly also, as in the 1590s, because the plague had closed the theaters. So also in 1608, *Pericles* and *Antony and Cleopatra* were entered in the Stationers' Register; the Quarto editions of *King Lear*, *Richard II*, and *Henry IV Part 1* were published. In the following year appeared both *Pericles* and *Troilus and Cressida*, and there was yet another edition of *Romeo and Juliet*. Of the most significant publication of that period, however, we cannot be certain if it was authorized or not.

As early as 1598 Francis Meres was able to praise Shakespeare's "sugared sonnets among his private friends." Sonnets 138 and 144 had been printed in *The Passionate Pilgrim* of 1599, and manuscript versions of sonnets 2 and 106 have survived from a tradition independent of the printed texts. During the sonnet-writing vogue in the 1590s, inaugurated by the publication of Sidney's *Astrophil and Stella* in 1591, Shakespeare was clearly aware of what was going on. He presents the writing of sonnets as a symptom of love-sickness on the part of the courtiers in *Love's Labour's Lost* (sonnets also reprinted in *The Passionate Pilgrim*); in *Romeo and Juliet* the lovers' first exchange miraculously distills itself into a sonnet, and the chorus uses the same form.

It was normal for sonnet sequences to tease their readers with the possibility of some actual events behind the elaborate poetic artifice, and Sidney's example was a powerful influence on later writers. But how the sonnets related to the real world is always problematic, elusive, mystifying. It was also normal for the predicament of the sonneteer to be one of frustration at the thwarted access to an idealized love object. So sequences usually include long and highly conventionalized descriptions of the beloved (commonly using the technique of the blazon, or list of the woman's physical qualities). Most common of all is the way the manner and style imitate the wretched situation of the petitioning, rejected lover. From Petrarch onward, he was depicted as torn by antithetical impulses, such as desire versus idealization, and he saw the world as structured by opposition and paradox—love understood as an icy fire, a warring peace, and so on. In Shakespeare's speaker's words:

> Two loves I have, of comfort and despair,
> Which like two spirits do suggest me still;
> The better angel is a man right fair,
> The worser spirit a woman coloured ill.

It was from this presentation of the divided consciousness of the speaker that the sonnet developed its role as a means of self-knowledge and self-examination. It became a parallel, for example, to the soliloquy as deployed by Shakespeare in his more psychologically focused plays. And the extreme self-consciousness extended also to a self-consciousness about art as well, about the value and purpose of writing poetry at all, and about the relationship between the poet and previous sonneteers.

The sonnet is a form that derives much from the sense of contributing to a genre being worked on by others at the same time; the drive to be unique, individual, different, was articulated within a highly conventional framework. The speaker of each sequence was characterized, and the sequence took much of its flavor from that. Sidney's Astrophil was markedly youthful, for instance, and hardly ever referred to the aspiration to immortalize himself or Stella in verse. Spenser, on the other hand, was at pains to structure his sequence as a meditation on the relationship between love, art, and time, and it was made sharper by his own revelation that he was an older man, and that the woman to whom he wrote was to be his second wife.

In Shakespeare's case, there are several clear signals of departure from convention—not least the fact that his mistress's eyes are nothing like the sun, and the speaker labors the point of his own antiquity. The sequence falls into two sections, each of which pushes aspects of the convention beyond normal limits. The latter part, Sonnets 127–152, celebrates the so-called "dark lady," who is presented in a way that stands in marked contrast to idealized poetic mistresses, muses, Ideas, Delias, and so on. And the first section (the first 126 poems) is written to a man.

This fact accounts for much of the ink that has been spilled over the centuries on the subject of the *Sonnets*. The first editor of the poems, Benson, in 1640, revised and reordered the sequence to suggest that the addressee was female. In later generations it was argued that the poems derived from a homosexual relationship and that they were made public in order to discredit Shakespeare—a view that owes more to the period that spawned it than to what we know about Jacobean London. Others argued, following a phrase of Benson's, that the poems were altogether removed from the real world, and were to be appreciated as "perfect eloquence" without reference to their context. Neither of these positions makes much sense.

Sonnet sequences usually deal in frustration and despair. Where romantic comedies, for example, show how love and sexual desire can be accommodated within society through unions that society blesses, the sonneteer is conventionally cut off from that consolation. What is more, the structure of many of the sequences suggests he is not alone. Several of the major collections end, like Shakespeare's, with a poem in which a woman complains at her desertion by a male lover. "A Lover's Complaint," as critics have increasingly come to recognize, rounds off the series of depictions of blocked, frustrated desire, of lost self-esteem and desolation. And if we look at the volume as a whole, and at the sequence, for points of connection, we are likely to find clusters of sonnets that are manifestly linked (106–9), and pairs of poems on related themes (50–1, 57–8, for example). So my advice, for what it is worth, is not to pluck out individual poems, nor to try to decode a story hidden behind the eloquence, but to try to read and experience the whole collection as a lyric and emotional continuity.

And if we set the *Sonnets* back in the time of their probable composition, back into the world of *Twelfth Night*, *Hamlet* and *As*

You Like It, we can recognize as familiar the exploration of identity and sexuality. The cross-dressing of the comedies, for instance, can be connected with the androgyny of the youth. But Shakespeare is cautious. He does not tell us much about the boy's appearance (in marked contrast to Marlowe's description of Leander in *Hero and Leander*), and many of the specific praises he offers can be paralleled in the long-established conventions through which intense male friendships were celebrated.

He makes a point of reminding us in Sonnet 20 that the love can have no physical outlet, but there is no doubt that the friendship is depicted in highly eroticized terms. This derives partly from the overlap between the language of desire and the language of client-age, an overlap encouraged by the way that, during Elizabeth's reign, so much of the language of politics and business was translated into the language of love. In his petitions, Shakespeare's speaker dwells on his own lack of rank, and he presents himself as old, worthless, jealous, and undervalued: all this in contrast to the ease, wealth, and eligibility of the youth.

What he—being blessed by nature rather than by fortune—can hope to offer to the young man is advice and immortality. But nothing is granted in return; the young patron is wooed by the claims of a rival poet (76–86), and then the "dark lady" herself goes to him. So intense is Shakespeare's depiction of the inner state of his rejected and humiliated speaker that it has conventionally been assumed that there is a real story behind it, and that one day, once the identities of the fair youth, the rival poet, and the dark lady have been established, all will be revealed.

The *Sonnets* appeared in 1609. They were published by Thomas Thorpe, who had earlier produced works by Jonson and Marston. We cannot know whether Shakespeare authorized the publication, and if so, what role he played in the preparation of the volume. Perhaps during the plague of 1608–9 Shakespeare gathered and shaped his sonnets (most of them written well before the turn of the century) into their present form before Thorpe acquired them, however that transaction was effected. In that sense, the volume is of a piece with other Elizabethan revivals in the period, with the new publication of Spenser's *Mutabilitie* cantos, for example, or the return of romance as a dramatic fashion.

The enigmatic title page is not much help:

TO. THE. ONLIE. BEGETTER. OF.
THESE. INSUING. SONNETS.
MR. W. H. ALL. HAPPINESSE.
AND. THAT. ETERNITE.
PROMISED.
BY.
OVR. EVER-LYING. POET.
WISHETH.
THE. WELL-WISHING.
ADVENTURER. IN.
SETTING.
FORTH.

T.T.

Some of those who favor the concept of unauthorized publication
would argue that W.H. was the "begetter" of the sequence in that
he acquired them and got them ready for publication. Another
tradition sees the begetter as the dedicatee. The two chief candidates
for the joint "role" of fair youth and "master W.H." are Henry
Wriothesley, the earl of Southampton, and William Herbert, third
earl of Pembroke and later dedicatee of the First Folio. Both men
have strong Shakespeare connections, but Herbert's youth (he was
born in 1580) is against him. The rank of both men, in an age when
noblemen were brought up to be decidedly prickly on such questions, is hardly reflected in the address to plain "Mr." We are no
nearer a "solution"; and that may be as Thorpe intended.

A strange book which has been thought, with varying degrees
of seriousness, to shed light on Shakespeare's personality and, perhaps, on the situation sometimes supposed to lie behind the *Sonnets*
was published in 1594. *Willobie his Avisa* is presented as a collection
of papers found by one "Hadrian Dorrell," of whom no record has
been found, and who may well be one of numerous fictional
"friends" in Elizabethan literature who take the liberty of publishing
the writings of someone close to them. Usually the relationship is
extremely close—gentleman authors often felt the need to create
elaborate fictions of this kind to excuse their descent into the vulgar
world of print. This "Dorrell" gives the public the poems of his
friend Henry Willobie, which depict the repudiation of a series of
suitors by a chaste woman named Avisa. The whole poem has
attracted ingenious allegorical interpretations over the years, but

the crucial passage that may relate to Shakespeare is a piece of prose just before Poem 44. The passage may have significance because there is a possibility that Willobie knew Shakespeare and that the initials "W.S." denote him. The connection, admittedly tenuous, is through Thomas Russell, whom Shakespeare would appoint in 1616 to oversee his will. In 1590 Russell had married Katharine Bampfield; a month earlier Katherine's sister Elinor had married William Willobie, the brother of the Henry Willobie who probably wrote the poems, and whose initials were a godsend for those desperate to decode the *Sonnets*. The passage runs:

> H.W. being suddenly infected with the contagion of a fantastical fit, at the first sight of A[visa], pineth awhile in secret grief. At length, not able any longer to endure the burning heat of so fervent a humour, bewrayeth the secret of his disease unto his familiar friend W.S., who not long before had tried the courtesy of the like passion, and was now newly recovered of the like infection. Yet, finding his friend let blood in the same vein, he took pleasure for a time to see him bleed, and, in stead of stopping the issue, he enlargeth the wound, with the sharp razor a willing conceit, persuading him that he thought it a matter very easy to be compassed, and no doubt—with pain, diligence, and some cost in time to be obtained. Thus this miserable comforter comforting his friend with an impossibility, either for that he now would secretly laugh at his friend's folly, that had given occasion not long before unto others to laugh at his own, or because he would see whether another could play the part better than himself, and in viewing far off the course of this loving comedy, he determined to see whether it would sort to a happier and for the new actor, than it did for the old player. But at length the comedy was like to have grown to a tragedy, by the weak and feeble estate that H.W. was brought into, by a desperate view of an impossibility of obtaining his purpose. . . .

Whatever we make of such intriguing oddities, the contrast with the publication of the narrative poems is striking, and the absence of specificity about the dedicatee means that we can hardly avoid the irony of Sonnet 18, "Shall I compare thee to a summer's day?" The poem recalls those sonnets in which Shakespeare's French contemporary Ronsard advises his Helen that her beauty will live on in his verses long after it has faded from her cheeks. It is also related to conventional appeals for patronage, where the favor of the patron is likened to the beams of the sun, with a suggestion that the golden glow is translated into coins. In return for such support the poet offers immortality through his verse—"So long lives this, and this gives life to thee." But the deal falls through. The poem, perhaps the most famous and most frequently anthologized of the *Sonnets*, has immortalized Shakespeare, not the unidentified and unremembered "thee."

It has been suggested that in the *Sonnets* Shakespeare developed, perhaps even invented, a novel way of representing human consciousness, of depicting an inner life. These poems, poised on the hinge between public and private communication, are at once the speaker's dramatic self-revelation and self-examination and a densely allusive, highly metaphorical sequence that gives its reader no rest, that challenges us, and nourishes us, with the same admiration, questioning, and ambiguity which Montaigne claimed were the only food for a generous spirit.

The plague kept the theaters closed from the summer of 1608 to the last month of 1609, and the King's Men were given a special reward for keeping together to prepare for the winter court season of 1608–9, or, in the words of the grant, "for their special practice in the time of infection."

When Shakespeare went into the Blackfriars he in effect took on two notable dramatic modes, one of the immediate past, the other emphatically of the present. The first was the distinctive dramatic manner and tone of the plays written by Marston, Chapman, Jonson, and others for the boys' companies. The second was the court masque.

By 1611, for instance, when *The Tempest* was performed, there had been no fewer than eleven great masques staged since the king's accession in 1603. From 1612, published texts of Jonson's masques show that the King's Men took the parts laid down for professional actors, and it is likely that they are the unnamed actors whose payment is recorded in earlier court shows.

The structure of the masques was simple: They displayed a movement from discord to concord, from disruption to harmony. The final resolution involves a turning outward, in which the action of the masque is supposed to be completed or achieved in the royal or noble spectators. Since those spectators are associated with harmony and resolution, the forces of disorder tend to be figured in terms of threats (moral, social, political) to that order. More specifically, the fount of virtue is invariably held to be the king, and he is shown to have a transforming power that can utterly change those powers that raise themselves in opposition to him. In the *Masque of Blackness*, for instance, James literally turns black to white. Elsewhere night becomes day, imprisonment freedom, ignorance illumination.

The masques share some important features with Mannerist and Baroque art. Three in particular are worth stressing. The first is a conscious emotionalism, a deliberate attempt directly to move the spectator or listener. The second is a disturbing disruption of expectations of harmony, often as part of an attempt to convey the idea that there is a higher unity above the seeming discords represented. The third is a tendency to disrupt conventional frames, to resist the shapes which art has conventionally imposed upon versions of existence. Shakespeare's late plays, possibly by analogy with such Baroque forms, place the ordinary spectator in the position the king enjoyed in royal masques. The play, as we shall see, was directed toward the spectator's emotions. Likewise, all of them seem consciously to flout conventional neoclassical notions of order and symmetry; and, above all, perhaps, their resolution is achieved in the mind and heart of the beholder, as the events of the play spill out of their frames and into the lives of the spectators.

Since Dowden proposed the term in the late nineteenth century, these plays have increasingly been grouped under the heading "romance." The term is only misleading if narrow definitions are applied to it. Romance in the Renaissance was a principle or a mode rather than a genre with precise rules. Indeed, it might almost be thought of as the quintessential Renaissance mode: not because it repudiates or escapes from neoclassical forms, but rather because it seeks to include them all—tragedy, comedy, satire, elegy, encomium, history—large and small. Romance offers a deliberate choice to avoid classic singleness of action. Variety, multiplicity, and inclusiveness were to be prized as qualitatively better ways of imitating nature.

Nature herself had been presented to the British reading public at about this time in the posthumous publication of a fragment of a lost seventh book of *The Faerie Queene*. In the *Cantoes of Mutabilitie*, Nature is presented as impossible to represent, as ultimately unknowable, as both old and young, male and female, comic and tragic. Where Art had been traditionally opposed to Nature, where the ruin of Time was inevitable for man-made monuments, be they pyramids or poems, Nature in this Spenserian guise is seen as a principle that embraces and includes Time in a paradoxical state that is both static and forever moving. From now on, I would argue, when Shakespeare set out to imitate Nature in his works he had before him a model of Nature as a state that was irreducible, that was double, that could not help but include life and death, both tragic and comic visions.

It happens that he turned to romance at a time when it was undergoing one of its periodic revivals, some of that revival being associated with the chivalric cult of the prince of Wales, Prince Henry. There were major new editions of Spenser and Sidney, and revivals of plays such as the popular Sidneian romance drama *Mucedorus;* even the most sophisticated audiences seem to have been involved in this conscious archaism and artful naïveté. And it involved a combination of material that was in one sense tragicomic— that is, combining tragic and comic elements—but in another sense wholly characteristic of romance in its Renaissance sense as a form that embraces other, smaller forms, and that represents a view of Nature as constantly changing and resistant to resolution.

Pericles enjoyed great and immediate success at the Globe. Some time between April 1607 and March 1608 the Venetian ambassador, Giustinian, made up a grand party to see this magnificent spectacle: He took the French ambassador, Boderie, with his wife, as well as the secretary of Florence, and the whole enterprise cost him a lot of money. In the words of a contemporary Venetian observer, such expeditions were part of the normal process of becoming acquainted with the ways of the British: "All the ambassadors who have come to England have gone to the play."

Blount's entry of the play in the Stationers' Register in May 1608 was presumably agreed to by the King's Men as a device to stop anyone else from bringing out an edition. But the strategy failed. That year saw the appearance of what we would nowadays call a "novelization" of the play, by the dramatist George Wilkins, whose *The Miseries of Enforced Marriage*, published in 1607, had been acted by the King's Men.

Shakespeare's play is presented not as a play at all, but as a "song that old was sung," and its singer, our host for the performance, is the medieval poet John Gower (who had told the story two hundred years earlier in his *Confessio Amantis*). And he, as befits an author of such distinction, is a much more interventionist chorus than Shakespeare has used before. His narrative constructs the frame of the story, other parts of which are told in pageant, dumb-show, or conventional stage action. Such a method makes it clear that a deliberate choice has been made as to the way in which each particular part of the story will be communicated—whether told or shown, performed silently, in darkness, or dully enacted.

> It hath been sung at festivals.
> On ember-eves and holy-ales;
> And lords and ladies in their lives
> Have used it for restoratives
> The purchase is to make men glorious,
> *Et bonum, quo antiquius, eo melius.*
> [And the older a good thing is, the better it gets.]

In the Prologue Gower asserts the relation between drama and religious ritual, and the value of repeated reenactment over the centuries; he argues that a primary justification for art is that for generations it has successfully been used "for restoratives."

The play is full of scenes of exceptional emotional intensity, as well as moments of great spectacle. But always Gower is there to guide and direct, as well as to proclaim the limits of his own power to tell or describe. When the play ends, he draws back from the passionate climax of the recognition scene, and describes the company onstage almost as if they were allegorical statues:

> In Helicanus you may well descry
> A figure of truth, of faith, of loyalty.
> In reverend Cerimon there well appears
> The worth that learned charity aye wears.

Thus each of the flesh-and-blood figures whose amazing exploits have been enacted with such vividness and spectacle is now "frozen" for a moment. Gower's words typify one of the most arresting features of these late plays, namely their oscillation between the searingly human and the coolly allegorical—or, to put it more strongly, their presentation of human existence as being simultaneously fleshly and abstract.

The story is one of redemption and regeneration, of tragic tales transformed through various agencies. In *Pericles* there are moments where healing is staged in a directly medical way (from 1607 Shakespeare's conversations with his learned son-in-law John Hall might conceivably have had some effect on the way he envisaged the process of healing), but we should note the magical, almost sacramental terms in which the healing is done. In the context of the language of the play, there is an obvious metaphorical association between the miraculous regenerations of the several healers in the play and the performance of Gower himself (and by extension, of Shakespeare, too).

Marina effects two of the most miraculous transformations simply by being herself—this was to become a common device in the late plays. When Lysimachus is confronted by her in the brothel, he is quite explicit in announcing the change she has wrought in him:

I brought hither a corrupted mind,
Thy speech hath alter'd it.

He sees her as "a piece of virtue" and goes away protesting that he has been reformed. Events prove this episode to be a rehearsal for the great recognition scene in which Marina confronts Pericles, who is in an inconsolable and apparently unbreakable silence. She persuades him to take notice of her by adopting the same riddling language that Helena deploys in *All's Well that Ends Well*. Two considerations move him: One is her evocation of abstract Justice and Truth; the other is much more emotional—"thou lookest/Like one I lov'd indeed." And so great is the magic of this transformation that it is effectively rewarded by the immediate appearance of a goddess, and Diana speaks to Pericles in a vision, and he is then reunited with Thaisa, his wife who had been presumed dead.

This is a moment that tells us a lot about the kind of art Shakespeare was creating in these late plays. In some paintings of this period, especially those of Caravaggio, the viewer is led into the painting by a glimmer of light, a glimpse of flesh, a shining jewel or some other immediate attraction. Once inside the frame, so to speak, the viewer's eye is led from point to point until the recognition dawns that these points are connected, that they tell a story or embody some allegorical meaning. In other words, the perception of the allegory follows on from an emotional experience on the observer's part. And so it is with Pericles. His response to Marina starts with the recognition of a lost love and leads to an apprehension of Truth and Justice. In these moments, I suggest, Shakespeare gives us a model of our own response to the miracles onstage, and a promise of a similar reward, as he shows what follows from Pericles' declaration of faith, "I will believe thee."

We know that audiences of the time were moved to tears by spectacle as much as by words, and there is at least one record that involves Shakespeare. In September 1610, Henry Jackson of Corpus Christi College wrote a letter in which he referred to a visit by the King's Men to Oxford, during which there were performances of Jonson's *The Alchemist* and Shakespeare's *Othello*. Parts of Jackson's letter were preserved by his friend William Fulman:

> Also they had tragedies, which they performed with decorum and fitness. In which tragedies they provoked tears not only through speaking but also through the way they acted certain things. But truly the celebrated Desdemona, she who was killed before our eyes by her husband, nevertheless moved us more after she had been slain: that was when, lying on her bed, she implored the pity of the beholders simply by her countenance.

Cymbeline engages in various ways, some oblique, some more direct, with the political circumstances of Jacobean Britain. In particular, it is a product of that extraordinary period between Prince Henry's creation as prince of Wales in 1608 and his much-lamented death at the age of only eighteen on November 6, 1612. With the splendid ceremonies held in 1610, Henry became the first prince of Wales to be invested in over a century. At the same time, he established his own substantial independent household, a gathering of remarkable individuals, by no means all of whom shared his severely puritan views. He was a patron of learning, the arts, and foreign trade, and constructed his image in terms of the militant, chivalric

Protestantism that Sidney, Essex, and Henri IV of France had been
held to embody.

Shakespeare's personal involvement with the prince is not recorded. In this he differed from some of the finest writers of that
exceptional age. Ralegh wrote his *History of the World* in prison for
Prince Henry; Jonson copiously annotated for the young man a
copy of the *Masque of Queens* in order to explain what the court
spectacle had really meant; Daniel composed shows for the prince
to perform in; Chapman's tragedies were essays in statecraft directed toward this apprentice Alexander. For two brief years between the founding of Henry's court ("as a courtly college or
collegiate court," in the words of a contemporary), and his death,
it was no longer possible to conceive of power in the simple, mon-
olithic way that the Tudors had fought for and that James had both
inherited and cultivated.

Henry did not live long enough to become a focus of discontent
or opposition on any substantial scale. But his presence opened up
new—not necessarily contradictory—ways of thinking about authority in all its forms. And the presence in public life of the king's
wife and three children, each (save perhaps Prince Charles, who
was too young) with a distinctive personal cult, subtly changed the
image of royalty as it was presented to the world. From being
unitary, directed solely on the monarch, attention was directed
increasingly to the royal family, of which the king was head, but
which stood as a collection—a consort, so to speak, of different
voices and images.

Shakespeare's romances participate in the new Jacobean vogue
for writing about the family. Even in the writings of the chief
dramatist of the King's Men, we see an increasing focus on the
family unit rather than on the solitary ruler. The very mixture and
hybridity of these plays may be thought of as embodying a new
attitude to literary authority, an attitude based on an ideal of full-
ness, comprehensiveness, and continuity. In the particular context
of the dynastic cult of James's family, we also see a developing
sense of the regenerative role of time.

Hybridity is certainly an appropriate term for *Cymbeline*, which
takes even further the relish for the broad sweep of history that
had characterized *Antony and Cleopatra* just a couple of years before.
The essential point about Cymbeline in the chronicles which Shake-

speare used as his sources was easy enough to grasp. His significance depended upon the simple fact that he was king of Britain at the time of the birth of Christ. This made him especially blessed in being chosen by God to preside over such a sacred time, and it also made him, in his small way, an English version of Augustus, a ruler whose establishment of peace was divinely ordained.

Cymbeline is a fable of union and peace. As such it enters the Jacobean controversies about the king's desire for a unified empire of the nations on the island of Britain. Probably Shakespeare returned to British history while revising *King Lear*. James saw his wishes as divinely inspired, and justified by the "fact" recorded in Geoffrey of Monmouth's history that the empire of Britain had been founded by Brutus, the son of Aeneas. The references to Wales allude to Prince Henry; those to Milford Haven to the accession of the Tudors in 1485, when the future Henry VII, whose destiny was to unite the kingdom, landed there to begin his campaign against Richard III. The numerous riddles and prophecies in the play add weight to this mythical and providential view of history. Wonder, amazement, and confusion are constantly evoked, not least in the unprecedentedly protracted and eventful recognition scene at the end.

But there are moments when authoritative interpretations are delivered. And when they are, we are brought firmly into the Jacobean present, as when the soothsayer deciphers Jupiter's message left on Posthumus's bosom, he says:

> The lofty cedar, royal Cymbeline
> Personates thee.

It also personated King James. The religious poet Joshua Sylvester called the king the "great, Royall Cedar of Mount Libanon"; many others who praised James figured him as a cedar (the tree associated with Solomon), whose branches were his children, and in whose shade the nation was sheltered. And the consequent peace treaty with Rome is a dramatization of the king's well-publicized desire for peace and aspiration to the title of *Rex Pacificus*.

The challenges that have to be overcome by the play's leading figures are paralleled by the challenges the audience is faced with in trying to make sense of what they see. It would be hard to imagine something further from Aristotelian prescriptions; to many critics, it has been hard to imagine anything further from common sense. Shakespeare's text is a highly self-conscious display of the fictional and of the marvelous. The great recognition scene goes even further than that at the end of *All's Well that Ends Well* in heaping up more and more improbable revelations. The difference from *The Winter's Tale* is sufficiently marked to reinforce the notion that the two plays were conceived as a contrasting pair. In that play, the opening is vague, uncertain, and unknowable, and at the end the offstage recognition scene is described. *Cymbeline* is crammed with numerous levels of fiction, and deploys many kinds of storytelling and presentation. We are spectators at a great variety of places: at the English court, in Wales, in Italy, in Ancient Rome. And Shakespeare excells himself in the use of a multiplicity of fictional kinds. The ingredients in his rich mixture of genres include tragedy, satire, elegy, tragicomedy, pastoral, city-comedy, masque, prophecy, and, above all, romance and epic. Posthumus, British though bearing a Roman name, is himself a mixture of the values of the two empires. At times he is closely identified with Aeneas, of course, and Imogen with Dido, while she further recalls symbolic representations of Britain—in particular those connected with Queen Elizabeth. And the diverse modes of presentation include battles, intimate scenes, lavish spectacles (such as Jupiter, and the scenes around the cave), darkness, pageants, and the use of a lifelike effigy (resembling Webster's practice).

The moment when Imogen's beauty causes Iachimo to desist from his planned rape is profoundly literary, and can be matched in countless romances. But it is more than just a cliché. Iachimo is transformed from a potential rapist into (quite literally) a writer—"I will write all down"—and a reader—"She hath been reading late/The tale of Tereus: here the leaf's turn'd down/Where Philomel gave up." Imogen's chaste beauty—let us not forget "she" was a boy actor—turns Iachimo from a stereotypical city-comedy hustler into either a detached aesthete making an inventory of the treasures the room contains, or into something more like an ancient Roman, moved to compare himself to Tarquin and to be shaken by the volume of Ovid by her bedside, which recalls both *Lucrece* and *Titus Andronicus*.

We in the audience are required to suppose that this miracle actually takes place, a suspension of disbelief that would have been easier in the shadows of the Blackfriars. And the question of "supposing," of fiction, is central to one of the most extraordinary episodes in the whole canon, a moment where epic and romance embrace lyric. Much of the writing of *Cymbeline* was contemporary with the final revision of the *Sonnets* volume. The prelude to the most intensely lyrical passage is musical; strange music sounds from the exiles' cave. And Guiderius announces a conventional aesthetic principle:

All solemn things
Should answer solemn accidents. The matter?
Triumphs for nothing, and lamenting toys,
Is jollity for apes, and grief for boys.

What then happens contradicts him. The boys deliver their exquisite laments over the body of Imogen, leading up to their dirge, "Fear no more the heat o'th'sun." Then the beheaded body of Cloten is brought in, and both corpses are left reverently in peace: "You were as flowers, now wither'd: even so/These herblets shall, which we upon you strew. . . ." We in the audience know that the boy they have laid to rest is "actually" Imogen, and we also know in a different way that the whole thing is a fiction, and that the boy-actor dressed as a girl dressed as a boy will be well enough to go home at the end of the show. But before we can ask ourselves if the mourners' ignorance devalues their mourning, a new complication arises. The "dead" Imogen wakes up—do we laugh? When she finds the body of Cloten she is convinced it is that of her husband Posthumus:

. . . I hope I dream;
. . . But 'tis not so.
'Twas but a bolt of nothing, shot at nothing,
Which the brain makes of fumes. Our very eyes
Are sometimes like our judgements, blind. Good faith,
I tremble still with fear; but if there be
Yet left in heaven as small a drop of pity
As a wren's eye, fear'd gods, a part of it!
The dream's here still; even when I wake, it is
Without me, as within me: not imagin'd, felt.

Her final words recall Pericles' suspension of disbelief. Everything we have seen has been—in a literal sense—wrong. The boys
lament someone they think of as Fidele, who is not in fact dead.
She laments her husband, but her husband is not dead, and the
body is that of the man who tried to rape her. But Shakespeare
challenges us either to find the laments absurd and meaningless
(since the "solemn things" do not "answer solemn accidents") or to
give assent to a notion that it is possible for there to exist a species
of truth that is somehow impervious to straightforward factual contradiction. I see this moment as the culmination of his lifelong
defense of "if," of "supposing," of Sidney's proposition that the
truest poetry is the most feigning. It is one of Shakespeare's most
powerful, eloquent, and unambiguous demonstrations of the power
of fiction, of the magic of art.

The resurrection of Hermione, one of Shakespeare's most memorable and magical scenes, connects *The Winter's Tale* with the world
from which it sprang. It may be, for instance, that the ceremonial,
almost liturgical quality of Paulina's instruction to Leontes: "It is
requir'd/You do awake your faith. . . ."—followed by her dismissal
of those who have doubts about her enterprise—"Or those that
think it is unlawful business/I am about, let them depart"—has
something to do with contemporary fascination at court with matters of ritual and faith. In particular it may allude—though the
purpose is now unknown—to the persistent rumor that Queen
Anne had become a Roman Catholic. At the same time (and Shakespeare would certainly have known this) the king was busy preparing a new tomb for his mother, Mary, Queen of Scots, who had
been executed by Elizabeth on February 9, 1587 and buried in
Peterborough. James arranged for a grand tomb to be constructed,
with a fine statue, in Westminster Abbey, next to the tomb of
Queen Elizabeth. The body was brought down from Peterborough
in 1613, and decoration continued for some time after that. The
gap of time between Mary's execution and James's accession to the
English throne was sixteen years, which parallels that between
tragedy and redemption in the play.

The play was a success at the Globe, where Simon Forman saw
it on May 15, 1611. It was also, as far as we can tell, a court

favorite. The play proved markedly popular; although records of Globe and Blackfriars performances are scanty, it presumably remained in the repertoire, as it was called for on no fewer than eight identifiable occasions, seven of them at court. The first recorded court performances were on November 5, 1611—the anniversary of the Gunpowder Plot—and during the wedding festivities in February 1613, as the court replaced its mourning for Prince Henry with spectacular nuptial celebrations for the wedding of his sister to the elector palatine.

Like *Cymbeline*, the play is part of the cultural response to the growing stature of Prince Henry—he has been identified with Florizel by some commentators. But the two occasions when it is known to have been performed are significant. Each was perceived at the time as a moment of deliverance. In the first, because divine providence had uncovered the work of the plotters and preserved the king and his family; in the second, as the grief of mourning was finally assuaged by a dynastic wedding, thereby uniting, in the words of many contemporary accounts, the Thames and Rhine.

The Winter's Tale probably owes something to Ben Jonson's masque *Oberon: The Fairy Prince*, which had been performed at court on New Year's Day 1611, with Prince Henry himself taking the role of Oberon. The dance of twelve rustics in Act IV, for example, may be the same dance with which twelve satyrs celebrated Oberon, and may have been performed by the same men. But unquestionably the major source is the short prose romance *Pandosto* (subtitled *The Triumph of Time*), first published in 1588 by the man who had seen himself as the grasshopper to the "upstart crow's" ant, namely Robert Greene. Shakespeare drew much of the situation, and many of the incidents, from Greene's story, though he changed the location and gave most of the characters names from Plutarch's *Lives*.

The most significant changes tell us a great deal about Shakespeare's conception of the play. The first is that in *Pandosto*, the onset of jealousy is slow, and presented as a festering sore in the king's mind. Shakespeare omits almost all of this psychologizing in Greene. The second is that the king's wife in *Pandosto* is actually dead, and is a genuine ghost when she appears to her husband. In Shakespeare's version, Hermione's status is very mysterious: She appears as a "ghost" of sorts, but she is not dead, though the audience has not much more clue than Leontes as to what is going on. The effect of Shakespeare's revisions is to add to the play's mystery, to focus our attention beyond the action onto what is not said, to what is not staged before our eyes.

Pandosto had been subtitled "The Triumph of Time," and on his title page Greene had cited the famous tag *temporis filia veritas*— Truth the daughter of Time. Greene explains that his story shows that "although by the means of sinister Fortune, Truth may be concealed, yet by Time in spite of Fortune it is most manifestly revealed." Shakespeare takes the unusual step of personifying Time at the heart of the play, and giving him a speech in which he outlines and then demonstrates his power. But time is manifested in other ways, too. In the midst of the extraordinary events at the center of the play, we are presented with a series of traditional ways of conceiving of time. The first is the violent storm (punning on tempest/*tempus*). The second is the bear—in romance narratives wild beasts (bears, lions, tigers, and so on) disrupt moments of pastoral stability, and stand for the onward march of Time. The third is the coincidence of the old man and the baby, which recalls a pictorial convention for representing Time that is still current in western culture.

Shakespeare conceals at least as much as he reveals, and places considerable weight upon the imagination of the audience, who are required to engage with the play very directly. Great stress is placed on things that are not represented. Many characters are given speeches in which they proclaim their inability to express what they want to say: In Camillo's words, "There is a sickness . . . but I cannot name the disease." Toward the end of the play, and in marked contrast to *Cymbeline*, the recognition scene is staged in our imaginations, as we have to supply the gaps in the descriptions of the event which are reported among a group of courtiers. As one of them tells Autolycus:

> . . . the changes I perceiv'd in the King and Camillo were very notes of admiration. They seem'd almost, with staring on one another, to tear the cases of their eyes. There was speech in their dumbness, language in their very gesture; they look'd as they had heard of a world ransom'd, or one destroy'd. A notable passion of wonder appear'd in them: but the wisest beholder, that knew no more but

seeing, could not say if th'importance were joy or sorrow; but in the extremity of the one, it must needs be.

The courtier has only his eyes to guide him. We can supply our experience of the play, and on the basis of that experience we know that his interpretation is inadequate. The reunion is neither extremely happy nor extremely sad. It is both, simultaneously. And this coincidence of tragedy with comedy is what makes *The Winter's Tale* less a tragicomedy than a tragical comedy. That is, it ends happily, but Antigonus is still dead; so is Mamillius, and the pain of the wrongs done cannot be argued away, no matter how joyful the restorations. This irreducible doubleness is mirrored in the responses of the leading players—which again we have to imagine.

Thus we hear of Paulina: "O the noble combat that twixt joy and sorrow was fought in Paulina! She had one eye declin'd for the loss of her husband, another elevated that the oracle was fulfilled" (this would have represented a major challenge for the boy actor taking the part had it occurred onstage!).

The role of the audience is more crucial to the resolution of the play and for *The Tempest* than it had been for *Cymbeline*. Here, it is partly a question of assenting to the fiction, of suspending disbelief. But it is also a matter of filling up the gaps in the narrative that Shakespeare leaves us to contemplate. To start with, there is the retirement for the exchange of experiences. Where those at the end of *Pericles* had gone off "to hear the rest untold," here there are still some mysteries and miracles to be explained. And Leontes asks Paulina: "lead us from hence, where we may leisurely/Each one demand, and answer to his part/Perform'd in this wide gap of time, since first/We were dissever'd." Our experience of the rest of the play—and perhaps of related moments in other romances, makes the task of imagining the event fairly straightforward, though the detail is harder to conceive. But the real challenge is to supply Hermione's silence, which is even more powerful than the very brief exchanges at the end of *All's Well that Ends Well*. After her revival, she speaks to Perdita, but says not a word to Leontes, and gives no indication of reconciliation or forgiveness. The tableau onstage (which includes Pollixenes) is full of contradictory emotions of loss and restoration, and Shakespeare makes no effort to sweep away its sorrows and pain. He leaves us this most densely charged moment to experience for ourselves, to come to terms with in our own hearts.

If significance can be read into a court performance of *The Winter's Tale* on the anniversary of the Gunpowder Plot, what is to be made of the performance of *The Tempest*, in the same Banqueting House with its new green carpet, four days earlier, on November 1, 1611? There are certainly features of the story that would be appropriate to a performance on the day after Halloween, when the dark forces are set aside in celebration of All Saints' Day. But a few years earlier *Othello* had also been performed on November 1, so *The Tempest* was not necessarily written with that occasion in mind. The play was almost certainly given at the Blackfriars, and is likely to have been staged at the Globe. It is also unwise to assume that it was centered on Prospero as an artist surrogate for Shakespeare, bidding farewell to the stage. It is by no means clear, for example, that *The Tempest* was the last-written or performed of these three romances. And Shakespeare, whose parents had lived to ripe ages, was still some way short of fifty, still had three plays in him, and seems to have had no reason to suspect an imminent demise.

Nevertheless, the play was no less implicated in the world from which it sprang than were *Cymbeline* and *The Winter's Tale*. Part of its magic lies in the way it transforms contemporary preoccupations, news sensations, political concerns, religious and philosophical theories, into something rich and strange.

Shakespeare might have had in mind William Thomas's book, *A History of Italy*, published in 1549; it tells the story of Prosper Adorno, duke of Genoa, who spent sixteen years in exile after being deposed by a rival court faction. When he came back, as deputy for the duke of Milan, his despotic rule caused civil unrest. He formed a defensive alliance with Ferdinando, king of Naples, whereupon he was attacked—unsuccessfully—by the Milanese army. Eventually he was deposed again. But Shakespeare knew lots of stories of deposed rulers—including perhaps the story of Prospero Colonna, told by Remigio Nannini in his *Civil Considerations upon Many and Sundry Histories* (1601), from which some of the supernatural elements and the name of Ferdinand's father might have derived. He had already written one of these stories himself in *Measure of Measure*, during the vogue for the subject in the early years of the new reign.

A good deal of the contemporaneity of *The Tempest* derives from its indebtedness to, or at least use of, several identifiable books and pamphlets of the time, and from its participation in controversies of the day. Even if the audience had not suspected as much from the preceding action, Gonzalo effectively opens up a debate early in the second act when he tells his companions how he would run his ideal commonwealth:

> . . . no kind of traffic
> Would I admit: no name of magistrate:
> Letters should not be known; riches, poverty,
> And use of service, none; contract, succession,
> Bourn, bound of land, tilth, vineyard, none:
> No use of metal, corn, or wine, or oil:
> No occupation, all men idle, all,
> And women too, but innocent and pure;
> No sovereignty. . . .
> All things in common nature should produce
> Without sweat or endeavour, Treason, felony,
> Sword, pike, knife, gun, or need of any engine
> Would I not have, but nature should bring forth
> Of its own kind all foison, all abundance,
> To feed my innocent people.

Gonzalo declares that his ambition, in his new Utopia, would be to govern with such "perfection" that his nation would "excel the golden age." His fantasy was a common one at the time and no less common are the two reactions it elicits. From Sebastian and Antonio comes scorn ("Yet would he be King on't"); from Alonso suppression—he tells Gonzalo he speaks "nothing" and orders him to be silent. The courtiers represent scepticism about human perfectibility, while the king displays an anxiety about the potential consequences of such free thoughts among his advisers.

The words of Gonzalo's reverie derive closely from Montaigne's essay "Of the Cannibals," which appeared in Florio's translation of the *Essays* in 1603. And they are part of the ways in which the practice and purpose of colonial government were debated. At the most basic level, it had to be decided whether a colony fell under the sway of the ruler of the colonists—did James's writ run in America?—or whether its laws should be derived from the specific circumstances of the place. And such questions were brought before the public's attention in 1609–10, when there was much excitement at the story of Sir Thomas Gates, who was reported lost at sea in 1609, and its consequences for the Virginia Company. The Company was relatively new: It had been founded in 1606, had established Jamestown in 1607, reformed itself as a joint stock company in 1609, and sent off a large flotilla of colonists—about four hundred of them—who enjoyed little success. In particular, the fleet was dispersed by a great storm—presumably a hurricane—which drove Gates (who was to have been governor of the colony) on to the shore of Bermuda.

In the latter part of 1610, Gates returned to England from Virginia. During the period when he had been presumed lost, dark rumors about the colony had begun to circulate. Investors were being discouraged by reports of unrest, indiscipline, and incompetence that seemed to indicate spectacular failure to establish an economically and socially viable colony. Shakespeare knew many of the leading investors in this enterprise—men like Christopher Brooke, the earl of Pembroke, and, above all, the earl of Southampton. Three official pamphlets were published at the time, and a further report circulated in manuscript; Shakespeare knew all of them, and was especially attentive to the manuscript, a letter by William Strachey (later published in *Purchas his Pilgrimes* 1625).

These pamphlets contain phrases which reveal succinctly some of the issues that Jacobeans felt were raised by the whole enterprise. The failures, for instance, are repeatedly attributed to lack of hard work—investors back home are in a way reassured that the raw material was good and the plan for the colony was well founded, but it was human frailty that caused the problems. In such a light, perhaps, Prospero's imposition of manual labor on his charges might be seen as part of a desirable discipline, and Gonzalo's advocacy of leisure a prescription for anarchy.

Then there was the lively contemporary debate (which the Spanish and other colonial powers also had) about the possibility of civilizing the natives. In the margins of Strachey's account, the contradictory positions are spelled out aphoristically—on the one hand, he asks, "Can the leopard change its spots?" while on the other he inquires, "Were not we ourselves made and not born civil in our progenitors' days? Were not Caesar's Britons as brutish as Virginians?" Such questions are posed in many places in the play, most firmly when Prospero, dressed once more (and for the first time onstage) as the duke of Milan announces, when confronted by Caliban (dressed in Prospero's discarded magician's robes), "This thing of darkness I acknowledge mine." Caliban's reply—"I'll be wise hereafter, and seek for Grace"—seems designed to prompt a debate in the audience.

The Virginia Company, like the King's Men, was a commercial operation with a group of shareholders to finance it. But the Jacobeans conceived of these activities in altogether loftier terms. Colonial expansion was understood as a religious duty and part of the British imperial destiny, derived ultimately from their ancestors, Brutus and the Trojans. And Shakespeare weaves into *The Tempest* material from the realm of epic, sometimes solemnly, sometimes in a more challenging way, as in the strange conversation about Tunis and Carthage and "widow Dido." The exchange may appear like a digression, but it is central to the structure of the play.

The Dido and Aeneas story is a tale of love, desertion, and suicide. Aeneas deserts Dido because the gods drive him on in his imperial destiny to found Rome, to leave Africa for Italy. Before ever they arrive on Prospero's island, the Italian party have been to Tunis (which stands where Carthage stood) to celebrate the dynastic marriage between Claribel, daughter of the king of Naples, and the prince of Tunis. In a sense, then, these seafarers have been, perhaps unwittingly, putting right an ancient wrong, soothing an ancient wound, by creating a union between nations that softens the memory of Dido's pain and Aeneas's desertion. It is the impulse to create a union that takes these people into Prospero's sphere of influence; it is their celebration of a marriage, rather than his power, that puts them in his hands.

The parallel with *The Winter's Tale* is obvious, and it is strengthened by Prospero's desire to avenge the personal wrongs he announces to Miranda that he has suffered. There is, both for him and the sea travelers, an unconscious coincidence of large, epic, and dynastic movements and purely personal concerns. And such a coming together underlines another set of themes in the play—

the internalization of the topics of governance, empire, exploration, control, and so on. The personal and the political are made to seem inseparable; and the parallels between Prospero and Caliban, between Prospero and Sycorax, generate new areas of investigation, of speculation.

That in itself is an important question raised by Prospero's story. The Renaissance was a great age of education and of educational theory, and there was intense interest about such questions as the desirability of mass education and the appropriate balance between "pure" academic study and practical skills. Sir Philip Sidney's mentor, the celebrated scholar-diplomat Hubert Languet, advised his brilliant charge not to become too academic if he hoped for a political career. "I regard as essential," he wrote, "those things it is discreditable for a man of high birth not to know, and which, one day, may be an ornament and a resource to you"—leaders were expected to be generalists rather than experts: in Languet's words, "I consider it absurd to learn the rudiments of many sciences simply for display and not for use." Likewise, King James warned Prince Henry of the dangers of learning that was not directed to specific purposes, apart from history. The king wrote, "for the study of the other liberal arts and sciences, I would have you reasonably versed in them, but not pressing to be a past-master in any of them: for that cannot but distract you from . . . your calling." Such remarks provide an important context for the audience's understanding of Prospero, and they make his journey through the play parallel those of Hamlet, Leontes, Lear, and the Duke in *Measure for Measure*.

Like Hamlet, Prospero eventually wakes up to the fact that the story through which he is living is one of revenge, and he has a choice (one to which Hamlet had aspired) of ending in deaths or marriages, in tragedy or comedy. We should not forget the transformation in the political order in Milan which the play effects. At the beginning of the action, after all, Antonio is the duke of Milan. At the end, Prospero wears the robes of that office, and the succession is established through the marriage of Miranda and Ferdinand. Antonio is cut out completely. Prospero can "retire," and let "every third thought . . . be my grave," secure in the knowledge that his revenge is completed.

In other words, Prospero's movement toward self-knowledge is a generic one; like so many of Shakespeare's rulers, he is shown facing up to the difference between his private preoccupations and the realities both of his life and of the historical and political circumstances in which he finds himself. What is surprising and novel is the way he involves the audience in his enterprise. The play's famous epilogue, stripped to its bones, is a request for applause. Most epilogues are, of course, but this is more explicit than many. We are told that everything depends on the assent of the observers: "Gentle breath of yours my sails must fill, or else my project fails."

As in *The Winter's Tale*, then, we are invited to imagine the conference in Prospero's cell, and then the journey back to Italy, the marriage and the new order that has been promised. And the sign that we are prepared to do that is our applause. Prospero seizes upon what was going to happen anyway, and tells us it has immense significance. Prospero's most potent magic occurs when he has given up the pursuit of magic—when he "converts" Caliban and secures the assent of the audience. Suddenly we are in the same position as the king was in the masques—the moment that usually signals the end of a stage show is here the moment when we join it. It is as if the frame of a picture dissolved and included its spectator. If a single moment had to stand for the combination of naturalism and allegory in the late plays, this would surely be it, where the most normal and everyday action—clapping at the end of a show— is magically reclassified from an act that concludes a work of art into an act that prolongs it.

Shakespeare's treatment of the family, sex, and marriage in these late plays can be seen as part of the cult of the family, of the dynasty, that was deliberately promoted by King James. From the moment when Isabella is drawn away from her solitary life into conjugality by the duke in *Measure for Measure*, the impulse toward union is presented as increasingly powerful. Most usually, the power of this familial imperative is displayed in its ability to overcome immense challenges to it—rejection, separation, persecution. Throughout, we are aware of the struggle to accommodate sexual desire, and the healing, regenerative roles played by women.

How the Jacobeans found them is unknown. But they were, as we have seen, popular in performance. There is a lengthy section among Simon Forman's papers for the months leading up to his death where he records seeing *Macbeth* on Saturday, April 20, 1611, then *Cymbeline*, and then, on Wednesday, May 15, *The Winter's Tale*, all at the Globe. Forman's accounts of the plots of the plays include some observations of a more general kind, abstracting lessons from what he had seen performed. This is the description of *The Winter's Tale*:

> Remember also the Rogue [Autolycus] that came in all tottered like coll-pixi [a fairy trickster]. And how he feigned him sick and to have been robbed of all that he had and how he cozened the poor man of all his money, and after came to the sheep-shearing with a peddlar's pack. And there cozened them again of all their money. And how he changed apparel with the King of Bohemia's son. And then how he turned courtier, etc.
>
> Beware of trusting feigned beggars or fawning fellows.

And it is with that homely reflection in mind that we, and Shakespeare, return to Stratford.

CHAPTER TWELVE

"Let's Go Off, and Bear Us Like the Time": The Last Years

In 1614 and 1615 the Stratford lawyer Thomas Greene referred to "my cosen Shakespeare," and it is probable that they were distantly related. Greene, together with his wife Lettice and children (named Anne and William—after the Shakespeares, perhaps?), stayed at New Place from 1609 until their new home, St. Mary's House, was ready for occupation. That may not have been until as late as 1611. Greene entered the Middle Temple in 1595 on the surety of John Marston of Coventry and his son of the same name, the poet and dramatist. He was town solicitor for Stratford in 1601, and was called to the bar in 1602.

Greene became a member of the literary circle that formed in the Inns of Court. John and Francis Beaumont and the antiquarian John Selden were acquaintances from the Inner Temple, while the Middle Temple group included George Sandys and the Midlands gentlemen Sir Henry Goodyer and Sir Henry Rainsford—both of whom were friends and patrons of Michael Drayton. Greene may well be the Thomas Greene who contributed a commendatory sonnet to Drayton's historical poem *The Barons' Wars* of 1603, as well as a panegyric to King James, *A Poet's Vision and a Prince's Glory*, of the same year.

He maintained an interest in letters and in British antiquities throughout his life, despite the pressures of a busy legal practice and public service. As steward of Stratford from 1603 to 1617, he spent a good deal of time negotiating on the town's behalf with the central authorities for a new charter. When he sold up and left Stratford in 1617, his house and lands were sold to Sir Henry Rainsford. Greene and Shakespeare shared many friends, and Greene was an able amateur poet; what is more, Greene was one of the few men at Stratford who had more than a spectator's acquaintance with the life of the court and the city in London. But perhaps he overstayed his welcome: Shakespeare did not mention him in his will.

Both men traveled easily and freely between the two worlds, and, as we have seen, each acted on behalf of fellow townsmen who were involved in business or litigation in London. On September 11, 1611, Shakespeare and Greene made a contribution—in company with more than sixty fellow townsfolk—toward the costs incurred in advancing a bill in Parliament for increased provision for highway maintenance. Shakespeare's name is added in the margin, which may indicate that he was not present when the original list was drawn up.

Although Shakespeare's company performed at court at least twenty times during the winter season beginning at the end of October and stretching through to April 26, 1612, no performances are recorded for the latter part of January or the first week of February, so it is possible that he was able to attend the burial of his younger brother Gilbert on February 3. Gilbert was just two years younger than William, and had acted as agent for him in Stratford on at least one occasion. The entry in the burial register calls him "adolescens"—which probably merely indicates that he died unmarried.

In 1612 Shakespeare became involved as a witness in a case at the Court of Requests in Westminster that related to events of almost a decade earlier. It took him back to the period, round about 1604, when he had had rooms in Christopher Mountjoy's house at the corner of Silver Street and Monkswell Street in Cripplegate. The case was brought by Stephen Belott, a former apprentice of Mountjoy's, who had married his master's daughter Mary but had still not received the dowry agreed at the time of the marriage. He called Shakespeare to testify to his good character and to the details of the financial arrangements. In the course of the evidence, it becomes clear that Shakespeare had acted as an intermediary between the Mountjoys and young Belott, though his memory about the precise terms of the discussions was imprecise.

The people involved were a colorful crew, straight out of a Jacobean city comedy. From the documents the old Huguenot Mountjoy comes out as irascible, ambitious, and protective of his daughter. His wife, also Mary, is known to have been involved in an affair with a neighboring tradesman, one Henry Wood, a mercer in Swan Alley. When she feared that she was pregnant by her lover she took her problems to the extraordinary Simon Forman, who recorded her visit in his diary. At another point in the diary Forman notes, "Mary Mountjoy alained" (that is, hidden)—conjuring up another of those Feydeau-like episodes in which the charismatic astrologer and physician delighted. Mountjoy consulted Forman (who also advised Mme. Mountjoy's lover on astrological aspects of his business ambitions and relationships) to find out the likely future prospect of his apprentices—perhaps he had in mind at that stage that one of them should be assimilated within the family. The successful suitor of the three, Stephen Belott, was almost a parody of the Protestant work ethic. He had risen through his own efforts as Mountjoy's apprentice, embarked on travels to broaden his mind and experience, and then returned to work with Mountjoy again.

The documents in the case relate to two hearings, on May 11 and June 19, 1612. Shakespeare attended the first but not the second, which suggests that he was out of town at the time. In addition, the fact that he is referred to as "from Stratford" indicates that by then he had no fixed London residence.

Several witnesses described the role Shakespeare had played in the negotiations. One of the family's servants, Joan Johnson, recalled, "As she remembereth, the defendant [Mountjoy] did send and persuade one Mr Shakespeare that lay in the house to persuade the plaintiff [Belott] to the same marriage." A family friend, Daniell Nicholas, was more precise, and his report of a conversation with Shakespeare was noted by the court:

Shakespeare told his deponent [Nicholas] that the defendant [Mountjoy] told him that if the plaintiff [Belott] would marry the said Mary . . . he would give them . . . a sum of money with her for a portion in marriage with her. . . . Shakespeare had told them that they should have a sum of money for a portion from the father, they were made sure by Mr Shakespeare by giving their consent, and agreed to marry.

"They were made sure by Shakespeare"—but for how much? Belott expected sixty pounds plus an inheritance of some two hundred pounds. Instead he got ten pounds and some household goods. Even after the couple moved back in to Silver Street on Mme. Mountjoy's death in 1606, and they became even more substantially involved in the business and the household, old Mountjoy withheld money and goodwill. Eventually they moved out, the father took to drink and other forms of unspecified debauchery, and it was rumored that he was going to cut them out of his will; hence the hearings.

Clearly Shakespeare's evidence was crucial. On the question of Belott's character and behavior when in Mountjoy's employment, the courts report states:

> . . . he [Shakespeare] did know the complainant [Belott] when he was servant with the defendant [Mountjoy] . . . during the time of his . . . service, [Belott] to this deponent's knowledge did well and honestly behave himself . . . this deponent sayeth that he verily thinketh that the . . . complainant was a very good and industrious servant in the said service.

He further affirmed that Belott had borne and shown "great good will and affection" toward Mountjoy; indeed, "he hath heard the defendant and his wife divers and sundry times say and report that the said complainant was a very honest fellow." Shakespeare reported that it had been Mountjoy who did "solicit and entreat" him "to move and persuade" Belott to marry her daughter—"and accordingly this deponent did move and persuade the complainant thereunto."

To the central question about the marriage settlement Shakespeare gave only a partial answer—his memory seems to have failed him. Because this report is as close as we can get to Shakespeare's own voice, it is quoted in full:

. . . this deponent saith that the defendant promised to give the said
complainant a portion in marriage with Mary his daughter, but what
certain portion he remembereth not, nor when to be paid, nor knoweth that the defendant promised the plaintiff two hundred pounds
with his daughter Mary at the time of his decease. But sayeth that
the plaintiff was dwelling with the defendant in his house, and they
had amongst themselves many conferences about their marriage
which afterwards was consummated and solemnised. And more he
cannot depose.

Shakespeare was not alone in his ignorance of the sums in question. All the other witnesses testify to Shakespeare's role, but they
are no more able than he to put a figure on the agreement. And
perhaps the Belotts themselves would not have made a fuss if old
Mountjoy had not become drunk and difficult in his old age. The
case was referred to the authorities of the French church in London,
who found cause for complaint in both Mountjoy and Belott, but
awarded the younger man twenty nobles (a noble was worth a third
of a pound—6s.8d.), which had still not been paid a year later, and
which had not curbed the energy with which Mountjoy pursued
his life of dissipation.

While the King's Men were busily preparing for their parts in
the royal wedding in 1613, Shakespeare's last surviving brother,
Richard, died. He was buried in Stratford on February 4. His only
appearance in the local records is when he is fined a shilling, to be
used for the relief of the poor, in July 1608 by the ecclesiastical court
at Stratford for an unidentified offense—most likely for not keeping
the Sabbath. It is not much to go on. After his death, of the whole
tribe of eight children, only William and his sister Joan were left.

There is no reason to suppose that the traditional view of Shakespeare's last years is other than substantially correct. In Nicholas
Rowe's famous words from his biography in 1709:

The latter part of his life was spent, as all men of good sense will
wish theirs may be, in ease, retirement, and the conversation of his
friends. He had the good fortune to gather an estate equal to his
occasion, and, in that, to his wish; and is said to have spent some
years before his death in his native Stratford.

It is known that he had business interests and investments in London, and was still connected with the King's Men. After 1612,

indeed perhaps from slightly earlier, he seems to have decided to use his talent more sparingly, and the surviving works from this period are all collaborative. His partner was John Fletcher, who had already written for the King's Men the successful *Philaster, or Love Lies A-Bleeding*, *A King and No King*, and *The Maid's Tragedy*, all three with Francis Beaumont, a family friend of Michael Drayton. Fletcher seems to have been seen as the company's most important rising young writer, whose gifts were already distinctive and who was helping to steer the audiences to appreciate new developments in theatrical taste. At the time of the collaboration with Shakespeare, the young man's writing partner Francis Beaumont was about thirty, newly married, and living outside London.

What Fletcher learned from Shakespeare—in particular from *Cymbeline* and *The Winter's Tale*—indicates that he saw what we think of as "the last plays" as a new beginning, as the opening up of new theatrical possibilities based on the extraordinary range and vitality of Shakespeare's most recent experiments. The relationship was by no means one-way. Fletcher brought on to the English stage the definitive modern tragicomedy, Guarini's *Il Pastor Fido*, which became *The Faithful Shepherdess*, published in 1608–9, with a preface in which the rules of the new genre are explained. This text played an important role in providing theoretical respectability, a certain intellectual *cachet*, to Shakespeare's formal experiments in *Pericles*— despite the fact that it was a commercial disaster. It gave a name to the form he had been practicing since *Much Ado*. And the artistic confidence of the next three plays may derive in some measure from the new model that Fletcher had made available, and which he translated into an artistically and theatrically vital form.

During the winter of 1612–13, in the period of mourning that followed the death of Prince Henry on November 6, the King's Men performed at court Shakespeare's new play *Cardenio*, now lost. They gave the piece again—also at court—to entertain the ambassador of the duke of Savoy, on June 8 of the following year, and on July 9 Heminges received on the company's behalf the sum of £6 13s. 4d. for their pains in presenting "Cardenna." The name Cardenio derives from the first part of *Don Quixote*—Thomas Shelton's English translation of which had just appeared. We can suppose that Shakespeare's play dramatized the story of Cardenio and Lucinda—even a cursory reading of Cervantes's narrative will show how closely its plot and tone resemble those of other late plays, in particular *The Winter's Tale*, *The Two Noble Kinsmen*, and *Pericles*. The madness of Cardenio, for instance, would probably have been a male counterpart to that of the jailer's daughter in *The Two Noble Kinsmen*, and would have resembled that of Pericles, Leontes, and Ferdinand in Webster's *The Duchess of Malfi*.

The last real trace of Shakespeare's play is a note in the Stationers' Register for 1653, where the publisher Humphrey Mosley entered a number of plays including "The History of Cardenio," attributed to "Mr Fletcher and Shakespeare." Lewis Theobald claimed that his 1728 publication *Double Falsehood* was based on a manuscript of Shakespeare's play; the piece had been staged with some success at Drury Lane in 1727–8. There were several revivals in later years. It was asserted that the manuscript was kept in the library of the Covent Garden playhouse, and that learned opinion held that it was rather more Fletcher's work than Shakespeare's. Theobald himself did not include the play in his edition of Shakespeare, and the matter was concluded after a fashion when a fire of 1808 destroyed the theater and its library. Modern scholars accept that there may well be a Jacobean original beneath Theobald's play (in which Cervantes's characters' names are changed and the story modified somewhat), though it requires a powerful effort of the imagination to reconstruct it in any satisfying way.

In early March 1613 Shakespeare bought a house in the Blackfriars complex, near to the new theater and close to the jetty at Puddle Wharf, from which he could speed across to the Bankside. He could hardly have chosen a more convenient or fashionable location, though it looks as though he never lived there. The property included the old gatehouse of what had been the Prior's lodgings before the Reformation. In Elizabeth's reign it had been a nest of dissidents, mainly disaffected Catholics; priests and their supporters had made use of the many places of concealment the apartments provided, the "sundry back doors and by-ways, and many secret vaults and corners," in the words of a contemporary. The lot that Shakespeare bought from Henry Walker, described as "citizen and minstrel of London," included, in addition to the rooms over the gatehouse, a patch of land enclosed on two sides by fences

and on the other by an old brick wall. It had been leased out for
twenty-five years in 1604 to a haberdasher, William Ireland (whose
name is preserved in Ireland Yard, which must be just south of the
site of Shakespeare's gatehouse).

Shakespeare made his purchase with three partners: William
Johnson, landlord of the Mermaid tavern, John Jackson, and John
Hemming—the last named presumably his fellow from the King's
Men. Jackson was related by marriage to Elias James, a brewer
who had premises at the foot of Puddle Dock Hill. Shakespeare
perhaps wrote an epitaph on this Elias James, who would have been
his neighbor. In the same Oxford manuscript that preserves "Shall
I die?," the text (which I have modernized) runs as follows:

> When God was pleased (the world unwilling yet),
> Elias James to Nature paid his debt,
> And here reposeth. As he liv'd, he died.
> The saying strongly in him verified,
> "Such life, such death." Then, a known truth to tell,
> He lived a godly life, and died as well.

These three friends were evidently to act as trustees for Shakespeare. He it was who put up all the money—the purchase price
was one hundred forty pounds, of which eighty was to be paid in
cash. On the following day the property was mortgaged back to
Walker for sixty pounds, the remainder of the original price. Apparently such a transaction was common enough, and it gave the
purchaser a little time to raise the full price—in this case until the
following September 29. A tenant, John Robinson, was installed
after Ireland's lease was surrendered (presumably during the preparation for the sale). In the documents Shakespeare is described as
living in Stratford, which explains the appointment of trustees. But
an additional consequence of this arrangement—and we can do no
more than guess at Shakespeare's motivation—was that, as long as
Shakespeare did not outlive the other trustees, Anne Shakespeare
would not be entitled to the usual widow's third interest in that
part of the estate.

In the same month, Shakespeare was moving in much grander
circles, in the world of conspicuous consumption and display of
aristocratic pageantry.

King James maintained for his own celebrations some Elizabethan rituals. In particular he held several tilts—a form of enter-tainment that had seemed fairly archaic even in the days of Sidney and Sir Henry Lee in the early 1580s, and which by 1613 was clearly part of a nostalgic revival of chivalry. This time, however, on March 24, 1613, Shakespeare's role was not to provide a play or show, but rather to work directly for an individual nobleman, Francis Manners, sixth earl of Rutland. The composer of the mottos and *imprese* (decorated shields) of the tournament in *Pericles* was commissioned to furnish the earl with a device for his shield, and the multitalented Burbage was employed to give practical expres-sion to Shakespeare's invention. Rutland's steward recorded the payment a week later: "Item, 31 Martii, to Mr Shakespeare in gold about my Lord's *impreso*, xliiiis; to Richard Burbage for painting and making it, in gold xliiiis" and he gives the total outlay as £4 8s., split equally between the two men.

This particular tilt seems to have featured an especially obscure and cryptic set of shield devices, which perhaps explains why Shakespeare was called in to pit his wits against other writers. In the words of a contemporary observer, the courtier and diplomat Sir Henry Wotton, "some were so dark [obscure], that their mean-ing is not yet understood, unless perchance that were their meaning, not to be understood." Wotton judged that the best devices had been worn by the Herbert brothers—later to be the dedicatees of the First Folio.

During the "Elizabethan revival" that occurred in the brief flow-ering of Prince Henry's court, as well as romances like *Mucedorus*, many other popular Elizabethan works were reissued. A major instance was the 1610 edition of *A Mirror for Magistrates*, and the structure and method of *Henry VIII* owe a good deal to the earlier work. In particular, the play's numerous tragedies make it almost rival the *Mirror*, and the direct statements by those who fall are often reminiscent of those found there—the best example is the fallen Wolsey's speech to Cromwell.

In the prologue, the writers announce that their play is designed to move the spectators to tears—"Be sad, as we would make ye"—and that it has a central core of veracity that is mediated by art; they call it "our chosen truth." The members of the audience, flatteringly called "the first and happiest hearers of the town," are told that they "may here find truth." And this early stress upon truth is surely related to the play's subtitle (*All is True*)—and perhaps, as some evidence indicates, *Henry VIII* became the title only later.

Such evidence as there is relates to the accident which led to the destruction of the Globe by fire during a performance of the play on June 29, 1613. This was St. Peter's Day—fitting the play's concern with the king who had replaced the pope as head of the Church. A letter of July 4, 1613 describes the event and also confirms that the performance was not the play's first. A young London merchant called Henry Bluett wrote to his friend Richard Weeks:

> On Tuesday last there was acted at the Globe a new play called *All is True*, which had been acted not passing two or three times before. There came many people to see it insomuch that the house was very full, and as the play was almost ended the house was fired with shooting off a chamber which was stopped with tow which was blown up into the thatch of the house and so burned down to the ground. But the people escaped all without hurt except one man who was scalded with the fire by adventuring in to save a child which otherwise had been burnt.

The best-known account of these events is to be found in a letter to Sir Edmund Bacon by Sir Henry Wotton, written two days earlier on July 2, 1613:

> The King's players had a new play, called *All is True*, representing some principal pieces of the reign of Henry VIII, which was set forth with many extraordinary circumstances of pomp and majesty, even to the matting of the stage: the Knights of the Order, with their Georges and garters, the Guards with their embroidered coats, and the like: sufficient in truth within a while to make greatness very familiar, if not ridiculous. Now, King Henry making a masque at the Cardinal Wolsey's house, and certain chambers being shot off at his entry, some of the paper, or other stuff, wherewith one of them was stopped, did light on the thatch, where being thought at first but an idle smoke, and their eyes more attentive to the show, it kindled inwardly, and ran around like a train, consuming within less than an hour the whole house to the very grounds.
> This was the fatal period of that virtuous fabric; wherein yet nothing did perish but wood and straw, and a few forsaken cloaks;

only one man had his breeches set on fire, that would perhaps have broiled him, if he had not by the benefit of a provident wit put it out with bottle ale.

Though the Globe saw the play, the Blackfriars is in it. The historical trial of Queen Katherine had taken place in the same great chamber at Blackfriars that was now the King's Men's theater, and it is reasonable to assume that the great set-piece in Act II, Scene IV was composed with a performance in that place in mind. Shakespeare exploits the potential of such a staging for creating a frisson as the present is suddenly joined to the past; by stressing the theatricality of the queen's show trial he inverts our categories, so that Henry's charade becomes the theatrical fiction, Shakespeare's presentation of the evidence the judgment of history on the trial.

The reign of Henry VIII was, and indeed still is, intensely controversial. Shakespeare organizes his pageants of rising and falling, of judging and interpreting, in such a way as to argue against a hierarchy of truth, and for the notion that Wolsey, for instance, can be both unjust and tragic. The long scene of Wolsey's humiliation and fall is a masterpiece of dramatic control, in which the audience's sympathies—naturally with the reforming nobles and against the axiomatically self-seeking prelate—are inverted. Pity is aroused for the fallen cardinal by means of his moving soliloquies, in which he discusses his fall as an illustration of human vanity:

> I have ventured
> Like little wanton boys that swim on bladders,
> This many summers in a sea of glory,
> But far beyond my depth; my high-blown pride
> At length broke under me, and now has left me,
> Weary and old with service, to the mercy
> Of a rude stream that must for ever hide me.
> Vain pomp and glory of this world, I hate ye!
> I feel my heart new opened. . . .

Like Parolles, he declares, "I know myself now, and I feel within me/A peace above all earthly dignities/A still and quiet conscience." Indeed, it is typical of the play that tragic falls (such as those of Buckingham and Katherine as well as Wolsey) are shown to possess both public and private dimensions, and to be affecting as well as illustrative. And the method seems to be designed for us to be able both to sympathize for Katherine and to entertain positive thoughts about Anne Bullen and to look forward to Queen Elizabeth (via Cranmer's prophecy) and to the marriage of the new Elizabeth, King James's daughter. All of these things are simultaneously "true." There is a notable sleight of hand in the treatment of More. Successive events, which might in a political or historical sense qualify or contradict one another, are presented in a strange evaluative limbo. There is no attempt to provide a central focus. Thus Wolsey and Cromwell discuss the future Catholic martyr in glowing terms, when his appointment as chancellor has been announced. Later, at Cranmer's trial, the lord chancellor who presides harshly over the proceedings is not named. The studied avoidance of reference to More is more notable in the study than on the stage. That is why the prologue lays such stress on the audience's feelings— "Those that can pity here/May, if they think it well, let fall a tear; /The subject will deserve it. . . ."

It is the role of the audience that connects the play's treatment of a contentious past for the benefit of the Jacobean present. The play displays Henry's strengths and weaknesses as an impresario, as a manipulator of the theatrical arts of power; and it shows how in the end his control over such figures as Katherine and Wolsey is limited to the merely physical and material. He embodies a certain order, a focus of authority within the stage events; but it is clear that there is another, providential order which stretches far beyond the zones where his writ runs.

Perhaps the play was originally conceived to some extent as a compliment to the future Henry IX, who died before it was finished. But its celebration of James and his daughter is clear enough: Henry represents an instructive contrast with his successor, and must have seemed a cruder, less enigmatic master of ceremonies than the new Solomon liked to think himself. And the play ends, in a "public" version of the ending of a masque, by opening itself out specifically to James. At the end of Cranmer's prophecy about the future Queen Elizabeth, cradled in his arms, he refers to her death and successor:

> . . . as when
> The bird of wonder dies, the maiden phoenix,

Her ashes new create another heir,
As great in admiration as herself;
So shall she leave her blessedness to one
. . . Who from the sacred ashes of her honour
Shall star-like rise, as great in fame as she was,
And so stand fixed. Peace, plenty, love, truth, terror,
That were the servants to this chosen infant,
Shall then be his, and like a vine grow to him;
Wherever the bright sun of heaven shall shine,
His honour and the greatness of his name
Shall be, and make new nations. He shall flourish,
And like a mountain cedar, reach his branches
To all the plains about him: our children's children
Shall see this, and bless heaven.

In Henry's view, Cranmer speaks "wonders." To James, as to the audience, the archbishop's words show that it is the audience's experience, its knowledge of the operations of history and providence, that enable the spectator to provide assent in the words of the title, that "All is True."

It has already been seen how poets grappled with the problem of accommodating within a single poem lament for Queen Elizabeth and praise of the new king, and how easy it was for them to give offense, as Drayton did, by getting the balance wrong. In the winter of 1612–13 there was a new challenge. After the universal and unprecedented outpouring of public grief that followed the sudden death of the heir to the throne on November 6, there was an abrupt change of gear as preparations resumed for the marriage of Princess Elizabeth to the German prince Frederick, the elector palatine. In William Basse's little volume of elegies on Prince Henry there is a gap after the last lament, followed by "A Morning after Mourning"—a collection of pieces on the wedding. Similarly abrupt transitions from mourning to celebration can be found in countless literary works of the period.

In *The Two Noble Kinsmen* Shakespeare and Fletcher got closer than anyone else to epitomizing the divided sentiments of that winter. But their play goes beyond its occasion, and continues the analysis of the human condition that had been developing in the other romances. It is Shakespeare's most explicit account of existence as irreducibly double, of the human lot as consisting of death and life, grieving and rejoicing, with neither capable of being argued away.

The celebrations for the royal wedding lasted several months, from February to mid-April, when the couple, accompanied by the king, traveled to Rochester to take ship for the continent. Dramatic shows and pageants of numerous kinds were presented before them wherever they went, and it is interesting how many of the plays they saw were tragicomedies such as *Much Ado* (twice), *Cardenio*, *The Winter's Tale*, *The Tempest* and *Philaster* (twice). Partly this was an accurate reflection of the latest theatrical fashion, of course, but it was also related to the widely shared perception of a close correspondence between recent historical events and this new dramatic form.

It is assumed that *The Two Noble Kinsmen* was performed at some stage in these festivities, almost certainly later than February 20, 1613. On that day, the third of the wedding masques, the *Masque of the Inner Temple and Gray's Inn*, by Francis Beaumont, was danced in the Banqueting House in Whitehall; the morris dance in Act III, Scene V of Shakespeare and Fletcher's play is taken from the masque. This confirms the increasing role taken by the King's Men in the staging of such royal entertainments from the time of Jonson's *Love Restored* in 1612.

The later theatrical history of the play is relatively simple. It was revived in 1619 for court performance, along with *Hamlet*, *The Winter's Tale*, and *Henry IV Part 2*. And since the Quarto text (published in 1634) refers in two places to the names of actors who were members of the King's Men in 1625–6 there was presumably another revival then, doubtless after November 1625, when the theaters, which had been closed because of the plague and the death of King James, eventually reopened. The title page of the Quarto claims that the play had been "Presented at the Blackfriars by the King's Majesty's Servants, with great applause." So while it may have been staged at the Globe, all the evidence is of performance— and successful performance—in the more intimate atmosphere of the court and Blackfriars.

The play stages the most extreme elements of tragicomedy— weddings and funerals. It opens and closes with the stark con-

junction of these ceremonies, and shows human beings torn between grief and rejoicing. Because of its powerful use of ceremony,
and its apparently strongly marked distinction between plot and
counterplot, the play has often, like *Henry VIII*, been taken as a
pageant, as a work preoccupied with externals, with spectacle.
Nothing could be further from the truth.

The main plot, the story of Palamon, Arcite, and Emilia, is a
reworking of the gravest, most epic, most chivalric of the tales told
by Chaucer's Canterbury pilgrims, *The Knight's Tale*, which Shakespeare had used on a rather more festive way as the framework for
A Midsummer Night's Dream. Part of the explanation for this new
"solemnity" is the implicit connection with recent events. Both
Henry and the elector were represented as champions of Protestant
chivalry, as the great hope of militant anti-Catholicism. Their mutual affection was constantly remarked—not least as a way of expressing the strength of a union between states cemented by a
dynastic marriage. And the close bond between the brother and
sister was often stressed. A fitness was claimed in the fact that
Henry's second name, Frederick, was the same as that of the elector.
So the main narrative could easily be decoded as a restaging of
Henry's relinquishing care for his sister to his dearest friend. But
the play has much more to offer than a crude political pageant.

It is structured on the basis of plot and counterplot, of frame
and details; the main events are themselves episodes in the bigger
story of Theseus and Hippolyta, and the subplot is bound fast to
the main love story from which it derives, which it echoes, and
upon which it comments. To focus solely on the play's dignity and
splendor is to ignore its savagery, passion, and madness.

Shakespeare and Fletcher add a crucial new dimension to Chaucer's tale. They place Palamon and Arcite in a world which they
affect, and where the consequences of their lofty cult of friendship,
greatness, and heroic love are worked out in the lives of their social
inferiors. The dramatists take what were conventionally two
jokes—the love of a poor woman for a prince, and the spectacle of
madness—and invest this material with a profound and harrowing
pathos.

In the figure of the jailer's daughter we are shown an illustration
of the cost of misplaced love, as she is shown to be a casualty of
that same courtly love which is elsewhere idealized. From the mo-

ment in the opening scene, when it has been established that parallels, comparisons, and contrasts are the play's staple, we are
invited to set the prince's sudden falling in love with Emilia alongside what happens to the jailer's daughter. The events are presented
in similar terms. As in *Henry VIII*, there is no suggestion of a
hierarchy of feeling—that one love is worth more than another.
Indeed, the play is organized around—and seems designed to
evoke—moments of pity, of empathy. In Theseus' words as he
shows compassion to the bereaved Third Queen, "As we are men,
Thus should we do." Later in the play he is similarly self-conscious—"Now I feel compassion"—and his responses provide an
important model and context for the audience.

But any social implications in Chaucer's "pitee renneth soone in
gentil herte" are dispelled by the compassion of those who try to
help the jailer's daughter. The predicament of the wooer is especially wretched. The doctor advises him to conduct himself in a
way familiar from chivalric romance: to pretend to be Palamon, to
sing to her, to entertain her, to "do anything—Lie with her if she
ask you." And they are packed off to bed on the medical advice
that the shock of defloration will bring her back to herself. The
whole painful episode with its anatomy of madness is utterly incomprehensible to the lofty beings in the main plot. For Palamon
and Arcite, their falling in love at first sight, and on principle, with
Emilia is sufficient to bring them to mortal combat and death. In
contrast, the jailer's daughter's affection for Palamon is altogether
unknown to the young prince; his casual rejection of her gives him
not a second's thought but plunges her into utter madness.

The play's image of the human condition is of a series of attempts,
some noble, some absurd, all flawed, to make sense of a universe
ruled by forces that cannot be reduced to human sense. It is compassion that brings the action back time and again from the brink
of absurdity, as scene after scene illustrates another battle in the
ceaseless war between love (or passion) and human reason. The
function of Theseus—a more impressive Albany or Gonzalo, as it
were—is to articulate rational responses to increasingly irrational
events. Like the king in *All's Well that Ends Well*, he is heard constantly summing up actions, persons, and speeches, only for his
certainty to be demolished by some surprising new event. Even at
the end of the play, when the most striking of all the reverses has

occurred—Arcite is crushed by his horse—he still tries to wrest the circumstances round into some sort of order, even if it is only to serve as an illustration of the power of the gods. "In the passage, the Gods have been most equal," he says, and then proceeds to try to decode the bizarre and enigmatic events through which he has lived. In his words:

> The gods my justice
> Take from my hand and they themselves become
> The executioners.

This gloomy, Sidneian view of mankind as the stars' tennis balls is only part of the story, however. The play is an extended dramatic homage to Chaucer, and through him to Bocaccio and Statius. In other words, the play is very obviously presented as an addition to an ancient literary tradition. By its very existence, the play demonstrates that art can have a life beyond the time of its first composition. As in *Pericles*, the stress upon antiquity is also a stress upon continuity and survival. So Shakespeare fixes himself and his young colleague within a community of poets stretching back into the mists of time. In addition, the very fact of the collaboration (and it is a collaboration that includes Beaumont as the provider of the morris dance) argues for an idea of poetic community in the present, a community that looks backward to great predecessors and draws strength from them; but it also reaches out to embrace contemporary and younger writers. In other words, *The Two Noble Kinsmen* is a meditation on poetic continuity and tradition—perhaps this was Shakespeare's real farewell to the stage, in which he self-consciously handed on the torch to his successors and reminded them of the tradition in which they were seeking to participate.

At the end of the play Palamon is rewarded for rejecting the world. As he faces execution with his knights, he spurns worldly glory and hands over a purse of money for the woman whose life he has destroyed:

> A right good creature, more to me deserving
> Than I can quite or speak of.

Quite so. We seem to be directed to pay special attention to his words after that, in particular his final speech as he contemplates his reprieve from execution, his betrothal to Emilia, and a victory that has left his dear friend Arcite mortally wounded as a result of a freakish accident:

> O cousin,
> That we should things desire, which do cost us
> The loss of our desire! That nought could buy
> Dear love, but loss of dear love!

These antitheses recall the gentleman's description of the "noble combat twixt joy and sorrow" fought in Paulina's face in *The Winter's Tale*. If Theseus's final words are indeed Shakespeare's farewell, they leave the audience in a similar position:

> A day or two
> Let us look sadly and give grace unto
> The funeral of Arcite, in whose end
> The visages of bridegrooms we'll put on
> And smile with Palamon, for whom an hour,
> But one hour since, I was as dearly sorry
> As glad of Arcite, and am now as glad
> As for him sorry. O you heavenly charmers,
> What things you make of us! For what we lack
> We laugh, for what we have, are sorry; still
> Are children in some kind. Let us be thankful
> For that which is, and with you leave dispute
> That are above our question.—Let's go off,
> And bear us like the time.

What are we to make of Shakespeare's last words to us? His final injunction, "bear us like the time," seems to be advice to frame a face, construct a behavior, that can match up equally to the griefs and sorrows, deaths and marriages, that express what it means to be human. In the case of his own life, his last years were to feature juxtapositions of rejoicing and sorrow entirely consistent with such a view of human life.

If his last years were touched with sadness as his parents and brothers died, Shakespeare had some compensation in the proximity of his children. Indeed, the only house in Stratford where it is known that his daughter and son-in-law the Halls lived is New Place, though there is a local tradition that they lived in a handsome house just a few yards away, known for part of its history as Cambridge House, and for the last hundred years or so as Hall's Croft. They were certainly living in New Place after Shakespeare's death in 1616, and it is possible that they moved in before that date.

Of the details of their lives precious little is known. But there was one major disturbance in 1613 of which record has survived. On July 15, 1613, Susanna Hall brought suit for defamation in the consistory court at Worcester Cathedral against John Lane, a ne'er-do-well descended from local gentry who had previously got himself into a variety of scrapes including drunkenness and libel suits. Mistress Hall claimed that, some five weeks earlier, Lane had "reported that the plaintiff had the runinge of the raynes & had bin naught with Rafe Smith"—in other words that she suffered from gonorrhea and had slept with Rafe Smith. Smith was a haberdasher and maker of hats, who is noted as an associate of Lane's in later documents. Speaking up for Mistress Hall was Robert Whatcott, who a couple of years later would witness her father's will. Lane decided not to show his face to answer the charges against him, and was accordingly excommunicated on July 27. To illustrate what a close-knit society Stratford was at this time, only a week before the case at Worcester, Susanna Hall's husband was appointed a trustee for the children of Richard Lane, the uncle of the man who had slandered his wife.

Legend has it that Shakespeare's famous wit struck home pointedly at least once in Stratford, and its target was one of the town's wealthiest men, the elderly bachelor John Combe. Combe, so the story goes, was a miserly man whose coffers had been swollen by the extortionate profits of a money-lending business. In Nicholas Rowe's 1709 version, Combe told Shakespeare that he planned to outlive all his contemporaries, and accordingly asked for his epitaph to be written while he lived and could enjoy the Bard's services. "Upon which," Rowe tells us, "*Shakespeare* gave him these four Verses":

Ten in the Hundred lies here ingrav'd,
'Tis a Hundred to Ten, his Soul is not sav'd:

If any Man ask, Who lies in this Tomb?
Oh! ho! quoth the Devil, 'tis my *John-a-Combe*.

A tradition associating Shakespeare with these verses or something very like them can be traced back to the 1630s. And a version
of the poem, described as an epitaph for Combe of Stratford, had
been published (with no reference to Shakespeare) in Richard
Braithwait's *Remains after Death* (1618). But the piece had appeared
earlier, and apparently independently, in Camden's *Remaines* (1614)
and in an anthology called *The More the Merrier* (1608). It was a
common practice for epitaphs to be applied to a variety of different
people and circumstances, and attribution is notoriously difficult.
Perhaps Shakespeare did tease his friend by applying to him—or
at least to his reputation as a hardhearted skinflint—verses he might
have picked up in London.

But what we know of Shakespeare's friendly relationship with
his neighbor, and indeed with his family, suggest that the legend
may be ill-founded. In his will the poet left his sword—always a
gesture rich in symbolic meaning—to Thomas Combe, John's
nephew and heir. John Combe was born three years before Shakespeare, in 1561, and he died two years earlier, in 1614. And the
two men had done business together over more than a decade without any suggestion of difficulty between them—no small achievement, given Combe's propensity for suing people. Combe had been
known to Shakespeare's parents, and they had chosen him to conduct important business for them in 1598. In his will, made on
January 28, 1613, he left money to endow an annual sermon, twenty
pounds for the poor of the parish, and, among the numerous bequests amounting to well over a thousand pounds, the sum of five
pounds to his friend William Shakespeare.

From the last years of Shakespeare's life came two further at-
tributions. One is of a poem on the frontispiece of the *Works* of
King James, published in 1616. The poem, which is not attributed
in the printed text, is engraved beneath a portrait of the crowned
king:

Crounes haue their compasse, length of dayes their date,
Triumphes their tombes, felicitie her fate:
Of more than earth, can earth make none partaker,
But knowledge makes the KING most like his maker.

Better known is the epitaph on Shakespeare's own tomb, which was often attributed to him and may well indeed be authentic. A modernized version runs:

Good friend, for Jesus' sake forbear
To dig the dust enclosed here:
Blest be the man that spares these stones,
And curst be he that moves my bones.

In 1614, most of what is known about Shakespeare concerns Stratford, though he was in London in November of that year. The Chamberlain's account book records, some time between March 21 and June 30, the visit of a preacher to the town and his entertainment by Shakespeare at New Place. The preacher's name is unknown, but he was in all probability an official visitor, invited to preach one of the three annual foundation sermons to the bailiff and council in the Gild Chapel. New Place, just across the street from the Gild Chapel, would have been a natural place for the preacher to stay, with the council picking up the bill. The account notes: "Item for one quart of sack and one quart of claret wine given to a preacher at the New Place, xxd."

In Queen Elizabeth's day Stratford had been devastated by fire in two successive years, 1594 and 1595, and puritan preachers had had no difficulty in uncovering the hand of God in these disasters, each of which took place on a Sunday. Thomas Beard told his readers in 1597 that "a whole town hath been twice burned, for the breach of the Sabbath by its inhabitants," and Lewis Bayly, preaching at Evesham in 1611, declared that the town had been consumed by flames "chiefly for prophaning the Lord's Sabbaths, and for contemning his word in the mouth of his faithful Ministers." On July 9, 1614—which was, perhaps as a token of the more godly lives of the townsfolk, a Saturday—another great fire broke out in Stratford. Fanned by strong winds all over the town, this time it threatened total destruction for some hours. This "sudden and terrible" fire destroyed fifty-four houses, as well as outbuildings, stores, and other goods, to a value of some eight thousand pounds—a catastrophe of huge proportions to the local economy and a personal tragedy for numerous people. Their situation was not helped by the cumbersome and possibly corrupt relief operation (much of

which did not properly get started until December), throughout
which there were complaints about maladministration and the greed
of those putting in disproportionate claims for compensation. The
name of one of the administrators, the older Richard Tyler, was
to be deleted at a later stage from Shakespeare's will. It looks as
though his relief work had alienated him from at least one prominent—and not easily angered—citizen.

It is easy to imagine the emotional temperature rising in Stratford
as the winter of 1614 drew closer. Everyone was affected by the
fire, and the need to do something to remedy disastrous loss was
felt as much by the better-off as by the paupers. Some of those
who had investments in the district were nervous about possible
losses; others saw the chaotic circumstances as an opportunity to
modernize the way the district was farmed, and to organize their
enterprises on a more businesslike footing. That, in the agricultural
world of the early seventeenth century, meant only one thing:
enclosures. And enclosures tended to benefit the larger landowners
at the expense of the smaller, and to the impoverishment of laborers,
most of whom would lose their jobs. Those who owned tithes of
small parcels of land, commonly used for grazing sheep, would find
their income sharply reduced, as sheep pastures yielded less than
the larger fields, which were used for hay or grain.

An earlier attempt to enclose land had failed, even though it had
been spearheaded by the local grandee Sir Edward Greville. This
time the scheme was supported by the young Thomas Combe
(John's nephew) and Arthur Mainwaring, steward of Lord Chancellor Ellesmere, and William Replingham (a solicitor who was
Mainwaring's cousin). It was clear that they were determined to
succeed. Thomas Greene began to prepare the council's defense,
and drew up a list of all the "Ancient freeholders" in the district:
Master Shakespeare is noted as the owner of only four small plots
and was not going to be much affected by the proposed scheme.

Nevertheless, Shakespeare found himself in the middle of a bitter
dispute. Stratford's opposition was chiefly based on fear of the
alarming economic consequences for a town already under severe
strain. On September 23 Greene secured a unanimous council vote
to resist the scheme. He was also motivated in part by the fact that
he had just sunk three hundred pounds into a half-interest in a
group of tithes; the other half or "moiety" was held by Shakespeare

himself, and some of their lands were being eyed by the enclosers. But Shakespeare was in touch with the other side. William Replingham agreed on October 28 to compensate Shakespeare for any losses he might incur in the short term by the enclosure of his land. Indeed, Replingham's letter includes Greene in its promises, presumably on the advice of his solicitor, Thomas Lucas. Lucas found himself in the difficult position of acting for both Greene and Shakespeare in a matter that was set to become acrimonious, as the enclosers tried to reach separate agreements with individual landowners and tithe-holders.

Greene tried hard to keep his group intact, to make sure the town's opposition was solid. But the Shakespeare/Replingham agreement was clearly an embarrassment. He set off for London to try to resolve that problem and also to have face-to-face discussions with Thomas Combe; Combe was not available, so Greene paid a call on his kinsman and partner. Greene wrote a note of the meeting which shows that Shakespeare was trying to calm him down, advising him that the whole project was going to take a long time to plan and that he and his son-in-law had reached the view that the plan would come to nothing. He wrote:

> 17 November. At my cousin Shakespeare: coming yesterday to town, I went to see him how he did. He told me that they assured him they meant to enclose no further than to Gospel Bush, and so up straight (leaving out part of the dingles to the field) to the gate in Cloptonhedge, and take in Salisbury's piece. And that they mean in April to survey the land, and then to give satisfaction and not before. And he and Master Hall say they think there will be nothing done at all.

But in fact Shakespeare had been taken in. Either that, or he was secretly on Mainwaring's side. A survey which he said would not take place until the spring was actually under way as he was reassuring Greene. When Greene got back to Stratford, he found that it had already happened. On December 10 he was chasing around Stratford looking for Replingham, who was presumably drawing up documents based on the survey but who he suspected might be at Shakespeare's house. Greene did eventually meet up with Combe, who smoothly claimed to be only a junior partner in the business, and suggested that the council should think twice about antagonizing a man so well connected as Mainwaring. They should bear in mind, he advised them, that they had "by stirring in this business got—he would not say the greatest, but *almost* the greatest men of England, to be [their] enemies."

The threat of bringing down the wrath of the lord chancellor did not, however, outface Greene, who kept the council busy and united. On December 23 he managed to get "almost all" of them to sign two letters. One was sent to Mainwaring, the other to Shakespeare. And when Greene recorded this, he added, "I also writ of myself to my cousin Shakespeare the copies of all our oathes made then. Also a note of the inconveniences [that] would grow by the enclosure." So a private appeal went in the same package as the official letter. On the same day the council wrote to solicit the support of neighboring landowners: Sir Francis Smith, who owned land at Welcombe, and Master Andrew Archer, the main landowner of Bishopton. Other local grandees, such as Lord Carew of Clopton and Lord Compton (who had backed antienclosure "diggers" in 1607), were thought to be sympathetic. The letter to Mainwaring, which presumably was similar to the one sent to Shakespeare, concentrated largely on the fragile state of the local economy, which already had some seven hundred paupers to maintain after the summer fire.

Greene's determination did not stop there. Two of his colleagues, William Walford (a draper who had served in various offices, including bailiff in 1610–11), and William Chandler, who owned some property in Stratford, were persuaded to buy a lease at Welcombe on January 6, 1615, thereby becoming tenants and acquiring the usual rights of a tenancy. These two unlikely peasant farmers were Greene's shock troops, and they were speedily into action. Combe's men had already begun work, now that the survey was complete, and had dug a trench almost three hundred yards long. Walford and Chandler hid some spades and, seizing the first opportunity, began three days later to fill in the ditch.

The ensuing struggle was unequal. Combe rode over to the site, bringing with him a party of workmen, and gathering a crowd of onlookers for what promised to be a winter afternoon's diversion. While Combe observed the scene from horseback, the two representatives of the council were manhandled into the ditch. To Combe, these two bourgeois worthies were not the threat that a peasant rising might have been. And there was clearly an element of relief as well as scorn in his voice when he mocked the council as "puritan knaves" and as people absurdly pretending to be peasants; this partly explains his theatrical hilarity—throughout the assault he "sat laughing on his horseback and said they were good football players."

In fact, Combe was very worried. He tried to bribe Greene into a negotiation with an inducement of ten pounds, but Greene remained adamant, even after a meeting over supper with Replingham, who reminded him before witnesses of the deal drawn up by Lucas and Shakespeare to protect their interests after any enclosure. Meanwhile, a popular rising of sorts, and one which Combe's henchmen could not so easily put down, took place. The very next day a troop of women and children from Stratford and Bishopton came and filled in their ditches.

Winter put an end to the work. Meanwhile, the council took their case to Warwick assizes, and secured an order restraining Combe until such time as a case for the enclosures could be established in open court. They also succeeded in dividing their opponents, by entreating Replingham and Mainwaring separately. Soon only Combe was left of the original consortium, but his commitment to the idea had become extreme. He went so far as to question the authority of the chief justice, Sir Edward Coke, to order a stay of enclosure. Then he set about beating and intimidating his tenants at Welcombe and depopulated the entire village, leaving only his own household. He threatened the recusant woollen draper Arthur Cawdrey that if he sowed wheat in his small fields, he (Combe) "would eat it up with his sheep"—this to a tenant who had, like Shakespeare, shown himself willing to discuss the project with the enclosers. Combe also showed himself irascible and difficult in his daily business in Stratford.

In September 1615, Greene noted "W. Shakespeare's telling J. Greene [Thomas's brother John] that I was not able to bear the enclosing of Welcombe." This is an enigmatic jotting. Perhaps "I" should read "he": or "bear" should read "bar"—Greene originally wrote "he . . ." but then crossed it out. It could be that Shakespeare was confiding to John Greene that his brother had become so personally involved in this unpleasant business that it had developed into an obsession for him, and was explaining why he had kept out of it, and had acted in their best interests from the outset. He may well have felt he had some explaining to do.

Finally, in the spring of 1616, the staying order was confirmed at the Court of King's Bench. Combe bounced back, with a new, less ambitious, scheme, which he offered to the council in a newly friendly spirit, addressing them oleaginously as "loving friends." But they resisted this and other approaches, not least because of his repeated small-scale enclosures of individual parcels of land over the next few years, despite the court order. Eventually, in 1619, he was told by the court once and for all to give up, and to return all the lands to their previous use. By then Greene had left Stratford, and William Shakespeare was dead.

These events can be read to show a disinterested Shakespeare, a Prospero to Greene's idealistic Gonzalo; or they can show him trying to strike compromises, to find common ground and goodwill in the midst of ever more heated exchanges; or they can, as in Edward Bond's play *Bingo*, show him as a hard-hearted encloser, a ruthless capitalist building his wealth on the destitution of his townsfolk. Was he, for instance, naïve or cunning to do his deal with Replingham? Was he the deceived or the deceiver when he said the survey would be delayed until April? We cannot know, but in the upshot—thanks admittedly in greater measure to Greene than to Shakespeare—his and Hall's assessment at the beginning proved to be correct. In the end, the Court of King's Bench would never allow it. And they didn't.

During the course of these events Shakespeare turned his mind to an altogether less contentious part of his estate. In the spring of 1615 an attempt was made by several owners of property in the Blackfriars complex to tidy up, in the light of Anne Bacon's recent death, some of the tangled legal interrelationships in the rabbit warren of buildings. Initially they petitioned the Court of Chancery to grant Mathias Bacon, Anne's heir, authority to surrender certain deeds and patents. The group consisted of Sir Thomas Bendish, Edward Newport, William Thoresby, Robert Dormer and his wife Mary, William Shakespeare, and Richard Bacon, and the documents in the seemingly uncontentious case are dated April 26, May 5, and May 22. On February 10, 1618, after Shakespeare's death, the three trustees conveyed the gatehouse to John Greene of Clement's Inn and Matthew Morris of Stratford, as their final act "in performance of the confidence and trust in them reposed by William Shakespeare . . . and . . . according to the true intent and meaning of the last will and testament of the said William Shakespeare." Matthew Morris had formerly been in the service of John Hall's father William, while John Greene was the brother of Shakespeare's former houseguest Thomas, and had many ties with the Shakespeare family; in this conveyance he was acting for Susanna Hall.

If Susanna Shakespeare followed her father's advice by taking a husband older than herself, his other daughter Judith (who may well, like her sister, have been illiterate—she endorsed documents with a mark) did not. This was not the only respect in which her life was to differ from the orderly and prosperous existence of the righteous Halls. She was just thirty-one when on February 10, 1616 she married Thomas Quiney, then aged twenty-seven. The couple were immediately in trouble with the ecclesiastical authorities for failing to obtain a license to permit a wedding at this time (the season when weddings were not usually permitted ran in that year from January 28 to April 7). As a result Thomas was excommunicated at the consistory court in Worcester, and it is possible that Judith suffered the same fate; though by November 23 of that year they were both in attendance when their first child, a boy named Shakespeare after his recently deceased grandfather, was christened. Their misdemeanor was neither great nor unusual, and the chances are that they had merely been unlucky to fall victim to an unscrupulous informer—in this case one Walter Nixon, who was later tried for falsifying evidence in proceedings of this kind.

Rather more serious was a hearing much closer to home. Quiney was summoned to appear before the so-called bawdy court at Stratford (the church court presided over by the vicar) on March 26 of the same year. The case he was required to answer was that, some months before his marriage to Judith Shakespeare, he had got with child Margaret Wheeler, and he had proceeded with his marriage (with irregular haste) despite the fact that his child by another woman was about to be born. This sorry episode took a tragic turn when Margaret Wheeler died in March, either in childbirth or very shortly afterward. Both she and her infant were buried on March 15. In court Quiney admitted having had carnal knowledge of the unfortunate woman, and was duly sentenced. John Rogers, the vicar, initially decreed that the appropriate penance was for Quiney to appear before the assembled congregation on three successive Sundays swathed in a white sheet. But for some reason the sentence was reduced to a less public humiliation. Quiney was fined five shillings; he was also obliged to attend the little chapel at Bishopton (within the parish of Stratford, and set amid fields that William Shakespeare owned), and make public and sincere admission of his misdemeanor. He was to perform this duty dressed not in a white sheet but rather *"in habito suo"*—in his own clothes.

The Quineys had three children. The first, Shakespeare, died in the first year of his life, in May 1617. They had two further sons: Richard was born in February 1618, Thomas in January 1620. Both died—perhaps of the plague—in 1639. And other suggestions of similar sorrow, of like unfulfilled promise, can be found elsewhere in the scant surviving records of the lives of Judith and Thomas Quiney.

By 1608 Quiney seems to have been in day-to-day charge of his mother's business, and was selling wine to the Stratford corporation. In 1611 he took on the lease of the tavern next door to his mother's house in High Street, before he and his wife moved to a new inn, the Cage, in July 1616, just a couple of months after Shakespeare's death. The Cage occupied a site at the corner of Bridge Street and High Street, and from these premises Quiney sold wine and tobacco. Over the years he held a number of middle-ranking local offices (burgess in 1617, chamberlain in 1621 and 1622), though he was never made an alderman, and he features in the records of several small court cases. His business did not thrive, and in 1633 the lease of the Cage was taken over by the trio of Dr. Hall, Richard Watts, the vicar of Harbury, and Thomas Nash, Hall's son-in-law. Eventually Richard Quiney took over, and after his death Thomas had an allowance of twelve pounds a year to live on. He was still active in small ways in these mid-century years, and probably died as late as 1662–3. His wife Judith died at the age of seventy-seven in 1661 or 1662.

Shakespeare's will is a document that has been pored over, and argued about, for many years. Shakespeare himself took a fair amount of time and trouble over it. The first draft was drawn up in January 1616, by the lawyer Francis Collins. A second version was drafted on March 25, and there was clearly a need for numerous revisions—not least because of Judith's marriage and the impending prosecution of her husband in the midst of a major town scandal. Each sheet was signed by Shakespeare, and on the last page appears, in a frail scrawl, the phrase "By me William Shakespeare." These signatures were the work of a dying man, though he was still able to declare himself, as convention required, "in perfect health and memory." Underneath the testator's final signature is a note in Latin to the effect that the will had been proved by Hall on June 22, 1616, and that an inventory follows. Not anymore. The inventory of William Shakespeare's goods at the time of his death has not surfaced, and is presumed lost.

The trouble with the will as a window on Shakespeare's soul is that it is so conventional. There are no emotional references to family and friends, which suggests that Collins wanted to keep his client to the well-tried formulas—possibly because of his failing health. The basic form of the will was designed primarily for Jacobean men of property, which explains its failure to mention what must have been one of Shakespeare's most treasured possessions—his library. His dramatic scripts had passed into the possession of the King's Men; but the printed books must have existed, and we can only assume that they passed into Hall's library on Shakespeare's death. In 1635, Baldwin Brook (who later became the town's bailiff) broke into New Place during a legal dispute with the Halls, and, according to Susanna, made off with "goods of great value" including "divers books." A happier dispersal took place eight years later in July 1643, when Queen Henrietta Maria, leading her army across country, stayed at New Place for two nights. Susanna Hall gave a book to Richard Grace, a colonel in the queen's forces and the duke of York's chamberlain. The book, Henri Estienne's *Marvellous Discourse upon the Life, Deeds, and Behaviours of Katherine de Medicis*, bears the inscription "Liber R: Gracei ex dono amicae D. Susanne Hall," and it could well have formed part of her father's library. It is now in the Library of the Shakespeare Birthplace Trust.

Although the will is silent about such important matters as his books, it nevertheless bears the marks of Shakespeare's intervention. In particular, he made amendments to the first draft that were designed to safeguard the interests of the newly married Judith, and to make her as independent as possible of her husband, whose disgrace was about to be publicly confirmed. He starts by altering the reference to "my son in law" to "my daughter Judith," and goes on to leave her one hundred pounds for her marriage portion plus a further fifty pounds if she gave up her claim on the Chapel Lane cottage. If Judith or any "children of her body" were still living three years after the will was signed, she or they would receive a further one hundred fifty pounds. As long as she remained married, she would be paid 10 percent annual interest rather than a capital sum. The only way Quiney could get his hands on these moneys would be if he were to settle lands worth the same amount on Judith and "children of her body." If Judith and any children should not survive, the money would be divided between his grandchild Elizabeth Hall (who would receive one hundred pounds) and his sister Joan Hart and her children. In another addition Judith is left "my broad silver and gilt bowl."

By far the largest proportion of the estate was left to Susanna and her husband John Hall; all the houses and lands, including New Place, were left to Susanna, then to her eldest son or male heir, and then to the son or male heir of Judith. Susanna and her husband were appointed chief executors, "for better enabling of her to perform this my will and towards the performance thereof." To her went his investments outside Stratford, too, including (unless they had already been sold) his shares in the Globe and Blackfriars, "and also all that messuage or tenement with the appurtenances wherein one John Robinson dwelleth, situate lying and being in the Blackfriars in London . . . and all my other lands tenements and heriditaments whatsoever."

To his sister Joan, Shakespeare left the sum of twenty pounds "and all my wearing appearel," and he willed that she be permitted to live out the rest of her days in her present Henley Street house for the annual rent of a shilling. Turning to the next generation, he left five pounds apiece to Joan's boys William, Michael, and Thomas, and his silver to Elizabeth Hall. In due course, it would be Joan's grandson Thomas who would inherit both of the Henley Street houses, now known as the Birthplace.

He left ten pounds for the relief of the poor of the town, his sword to Thomas Combe (John's nephew), twenty marks (£31 6s. 8d.) to Francis Collins, and five pounds to Thomas Russell. He also left money for the purchase of memorial rings by some of his neighbors and oldest acquaintances in Stratford: Hamnet Sadler, William Reynolds, and the brothers Anthony and John Nash. Then follows another late addition—"& to my Fellows John Hemminge, Richard Burbage & Henry Cundell xxvjs viijd A peece to buy them Ringes"—as he remembered his colleagues from the King's Men. They would cherish and preserve his memory better than he could have imagined as he lay dying in Stratford in that sad spring.

It is the final addition that has provoked the most comment. On the last page, in a passage tidying up small bequests and making administrative provisions, there appears the enigmatic insertion, "Item I gyve vnto my wief my second best bed with the furniture." The "furniture" meant the mattress, hangings, linen, and so forth. This is the only reference to Anne Shakespeare in the will, and its tone is impossible to identify. It could be a callous and derisive bequest; it could equally be an affectionate gesture—we can assume the best bed was reserved for the many guests who came to New Place, and perhaps had been specially constructed for that grand house. In such circumstances, the second-best bed would be the marital bed—perhaps, as some have speculated, a bed they had shared since Anne moved in more than thirty years earlier. Centuries of investigation have thrown up at least one local parallel, in Leamington in 1573. A man called William Palmer left his wife their "second best featherbed" in the context of a will that was extremely generous to her in numerous other ways.

What is striking is how little Anne—then aged about sixty—features throughout the will. We must infer from this that her treatment would depend on local customs that were so well known and so securely established that they would not need to be spelled out. But the Stratford view of the so-called "widow's portion" has not been identified. In London at the time, a widow was entitled to a life interest of a third of the husband's estate, as well as the right to remain in the family home. It is possible that the Stratford practice was for this right to have applied primarily to land rather than goods or property (which may explain the nature of the Blackfriars arrangement). So Anne would have been comfortably provided for, and would have seen out the rest of her days in New Place. Anne was to die in the summer of 1623, the year of the publication of the Folio, and was laid to rest on August 8 next to her husband's grave and just below the monument. She was sixty-seven years old; despite her longevity, of her life, her appearance, her actions, and her feelings nothing remains.

Shakespeare appointed Collins and Thomas Russell as overseers, and the last sheet was signed by Collins, July Shaw, John Robinson, Hamnet Sadler, and Robert Whatcott. Shaw was the son of Ralph Shaw, whose property had been valued by John Shakespeare in 1592. He lived in the second house down from the Shakespeares in Chapel Street, and traded successfully in wool and malt. By 1613 he was styled "gentleman," having begun life as a yeoman, and served as alderman; in 1616 he was bailiff, an office he was to hold again in 1627–8. He died in 1629. Robinson worked as a laborer, possibly attached to the Shakespeare-Hall households. Whatcott, as we have seen, had testified on behalf of Susanna in 1613; he was probably also an employee of the household. Sadler was one of the dying man's oldest friends, and had been godfather to the little boy who bore his name.

William Shakespeare faced his last weeks on earth as a wealthy and well-regarded man who had constructed a substantial estate, and he was anxious to preserve what he had built up. He seems to have been a good deal less concerned about the offspring of his brain than about the material security of his family. Others would deal with his literary remains out of love and respect for him. The whole edifice was threatened by the looming specter of disgrace, of public humiliation, that had haunted his life since adolescence. Like Wolsey, like Essex, like Falstaff, like his father, he faced a sudden loss of standing, an evaporation of esteem. With the amendments to his will he did what he could, and doubtless was comforted by his daughters and by the presence of his grandchild Elizabeth. And the unfortunate Judith herself was in the first months of a pregnancy. He would also have had the reassurance of his son-in-law's presence to nurse him through his last days.

What his illness was is unknown; at any rate, it seems that Shakespeare was in failing health for some weeks before his death. A piece of local gossip—from the same source (Stratford's vicar, John Ward, writing in the 1660s) that claimed absurdly that the poet spent at the rate of a thousand pounds per year—is all that survives. Ward wrote: "Shakespear, Drayton, and Ben Johnson, had a merry meeting, and itt seems drank too hard, for Shakespear

died of a feavour there contracted. . . ." The report may tell us
more about the vogue, which developed in the mid-seventeenth
century, for stories about Shakespeare as a robust, no-nonsense,
hard-drinking fellow. But it is possible that Shakespeare entertained
his two friends at some point in the early months of 1616. Drayton
was often in the area, and spent much of his time just a couple of
miles away at Clifford Chambers. Jonson was mainly engaged in
overseeing the production of his Folio *Works*—published in the
summer of 1616—and he had just been granted a royal pension of
one hundred marks per year for the rest of his life. Perhaps the
three were together for Judith's wedding in March. But the story,
in its melancholy way, encapsulates the way that celebration and
sadness go hand in hand in Shakespeare's life as in his art. Such
speculation ends with his death on April 23. He was buried two
days later in the chancel off Holy Trinity.

Shakespeare left money in his will to provide for a monument
in the church, to be carved by Gheerart Janssen (anglicized to
"Gerard Johnson"), one of the sons of Gheerart Janssen the elder,
who had a stonemason's yard in Southwark, close to the Globe,
from the late 1560's. The elder Janssen and his four sons carried
on a prosperous business, and their clients included aristocrats such
as the earls of Rutland (for whom Shakespeare and Burbage also
worked, as we have seen). The Shakespeare monument combines
convention with specificity; it is a reworking of an earlier (1615)
model of a writer's tomb by the same team, namely that of the
great antiquarian John Stow in St. Nicholas Undershaft in London.

This, with the Droeshout engraving in the Folio, is as close as
we can get to his physical appearance. Stow had been depicted
gazing down at a desk, in a book-filled room. In the Stratford
monument Shakespeare looks out, his right hand lying on a cushion
while his left hand holds a sheet of paper which he has just filled.
The poet's hand and his writings rest on a cushion that may be
leather stuffed with wool—a symbolic representation of the sources
of his wealth, perhaps. The contrast between the two monuments
is the familiar humanist distinction between the scholar and the
orator. Where Stowe is wrapped in a brooding study, Shakespeare's
unfurrowed brow looks confidently out on the world, above a mouth
that is open to declaim the verses he has just written.

It is with that image that I end, as Shakespeare's brief existence as a private man came to a close, his human joys and griefs smoothed away into a serene mask. But that is only part of the story. For the monument proclaims another message, one that history has confirmed. Though his pen is stilled, his words continue to sound:

> Think ye see
> The very persons of our noble story
> As they were living. Think ye see them great
> And followed with the general throng and sweat
> Of thousand friends; then, in a moment, see
> How soon this mightiness meets misery:
> And if you can be merry then, I'll say
> A man may weep upon his wedding day.

Notes and References

This book was designed to be read without footnotes, without the sometimes off-putting apparatus of scholarly references and citations. But I
hope that some of its readers will become interested enough in the issues
raised to want to check my sources, and follow up some of the ideas
explored here.

Given the constraints of space, it has not been possible to acknowledge
in detail the extent to which my account is inevitably based on several
indispensable repositories of primary source material, and indebted to the
labors of many generations of scholars. I have confined myself largely to
general information for each chapter. Because the material I refer to is
excellently indexed, and because much of it will be readily accessible to
students, I have kept my own citations to a brief minimum; anyone wishing
to explore this material further should have no difficulty in tracing chapter
and verse.

Quotations from Shakespeare's plays and poems are taken from a variety
of editions, though the single-volume text I have used most frequently is
The Riverside Shakespeare, editor, G. B. Evans (Boston, Mass., 1974). For
each text I have consulted all available modern editions. In particular I
have worked with the Arden, the New Penguin, the Oxford (where available) and the New Cambridge (where available), as well as the single-
volume Oxford *Works*, editors, Stanley Wells and Gary Taylor. Unless

otherwise noted, material relating to dating and textual matters is drawn from these editions. On sources, again unless otherwise indicated, I have used these editions, as well as Geoffrey Bullough's eight-volume *Narrative and Dramatic Sources of Shakespeare.*

As far as traditions of criticism of individual plays is concerned, the handiest modern guide is *Shakespeare, A Bibliographical Guide*, editor, Stanley Wells (Oxford, 1990). Only occasionally do I have space to note the titles of individual critical studies; those cited are either very recent or especially influential. Readers wishing to pursue criticism further should use Wells, or consult the excellent and pithy guide to the field in Philip Edwards, *Shakespeare. A Writer's Progress* (Oxford, 1986), pps. 185–95. The Bibliography in the *Riverside Shakespeare* is full and up-to-date. The new *Cambridge Companion to English Drama*, editors, A. R. Braunmuller and M. Hattaway (Cambridge, 1990), is a very valuable modern guide to the subject, and there is a helpful selection of primary source material in *Elizabethan-Jacobean Drama*, editor, G. B. Evans (1988).

In the references, the place of publication is London unless indicated otherwise.

ABBREVIATIONS

In the notes that follow I have used the following shortened designations:

Bullough Geoffrey Bullough, *Narrative and Dramatic Sources of Shakespeare*, 8 vols. (1957–75)

Eccles Mark Eccles, *Shakespeare in Warwickshire* (Madison, Wisc., 1961)

EKC E. K. Chambers, *William Shakespeare: A Study of Facts and Problems* (Oxford, 1930; repr. 1990)

ES E. K. Chambers, *The Elizabethan Stage*, 4 vols. (Oxford, 1923).

Oxford Works *William Shakespeare: The Complete Works*, eds. Stanley Wells and Gary Taylor (Oxford, 1986; compact edn. 1988)

Riverside *The Riverside Shakespeare*, ed. G. B. Evans (Boston, Mass., 1974)

SS DOC Samuel Schoenbaum, *William Shakespeare: A Documentary Life* (Oxford, 1975)

SS Samuel Schoenbaum, *William Shakespeare: A Compact Documentary Life* (Oxford, 1977)

Wells *Shakespeare, A Bibliographical Guide*, ed. Stanley Wells (Oxford, 1990)

CHAPTER 1

(pages 17–30)

The documents cited in this chapter are reproduced in SS DOC, and transcribed in EKC, Vol. II, Appendix A, pp. 1–40 (the quotation from Thomas Plume is on p. 247). My accounts of the Shakespeare family and Stratford are drawn from Eccles, chs. 1–3, and from SS, chs. 1–4.

(pages 30–38)

The information on John Shakespeare's business dealings is supplemented by D. L. Thomas and N. E. Evans, "John Shakespeare in the Exchequer," *Shakespeare Quarterly* 35 (1984), pp. 315–8. On the economic recession from which he suffered, see D. Hamer's review of Schoenbaum's *Shakespeare's Lives* (1970), in *The Review of English Studies*, n.s. 32 (1971), pp. 483–4.

CHAPTER 2

(pages 39–52)

See also the accounts of Shakespeare's upbringing and education in Eccles, ch. 4 and in SS, ch. 6. The standard study of the education available to Shakespeare at Stratford is still T. W. Baldwin's massive *William Shakespeare's Petty School* (1943) and *William Shakespeare's Small Latine and Lesse Greeke* (1944).

CHAPTER 3

(pages 53–57)

For narratives of Shakespeare's marriage and details about Anne's family, see Eccles, ch. 5 and SS ch. 7. More generally, see L. Stone, *The Family, Sex and Marriage in England, 1500–1800* (1977); A. McFarlane, *Marriage and Love in England: Modes of Reproduction 1300–1800*; and R. Houlbrooke, *The English Family 1450–1700* (1984).

(pages 58–70)

On the so-called lost years, see P. Millward, *Shakespeare's Religious Background* (1973); SS, ch. 8; E. A. J. Honigmann, *Shakespeare: The Lost Years* (Manchester, 1985). Early allusions to Shakespeare are collected and transcribed in EKC, II, Appendices C and D. The mythos is discussed in Richard Dutton, *William Shakespeare: A Literary Life* (1989), ch. 1. By far the fullest and most entertaining account of the legends that have grown up around Shakespeare's life is Schoenbaum's excellent *Shakespeare's Lives.* For inspections of the relationships between the Shakespeare myths and British culture more generally, see Graham Holderness, ed., *The Shakespeare Myth* (Manchester, 1988); and Gary Taylor, *Reinventing Shakespeare* (1989).

CHAPTER 4
(pages 71–86)

The most illuminating primary source of information about Tudor London is John Stow, *A Survey of London* (1603). The standard edition is by G. L. Kingsford (Oxford 1908), and there is an Everyman edition by H. B. Wheatley. I have also used the following, among others: SS, ch. 9; *The A to Z of Elizabethan London*, compiled by A. Prockter and R. Taylor (1979); *London 1500–1700: The Making of the Metropolis*, eds. A. L. Beir and R. Findlay (1986); *London in the Age of Shakespeare: An Anthology*, ed. L. Manley (1986); and F. J. Fisher, *London and the English Economy 1500–1700* (1990).

(pages 86–95)

The documents concerning the theaters and dramatic companies are cited chiefly from ES. I have also used *Henslowe's Diary*, eds. R. A. Foakes and R. T. Rickert (Cambridge 1961); A. Gurr's admirable *The Shakespearean Stage, 1574–1642* (2nd. edn. Cambridge, 1980); and *Documents of the Rose Playhouse*, ed. C. C. Rutter (1984).

CHAPTER 5
(pages 96–119)

See the account by M. Hattaway of the criticism of the early histories in Wells, pp. 321–35. I have used Hattaway's edition of *Henry VI Part 1* (Cambridge 1900). Of earlier studies, I recommend Emrys Jones, *The Origins of Shakespeare* (Oxford 1977). There are chapters on these plays in several recent books, including: Annabel Patterson, *Shakespeare and the Popular Voice* (Oxford 1989); Leah Marcus, *Puzzling Shakespeare: Local Reading and its Discontents* (Berkeley, Cal., 1988); and Phyllis Rackin, *Stages of History: Shakespeare's English Chronicles* (Ithaca, NY, 1990).

(pages 119–143)

References to the sources and occasion of *The Comedy of Errors* are taken from EKC, Bullough, and from the Arden edition by R. A. Foakes. Erasmus's *De Ratione Studii* is cited from the Toronto edition of *The Collected Works of Erasmus*, Vol. 24. The distinction between "defining" and "exploring" in Tudor drama is taken from Joel B. Altman, *The Tudor Play of Mind* (Berkeley, Cal., 1978), pp. 13–30. My readings of *The Shrew and Titus* are influenced by Emrys Jones, *Scenic Form in Shakespeare* (Oxford 1970). I have used the informative new editions of *Titus* by E. M. Waith (Oxford 1984), and of *The Shrew* by Brian Morris (Arden 1981) and by H. J. Oliver (Oxford 1982).

CHAPTER 6
(pages 144–152)

On the plague, see Paul Slack, *The Impact of the Plague in Tudor and Stuart England* (1985); Beir and Findlay, eds., *London, 1500–1700;* SS, ch. 11. I cite *The Plague Pamphlets of Thomas Dekker*, ed. F. P. Wilson, (Oxford 1925). There is a modern selection of Dekker's prose by E. D. Pendry in the Stratford-upon-Avon Library (1967).

(pages 152–169)

Information on the dramatic companies is drawn from: ES, Vol. II; Gurr, *Shakespeare Stage*, ch. 2; SS ch. 9; and G. E. Bentley, *The Professions of Dramatist and Player in Shakespeare's Time* (Princeton, NJ, 1986). See also Rutter, ed., *Documents of the Rose Playhouse*, and M. Hattaway, *Elizabethan Popular Theatre* (1982). On Greene, see SS, ch. 10, and the thought-provoking study by E. A. J. Honigmann, *Shakespeare's Impact on his Contemporaries* (1982). On Shakespeare's relations with Southampton, the two fullest studies are A. L. Rowse, *Shakespeare's Southampton* (1965), and G. P. V. Akrigg, *Shakespeare and the Earl of Southampton* (1968); also see SS, ch. 11.

Chapter 7

(pages 170–176)

For documents concerning Shakespeare's London residences, see SS, pp. 121–3, 221–3; Stow, *Survey;* and EKC, Vol. II, pp. 87–90. The most recent study of the Lord Chamberlain's Men is P. Thompson, *Shakespeare's Theatre* (1983); see also SS, ch. 12; also the detailed information in ES; Gurr, *Shakespearean Stage*; and Bentley, *Professions of Dramatist and Player.*

(pages 176–206)

A full survey of the controversies that have raged about *King John* will be found in the new Oxford edition by A. R. Braunmuller (1989); see also the "early start" arguments proposed by Honigmann in *Shakespeare's Impact on his Contemporaries*. There is a new edition of *Sir Thomas More*, "by Anthony Munday and others," eds. V. Gabrieli and G. Melchiori, in the Revels Plays (Manchester, 1990); a reproduction and transcript of the Shakespearean material can be seen in the *Riverside Shakespeare*. For *Love's Labour's Lost* I have used the two modern editions: the Penguin by John Kerrigan (1982); and the Oxford by G. R. Hibbard (1989). The fullest edition of *A Midsummer Night's Dream* is the Arden by Harold Brooks (1979); and the New Cambridge edition by R. A. Foakes (1984) has a lively introduction. The most influential of modern studies of the play is Louis Adrian Montrose, "Shaping Fantasies: Figurations of Gender and Power in Elizabethan Culture," in S. Greenblatt, ed., *Representing the English Renaissance* (Berkeley, Cal., 1988). I have used the Arden edition of *Romeo and Juliet* by Brian Gibbons (1980), as well as the New Cambridge text by G. B. Evans (1984). There is an excellent New Cambridge edition of *Richard II* by Andrew Gurr (1984), which, like all editions of the history plays, deals thoroughly with the sources. Texts of the sources are most easily consulted in Bullough.

(pages 206–212)

The record of the burial of Hamnet Shakespeare is transcribed in EKC, Vol. II, p. 4, and reproduced in SS DOC, p. 164. The documents concerning the application for a coat of arms may be similarly consulted in EKC, Vol. II, pp. 18–32, and SS DOC, pp. 166–73; see also SS, pp. 227–32. A reproduction of the letter from Richard Quiney to Shakespeare is in SS DOC, p. 180; and there are transcripts of the whole exchange in EKC, Vol. II, pp. 101–7. See also Eccles, pp. 92–9.

(pages 212–227)

Henry IV is available in two modern editions: Part 1 in the Oxford series by David Bevington, and Part 2 in the New Cambridge series by Georgio Melchiori (1989); the two Arden volumes by A. R. Humphreys (1960) are still valuable, especially for their treatment of the sources. On the Falstaff/Oldcastle controversy, see Bevington's edition, pp. 1–10; Dutton, *William Shakespeare*, pp. 62–6; SS, pp. 192–6; and the editorial matter in the Oxford *Works*. I have used the Oxford edition of *The Merry Wives of Windsor*, by T. W. Craik (1990), and the New Cambridge edition of *The Merchant of Venice*, by M. M. Mahood (1987). Some of my comments on *The Merchant* are indebted to the chapter on Shakespeare and the law in Terry Eagleton, *William Shakespeare* (1986), pp. 35–63.

(pages 227–242)

The full passage from Meres, *Palladis Tamia* (1598) is reproduced in EKC, Vol. II, pp. 193–5, and in the *Riverside*. On the building of the Globe, see SS, pp. 206–10. For *Much Ado About Nothing* I have used the Arden edition by A. R. Humphreys (1981), supplemented by the New Cambridge edition by F. H. Mares (1988).

CHAPTER 8

(pages 243–256)

I have used the Oxford edition of *Henry V* by Gary Taylor (1982). In addition to works cited in Wells, see also Patterson, *Shakespeare and the Popular Voice;* Greenblatt, *Shakespeare Negotiations;* Rackin, *Stages of History.* On Ben Jonson's career at this time, see D. Riggs, *Ben Jonson: A Life* (Cambridge, Mass., 1989), ch. 4. The best modern edition of *Julius Caesar*, with excellent information on sources, reception, and stage history, is by A. R. Humphreys in the Oxford series (1984), and there is also a New Cambridge text by M. Spevack (1988). On the world/stage metaphor, the classic study is Anne Barton, *Shakespeare and the Idea of the Play* (1962); a more recent treatment is S. Mullaney, *The Place of the Stage* (Chicago, Ill., 1989). The Montaigne passage, like all such in these pages, is from the three-volume Everyman edition (1912, often reprinted) of John Florio's 1603 translation, which was the text Shakespeare knew and used.

(pages 256–265)

The standard modern account of the theatrical styles of Kemp and Armin is David Wiles, *Shakespeare's Clown: Actor and Text in the Elizabethan Playhouse* (Cambridge, 1987). I have used Agnes Latham's edition of *As You Like It* (1975), supplemented with the New Variorum edition (ed. D. Knowles, 1977), which contains a full text of Lodge's *Rosalynde*. Lodge's novel can also be read in Bullough. The most accessible study of literary melancholy in the period is B. G. Lyons, *Voices of Melancholy* (1971). For more on Shakespeare's names, see Anne Barton, *The Names of Comedy* (Oxford 1990).

(pages 264–271)

For an account of the Essex rebellion, see Mervyn James, "At a Crossroads of the Political Culture: The Essex Revolt, 1601," in his book *Society, Politics and Culture* (Cambridge 1986), pp. 416–65. Extracts from documents relating to the involvement of the Lord Chamberlain's Men in the events of February 1601 are printed in EKC, Vol. II, pp. 323–7; see also SS, pp. 217–19, and Dutton, *Shakespeare*, pp. 125–5. The text of Essex's poem is cited from *English Madrigal Verse 1588–1632*, ed. E. H. Fellowes (3rd. edn. rev., F. W. Sternfeld and D. Greer, Oxford, 1967), p. 504. The longer passage from Manningham's Diary is found in all modern editions, as well as EKC, Vol. II, pp. 327–8, and SS, pp. 205–6. I have used for this extract and others below *The Diary of John Manningham of the Middle Temple, 1602–1603*, ed. R. P. Sorlien (Hanover, NH, 1976). For *Twelfth Night* I have used the New Cambridge edition by Elizabeth Story Donno (1985). On crossdressing, see the chapter "Fiction and Friction" in Greenblatt, *Shakespearean Negotiations*, and the article by Jean Howard, "Crossdressing, the Theatre and Gender Struggle in Early Modern England," in *Shakespeare Quarterly* 39 (1988), pp. 418–40.

(pages 271–274)

Jonson's observations, from *Timber, or Discoveries*, are available in Chambers, Vol. II, p. 210. For accounts of the textual history of the miscellaneous poems discussed here, see the Oxford *Works*; all except "Shall I die?" can also be found in EKC. On the Stanley epitaphs, see Honingmann, *Shakespeare: the "lost years,"* ch. 7; and ch. 9 for an account of *The Phoenix and the Turtle*.

(pages 275–286)

Of recent editions of *Hamlet*, I have consulted the Penguin by T. J. B. Spencer with an introduction by Anne Barton (1980); the Arden by Harold

Jenkins (1982); the New Cambridge by Philip Edwards (1985); and the Oxford by G. R. Hibbard. A massive contextualizing study is R. M. Frye, *The Renaissance Hamlet: Issues and Responses in 1600* (Princeton, NJ, 1984). For *Troilus and Cressida*, I have relied on the Arden by Kenneth Palmer (1982), supplemented by the Oxford text by Kenneth Muir (1982). It should be noted that, whereas these editions are based on the Quarto text, the Oxford *Works* adopts the Folio text, on the basis of an argument that it incorporates Shakespeare's later revisions of the material.

CHAPTER 9

(pages 287–290)

For investigations of the relationship between the new king and English literary culture, see Jonathan Goldberg, *James I and the Politics of Literature* (Stanford, 1983), and Marcus, *Puzzling Shakespeare*, ch. 3. There is an excellent anthology of contemporary accounts of the king in *James I by his Contemporaries*, ed. R. Ashton (1969), from which my text of Weldon is taken. The king's speech to parliament is quoted from *The Political Works of James I*, ed. C. H. McIlwain (Cambridge, Mass., 1918); it is cited also by Marcus at p. 110.

(pages 290–311)

On the King's Men, see ES, Vol. II, pp. 192–220; Gurr, *Shakespearean Stage, passim*, also his *Playgoing in Shakespeare's London* (Cambridge, 1987); SS, pp. 249–53. On patronage, see Jonathan Goldberg, *James I*, and Annabel Patterson, *Censorship and Interpretation* (Madison, Wisc., 1984); and G. Lytle and S. Orgel, eds., *Patronage in the Renaissance* (Princeton, NJ, 1981). The sources of *Othello* are fully cited in Bullough. My own reading of the play is indebted to those of Jones, in *Scenic Form in Shakespeare*, and of Barbara Everett, whose article "Spanish *Othello*" is reprinted in her *Young Hamlet* (Oxford 1989), ch. 9. The Montaigne passage is from *Essays*, I, p. xviii. There is a New Variorum edition of *Measure for Measure* by Mark Eccles (1980); I have also used the Arden edition by J. W. Lever (1965). See also Marcus, *Puzzling Shakespeare*, pp. 161–202, and L. Tennenhouse, *Power on Display: The Politics of Shakespeare's Genres* (1986), pp. 154–71. For *All's Well that Ends Well*, I have used Russell Fraser's New Cambridge edition (1985), alongside those of G. K. Hunter (Arden, 1959), and Barbara Everett (Penguin, 1970). The passage from Montaigne's Essay "Of Experience" is taken from *Essays*, III, ch. 13, p. 326.

(pages 311–321)

The standard study of the Gowrie affair is still W. F. Arbuckle, in *The Scottish Historical Review* 36 (1957). The new Oxford Shakespeare Complete Works prints both the Quarto and Folio texts of *King Lear*. The presentation of the text in the *Riverside* makes it possible for the reader—with some effort—to reconstruct the two versions of the play. For some important studies of the text of the play, see *The Division of the Kingdoms*, eds. G. Taylor and M. Warren (Oxford 1986). My text of *King Leir* is cited from Bullough. The anecdote about the Italian furrier is taken from a novel by Giovanni Sercambi cited in *A History of Private Life*, eds. P. Ariès and G. Duby (Cambridge, Mass., 1988), Vol. II, p. 568. There is a modern edition of Witney's *Choise of Emblemes* (1587) by J. Manning (1990). The classic study of "Veritas filia temporis" is found in D. J. Gordon, *The Renaissance Imagination*, ed. S. Orgel (Berkeley, Cal., 1975). The most up-to-date edition of *Macbeth* is by Nicholas Brooke (Oxford 1990); and there is a valuable survey of scholarship and criticism by R. A. Foakes in Wells, ch. 13.

(pages 321–323)

The Donne passage is cited from *The Sermons of John Donne*, eds. G. R. Potter and E. M. Simpson, 10 vols. (Berkeley, Cal., 1953–62), Vol. VII, p. 72; later in the same volume, Donne remarks that people "need such glasses and such Images, as God shews us himself in the King" (p. 357).

CHAPTER 10

(pages 324–344)

For the documents relating to Shakespeare's lawsuits and land purchases in Stratford, see EKC, Vol. II, pp. 107–27; SS DOC, pp. 188–92 (plus illustrations); SS, pp. 247–7; for more detail on Hall, see Eccles, pp. 111–16, 129–42; and SS, pp. 287–92. At present the standard editions of *Timon of Athens* are the Arden by H. J. Oliver (1963) and the Cambridge by J. C. Maxwell (1964): but see the textual introduction in the Oxford *Works*. The major edition of *Coriolanus* remains the Arden by Philip Brockbank. The major sources are available in Bullough, but a handy single volume is the Penguin *Shakespeare's Plutarch*, ed. T. J. B. Spenser (repr. 1991). There is an account of *Coriolanus* in the political context of its age in Patterson, *Shakespeare and the Popular Voice*, ch. 6; see also Marcus, *Puzzling Shakespeare*, pp. 202–11. An influential article is Anne Barton,

"Livy, Machiavelli, and Shakespeare's *Coriolanus*," *Shakespeare Survey* 38 (1985), pp. 115–29. For *Antony and Cleopatra* I have used the fine New Cambridge edition by David Bevington (1990).

(pages 344–348)

There are numerous accounts of the Blackfriars theater: for physical detail and documentary evidence, see EKC, Vol. II, pp. 52–71; ES, Vol. IV, pp. 475–514; SS, pp. 264–7; also the many references in Gurr's *Shakespearean Stage* and *Playgoing in Shakespeare's London*. For more detail on the seaborne performance of *Hamlet* and *Richard II* in 1607–8, see EKC, Vol. II, pp. 334–5.

CHAPTER 11

(pages 349–358)

For details of the burial of Edmund Shakespeare, see EKC, Vol. II, p. 18; Edgar Fripp, *Shakespeare, Man and Artist* (1938), Vol. II, p. 687; and SS, pp. 28–9. The most copious and informative editions of the *Sonnets* are Stephen Booth, *Shakespeare's Sonnets: Edited with an Analytic Commentary* (New Haven, Conn., 1977); and John Kerrigan's Penguin edition (1986). There is a facsimile edition published by the Scolar Press (1968, often repr.). The relevant passages of *Willobie His Avisa* are cited in EKC, Vol. II, p. 191, in the *Riverside;* and in SS, pp. 180–2. There is also a modern edition, *The Queen Denied* (Oxford 1970), by B. N. Luna, whose theories have failed to secure general acceptance.

(pages 358–361)

Of texts of *Pericles*, I mainly used those by Philip Edwards (Penguin, 1976); F. D. Hoeniger (Arden, 1963); and J. C. Maxwell (Cambridge, 1956). The Oxford *Works* contains some challenging work on the text, especially on its relation to George Wilkins's *The Painful Adventures of Pericles Prince of Tyre*. There is an account of a court performance of *Pericles* in May 1619 to honor a departing group of French dignitaries (EKC, Vol. II, p. 346). For more information on the performance of Othello in Oxford, see the original Latin text provided in the *Riverside*, p. 1852.

(pages 361–366)

For a text of *Cymbeline*, I have used the Arden edition by J. M. Nosworthy (1955). On connections between *Cymbeline* (and the other late plays) and the events at the Jacobean court, see D. M. Bergeron, *Shakespeare's Romances and the Royal Family* (Lawrence, Kans., 1985). For accounts of the life and influence of Prince Henry, see G. Parry, *The Golden Age Restor'd: The Culture of the Stuart Court* (Manchester, 1981); Roy Strong, *Henry Prince of Wales and England's Lost Renaissance* (1986); and Dennis Kay, *Melodious Tears: The English Funeral Elegy from Spenser to Milton* (Oxford 1990), ch. 5.

(pages 366–370)

I have used the Arden edition of *The Winter's Tale* by J. H. P. Pafford (1963); details about the tomb of Mary, Queen of Scots are from Bullough, Vol. VIII, pp. 115–7. Eccles, p. 107, records that at the time Shakespeare was suing John Addenbrooke at the Stratford Court of Record (1608), another suitor was named Elorisell Bovey. For Shakespeare to encounter this heroic name—deriving from *Amadis de Gaule*—may have given him the idea for a name for a character in *The Winter's Tale*. For a text of Greene's *Pandosto* see Paul Salzman, ed., *An Anthology of Elizabethan Prose Fiction* (Oxford 1987).

(pages 370–376)

The two major editions of *The Tempest* are those by Frank Kermode (Arden, often revised and updated), and by Stephen Orgel (Oxford 1987). I have cited the source material mainly from Bullough. See also the two influential essays by Stephen Greenblatt, "Martial Law in the Land of Cockayne," in *Shakespearean Negotiations*, and "Learning to Curse: Aspects of Linguistic Colonialism in the Sixteenth Century," in his collection of essays, *Learning to Curse* (1991). Forman's comments on performances of Shakespeare's plays are given in EKC, Vol. II, pp. 337–41; they are also available in the *Riverside*, and in the edition by A. L. Rowse, *The Case Books of Simon Forman* (1974).

CHAPTER 12

(pages 377–383)

On Greene, see the many references in Eccles, especially pp. 131–9; also SS, pp. 282–5. For a narrative of the Bellott/Mountjoy suit, see SS, pp. 260–4. The documents in the case are transcribed in EKC, Vol. II, pp. 90–5, and are reproduced in SS, DOC, pp. 209–13. Information about the King's Men is drawn chiefly from ES, Gurr, *Shakespearean Stage*; and Bentley, *Professions of Dramatist and Player*. The source of the lost *Cardenio* is Cervantes's *Don Quixote*, Part One, chs. 23–7, which is also the source of the subplot of *The Second Maiden's Tragedy*, an anonymous play attributed to Middleton in which Shakespeare may have had a hand.

(pages 383–394)

Texts of all the miscellaneous poems—including the piece from the frontispiece of the *Works* of King James—are provided in the Oxford *Works*. For more detail on the epitaph on Elias James, see EKC, Vol. II, p. 153; and SS, p. 272. I have used both R. A. Foakes's Arden edition of *Henry VIII* (1954, often repr.), and the new Cambridge edition by John Margeson (1990), which uses the recent (1981) discovery of a second account of the Globe fire. For *The Two Noble Kinsmen*, I have used the Oxford edition by E. M. Waith (1989), as well as the Penguin by N. Bawcutt (1977), and the Regent's Renaissance by Richard Proudfoot (1970).

(pages 394–410)

On the Welcombe enclosure, the documents are transcribed in EKC, Vol. II, pp. 141–52, and reproduced in SS DOC, pp. 230–4; there is a brief narrative in both Eccles, pp. 136–9 and SS, pp. 281–5. On the Blackfriars purchase, see the transcripts in EKC, Vol. II, pp. 154–69, the reproduction in SS DOC, p. 125, and the account in SS, pp. 272–5. For a narrative of the difficulties in Shakespeare's family in his latter years, see SS, pp. 292–6. The text of the will can be studied in the *Riverside*, in SS, pp. 297–306, and in EKC, Vol. II, pp. 169–80 (with reduced facsimiles). There is a full-size reproduction in SS, DOC, pp. 243–5. The title page of Susanna Hall's book, *The Nervaylous Discourse . . . etc*, is reproduced in SS DOC, p. 249. Images of Shakespeare's monument have often been reproduced; but the contrast I develop with the monument of Stow can be compared with the reproduction of both monuments in SS DOC, pp. 253–4. The final lines are from the prologue to *Henry VIII: Or, All is True*.

Index